WOMEN'S WRITING OF THE VICTORIAN PERIOD 1837–1901: AN ANTHOLOGY

Edited by

Harriet Devine Jump

EDINBURGH UNIVERSITY PRESS

© Harriet Devine Jump, 1999

Edinburgh University Press
22 George Square, Edinburgh

Typeset in Bulmer
by Pioneer Associates, Perthshire, and
printed and bound in Great Britain by
MPG Books, Bodmin

A CIP record for this book is available from the
British Library

ISBN 0 7486 0927 X (hardback)
ISBN 0 7486 0891 5 (paperback)

CONTENTS

INTRODUCTION

'[M]y idea of a perfect woman is one who can write but won't'
(George Henry Lewes, 'A Gentle Hint to
Writing Women', 1850)

George Henry Lewes's idea of perfection presumably had to be modified a few years later, when he became the common-law husband of George Eliot, arguably the most formidable woman writer of the Victorian period. His essay is partly ironic, of course, but it is based in a perceptible anxiety which owes its existence to the fact that 'the group of female authors is becoming every year more multitudinous and more successful' (Lewes, 1850, p. 929). Lewes was not alone in worrying about the perceived invasion of the literary market-place by women writers: there seems to have been a general, though almost certainly ill-founded, feeling that the male preserve of letters was being swamped by large numbers of 'women, children and ill-trained troops', as Lewes himself had expressed it a few years earlier (Lewes, 1847, p. 285). In fact, although the figures have been much disputed, it seems likely that only about 20 per cent of the total number of practising writers in the nineteenth century were female. Of these, a recent study has estimated, about one third were novelists, half were writers for children, 14 per cent were poets, and only 3 per cent wrote works of non-fictional prose on subjects such as history, philosophy or economics (Cross, 1985, p. 167).

These figures, however, are based on the listings of book-length texts in the *Cambridge Bibliography of English Literature*. Left out of these calculations are the ever- increasing number of professional women writers who contributed articles and reviews to the rapidly expanding market-place offered by the weekly, fortnightly, monthly or quarterly periodicals and, increasingly towards the end of the century, to the daily papers. A conservative estimate made in 1979 suggested a figure of 14 per cent for female involvement in this sphere of literary production, but acknowledged that the total was almost certainly much greater, owing to the many reviews and articles which appeared either anonymously or pseudonymously

(Houghton, 1979, p. xvi). Among the many women whose financial sur-
vival depended at least in part on journalism, honourable mention should
be made of Harriet Martineau, Geraldine Jewsbury, George Eliot, Margaret
Oliphant, Frances Power Cobbe, and Fliza Lynn Linton. Martineau wrote
for numerous periodicals and newspapers, while Jewsbury's reviews and
articles were a regular feature of *The Athenaeum* from 1849 to 1880. Eliot
began her professional career writing for periodicals such as *The Leader*
and the *Westminster Review*, for which she acted as assistant editor in the
early 1850s, and Oliphant wrote extensively for *Blackwood's* and other
periodicals for almost 40 years. Cobbe, who was all but disinherited after
her father's death, supplemented her meagre income by prolific journalism,
although she commented towards the end of her life that the total of
£5,000 she had earned by that means was less than her eldest brother's
annual income from the family estate (Cobbe, 1894, ii 76). Eliza Lynn
Linton, the first woman journalist to be employed by a daily paper, wrote
for the *Morning Chronicle* between 1848 and 1851, and later contributed
a stream of articles to the *Saturday Review*. Much of the prose which has
been included in this anthology has been taken from these sources.

What were women writers of the Victorian period writing about?
Inevitably, the 'Woman Question' of the earlier part of the era, and the
debates on sexual emancipation associated with the 'New Woman' in the
1890s, tend to cast their shadow over almost all of the women's writing of
the period. The issues raised were obviously of primary importance, and
extended widely to encompass all aspects of women's lives, both public
and private. Not all women writers supported what we today call feminism:
some, such as the notoriously conservative Sarah Ellis at the beginning of
the era, and the eccentric Ouida towards its close, were strongly opposed
to it. Even among those who did support it, although they were broadly in
agreement that women should have equal legal and political rights, there
were clear differences. Perhaps the most important fundamental divergence
was between those who argued that men and women were essentially
similar intellectually and morally (although even the 'equality feminists'
tended to see women as morally superior to men) and those who stressed
the differences between the sexes (with women seen as innately nurturant).
Many writers were concerned with political issues affecting women, such
as the Married Women's Property Act, the Contagious Diseases Acts, the
divorce laws and, of course, female suffrage. Educational opportunities
were a recurring preoccupation, and the issue of women's training for
the medical profession in particular was highlighted in the 1870s. While
some women discussed the difficulties faced by married women (male
violence was a recurring theme), other writers were more concerned with

the position of, and opportunities available to, the increasing number of women who remained single, either by choice or lack of opportunity. Towards the end of the century, the 'New Woman' put in an appearance (the term was actually coined by Sarah Grand in 1894) to act as a locus for debates on a number of issues ranging from dress and behaviour (smoking, drinking, swearing) to sexual mores such as the use of birth control, with its concomitants of free love and the rejection of motherhood.

Given the proliferation of articles, pamphlets and books generated by these debates, it would have been quite easily possible to have devoted an entire anthology to works which directly address these issues. I have wished, however, to cast my net more broadly. Thus, although I have tried to do justice to the obvious importance of this area, readers will find included here examples of less obviously didactic forms of prose writing by women. Book reviews and literary criticism, travel writing and religious debate, discussions of slavery and of the duties of servants, memoirs and autobiography are among the themes of the 'public' (or published) writing included. Private writing has found a place as well, in the form of diaries and journals. Inevitably, however, in a century when issues affecting women's lives and their legal and social position were so much to the fore, all these forms tend to refer to the 'Woman Question' more or less obliquely.

The recent movement generated by feminist literary historians to recover and validate literary texts by women writers could be said to have had its roots in the nineteenth century. Elizabeth Barrett Browning's well known lament: 'I look everywhere for Grandmothers and see none' (Kelley and Lewis, 1992, p. 3) seems to express a desire found in many other women of the period to acknowledge the contribution made by earlier writers. Certain names recur. The poet Letitia Landon ('L. E. L.') quickly became an icon following her mysterious and tragic death (murder? suicide?) in Africa shortly after her marriage, and the difficulties she faced both as a woman and a writer are confronted by two of her most celebrated successors, Barrett Browning and Rossetti. Charlotte Brontë, under attack shortly after her death by Elizabeth, Lady Eastlake among others, rises to heroic status following her friend Elizabeth Gaskell's sensitive biography. A quarter of a century later, Edith Simcox voices her grief at the loss of her adored friend George Eliot in an adulatory memoir. Jane Austen is awarded cautious praise (although her irony is deplored as an unfortunate habit) by the literary historian Julia Kavanagh. Although not in the field of literary history, a similar interest in the lives of successful and creative women can be found in the tribute to the great woman photographer Julia Margaret Cameron by the celebrated memorialist Anne Thackeray Ritchie.

There was a clear tendency, throughout the century, for women, aware in their own lives of oppression by the patriarchal hegemony, to identify with other oppressed groups. The emotive issue of slavery, which had preoccupied so many writers in the late eighteenth and early nineteenth centuries, remained a pressing concern. Those women who had viewed it in operation at first hand, such as Harriet Martineau, who toured America in the late 1830s, or Frances Anne Kemble, who visited her husband's Georgian plantations at about the same time, wrote about it with an especial edge, and show an obvious sympathy with the condition of the female slaves in particular. Closer to home, women writers (themselves predominantly middle-class) increasingly concerned themselves with the rights of working-class women. In this anthology, Josephine Butler's campaigning writing on behalf of prostitutes, Clementina Black's article, which gives a voice to a 'working woman', and Frances Power Cobbe's comments on marital violence all foreground the abuses to which less privileged and confident women were subjected. Among the few working-class women who did write and get published, Eliza Cook drew the attention of her mainly middle-class readership to the plight of female servants, and Ellen Johnston ('the factory girl') wrote movingly of the struggles and sufferings of her own life at the lowest end of the social scale. By the end of the century, campaigners for class and monetary equality were making themselves heard, among them the anarchist poet Louisa Bevington.

It is well known that the nineteenth century was the great age of the woman traveller and travel writer. These fearless female tourists – celebrated by Elizabeth, Lady Eastlake in her 1845 article for their possession of 'the four cardinal virtues of travelling – activity, punctuality, courage, and independence' – astonish us today by their resourcefulness and adventurousness. Nothing could apparently be further from the Victorian construction of domestic woman than Anna Jameson, in the 1830s, shooting the rapids in a canoe and living with Native Americans for protracted periods of time. Even more extraordinary are the exploits of the remarkable Isabella Bird, whether narrowly escaping drowning while exploring Hawaii with her native guides or developing an intense emotional relationship with a 'Mountain Man' while snowed up with two young men in a cabin in the Rockies. Bird would almost certainly have been surprised (Jameson probably less so) by the suggestion that their activities and texts could be read as powerful arguments for the feminist cause simply by virtue of their demonstration of women's strength and capabilities. Towards the end of the century, this fact is clearly acknowledged by the young New Woman writer Ménie Muriel Dowie, whose travel book deliberately shocked her readers by its revelations that she travelled alone and not only smoked and drank but also wore a pair of very fetching breeches (her masculine attire is not only described, but also illustrated within the text).[1]

In the Romantic period, the popularity of travel writing for women writers lay partly in the fact that it was one of the few ways a woman could acceptably write autobiography. This was no longer true by the Victorian era, as the increasing number of female autobiographies and memoirs clearly shows. Not all autobiographers were as controversial as Frances Anne Kemble, actress and abolitionist, who shocked and alienated the citizens of her adopted America by her publication of her injudiciously critical journals in the early 1830s, and who, in 1863, deliberately set out to produce a powerful effect by publishing her autobiographical account of the horrifying conditions on her husband's plantations in Georgia. By their very nature, however, autobiographies from this period tell us much about the way women's lives were constrained and oppressed: at two diametrically opposite ends of the class scale, Caroline Norton's and Ellen Johnston's experiences are obvious cases in point. Happily, however, they often celebrate the ways in which some women (Harriet Martineau is a supreme example) managed to break through the prevailing, and debilitating, constructions of gender to make successful and powerful careers for themselves.

Although some autobiographical writings originated in diaries which were later published by the diarists themselves (most notably those of Queen Victoria, one of the entries from which opens this volume), other unpublished diaries and journals of the era give an insight into the hidden lives of women. Some of Caroline Clive's revelations of her experiences of pregnancy and motherhood were censored as too coarse by the distant descendant who edited her diaries in the 1940s, but enough remains for us to appreciate the writer's refreshing cheerfulness and honesty. Censorship for other reasons was demonstrated when Margaret Oliphant's nieces removed some of the keen anguish she expressed in her diary after her nine-year-old daughter's sudden death. However the depth of her feelings is still apparent here, as it is again in her final entry, written shortly after the death of her only remaining child thirty five years later. Other diaries remained private until many years after the death of their authors. Among them is Hannah Cullwick's account of her life as a servant, and of her extraordinary relationship with her 'Massa', which was not made public until nearly eighty years after her death, and which provides a remarkable insight into Victorian society and sexual mores. Just as fascinating are the journals of the lesbian couple (aunt and niece) who wrote jointly under the name Michael Field: one of the extracts included here tells a tragi-comic story of a German nurse falling under the spell of a powerful, though only partly understood, sexual attraction for one of them.

As the nineteenth century draws to a close, and with it the life of Queen Victoria, there is a clear sense that women writers, both public and private, are reflecting on their own age and on the changes, for good and bad, that they perceive as pointers towards the twentieth century. The difficult, opinionated Ouida, who had turned to journalism following the waning of her hugely successful career as a novelist, reflects with distaste on what she sees as the regrettable manners and morals of the New Woman and, in the first year of the new century, on what she calls the 'Ugliness of Modern life'. Sarah Grand, always Ouida's declared opponent, writes with cautious optimism about 'the Modern Man and Maid', but shows an awareness, in 'The Human Quest', of the great distance which women and society still have to travel. The anthology ends with Michael Field's private expression of grief at the death of the queen after whom the age, and this volume, have come to be named.

Editorial Matters

Once again, I apologise to anyone who finds my choice of extracts odd or inadequate, or who thinks they fail to do justice to the range of available materials. Much has, of course, had to be excluded in order to make the volume of manageable size. Inevitably, the selection reflects my own interests, but also my own enjoyment of the texts and authors I have included. I hope teachers and students will agree with me.

In common with the previous volume in this series, this volume is not arranged thematically or by chronological date of birth of the author, but instead by date of publication of the text. A thematic arrangement seemed to me too reductive, although an index of themes has been included for those who wish to follow ideas through the period. Author-based grouping has also been rejected, though again, readers who are interested in the authors will find short biographical notes on each on pp. 344–65. Through the present arrangement, I hope to show more clearly both the way in which these texts fit into the context of the period as a whole (a chronological table of the whole period, including historical events and significant publications is also included on pp. xxi–xxiv) and the ways in which the texts react and respond to each other. Writing does not exist in a vacuum: it comes into being as a result of a complex interplay of historical, social, and cultural pressures which will, I hope, be revealed more adequately by this arrangement than by the usual and more conventional one.

This being said, however, some editorial decisions have been taken which have resulted in a picture which is by no means wholly representative. It has recently been estimated that ' [i]f one includes those writers who wrote for children, about 80 per cent of all professional women writers in the nineteenth century wrote fiction' (Pykett, 1996, p. 153). In the present anthology, however, fiction has been excluded altogether. This is partly owing to pressures of space, but also, and equally important, because I felt that while it is possible to make excerpts from non-fictional prose without doing it too much damage, the same cannot be said of novels. This has led to a slightly skewed perspective, and readers should be aware of the fact that some important female writers of the era are either missing altogether (Anne Brontë, Mary Elizabeth Braddon, Ellen Wood, George Egerton, for example) or represented only by what might be regarded as the more marginal elements of their total output (Charlotte and Emily Brontë, Elizabeth Gaskell, George Eliot).

Poetry has presented a different kind of problem. Two excellent anthologies, Leighton and Reynolds (1995) and Armstrong et al. (1996), have made nineteenth-century women's poetry readily accessible to the general reader in the last few years. Even so, in order to represent the period as broadly as possible, a limited amount of poetry has been included here. Selection was particularly difficult given the fact that the period produced a large number of impressive women poets. In the interest of keeping to a manageable word-limit, I have included only short poems, ruling out extracts from long works. This has meant that some important long narrative poems – Barrett Browning's *Aurora Leigh*, 1857, and Rossetti's *Goblin Market*, 1862, for example – are not represented here, and nor are Augusta Webster's fine dramatic monologues. I would hope that readers who enjoy the relatively small number of poems in this volume will be encouraged to seek out more work by their authors.

In the case of prose, an attempt has been made to strike a balance between the desire to give as wide a range of material as possible and the wish not to confine the contents solely to short extracts taken from larger works. While book-length texts have had to be severely shortened, as many essays as possible have been given in their entirety.

Although most of the texts included here did find their way into the public domain, I have been aware of the need to do justice to those writers who, for whatever reason, avoided publication for some or all of their literary productions. This unpublished material is represented by journal entries. Letters have been excluded on the grounds of lack of space.

In general, the copy-texts of the works included are those of the first published editions. Obvious printers' errors have been silently corrected, and proper names have been adjusted. Texts have in general been modernised as far as spelling is concerned.

The notes on pp. 331–343 give the source for each text. Brief contextual background and explanatory notes have been added where necessary. Notes provided by the authors themselves were often copious, and have not always been given in full.

Notes

1. Isabella Bird's 'Hawaiian riding dress', which she took with her to the Rockies, consisted of a pair of trousers which enabled her to sit astride her horse, but she is careful to point out that it also had a skirt over the top for appearances' sake.

ACKNOWLEDGEMENTS

I am grateful to Edge Hill University College for financial support and for a period of research leave which has enabled me to complete this volume. Professor John Simons and Dr Gill Davies have been consistently helpful and supportive and I thank them especially. Margaret Forsyth, a model research student, has been a help and an inspiration, and colleagues have helped to elucidate various puzzling references. My thanks also go to the staff of the Bodleian Library, the British Library, the Sidney Jones Library, University of Liverpool, the John Rylands Library, University of Manchester and the Portico Library, Manchester. As always, I must thank my family and friends for their encouragement and tolerance.

CHRONOLOGY

1837   Death of William IV; accession of Queen Victoria; Dickens, *The Pickwick Papers, Oliver Twist*

1838   Coronation of Queen Victoria; Anti-Corn Law League established; People's Charter drafted; Great Western Railway opens; Afghan Wars (1838–42)

1839   Chartist riots; 'Opium War' (1839–40)

1840   Penny post instituted; marriage of Queen Victoria to Albert

1841   Tories in power; 'Hungry forties' depression begins

1842   Railway links Manchester and London; Mines and Collieries Act forbids underground work for women, girls and boys under ten

1843   National Temperance Society founded; Ruskin, *Modern Painters* I; Dickens, *A Christmas Carol*; Carlyle, *Past and Present*

1844   Railway mania begins

1845   Potato famine in Ireland begins; Engels, *Condition of the Working Class in England*; Sikh War (1845–6)

1846   Corn Laws suspended; Whigs in power

1847   Urania Cottage shelter for fallen women established by Angela Burdett-Coutts; Charlotte Brontë, *Jane Eyre*; Emily Brontë, *Wuthering Heights*; Anne Brontë, *Agnes Grey*; Tennyson, *The Princess*; Thackeray, *Vanity Fair*

1848   Cholera epidemic (1848–9); Public Health Act; Queen's College opens higher education for women; Anne Brontë, *The Tenant of Wildfell Hall*; Dickens, *Dombey and Son*; Gaskell, *Mary Barton*; Thackeray, *Pendennis*

1849   Corn laws abolished; Bedford College for women established; Charlotte Brontë, *Shirley*; Dickens, *David Copperfield*

1850   Death of Wordsworth; Wordsworth, *The Prelude*; Tennyson, *In Memoriam*

1851   Great Exhibition

1852   Burmese War (1852–3); Dickens, *Bleak House*

1853   Charlotte Brontë, *Villette*; Gaskell, *Cranford, Ruth*

1854   Crimean War (1854–6); birth of Oscar Wilde; Coventry Patmore, *The Angel in the House*; Dickens, *Hard Times*

1855   Married Women's Property Committee formed; Dickens, *Little Dorrit*; Gaskell, *North and South*; Browning, *Men and Women*; Tennyson, *Maud and Other Poems*

1856   Crimean War ends

1857   Second 'Opium War' opens China to trade with Europe; Indian Mutiny (1857–8); Matrimonial Causes Act makes divorce available without an act of parliament; Eliot, *Scenes of Clerical Life*

1858   Darwin and Wallace propose theory of evolution at Linnean Society

1859   Elizabeth Blackwell registered as qualified physician; Darwin, *Origin of Species*; George Eliot, *Adam Bede*: Dickens, *A Tale of Two Cities*; Tennyson, *Idylls of the King*; J. S. Mill, *On Liberty*

1860   Nightingale Training School for nurses established; Victoria Press founded by Emily Faithfull; George Eliot, *The Mill on the Floss*; Dickens, *Great Expectations*; Collins, *The Woman in White*

1861   Death of Albert, Prince Consort

1862   Contagious Diseases Act passed; Wood, *East Lynne*; Braddon, *Lady Audley's Secret*

1863   Death of Thackeray; Cambridge Local Examinations admit girls; Gaskell, *Sylvia's Lovers*

1864   Contagious Diseases Acts passed; Dickens, *Our Mutual Friend*; Browning, *Dramatis Personae*

1865   Carroll, *Alice in Wonderland*

1866   J. S. Mill presents Womens' Suffrage Petition to parliament; Gaskell, *Wives and Daughters*

1867   Reform Act extends suffrage to all male householders satisfying one-year residential requirement; Abyssinian War (1867–8)

1868   London University admits women to examinations; Collins, *The Moonstone*

1869   Suez Canal opens; Irish Church disestablished; Ladies' National Association for Repeal of the Contagious Diseases Acts founded; women's residence in Cambridge (to become Girton College) opens; Arnold, *Culture and Anarchy*

1870   Married Women's Property Act extends rights of women in marriage; English Elementary Education Act; Irish Land Act; death of Dickens

1871   Women's Education Union founded; George Eliot, *Middlemarch*

1872   Slade School of Art opens to women; Scottish Education Act

1873   College for women established in Oxford; J. S. Mill, *Autobiography*

1874 London Medical College for Women established; George Eliot, *Daniel Deronda*
1876 Medical licensing bodies given power to examine women; telephone invented; Victoria proclaimed Empress of India
1877 Trial of Annie Besant and Charles Bradlaugh for publication of book on birth control
1878 Women admitted to lectures in Oxford; London University degrees open to women; Zulu War (1878–9); Hardy, *Return of the Native*
1879 Lady Margaret Hall and Somerville Hall, Oxford colleges for women, established
1880 First Anglo-Boer War (1880–1); compulsory elementary education established
1881 Women allowed to take Cambridge honours examinations
1882 Britain occupies Egypt; Stevenson, *Treasure Island*; birth of Virginia Woolf
1883 Schreiner, *Story of an African Farm*
1884 Reform Act extends suffrage to all male householders; co-educational Victoria University, Manchester, opens; *Oxford English Dictionary* begins publication
1885 Death of Gordon at Khartoum; Burma annexed
1886 Liberal government introduces Home Rule Bill for Ireland; Contagious Diseases Acts repealed; Stevenson, *Dr Jekyll and Mr Hyde*
1887 Queen Victoria's Silver Jubilee celebrated; British East Africa Company chartered; Conan Doyle, *A Study in Scarlet*
1888 Bryant and May matchworkers strike; 'Jack the Ripper' murders; Wilde, *The Happy Prince*
1889 London Dock strike; British South Africa Company chartered; death of Browning; Yeats, *Wanderings of Oisin*
1890 Morris, *News from Nowhere*; Frazer, *The Golden Bough*
1891 Abolition of fees in most state elementary schools; Wilde, *The Picture of Dorian Gray* Hardy, *Tess of the D'Urbervilles*, Gissing, *New Grub Street*
1892 Wilde, *Lady Windermere's Fan*; death of Tennyson
1893 Second Irish Home Rule Bill rejected by Lords; Independent Labour Party founded; 25% pay cut avoided by miners' strike; women no longer required to be chaperoned at Oxford University lectures
1895 Imprisonment of Wilde; Hardy, *Jude the Obscure*; Allen, *The Woman Who Did*; Wilde, *Salome*, *The Importance of Being Earnest*
1896 First cinema (Empire Theatre) opens

1837

1. Queen Victoria
from *Diary*

20 June.

I was awoke at 6'oclock by Mamma, who told me that the Archbishop of Canterbury and Lord Conyngham were here, and wished to see me. I got out of bed and went into my sitting-room (only in my dressing-gown), and *alone*, and saw them. Lord Conyngham (the Lord Chamberlain) then acquainted me that my poor Uncle, the King, was no more, and had expired at 12 minutes p. 2 this morning, and consequently that I am *Queen*. Lord Conyngham knelt down and kissed my hand, at the same time delivering to me the official announcement of the poor King's demise. The Archbishop then told me that the Queen was desirous that he should come and tell me the details of the last moments of my poor, good Uncle; he said that he had directed his mind to religion, and had died in a perfectly happy, quiet state of mind, and was quite prepared for his death. He added that the King's sufferings at the last were not very great but that there was a good deal of uneasiness. Lord Conyngham, whom I charged to express my feelings of condolence and sorrow to the poor Queen, returned directly to Windsor. I then went to my room and dressed.

Since it has pleased Providence to place me in this station, I shall do my utmost to fulfil my duty towards my country; I am very young and perhaps in many, though not in all things, inexperienced, but I am sure, that very few have more real good will and more real desire to do what is fit and right than I have.

2. Sara Coleridge
One Face Alone

One face alone, one face alone,
    These eyes require;
But, when that longed-for sight is shewn,
    What fatal fire
Shoots through my veins a keen and liquid flame,
That melts each fibre of my wasting frame!

One voice alone, one voice alone,
    I pine to hear;
But, when its meek; mellifluous tone
    Usurps mine ear,
Those slavish chains about my soul are wound,
Which ne'er, till death itself, can be unbound.

One gentle hand, one gentle hand,
    1 fain would hold;
But, when it seems at my command,
    My own grows cold;
Then low to earth I bend in sickly swoon,
Like lilies drooping, 'mid the blaze of noon.

3. Letitia Landon
Gifts Misused

Oh, what a waste of feeling and of thought
Have been the imprints of my roll of life!
What worthless hours! to what use have I turned
The golden gifts which are my hope and pride!
My power of song, unto how base a use
Has it been put! with its pure ore I made
An idol, living only on the breath
Of idol worshippers. Alas! that ever
Praise should have been what praise has been to me –
The opiate of the mind!

4. Letitia Landon
The Marriage Vow

The altar, 'tis of death! for there are laid
The sacrifice of all youth's sweetest hopes.
It is a dreadful thing for woman's lip
To swear the heart away; yet know that heart
Annuls the vow while speaking, and shrinks back
From the dark future that it dares not face.
The service read above the open grave
Is far less terrible than that which seals
The vow that binds the victim, not the will:
For in the grave is rest.

1838

5. Anna Jameson
from *Winter Studies and Summer Rambles*

January 29.

Well! I have seen these Cataracts of Niagara, which have thundered in my mind's ear ever since I can remember – which have been my "childhood's thought, my youth's desire," since first my imagination was awakened to wonder and to wish. I have beheld them, and shall I whisper it to you? – but, O tell it not among the Philistines! – I wish I had not! I wish they were still a thing unbeheld – a thing to be imagined, hoped, and anticipated – something to live for: – the reality has displaced from my mind an illusion far more magnificent than itself – I have no words for my utter disappointment: yet I have not the presumption to suppose that all I have heard and read of Niagara is false or exaggerated – that every expression of astonishment, enthusiasm, rapture, is affectation or hyperbole. No! it must be my own fault. Terni, and some of the Swiss cataracts leaping from their mountains, have affected me a thousand times more than all the immensity of Niagara. O I could beat myself ! and now there is no help! – the first moment, the first impression is over – is lost; though I should live a thousand years, long as Niagara itself shall roll, I can never see it again for the first time. Something is gone that cannot be restored. What has come over

my soul and senses? – I am no longer Anna – I am meta-morphosed – I
am translated – I am an ass's head, a clod, a wooden spoon, a fat weed
growing on Lethe's bank, a stock, a stone, a petrifaction, – for have I not
seen Niagara, the wonder of wonders; and felt – no words can tell *what*
disappointment!

But, to take things in order: we set off for the falls yesterday morning,
with the intention of spending the day there, sleeping, and returning the
next day to Niagara The distance is fourteen miles, by a road winding
along the banks of the Niagara river, and over the Queenston heights; –
and beautiful must this land be in summer, since even now it is beautiful.
The flower garden, the trim shrubbery, the lawn, the meadow with its
hedgerows, when frozen up and wrapt in snow, always give me the idea of
something not only desolate but dead: Nature is the ghost of herself, and
trails a spectral pall; I always feel a kind of pity – a touch of melancholy
– when at this season I have wandered among withered shrubs and buried
flower-beds; but here, in the wilderness, where Nature is wholly independent of art, she does not die, nor yet mourn; she lies down to rest on the
bosom of Winter, and the aged one folds her in his robe of ermine and
jewels, and rocks her with his hurricanes, and hushes her to sleep. How
still it was! how calm, how vast the glittering white waste and the dark
purple forests! The sun shone out, and the sky was without a cloud; yet we
saw few people, and for many miles the hissing of our sleigh, as we flew
along upon our dazzling path, and the tinkling of the sleigh-bells, were
the only sounds we heard. When we were within four or five miles of
the falls, I stopped the sleigh from time to time to listen for the roar of
the cataracts, but the state of the atmosphere was not favourable for the
transmission of sound, and the silence was unbroken.

Such was the deep, monotonous tranquillity which prevailed on every
side – so exquisitely pure and vestal-like the robe in which all Nature lay
slumbering around us, I could scarce believe that this whole frontier
district is not only remarkable for the prevalence of vice – but of dark and
desperate crime.

Mr. A., who is a magistrate, pointed out to me a lonely house by the
way-side, where, on a dark stormy night in the preceding winter, he had
surprised and arrested a gang of forgers and coiners; it was a fearful
description. For some time my impatience had been thus beguiled –
impatience and suspense much like those of a child at a theatre before the
curtain rises. My imagination had been so impressed by the vast height of
the Falls, that I was constantly looking in an upward direction, when, as we
came to the brow of a hill, my companion suddenly checked the horses,
and exclaimed, "The Falls!"

I was not, for an instant, aware of their presence; we were yet at a distance, looking *down* upon them; and I saw at one glance a flat extensive plain; the sun having withdrawn its beams for the moment, there was neither light, nor shade, nor colour. In the midst were seen the two great cataracts, but merely as a feature in the wide landscape. The sound was by no means overpowering, and the clouds of spray, which Fanny Butler called so beautifully the "everlasting incense of the waters," now condensed ere they rose by the excessive cold, fell round the base of the cataracts in fleecy folds, just concealing that furious embrace of the waters above and the waters below. All the associations which in imagination I had gathered round the scene, its appalling terrors, its soul subduing beauty, power and height, and velocity and immensity, were all diminished in effect, or wholly lost.

❊ ❊ ❊ ❊

I was quite silent – my very soul sank within me. On seeing my disappointment (written, I suppose, most legibly in my countenance) my companion began to comfort me, by telling me of all those who had been disappointed on the first view of Niagara, and had confessed it. I *did* confess; but I was not to be comforted.

❊ ❊ ❊ ❊

In what regards government and politics, do we not find the interest of the many sacrificed to the few; while, in all that regards society, the morals and the happiness of individuals are sacrificed to the many? and both are wrong. I never can bring myself to admire a social system, in which the honour, rights, or happiness of any individual, though the meanest, is made to yield to a supposed future or general good. It is a wicked calculation, and it will be found as inexpedient as it is wicked.

We women have especial reason to exclaim against this principle. We are told openly by moralists and politicians, that it is for the general good of society, nay, an absolute necessity, that one-fifth part of our sex should be condemned as the legitimate prey of the other, predoomed to die in reprobation, in the streets, in hospitals, that the virtue of the rest may be preserved, and the *pride* and the passions of men both gratified. But I have a bitter pleasure in thinking that this most base, most cruel conventional law is avenged upon those who made and uphold it; that here the sacrifice of a certain number of one sex to the permitted license of the other is no general good, but a general curse – a very ulcer in the bosom of society.

The subject is a hateful one – more hateful is it to hear it sometimes alluded to with sneering levity, and sometimes waved aside with a fastidious or arrogant prudery. Unless we women take some courage to look upon the evil, and find some help, some remedy within ourselves, I know not where it is to come from.

F. told me yesterday a story which I must try to note down for you, if I can find fit words in which to relate it. It is another proof that the realities of life transcend all fiction. I have known – have seen with these mine own eyes, more of tragedy and romance than I would dare to reveal – and who has not?

F. told me, that when he was serving in the army in the Lower Province, a young officer, one of his own friends, (mentioning his name,) seduced from her parents a very pretty girl, about fifteen or sixteen. F. knew something of her family, which was respectable, and tried to save her, but in vain. After some months, the officer S. became tired of his victim, and made her over to a brother officer. F. again interfered, and the poor girl did for a time return to her parents, who gladly and gratefully received her; but she was spoiled for her home, and her home was spoiled for her; the sources of innocent pleasure were poisoned, and why should we wonder and exclaim, if a woman who has once known the flatteries and caresses of love, find it hard – most hard – to resign her self to days and nights, solitary, toilsome, joyless, unendeared? After a while, the colonel of the regiment found means to allure her again from her home; he became strongly attached to her, she was faithful and devoted to him, and he took her with him to England.

Years had passed away, when S., who had left the army, also returned to England. While he was roaming about London, amusing himself as young men are wont to do after a long absence from the central mart of pleasure and dissipation, he betook himself one evening, after a tavern dinner, to some house of infamous resort, and one of the wretched women of the establishment was sent to him as a companion. As she entered the room, S. started from the sofa to encounter in the impudent, degraded, haggard, tawdry thing before him, the poor child who had been his victim in Canada; but long years of vice and misery had not yet utterly hardened her. They stood face to face for few seconds, and looked in silence upon each other, (and who can tell what in those few seconds may have passed through the minds of each?) and then the miserable girl fell senseless on the floor.

He raised her up, and, in the remorse and agony of the moment, offered her all he had in the world; – poor, poor compensation! He urged her return to Canada: – he would pay all her expenses – place her beyond the reach of want – but it was all in vain.

After the first burst of feeling was over, the wretched girl shook him from her with sullen scorn and despair, and not only refused to return to the home she had disgraced, but even to accept from him anything whatever – and thus she left him. He it was – *himself* – who described the scene to F.

"Poor fellow!" said F., in conclusion, "he did not recover it for a long time – he felt it very much!"

Poor fellow! – and yet he was to be pitied; he did not make the system under which he was educated.

"What became of Captain S.?" I asked.

"O, he married well; he is now a very respectable and excellent man – father of a family."

"He has children, then?"

"Yes; several."

"Daughters?"

"Yes."

"No doubt," thought I, "he will take care of *them*."

And yet one word more before I throw down my pen. I have wandered far from the fire in King-street – but no matter.

How often we hear repeated that most false and vulgar commonplace, that the rakes and the libertines of the other sex are sure to find favour with women – even the most virtuous women! This has been repeated over and over again by wits and playwrights till foolish women take the thing for granted, and foolish men aim at such a reputation as a means of pleasing us. O the folly in them, – the insult to us! No man ever pleased a woman because he was a libertine. What virtuous woman has the least idea of what a libertine really is? What fair, innocent girl, who hears a very agreeable and perfectly well-bred man stigmatised as such, images the thing to herself? Does she know what it means? Can *she* follow such a man into his daily life, his bought pleasures, his shameful haunts? Luckily – or shall I not say unluckily? – she has no knowledge, no conception even, of all this. If the truth were laid open to her, how she would shrink away from all contact with such a being, in the utter disgust which a pure-hearted and pure-minded being would naturally feel! . . . And so that which is the result of the ignorance, the innocence, the purity of women, is oddly enough converted into a reproach against us.

No; there is no salvation for women but in ourselves: in self-knowledge, self-reliance, self-respect, and in mutual help and pity; no good is done by a smiling abuse of the "wicked courses" of men, while we trample into irrecoverable perdition the weak and erring of our own sex.

❋ ❋ ❋ ❋

THAT the poor Indians to whom reserved lands have been granted, and who, on the faith of treaties, have made their homes and gathered themselves into villages on such lands, should, whenever it is deemed expedient, be driven out of their possessions, either by purchase, or by persuasion, or by force, or by measures which include all three, and sent to seek a livelihood in distant and strange regions – as in the case of these Delawares – is horrible, and bears cruelty and injustice on the face of it. To say that they cannot exist in amicable relation with the whites, without depravation of their morals, is a fearful imputation on us as Christians; – but thus it is. And I do wish that those excellent and benevolent people who have taken the cause of the aborigines to heart, and are making appeals in their behalf to the justice of the government and the compassion of the public, would, instead of theorising in England, come out here and behold the actual state of things with their own eyes – and having seen all, let, them say *what* is to be done, and what chances exist, for the independence, and happiness, and morality of a small remnant of Indians residing on a block of land, six miles square, surrounded on every side by a white population. To insure the accomplishment of those benevolent and earnest aspirations, in which so many good people indulge, what is required? what is expected? Of the white men such a pitch of lofty and self-sacrificing virtue, of humane philosophy and christian benevolence, that the future welfare of the wronged people they have supplanted shall be preferred above their own immediate interest – nay, their own immediate existence: of the red man, that he shall forget the wild hunter blood flowing through his veins, and take the plough in hand, and wield the axe and the spade instead of the rifle and the fish-spear! Truly they know not what they ask, who ask this; and among all those with whom I have conversed – persons familiar from thirty to forty years together with the Indians and their mode of life – I never heard but one opinion on the subject. Without casting the slightest imputation on the general honesty of intention of the missionaries and others delegated and well paid by various societies to teach and protect the Indians, still I will say that the enthusiasm of some, the self-interest of others, and an unconscious mixture of pious enthusiasm and self-interest in many more, render it necessary to take their testimony with some reservation; for often with them "the wish is father to the thought" set down; and feeling no lack of faith in their cause or in themselves, they look for miracles, such as waited on the missions of the apostles of old. But in the mean time, and by human agency, what is to be done? Nothing so easy as to point out evils and injuries, resulting from foregone events, or deep-seated in natural and necessary causes, and lament over them with resistless eloquence in verse and prose, or hold them up to the sympathy and indignation of the universe; but let the real friends of religion, humanity, and the poor Indians, set down a probable and feasible remedy for their wrongs and miseries; and follow it up, as the advocates for the abolition of the slave-trade followed up their just and glorious purpose. With a definite object and plan, much might be done; but mere declamation against the evil does little good. The people who propose remedies, forget that there are two parties concerned.

❀ ❀ ❀

The more I looked upon those glancing, dancing rapids, the more resolute I grew to venture myself in the midst of them. George Johnston went to seek a fit canoe and a dexterous steersman, and meantime I strolled away to pay a visit to Wayish,ky's family, and made a sketch of their lodge, while pretty Zah,gàh,see,gah,qua, held the umbrella to shade me from the sun.

The canoe being ready, I went to the upper end of the portage, and we launched into the river. It was a small fishing canoe about ten feet long, quite new, and light and elegant and buoyant as a bird on the waters. I reclined on a mat at the bottom, Indian fashion, (there are no seats in a genuine Indian canoe;) in a minute we were within the verge of the rapids, and down we went with a whirl and a splash! – the white surge leaping around me – over me. The Indian with astonishing dexterity kept the head of the canoe to the breakers, and somehow or other we danced through them. I could see, as I looked over the edge of the canoe, that the passage between the rocks was sometimes not more than two feet in width, and we had to turn sharp angles – a touch of which would have sent us to destruction – all this I could see through the transparent eddying waters, but I can truly say I had not even a momentary sensation of fear, but rather of giddy, breathless, delicious excitement. I could even admire the beautiful attitude of a fisher, past whom we swept as we came to the bottom. The whole affair, from the moment I entered the canoe till I reached the landing-place, occupied seven minutes, and the distance is about three quarters of a mile.

My Indians were enchanted, and when I reached *home*, my good friends were not less delighted at my exploit: they told me I was the first European female who had ever performed it, and assuredly I shall not be the last. I recommend it as an exercise before breakfast. Two glasses of champagne could not have made me more tipsy and more self-complacent .

❀ ❀ ❀

There is one subject on which all travellers these regions – all who have treated of the manners and modes of life of the north-west tribes, are

accustomed to expatiate with great eloquence and indignation, which they
think it incumbent on the gallantry and chivalry of Christendom to
denounce as constituting the true badge and distinction of barbarism and
heathenism, opposed to civilisation and Christianity: – I mean the treatment
and condition of their women. The women, they say, are "drudges," "slaves,"
"beasts of burthen," victims, martyrs, degraded, abject, oppressed; that not
only the cares of the household and maternity, but the cares and labours
proper to the men, fall upon them; and they seem to consider no expression
of disapprobation, and even abhorrence, too strong for the occasion. . . .

Under one aspect of the question, all these gentlemen travellers are
right: they are right in their estimate of the condition of the Indian squaws –
they *are* drudges, slaves: and they are right in the opinion that the condition of the women in any community is a test of the advance of moral and
intellectual cultivation in that community; but it is not a test of the virtue
or civilisation of the man; in these Indian tribes, where the men are the
noblest and bravest of their kind, the women are held of no account, are
despised and oppressed. But it does appear to me that the woman among
these Indians holds her true natural position relatively to the state of the
man and the state of society; and this cannot be said of all societies.

Take into consideration, in the first place, that in these Indian communities the task of providing subsistence falls solely and entirely on the men.
When it is said, in general terms, that the men do nothing but *hunt* all day,
while the women are engaged in perpetual *toil*, I suppose this suggests
to civilised readers the idea of a party of gentlemen at Melton, or a turn-out
of Mr. Meynell's hounds; – or at most a deer-stalking excursion to the
Highlands – a holiday affair; – while the women, poor souls! must sit at
home and sew, and spin, and cook victuals. But what is the life of an Indian
hunter? – one of incessant, almost killing toil, and often danger. A hunter
goes out at dawn, knowing that, if he returns empty, his wife and his little
ones must *starve* – no uncommon predicament! He comes home at sunset,
spent with fatigue, and unable even to speak. His wife takes off his moccasins, places before him what food she has, or, if latterly the chase has
failed, probably no food at all, or only a little parched wild rice. She then
examines his hunting-pouch, and in it finds the claws, or beak, or tongue
of the game, or other indications by which she knows what it is, and where
to find it. She then goes for it, and drags it home. When he is refreshed, the
hunter caresses his wife and children, relates the events of his chase, smokes
his pipe, and goes to sleep – to begin the same life on the following day.

Where, then, the whole duty and labour of providing the means of
subsistence, ennobled by danger and courage, fall upon the man, the
woman naturally sinks in importance, and is a dependent drudge. But she

is not therefore, I suppose, so *very* miserable, nor, relatively, so very abject; she is sure of protection; sure of maintenance, at least while the man has it; sure of kind treatment; sure that she will never have her children taken from her but by death; sees none better off than herself, and has no conception of a superior destiny; and it is evident that in such a state the appointed and necessary share of the woman is the household work, and all other domestic labour. As to the necessity of carrying burthens, when moving the camp from place to place, and felling and carrying wood, this is the most dreadful part of her lot; and however accustomed from youth to the axe, the paddle, and the carrying-belt, it brings on internal injuries and severe suffering – and yet it *must* be done. For a man to carry burthens would absolutely incapacitate him for a hunter, and consequently from procuring sufficient meat for his family. Hence, perhaps, the contempt with which they regard it. And an Indian woman is unhappy, and her pride is hurt, if her husband should be seen with a load on his back; this was strongly expressed by one among them who said it was "unmanly;" and that "she could not bear to see it!"

Hence, however hard the lot of woman, she is in no *false* position. The two sexes are in their natural and true position relatively to the state of society, and the means of subsistence . . .

Then, when we speak of the *drudgery* of the women, we must note the equal division of labour; there is no class of women privileged to sit still while others work. Every squaw makes the clothing, mats, moccasins, and boils the kettle for her own family. Compare her life with the refined leisure of an elegant woman in the higher classes of our society, and it is wretched and abject; but compare her life with that of a servant-maid of all work, or a factory girl, – I do say that the condition of the squaw is gracious in comparison, dignified by domestic feelings, and by equality with all around her. If women are to be exempted from toil in reverence to the sex, and as *women*, I can understand this, though I think it unreasonable; but if it be merely a privilege of station, and confined to a certain set, while the great primeval penalty is doubled on the rest, then I do not see where is the great gallantry and consistency of this our Christendom, nor what right we have to look down upon the barbarism of the Indian savages who make *drudges* of their women.

I will just mention here the extreme delicacy and personal modesty of the women of these tribes, which may seem strange when we see them brought up and living in crowded wigwams, where a whole family is herded within a space of a few yards: but the lower classes of the Irish, brought up in their cabins, are remarkable for the same feminine characteristic: it is as if true modesty were from within, and could hardly be outwardly defiled.

But to return. Another boast over the Indian savages in this respect is, that we set a much higher value on the chastity of women.

We are told (with horror) that among some of the north-west tribes the man offers his wife or sister, nothing loth, to his guest, as a part of the duty of hospitality; and this is, in truth, *barbarism*! – the heartless brutality on one side, and the shameless indifference on the other, may well make a woman's heart shrink within her. But what right have civilised *men* to exclaim, and look sublime and self-complacent about the matter? . . . .

Such women as those poor perverted sacrificed creatures who haunt our streets, or lead as guilty lives in lavish splendour, are utterly unknown among the Indians.

With regard to female right of property, there is no such thing as real property among them, except the hunting-grounds or territory which are the possession of the tribe. The personal property, as the clothing, mats, cooking and hunting apparatus, all the interior of the wig-wam, in short, seems to be under the control of the woman; and on the death of her husband the woman remains in possession of the lodge, and all it contains, except the medal, flag, or other insignia of dignity, which go to his son or male relatives. The corn she raises, and the maple sugar she makes, she can always dispose of as she thinks fit – they are *hers*.

It seems to me a question whether the Europeans, who, Heaven knows, have much to answer for in their intercourse with these people, have not, in some degree, injured the cause of the Indian women: – first, by corrupting them; secondly, by checking the improvement of all their own peculiar manufactures. They prepared deer skins with extraordinary skill; I have seen dresses of the mountain sheep and young buffalo skins, richly embroidered, and almost equal in beauty and softness to a Cashmere shawl; and I could mention other things. It is reasonable to presume that as these manufactures must have been progressively improved, there might have been farther progression, had we not substituted for articles they could themselves procure or fabricate, those which we fabricate; we have taken the work out of their hands, and all motive to work, while we have created wants which they cannot supply. We have clothed them in blankets – we have not taught them to weave blankets. We have substituted guns for the bows and arrows – but they cannot make guns: for the natural progress of arts and civilisation springing from within, and from their own intelligence and resources, we have substituted a sort of civilisation from without, foreign to their habits, manners organisation: we are making paupers of them; and this by a kind of terrible necessity. . . .

I must stop here: but do you not think, from the hints I have rather illogically and incoherently thrown together, that we may assume as a general principle, that the true importance and real dignity of woman is every-where, in savage and civilised communities, regulated by her capacity of being useful; or, in other words, that her condition is decided by the share she takes in providing for her own subsistence and the well-being of society as a productive labourer? Where she is idle and useless by privi-lege of sex, a divinity and an idol, a victim or a toy, is not her position quite as lamentable, as false, as injurious to herself and all social progress, as where she is the drudge, slave, and possession of the man?

6. Harriet Martineau
from *Retrospect of Western Travel*

FROM the day of my entering the States till that of my leaving Philadelphia, I had seen society basking in one bright sunshine of good will. The sweet temper and kindly manners of the Americans are so striking to foreigners, that it is some time before the dazzled stranger perceives that, genuine as is all this good, evils as black as night exist along with it. I had been received with such hearty hospitality everywhere, and had lived among friends so conscientious in their regard for human rights, that though I had heard of abolition riots, and had observed somewhat of the degradation of the blacks, my mind had not yet been really troubled about the enmity of the races. The time of awakening must come. It began just before I left Philadelphia.

I was calling on a lady whom I had heard speak with strong horror of the abolitionists (with whom I had then no acquaintance); and she turned round upon me with the question whether I would not prevent, if I could, the marriage of a white person with a person of colour. I saw at once the beginning of endless troubles in this inquiry, and was very sorry it had been made: but my determination had been adopted long before, never to evade the great question of colour; never to provoke it; but always to meet it plainly in whatever form it should be presented. I replied that I would never, under any circumstances, try to separate persons who really loved, believing such to be truly those whom God hath joined: but I observed that the case she put was one not likely to happen, as I believed the blacks were no more disposed to marry the whites than the whites to marry the blacks. "You are an amalgamationist!" cried she. I told her that the party term was new to me; but that she must give what name she pleased to the principle I had declared in answer to her question. This lady is an eminent religionist, and denunciations spread rapidly from her. The day before I left Philadelphia, my old shipmate, the Prussian physician, arrived there, and lost no time in calling to tell me, with much agitation, that I must not go a step further south; that he had heard on all hands, within two hours of his arrival, that I was an amalgamationist, and that my having published a story against slavery would be fatal to me in the slave States. I did not give much credit to the latter part of this news; and saw plainly that all I had to do was to go straight on. I really desired to see the working of the slave system, and was glad that my having published against its principles divested me altogether of the character of the spy, and gave me an unquestioned liberty to publish the results of what I might observe. In order to see things as they were, it was necessary that people's minds should not be prepossessed by my friends as to my opinions and conduct; and I therefore forbade my Philadelphia friends to publish in the newspapers, as they wished, an antidote to the charges already current against me.

The next day I first set foot in a slave State, arriving in the evening at Baltimore. I dreaded inexpressibly the first sight of a slave, and could not help speculating on the lot of every person of colour I saw from the windows, the first few days. The servants in the house where I was were free blacks.

Before a week was over, I perceived that all that is said in England of the hatred of the whites to the blacks in America is short of the truth. The slanders that I heard of the free blacks were too gross to injure my estimation of any but those who spoke them. In Baltimore the bodies of coloured people exclusively are taken for dissection, "because the whites do not like it, and the coloured people cannot resist." It is wonderful that the bodily structure can be (with the exception of the colouring of the skin) thus assumed to be the pattern of that of the whites; that the exquisite nervous system, the instrument of moral as well as physical pleasures and pains, can be nicely investigated on the ground of its being analogous with that of the whites; that not only the mechanism, but the sensibilities of the degraded race should be argued from to those of the exalted order, and that men come from such a study with contempt for these brethren in their countenances, hatred in their hearts, and insult on their tongues. These students are the men who cannot say that the coloured people have not nerves that quiver under moral injury, nor a brain that is on fire with insult, nor pulses that throb under oppression. These are the men who should stay the hand of the rash and ignorant possessors of power who crush the being of creatures, like themselves, "fearfully and wonderfully made." But to speak the right word, to hold out the helping hand, these searchers into man have not light nor strength. . . .

A lady from New England, staying in Baltimore, was one day talking over slavery with me, her detestation of it being great, when I told her I dreaded seeing a slave. "You have seen one," said she. "You were waited on by a slave yesterday evening." She told me of a gentleman who let out and lent out his slaves to wait at gentlemen's houses, and that the tall handsome mulatto who handed the tea at a party the evening before was one of these. I was glad it was over for once; but I never lost the painful feeling caused to a stranger by intercourse with slaves. No familiarity with them, no mirth and contentment on their part ever soothed the miserable restlessness caused by the presence of a deeply-injured fellow-being. No wonder or ridicule on the spot avails anything to the stranger. He suffers, and must suffer from this, deeply and long, as surely as he is human and hates oppression.

The next slave that I saw, knowing that it was a slave, was at Washington, where a little negro child took hold of my gown in the passage of our boarding-house, and entered our drawing-room with me. She shut the door softly, as asking leave to stay. I took up a newspaper. She sat at my feet, and began amusing herself with my shoe-strings. Finding herself not discouraged, she presently begged play by peeping at me above and on each side the newspaper. She was a bright-eyed, merry-hearted child, – confiding, like other children, and dreading no evil, but doomed, hopelessly doomed to ignorance, privation, and moral degradation. When I looked at her, and thought of the fearful disobedience to the first of moral laws, the cowardly treachery, the cruel abuse of power involved in thus dooming to blight a being so helpless, so confiding, and so full of promise, a horror came over me which sickened my very soul. To see slaves is not to be reconciled to slavery.

❄ ❄ ❄ ❄

There is something inexpressibly disgusting in the sight of a slave woman in the field. I do not share in the horror of the Americans at the idea of women being employed in out-door labour. It did not particularly gratify me to see the cows always milked by men (where there were no slaves); and the hay and harvest fields would have looked brighter in my eyes if women had been there to share the wholesome and cheerful toil. But a negro woman behind the plough presents a very different object from the English mother with her children in the turnip field, or the Scotch lassie among the reapers. In her pre-eminently ugly costume, the long, scanty, dirty woollen garment, with the shabby large bonnet at the back of her head, the perspiration streaming down her dull face, the heavy tread of the splay foot, the slovenly air with which she guides her plough, – a more hideous object cannot well be conceived; unless it be the same woman at home, in the negro quarter, as the cluster of slave dwellings is called. . . .

Meantime, you attempt to talk with the slaves. You ask how old that very aged man is, or that boy; they will give you no intelligible answer. Slaves never know, or never will tell, their ages; and this is the reason why the census presents such extraordinary reports on this point; declaring a great number to be above a hundred years old. If they have a kind master, they will boast to you of how much he gave for each of them, and what sums he has refused for them. If they have a hard master, they will tell you that they would have more to eat, and be less flogged, but that massa is busy, and has no time to come down, and see that they have enough to eat. Your hostess is well known on this plantation, and her kind face has been recognized from a distance; and already a negro woman has come to her with seven or eight eggs, for which she knows she shall receive a quarter dollar. You follow her to the negro quarter, where you see a tidy woman knitting, while the little children who are left in her charge are basking in the sun, or playing all kinds of antics in the road; little shining, plump, clear-eyed children, whose mirth makes you sad, when you look round upon their parents, and see what these bright creatures are to come to. You enter one of the dwellings, where every thing seems to be of the same dusky hue: the crib against the wall, the walls themselves, and the floor, all look one yellow. More children are crouched round the wood fire, lying almost in the embers. You see a woman pressing up against the wall, like an idiot, with her shoulder turned towards you, and her apron held up to her face. You ask what is the matter with her, and are told that she is shy. You see a woman rolling herself about in a crib, with her head tied up. You ask if she is ill, and are told that she has not a good temper; that she struck at a girl she was jealous of with an axe; and the weapon being taken from her, she threw herself into the well, and was nearly drowned before she was taken out, with her head much hurt.

7. Caroline Clive
from *Diary*

Saturday, July 14th.

The steamboat set off at half-past eight. I met with the Dinan passengers again and found that instead of merchants they were artillery officers making a tour on a short leave. I began to talk with them once more, but presently sickness began all over the vessel and the soul of nobody was their own, with exceptions, however. I and two ladies escaped, and a few gentlemen, but all the rest were more or less sick and looked as if not only they, but nobody else, had ever suffered so before. All round rose the most hideous gurging mixed with groans and crying. Basins were handed about on all sides and when a wretch leaned over the vessel's side the boatswain came with his mop and wiped away the atrocities before his eyes. '*Boy*,' cried a voice of detestation, 'Boy, go to the leeward, the wind is sending it all over us.' An unfortunate father and husband took care of a wife who was sick, sick children and a sick friend. He held the basin for each, calling aloud at intervals, '*Garçon, encore un bassin.*' One brute of a woman came beside me to the spot whither I had gone to escape the thick of the sights and leaning over the side asked if I thought looking at the sea would make her sick. I said indeed I was afraid so and she had better turn her eyes anywhere else, but she answered that on the contrary she was trying the experiment on purpose, for not being in health, she thought it might do her good; and then she stood close to me and tried to bring it to bear. I am thankful to say health was denied her. In the midst of this anguish I felt not only indifferent to the sufferings of those around but full of hate and detestation, and when a Jersey man came and sat by me and I found he was as well as I was, I considered him and his affairs the most respectable on board. I learned that he had a son who was '*ce que vous appellez crackbrain.*'

It was a fine sea, agitated but not rough and became rougher as we drew near to Jersey. This was a trial to the few who had hitherto escaped. Among them was an old lady sitting on the bench in the middle of the deck, and reading for her life at *The Robber*, an English novel, evidently published in France by its yellow paper cover and state of single volume-ness. Now and then as the sea became rougher, she got up and was sick over the side of the vessel and then sat smiling down again and went on with her book. A rather younger woman with small feet in thin black silk stockings sat by her and read equally hard at another book. A still younger man sat on the same bench and when the old lady was sick, held her at the back of the waist at the vessel's side. Presently when we had passed the Race of Alderney he fetched out of the cabin a young lady, very pretty, dressed in pink with a black mantilla and a delicate cap with blue ribbons. She tottered along, so giddy that she seemed at the mercy of her conductor, and sat down holding her face on both sides with her white hands. Her hair was bound across her forehead, and there she sat, giddy, pretty, pale, her eyes closed. He brought a smelling bottle, folded her shawl about her (which fell off for ever) and tried to talk to the others in order to amuse her. At last she began to lift up her large blue eyes upon him and some times to smile briefly, and then unhappily she showed that she thought herself uncommonly pretty; but as for her cavalier it was evident that he had but one current of ideas about her.

———

1839

8. Queen Victoria
from *Diary*

Tuesday, 15th October.

At about $\frac{1}{2}$ p. 12 I sent for Albert; he came to the Closet where I was alone, and after a few minutes I said to him, that I thought he must be aware *why* I wished them to come here, – and that it would make me *too happy* if he would consent to what I wished (to marry me). We embraced each other, and he was *so* kind, *so* affectionate. I told him I was quite unworthy of him, – he said he would be very happy "das Leben mit dir zu zubringen," and was so kind, and seemed so happy, that I really felt it was the happiest brightest moment in my life. I told him it was a great sacrifice, – which he wouldn't allow; I then told him of the necessity of keeping it a secret, except to his father . . . I feel the happiest of human beings.

———

1840

9. Mary Shelley
from *The Poetical Works of Shelley*

Obstacles have long existed to my presenting the public with a perfect edition of Shelley's Poems. These being at last happily removed, I hasten to fulfil an important duty, – that of giving the productions of a sublime genius to the world, with all the correctness possible, and of, at the same time, detailing the history of those productions, as they sprung, living and warm, from his heart and brain. I abstain from any remark on the occurrences of his private life; except, inasmuch as the passions which they engendered, inspired his poetry. This is not the time to relate the truth; and I should reject any colouring of the truth. No account of these events has ever been given at all approaching reality in their details, either as regards himself or others; nor shall I further allude to them than to remark, that the errors of action, committed by a man as noble and generous as Shelley, may, as far as he only is concerned, be fearlessly avowed, by those who loved him, in the firm conviction, that were they judged impartially, his character would stand in fairer and brighter light than that of any contemporary. Whatever faults he had, ought to find extenuation among his fellows, since they proved him to be human; without them, the exalted nature of his soul would have raised him into something divine.

The qualities that struck any one newly introduced to Shelley, were, first, a gentle and cordial goodness that animated his intercourse with warm affection, and helpful sympathy. The other, the eagerness and ardour with which he was attached to the cause of human happiness and improvement. To defecate life of its misery and its evil, was the ruling passion of his soul: he dedicated to it every power of his mind, every pulsation of his heart. He looked on political freedom as the direct agent to effect the happiness of mankind; and thus any new-sprung hope of liberty inspired a joy and an exultation more intense and wild than he could have felt for any personal advantage. Those who have never experienced the workings of passion on general and unselfish subjects, cannot understand this; and it must be difficult of comprehension to the younger generation rising around, since they cannot remember the scorn and hatred with which the partizans of reform were regarded some few years ago, nor the persecutions to which they were exposed. He had been from youth the victim of the state of feeling inspired by the reaction of the French Revolution; and believing firmly in the justice and excellence of his views, it cannot be wondered that a nature as sensitive, as impetuous, and as generous as his, should put its whole force into the attempt to alleviate for others the evils of those systems from which he had himself suffered. Many advantages attended his birth; he spurned them all when balanced with what he considered his duties. He was generous to imprudence, devoted to heroism.

These characteristics breathe throughout his poetry. The struggle for human weal; the resolution firm to martyrdom; the impetuous pursuit; the glad triumph in good; the determination not to despair. Such were the features that marked those of his works which he regarded with most complacency, as sustained by a lofty subject and useful aim.

In addition to these, his poems may be divided into two classes, – the purely imaginative, and those which sprung from the emotions of his heart. Among the former may be classed "The Witch of Atlas," "Adonais," and his latest composition, left imperfect, "The Triumph of Life." In the first of these particularly, he gave the reins to his fancy, and luxuriated in every idea as it rose; in all, there is that sense of mystery which formed an essential portion of his perception of life – a clinging to the subtler inner spirit, rather than to the outward form – a curious and metaphysical anatomy of human passion and perception.

The second class is, of course, the more popular, as appealing at once to emotions common to us all; some of these rest on the passion of love, others on grief and despondency; others on the sentiments inspired by natural objects. Shelley's conception of love was exalted, absorbing, allied to all that is purest and noblest in our nature, and warmed by earnest passion; such it appears when he gave it a voice in verse. Yet he was usually averse to expressing these feelings, except when highly idealised; and many of his more beautiful effusions he had cast aside, unfinished, and they were never seen by me till after I had lost him. Others, as for instance, "Rosalind and Helen," and "Lines written among the Euganean Hills," I found among his papers by chance; and with some difficulty urged him to complete them. There are others, such as the "Ode to the Sky Lark," and "The Cloud," which, in the opinion of many critics bear a purer poetical stamp than any other of his productions. They were written as his mind prompted, listening to the carolling of the bird, aloft in the azure sky of Italy; or marking the cloud as it sped across the heavens, while he floated in his boat on the Thames.

No poet was ever warmed by a more genuine and unforced inspiration. His extreme sensibility gave the intensity of passion to his intellectual pursuits; and rendered his mind keenly alive to every perception of outward objects, as well as to his internal sensations. Such a gift is, among the sad vicissitudes of human life, the disappointments we meet, and the galling sense of our own mistakes and errors, fraught with pain; to escape from such, he delivered up his soul to poetry, and felt happy when he sheltered himself from the influence of human sympathies, in the wildest regions of fancy. His imagination has been termed too brilliant, his thoughts too subtle. He loved to idealise reality; and this is a taste shared by few. We are willing to have our passing whims exalted into passions, for this gratifies our vanity; but few of us understand or sympathise with the endeavour to ally the love of abstract beauty, and adoration of abstract good, the τὸ ἀγαθὸν καὶ τὸ καλὸν of the Socratic philosophers, with our sympathies with our kind. In this Shelley resembled Plato; both taking more delight in the abstract and the ideal, than in the special and tangible. This did not result from imitation; for it was not till Shelley resided in Italy that he made Plato his study; he then translated his Symposium and his

Ion; and the English language boasts of no more brilliant composition, than Plato's Praise of Love, translated by Shelley. To return to his own poetry. The luxury of imagination, which sought nothing beyond itself, as a child burthens itself with spring flowers, thinking of no use beyond the enjoyment of gathering them, often showed itself in his verses: they will be only appreciated by minds who have resemblance to his own; and the mystic subtlety of many of his thoughts will meet the same fate. The metaphysical strain that characterises much of what he has written, was, indeed, the portion of his works to which, apart from those whose scope was to awaken mankind to aspirations for what he considered the true and good, he was himself particularly attached. There is much, however, that speaks to the many. When he would consent to dismiss these huntings after the obscure, which, entwined with his nature as they were, he did with difficulty, no poet ever expressed in sweeter, more heart-reaching, or more passionate verse, the gentler or more forcible emotions of the soul.

A wise friend once wrote to Shelley, "You are still very young, and in certain essential respects you do not yet sufficiently perceive that you are so." It is seldom that the young know what youth is till they have got beyond its period; and time was not given him to attain this knowledge. It must be remembered that there is the stamp of such inexperience on all he wrote; he had not completed his nine and twentieth year when he died. The calm of middle life did not add the seal of the virtues which adorn maturity to those generated by the vehement spirit of youth. Through life also he was a martyr to ill health, and constant pain wound up his nerves to a pitch of susceptibility that rendered his views of life different from those of a man in the enjoyment of healthy sensations. Perfectly gentle and forbearing in manner, he suffered a good deal of internal irritability, or rather excitement, and his fortitude to bear was almost always on the stretch; and thus, during a short life, had gone through more experience of sensation, than many whose existence is protracted. "If I die to-morrow," he said, on the eve of his unanticipated death, "I have lived to be older than my father." The weight of thought and feeling burdened him heavily; you read his sufferings in his attenuated frame, while you perceived the mastery he held over them in his animated countenance and brilliant eyes.

He died, and the world shewed no outward sign; but his influence over mankind, though slow in growth, is fast augmenting, and in the ameliorations that have taken place in the political state of his country, we may trace in part the operation of his arduous struggles. His spirit gathers peace in its new state from the sense that, though late, his exertions were not made in vain, and in the progress of the liberty he so fondly loved.

He died, and his place among those who knew him intimately, has never been filled up. He walked beside them like a spirit of good to comfort and benefit – to enlighten the darkness of life with irradiations of genius, to cheer it with his sympathy and love. Any one, once attached to Shelley, must feel all other affections, however true and fond, as wasted on barren soil in comparison. It is our best consolation to know that such a pure-minded and exalted being was once among us, and now exists where we hope one day to join him; – although the intolerant, in their blindness, poured down anathemas, the Spirit of Good, who can judge the heart, never rejected him. In the notes appended to the poems, I have endeavoured to narrate the origin and history of each. The loss of nearly all letters and papers which refer to his early life, renders the execution more imperfect than it would otherwise have been. I have, however, the liveliest recollection of all that was done and said during the period of my knowing him. Every impression is as clear as if stamped yesterday, and I have no apprehension of any mistake in my statements, as far as they go. In other respects, I am, indeed, incompetent; but I feel the importance of the task, and regard it as my most sacred duty. I endeavour to fulfil it in a manner he would himself approve; and hope in this publication to lay the first stone of a monument due to Shelley's genius, his sufferings, and his virtues.

❦ ❦ ❦ ❦

MY task becomes inexpressibly painful as the year draws near that which sealed our earthly fate; and each poem and each event it records, has a real or mysterious connexion with the fatal catastrophe. I feel that I am incapable of putting on paper the history of those times. The heart of the man, abhorred of the poet,

Who could peep and botanize upon his mother's grave,

does not appear to me less inexplicably framed than that of one who can dissect and probe past woes, and repeat to the public ear the groans drawn from them in the throes of their agony.

The year 1821 was spent in Pisa, or at the baths of San Giuliano. We were not, as our wont had been, alone – friends had gathered round us. Nearly all are dead; and when memory recurs to the past, she wanders among tombs: the genius with all his blighting errors and mighty powers; the companion of Shelley's ocean-wanderings, and the sharer of his fate, than whom no man ever existed more gentle, generous, and fearless; and others, who found in Shelley's society, and in his great knowledge and warm sympathy, delight, instruction and solace, have joined him beyond the grave. A few survive who have felt life a desert since he left it. What misfortune can equal death? Change can convert every other into a blessing, or heal its sting – death alone has no cure; it shakes the foundations of the earth on which we tread, it destroys its beauty, it casts down our shelter, it exposes us bare to desolation; when those we love have passed into eternity, "life is the desert and the solitude," in which we are forced to linger – but never find comfort more. . . .

Shelley's favourite taste was boating; when living near the Thames, or by the lake of Geneva, much of his life was spent on the water. On the shore of every lake, or stream, or sea, near which he dwelt, he had a boat moored. He had latterly enjoyed this pleasure again. There are no pleasure-boats on the Arno, and the shallowness of its waters except in winter time, when the stream is too turbid and impetuous for boating, rendered it difficult to get any skiff light enough to float. Shelley, however, overcame the difficulty; he, together with a friend, contrived a boat such as the huntsmen carry about with them in the Maremma, to cross the sluggish but deep streams that intersect the forests, a boat of laths and pitched canvas; it held three persons, and he was often seen on the Arno in it, to the horror of the Italians, who remonstrated on the danger, and could not understand how any one could take pleasure in an exercise that risked life. "Ma va per la vita!" they exclaimed. I little thought how true their words would prove. He once ventured with a friend, on the glassy sea of a calm day, down the Arno and round the coast, to Leghorn, which by keeping close in shore was very practicable. They returned to Pisa by the canal, when, missing the direct cut, they got entangled among weeds, and the boat upset; a wetting was all the harm done, except that the intense cold of his drenched clothes made Shelley faint. Once I went down with him to the mouth of the Arno, where the stream, then high and swift, met the tideless sea and disturbed its sluggish waters; it was a waste and dreary scene; the desert sand stretched into a point surrounded by waves that broke idly though perpetually around; it was scene very similar to Lido, of which he had said,–

> I love all waste
> And solitary places; where we taste
> The pleasure of believing what we see
> Is boundless, as we wish our souls to be;
> And such was this wide ocean, and this shore
> More barren than its billows.

Our little boat was of greater use, unaccompanied by any danger, when we removed to the baths. Some friends lived at the village of Pugnano, four miles off, and we went to and fro to see them, in our boat, by the canal; which, fed by the Serchio, was though an artificial, a full and picturesque stream, making its way under verdant banks sheltered by trees that dipped their boughs into the murmuring waters. By day, multitudes of ephemera darted to and fro on the surface; at night, the fire-flies came out among the shrubs on the banks; the cicale at noon day kept up their hum: the aziola cooed in the quiet evening. It was a pleasant summer, bright in all but Shelley's health and inconstant spirits; yet he enjoyed himself greatly, and became more and more attached to the part of the country where chance appeared to cast us. Sometimes he projected taking a farm, situated on the height of one of the near hills, surrounded by chesnut and pinewoods, and overlooking a wide extent of country; or of settling still further in the maritime Apennines, at Massa. Several of his slighter and unfinished poems were inspired by these scenes, and by the companions around us. It is the nature of that poetry however which overflows from the soul oftener to express sorrow and regret than joy; for it is when oppressed by the weight of life, and away from those he loves, that the poet has recourse to the solace of expression in verse.

Still Shelley's passion was the ocean; and he wished that our summers, instead of being passed among the hills near Pisa, should be spent on the shores of the sea. It was very difficult to find a spot. We shrank from Naples from a fear that the heats would disagree with Percy; Leghorn had lost its only attraction, since our friends who had resided there were returned to England; and Monte Nero being the resort of many English, we did not wish to find ourselves in the midst of a colony of chance travellers. No one then thought it possible to reside at Via Reggio, which latterly has become a summer resort. The low lands and bad air of Maremma stretch the whole length of the western shores of the Mediterranean,till broken by the rocks and hills of Spezia. It was a vague idea; but Shelley suggested an excursion to Spezia to see whether it would be feasible to spend a summer there. The beauty of the bay enchanted him – we saw no house to suit us – but the notion took root, and many circumstances, enchained as by fatality, occurred to urge him to execute it.

❋ ❋ ❋ ❋

He spent a week at Pisa, employed in kind offices toward his friends, and enjoying with keen delight the renewal of their intercourse. He then embarked with Williams, the chosen and beloved sharer of his pleasures and his fate, to return to us. We waited for them in vain; the sea by its restless moaning seemed to desire to inform us of what we would not learn: – but a veil may well be drawn over such misery. The real anguish of those moments transcended all the fictions that the most glowing imagination ever portrayed: our seclusion, the savage nature of the inhabitants of the

surrounding villages, and our immediate vicinity to the troubled sea, combined to imbue with strange horror the days of our uncertainty. The truth
was at last known, – a truth that made our loved and lovely Italy appear a
tomb, its sky a pall. Every heart echoed the deep lament, and my only consolation was in the praise and earnest love that each voice bestowed and
each countenance demonstrated for him we had lost, – not, I fondly hope,
for ever: his unearthly and elevated nature is a pledge of the continuation
of his being, though in an altered form. Rome received his ashes, they are
deposited beneath its weed-grown wall, and 'the world's sole monument'
is enriched by his remains.

---

10. Queen Victoria
from *Diary*

Monday, 10th February.
Got up at a $\frac{1}{4}$ to 9 – well, and having slept well; and breakfasted at $\frac{1}{2}$ p. 9.
Mamma came before and brought me a Nosegay of orange flowers.

Had my hair dressed and the wreath of orange flowers put on. Saw
Albert for the *last* time *alone*, as my *Bridegroom*. Dressed. . . .

At $\frac{1}{2}$ p. 12 I set off, dearest Albert having gone before. I wore a white
satin gown with a very deep flounce of Honiton lace, imitation of old. I
wore my Turkish diamond necklace and earrings, and Albert's beautiful
sapphire brooch. Mamma and the Duchess of Sutherland went in the
carriage with me. I never saw such crowds of people as there were in the
Park, and they cheered most enthusiastically. When I arrived at St. James's,
I went into the dressing-room where my 12 young Train-bearers were,
dressed all in white with white roses, which had a beautiful effect. Here I
waited a little till dearest Albert's Procession had moved into the Chapel.
I then went with my Train-bearers and ladies into the Throne-room,
where the Procession formed . . .

Queen Anne's room was full of people, ranged on seats one higher than
the other, as also in the Guard room, and by the Staircase, – all very
friendly; the Procession looked beautiful going downstairs. Part of the
Colour Court was also covered in and full of people who were very civil.
The Flourish of Trumpets ceased as I entered the Chapel, and the organ
began to play, which had a beautiful effect. At the Altar, to my right, stood
Albert; Mamma was on my left . . .

Lord Melbourne stood close to me with the Sword of State. The
Ceremony was very imposing, and fine and simple, and I think OUGHT to

make an everlasting impression on every one who promises at the Altar to *keep* what he or she promises. Dearest Albert repeated everything very distinctly. I felt so happy when the ring was put on, and by Albert. As soon as the Service was over, the Procession returned as it came, with the exception that my beloved Albert led me out. The applause was very great, in the Colour Court as we came through; Lord Melbourne, good man, was very much affected during the Ceremony and at the applause. We all returned to the Throne-room, where the Signing of the register took place.

We then went into the Closet, and the Royal Family waited with me there till the ladies had got into their carriages. I gave all the Train-bearers as a brooch a small *eagle* of turquoise. I then returned to Buckingham Palace alone with Albert; they cheered us really most warmly and heartily; the crowd was immense; and the Hall at Buckingham Palace was full of people; they cheered us again and again. The great Drawing-room and Throne-room were full of people of rank, and numbers of children were there. . . .

I went and sat on the sofa in my dressing-room with Albert; and we talked together there from 10 m. to 2 till 20 m. p. 2. Then we went downstairs where all the Company was assembled and went into the dining-room – dearest Albert leading me in, and my Train being borne by 3 Pages. . . .

I sat between dearest Albert and the Duke of Sussex. My health and dearest Albert's were drunk. The Duke was very kind and civil. Albert and I drank a glass of wine with Lord Melbourne, who seemed much affected by the whole. I talked to all after the breakfast, and to Lord Melbourne, whose fine coat I praised. . . .

I went upstairs and undressed and put on a white silk gown trimmed with swansdown, and a bonnet with orange flowers. Albert went downstairs and undressed. At 20 m. to 4 Lord Melbourne came to me and stayed with me till 10 m. to 4. I shook hands with him and he kissed my hand. Talked of how well everything went off. "Nothing could have gone off better," he said, and of the people being in such good humour and having also received him well; of my receiving the Addresses from the House of Lords and Commons; of his coming down to Windsor in time for dinner. I begged him not to go to the party; he was a little tired; I would let him know when we arrived; I pressed his hand once more, and he said, "God bless you, Ma'am," most kindly, and with such a kind look. Dearest Albert came up and fetched me downstairs, where we took leave of Mamma and drove off at near 4; I and Albert alone.

11. Sydney Owenson, Lady Morgan
from *Woman and her Master*

In the great and general progress of knowledge, much has been neglected, much overstepped; and, amidst the most beneficial reforms and sagacious improvements, great moral incoherences still linger, which require to be eliminated, before the interests of humanity can be based upon a system, consonant with nature, and conducive to general happiness.

But where lies the oversight? Can it be one, astounding in its obviousness, and all-important in its mischiefs? While codes have been reformed, institutes rationalized, and the interests of orders and classes have been minutely attended to, has one half of the human species been left, even to the present moment, where the first rude arrangements of a barbarous society and its barbarous laws had placed it. Is woman still a thing of sufferance and not of rights, as in the ignorant infancy of early aggregation, when the law of the strongest was the only law acted on? and in the great impulsion to a regenerating reform, has that most applicable and intelligible instrument of social improvement and national well being, has Woman, been forgotten ?

Even now, when supremacy has been transferred from muscle to mind, has that most subtle spirit, that being of most mobile fibre, that most sensitive and apprehensive organization – has she, whom God has placed, to be a "mate and a help to man," at the head of his creation, the foundress of nations, the embellisher of races, has she alone been left behind, at the very starting-post of civilization, while around her all progresses and improves? And is man still "the master," and does he, by a misdirected self-love, still perpetuate her ignorance and her dependance, when her emancipation and improvement are most wanting, as the crowning element of his own happiness? If, in the progress of refinement, he has brightened instead of breaking the chain of his slave, he has only linked a more shewy nucleus of evil to his own destiny, and bound up, with his noblest views of national and social development, a principle that too often thwarts the progress and enfeebles the results of his best reforms.

If, in the first era of society, woman was the victim of man's physical superiority, she is still, in the last, the subject of laws, in the enactment of which she has had no voice – amenable to the penalties of a code, from which she derives but little protection. While man, in his first crude attempts at jurisprudence, has surrounded the sex with restraints and disabilities, he has left its natural rights unguarded, and its liberty unacknowledged. Merging the very existence of woman in his own, he has allowed her no separate interest, assigned her no independent possessions: "for," says the law – the law of man – "the husband is the head of the wife, and all that she has belongs to him." Even the fruit of her own labour is torn from her, unless she is protected by the solitary blessedness of a derided but innocent celibacy, or by an infamous frailty. Thus, (to adopt the barbarous jargon of these barbarous laws,) as *femme sole*, or *femme couverte*, she is equally the victim of violence and injustice, those universal and invariable attributes of the law of the strongest.

But there is still a more terrible outrage committed against all that is most dear to her nature; she may be deprived of the possession of her own child – of that child, which, but an hour before, was shrined in her bosom, a portion of herself, flesh of her flesh, and bone of her bone – her infant may be torn from her while it is still drawing its nourishment from her breast, and while she is still "thanking the gods for all her labour past," as she gazes tenderly on its helplessness.

In the progress of moral improvement, it is true, some faint rays of light have broken on the darkness of these wrongs; and equity, the common sense of advancing civilization, has endeavoured, by a system of fictions, to defeat the law. Timidly admitting the possible injustice of early institutes, it hesitatingly evades the consequences, and ventures not to touch the principle. Thus has the destiny of woman become only more complicated and uncertain; and rights, on which the nature of things has already decided, are kept for years at anxious issue, through the incoherences and contradictions of the machinery by which they have been bolstered, until a life of hope deferred may be worn out, before the industry and intelligence of its defenders can acquire a mastery of the case, and ripen it to a decision.

But in vain has opinion, the new depository of power, the antagonist of physical force, opened its tribunals to the wrongs of the aggrieved! Even there her master meets her, citing against her what *he* calls philosophy and science; and if, even while these lines are tracing, a scanty measure of partial and reluctant amelioration has been wrung from the legislature, the exceptional fact has only been made an occasion for the sterner assertion of the outrageous principle. The natural dependance of the sex on its master, its imputed inaptitude for the higher intellectual pursuits, and presumed incapacity for concentration, are still insisted upon; and, while woman is permitted to cultivate the arts which merely please, and which frequently corrupt, she is denounced as a thing unsexed, a *lusus naturæ*, if she directs her thoughts to pursuits which aspire to serve, and which never fail to elevate.

Educating her for the Harem, but calling on her for the practices of the Portico, man expects from his odalisque the firmness of the stoic, and demands from his servant the exercise of those virtues which, placing the *élite* of his own sex at the head of its muster-roll, give immortality to the master. He tells her "that obscurity is *her* true glory, insignificance her distinction, ignorance her lot, and passive obedience the perfection of her nature;" yet he expects from her, as the daily and hourly habit of her existence, that conquest over the passions by the strength of reason, that triumph of moral energy over the senses and their appetites, and that endurance of personal privations and self-denials, which with him (even under all the excitements of ambition and incentives to renown) are qualities of rare exception, the practices of most painful acquirement.

Such has been the destiny of woman amongst the most highly-organized and intellectual of the human races, and in the regions most favourable to their moral development. Among the inferior varieties, and in less temperate regions, she is even yet more degraded and helpless. The object and the victim of a brutal sensuality, her life passes in humiliating restriction and debasing ignorance; while her death is not unusually an act of murderous violence, or of refined torture.

But how has this Pariah of the species, this alien to law, this dupe of fictions and subject of force – how has she felt, how acted, how borne the destiny assigned her? Has she bowed her head to the yoke with tame acquiescence, as one for whose nature it was fitted and adapted? or has she, as slave, concubine, or wife, felt and protested? Has she not, under the corrupting influence of oppression,sometimes converted those qualities of her sex, which were designed as the supplement of the intellectual system of the species, as an aid to man in his war with the elements, into weapons against him? Has not her quick apprehension often degenerated into cunning under his misrule? Has she not, in discovering how little was to be hoped from his justice, succeeded in founding an empire over his passions? And has not man, who denies every right that interferes with his own supremacy, submitted to the spell which undermines it; and, by thus giving influence, direct or indirect, where he has withheld knowledge and denied rights, established an insidious, ignorant tyranny that perpetually thwarts his own designs, injures the best interests of society, and retards its progress to reform?

Still, notwithstanding her false position, woman has struggled through all disabilities and degradations, has justified the intentions of Nature in her behalf, and demonstrated her claim to share in the moral agency of the world. In all outbursts of mind, in every forward rush of the great march of improvement, she has borne a part; permitting herself to be used as an instrument, without hope of reward, and faithfully fulfilling her mission, without expectation of acknowledgment. She has, in various ages, given her secret services to her task-master, without partaking in his triumph, or sharing in his success. Her subtlety has insinuated views which man has shrank from exposing, and her adroitness found favour for doctrines, which he had the genius to conceive, but not the art to divulge. Priestess, prophetess, the oracle of the tripod, the sibyl of the cave, the veiled idol of the temple, the shrouded teacher of the academy, the martyr or missionary of a spiritual truth, the armed champion of a political cause, she has been covertly used for every purpose, by which man, when he has failed to reason his species into truth, has endeavoured to fanaticise it into good; whenever mind has triumphed by indirect means over the inertia of masses.

In all moral impulsions, woman has aided and been adopted; but, her efficient utility accomplished, the temporary part assigned her for temporary purposes performed, she has been ever hurled back into her natural obscurity, and conventional insignificance: no law against her has been repealed, no injury redressed, no right admitted. Alluded to, rather as an incident than a principal in the chronicles of nations, her influence, which cannot be denied, has been turned into a reproach; her genius, which could not be concealed, has been treated as a phenomenon, when not considered as monstrosity!

But where exist the evidences of these merits unacknowledged, of these penalties unrepealed? They are to be found carelessly scattered through all that is known in the written history of mankind, from the first to the last of its indited pages. They may be detected in the habits of the untamed savage, in the traditions of the semi-civilized barbarian! and in those fragments of the antiquity of our antiquity, scattered through undated epochs, – monuments of some great moral *débris*, which, like the fossil remains of long-imbedded and unknown species, serve to found a theory, or to establish a fact.

Wherever woman has been, there has she left the track of her humanity, to mark her passage – incidentally impressing the seal of her sensibility and her wrongs upon every phasis of society, and in every region, "from Indus to the Pole."

1842

12. Sarah Ellis
from *The Women of England*

How often has man returned to his home with a mind confused by the many voices, which in the mart, the exchange, or the public assembly, have addressed themselves to his inborn selfishness, or his worldly pride; and while his integrity was shaken, and his resolution gave way beneath the pressure of apparent necessity, or the insidious pretences of expediency, he has stood corrected before the clear eye of woman, as it looked directly to the naked truth, and detected the lurking evil of the specious act he was about to commit. Nay, so potent may have become this secret influence, that he may have borne it about with him like a kind of second conscience, for mental reference, and spiritual counsel, in moments of trial; and when the snares of the world were around him, and temptations from within and without have bribed over the witness in his own bosom, he has thought of the humble monitress who sat alone, guarding the fireside comforts of his distant home; and the remembrance of her character, clothed in moral beauty, has scattered the clouds before his mental vision, and sent him back to that beloved home, a wiser and a better man.

❀ ❀ ❀ ❀

IT may appear somewhat paradoxical to commence a chapter on the uses of conversation, by pointing out the uses of being silent; yet such is the importance to a woman, of knowing exactly when to cease from conversation, and when to withhold it altogether, that the silence of the female sex seems to have become proverbially synonymous with a degree of merit almost too great to be believed in as a fact. There could be no agreeable conversation carried on, if there were no good listeners, and from her position in society, it is the peculiar province of a woman, rather to lead others out into animated and intelligent communication, than to be intent upon making communications from the resources of her own mind.

Besides this, there are times when men, especially if they are of moody temperament, are more offended and annoyed by being talked to, than they could be by the greatest personal affront from the same quarter; and a woman of taste will readily detect the forbidding frown, the close-shut lips, and the averted eye, which indicate a determination not to be drawn out. She will then find opportunity for the indulgence of those secret trains of thought and feeling which naturally arise in every human mind; and while she plies her busy needle, and sits quietly musing by the side of her husband, her father, or her brother, she may be adding fresh materials from the world of thought, to that fund of conversational amusement, which she is ever ready to bring forward for their use.

❀ ❀ ❀ ❀

Besides the cases already described, there are some darker passages in human life, when women are thrown upon the actual *charm* of their conversation, for rendering more alluring, the home that is not valued as it should be. Perhaps a husband has learned before his marriage the fatal habit of seeking recreation in scenes of excitement and convivial mirth. It is but natural that such habits should with difficulty be broken off, and that he should look with something like weariness upon the quiet and monotony of his own fireside. Music cannot always please, and books to such a man are a tasteless substitute for the evening party. He may possibly admire his wife, consider her extremely good-looking, and, for a woman, think her very pleasant; but the sobriety of matrimony palls upon his vitiated taste, and he longs to feel himself a free man again amongst his old associates.

Nothing would disgust this man so much, or drive him away so effectually, as any assumption the part of his wife, of a *right* to detain him. The next most injudicious thing she could do, would be to exhibit symptoms of grief – of real sorrow and distress at his leaving her; for whatever may be said in novels on the subject of beauty in tears, seems to be rendered null and void by the circumstance of marriage having taken place between the parties.

The rational woman, whose conversation on this occasion is to serve her purpose more effectually than tears, knows better than to speak of what her husband would probably consider a most unreasonable subject of complaint. She tries to recollect some incident, some trait of character, or some anecdote of what has lately occurred within her knowledge, and relates it in her most lively and piquant manner. If conscious of beauty, she tries a little raillery, and plays gently upon some of her husband's not unpleasing peculiarities, looking all the while as disengaged and unsuspecting as she can. If his attention becomes fixed, she gives her conversation a more serious turn, and plunges at once into some theme of deep and absorbing interest. If her companion grows restless, she changes the subject, and again recollects something laughable to relate to him. Yet all the while her own poor heart is aching with the feverish anxiety that vacillates between the extremes of hope and fear. She gains courage, however, as time steals on, for her husband is by her side, and with her increasing courage her spirits become exhilarated, and she is indeed the happy woman she has hitherto but appeared; for at last her husband looks at his watch, is astonished to find it is too late to join his friends; and while the evening closes in, he wonders whether any other man has a wife so delightful and entertaining as his own.

✱ ✱ ✱ ✱

All that I have written in this volume, imperfect as it is, has been stimulated by a desire to increase the moral worth of my countrywomen, and enhance the domestic happiness of my native land. In order that this should be done effectually, it seems to me indispensably necessary, that women, whose parents are possessed of slender means, or engaged in business, and who can with extreme difficulty accomplish even so much as what is called "making their way," – that women in this class should be educated, not simply for ladies, but for useful and active members of society – and for this purpose, that they also should consider it no degradation to render their activity conducive to the purposes of trade.

It is a curious anomaly in the structure of modern society, that gentlemen may employ their hours of business in almost any degrading occupation, and, if they have but the means of supporting a respectable establishment at home, may be gentlemen still; while, if a lady does but touch any article, no matter how delicate, in the way of of trade, she loses caste, and ceases to be a lady.

I say this with all possible respect for those who have the good sense and the moral courage to employ themselves in the business of their fathers and their husbands, rather than to remain idle and dependent; because I know that many of them *are* ladies in the best acceptation of the word – ladies in the delicacy and propriety of their feelings, and more than ladies in the noble dignity of their general conduct. Still I doubt not they have had their difficulties to encounter from the influence of public opinion, and that their generous feelings have been often wounded by the vulgar prejudices prevailing in society against their mode of life.

With the improvements of art, and the increase of manufactures, there must be an increased demand for mechanics and work-people of every description; and supposing English society to be divided, as it soon must be, into four classes, there surely can be no reason why the second class of females should not be so trained, as to partake in the advantages resulting from this extended sphere of active and useful occupation. – The only field at present open for what is considered lady-like employment, is that of educating the young; and hence the number of accomplished young women, too refined for common usefulness, whose claims to public attention as governesses tend so much to reduce the value of their services in that important sphere.

There are, however, many descriptions of occupation connected with business in its varied forms, which are by no means polluting to the touch, or degrading to the mind; and it would be an unspeakable advantage to hundreds of young females, if, instead of useless accomplishments, they could be instructed in these. In addition to all kinds of fancy millinery, the entire monopoly of which they might surely be permitted to enjoy, I would point out especially to their attention, the art of engraving, which might very properly call into exercise the taste and ingenuity of the female sex, without taxing too severely their mental or bodily powers. To this I would add, the art of drawing patterns for the muslin and calico printers, an occupation which appears peculiarly adapted to the female taste, and which might be carried on without the least encroachment upon the seclusion of domestic life, and the delicacy of the female character. I have been led to understand that this branch of business is almost exclusively carried on by men; and I cannot but regret, that an employment, which offers a tempting luxury to those who suffer from the combined evils of idleness and scanty means, should not also be rendered productive of pecuniary benefit to women.

It seems, however, to be from this pecuniary benefit that they shrink; for when we observe the nature of their daily occupations, their common stitchery, their worsted work, their copied music, their ingeniously-invented articles for bazaars, it would be difficult to say in what sense they are more agreeable, or more dignified, than many branches of art connected with trade. It must therefore be the fact of receiving money for what they do, which renders the latter so objectionable; and it is a strange paradox in our daily experience, that this money should all the while be the very thing of which they are most in want.

The degradation of what is vulgarly called *making their own living*, is, I believe, the obstacle of paramount difficulty; and therefore it is to reduce this difficulty, and to render it more easily surmountable, that our solicitude for the well-being of society, with all our influence, and all our talent, ought to be employed.

13. Caroline Clive
from *Diary*

February 21st.

Three weeks and a day since our boy was born. I did not care very much about him the two first days, except when Archer brought him to me first. He seemed to me scarcely alive, or really in the world. Since then I have grown to love him beyond everything except Archer, and to think his society, when he comes to feed upon me, perfectly delightful. He weighed seven pounds six ounces when he was born and measured twenty-one inches. He has dark blue eyes and brown hair, but is not the least pretty as yet. He is very well made and has nice little red hands, mottled, and white nails. His snub nose excites Archer's daily rebuke. He says it is the Clive nose as to the bottle, but wants the bridge. Bad as the pain of his birth was, I thought to myself several times that I wondered people imagined they were going to die in consequence. It did not seem at all like dying, and afterwards when I was really in danger, I did not know what was going on. I merely remember an inclination to sleep. Nothing else than the common wish to sleep after fatigue. Death would be very easy if I was near dying then – no parting, no quitting of the world; mere sleep without waking. It is something to be remembered that one has entered within the shadow of death.

My nurse is very quiet and lets me have my own way. She manages the boy very well, and I manage myself. I have done boldly and eaten fruit and vegetables though ordered not. They said my milk would suffer and disagree with the boy; but he was in torments of pain in consequence of a dose of castor oil which I took without any effect upon myself, and now I do well with my usual diet and it does him no harm. My doctors have taken leave of me, and I am sitting again in the library, dining at the usual hour and getting up to breakfast. The nurse has sundry superstitions. She asked me one day with apologies whether I had wished for anything during my pregnancy without succeeding in getting it. I said no, and enquired why she asked. She said the baby had a habit of licking his lips and rolling his tongue as if he wanted something, and she supposed my unsatisfied longing reappeared in him. The remedy she suggested was some sacramental wine, a *leetle* drop, and then he would be contented.

✳ ✳ ✳

March 9th.

Mrs Hands told me that Mrs. Harding's precaution against thrush was, when she was expecting a baby, to catch a frog and keep it in water till the baby came into the world. If any symptoms of thrush appeared, the frog was sewn into a muslin bag and its head put into the child's mouth, who was induced, if possible, to suck it. The rationale, as set forth by Mrs. Harding, was that the frog's breath drew away the thrush. 'The frog always dies,' added Mrs. Hands.

1843

14. Caroline Clive
from *Diary*

October 29th.

Archer sat up to finish his sermon and came to bed at one. About three hours after I found the first sign of parturition come on and then some pain. Archer spoke to me at half-past five, saying it was cold. Then I told him. 'What, to-day, my darling?' he said in rather a sleepy tone of reproach as if I might as well have put it off till after the Charity Sermon Sunday. And indeed, I did not expect it for a fortnight., Soon after, he got up and sent for the nurse, and also to Hodgson saying the carriage should fetch him about two, for he supposed things would go upon the mode of last time. After that I continued between sleep and pain till past eight, and then the violent anguish came on. Lowe was about twenty minutes in the house and at a quarter before nine a little girl was born. I was beside myself when I saw her and heard her loud crying. It is a bewildering thing to see a human being, one's own child, where just before there was nothing, and I cried out alternately 'My child, thank God, my child, thank God, thank God.' Though Lowe said the event was very near, Archer little thought it was so close and had gone to the Garbetts to say how matters stood, and when he came back, Robinson met him in the passage and told him the child was born.

1844

15. Elizabeth Barrett Browning
L. E. L.'s Last Question

'Do you think of me as I think of you?'

From HER POEM WRITTEN DURING THE
VOYAGE TO THE CAPE.

'Do you think of me as I think of you,
My friends, my friends?' – She said it from the sea,
The English minstrel in her minstrelsy,
While, under brighter skies than erst she knew,
Her heart grew dark, and groped there, as the blind,
To reach, across the waves, friends left behind –
'Do you think of me as I think of you?'

It seemed not much to ask – As *I* of *you*?
We all do ask the same. No eyelids cover
Within the meekest eyes, that question over.
And little, in the world, the Loving do
But sit (among the rocks?) and listen for
The echo of their own love evermore –
'Do you think of me as I think of you?'

Love learnèd she had sung of love and love, –
And like a child that, sleeping with dropt head
Upon the fairy-book he lately read,
Whatever household noises round him move,
Hears in his dream some elfin turbulence, –
Even so, suggestive to her inward sense,
All sounds of life assumed one tune of love.

And when the glory of her dream withdrew,
When knightly gestes and courtly pageantries
Were broken in her visionary eyes,
By tears the solemn seas attested true, –
Forgetting that sweet lute beside her hand
She asked not, – Do you praise me, O my land? –
But, 'Think ye of me, friends, as I of you?'

Hers was the hand that played for many a year
Love's silver phrase for England, – smooth and well!
Would God, her heart's more inward oracle
In that lone moment, might confirm her dear!
For when her questioned friends in agony
Made passionate response, – 'We think of thee' –,
Her place was in the dust, too deep to hear.

Could she not wait to catch their answering breath?
Was she content, – content, – with ocean's sound,
Which dashed its mocking infinite around
One thirsty for a little love? – beneath
Those stars, content, where last her song had gone, –
They mute and cold in radiant life, – as soon
Their singer was to be, in darksome death?

Bring your vain answers—cry, 'We think of *thee*!'
How think ye of her? warm in long ago
Delights?—or crowned with budding bays? Not so.
None smile and none are crowned where lieth she, –
With all her visions unfulfilled save one, –
Her childhood's – of the palm-trees in the sun –
And lo! their shadow on her sepulchre!

'Do ye think of me as I think of you?' –
O friends, – O kindred, – O dear brotherhood
Of all the world! what are we, that we should
For covenants of long affection sue?
Why press so near each other when the touch
Is barred by graves? Not much, and yet too much,
Is this 'Think of me as I think of you'.

But while on mortal lips I shape anew
A sigh to mortal issues, – verily
Above the unshaken stars that see us die,
A vocal pathos rolls; and HE who drew
All life from dust, and for all, tasted death,
By death and life and love, appealing, saith,
Do you think of me as I think of you?

1845

16. Elizabeth Rigby, Lady Eastlake
from *Lady Travellers*

THAT there are peculiar powers inherent in ladies' eyes, this number of the Quarterly Review was not required to establish; but one in particular, of which we reap all the benefit without paying the penalty, we must in common gratitude be allowed to point out. We mean that power of observation which, so long as it remains at home counting canvass stitches by the fireside, we are apt to consider no shrewder than our own, but which once removed from the familiar scene, and returned to us in the shape of letters or books, seldom fails to prove its superiority. Who, for instance, has not turned from the slap-dash scrawl of your male correspondent – with excuses at the beginning and haste at the end, and too often nothing between but sweeping generalities – to the well-filled sheet of your female friend, with plenty of time bestowed and no paper wasted, and overflowing with those close and lively details which show not only that observing eyes have been at work, but one pair of bright eyes in particular? Or who does not know the difference between their books – especially their books of travels – the gentleman's either dull and matter-of-fact, or off-hand and superficial, with a heavy disquisition where we look for a light touch, or a foolish pun where we expect a reverential sentiment, either requiring too much trouble of the reader, or showing too much carelessness in the writer – and the lady's – all ease, animation, vivacity, with the tact to dwell upon what you most want to know, and the sense to pass over what she does not know herself; neither suggesting authorly effort, nor requiring any conscious attention, yet leaving many a clear picture traced on the memory, and many a solid truth impressed on the mind? It is true the case is occasionally reversed. Ladies have been known to write the dullest and emptiest books – a fact for which there is no accounting – and gentlemen the most delightful; but here probably, if the truth were told, their wives or daughters helped them.

But, in truth, every country with any pretensions to civilization has a twofold aspect, addressed to two different modes of perception, and seldom visible simultaneously to both. Every country has a home life as well as a public life, and the first quite necessary to interpret the last. Every country therefore, to be fairly understood, requires reporters from both sexes. Not that it is precisely recommended that all travellers should hunt the world in couples, and give forth their impression in the double columns of holy wedlock; but that that kind of partnership should be tacitly formed between books of travel which, properly understood, we should have imagined to have been the chief aim of matrimony – namely, to supply each other's deficiencies, and correct each other's errors, purely for the good of the public.

It may be objected that the inferiority of a woman's education is, or ought to be, a formidable barrier; but without stopping to question whether the education of a really well-educated English-woman be on the whole inferior to her brother's, we decidedly think that in the instance of travelling the difference between them is greatly in her favour. If the gentleman knows more of ancient history and ancient languages, the lady knows more of human nature and modern languages; while one of her greatest charms, as a describer of foreign scenes and manners, more even than the closeness or liveliness of her mode of observation, is that very purposelessness resulting from the more desultory nature of her education. A man either starts on his travels with a particular object in view, or, failing that, drives a hobby of his own the whole way before him; whereas a woman, accustomed by habit, if not created by nature, to diffuse her mind more equally on all that is presented, and less troubled with preconceived ideas as to what is most important to observe, goes picking up materials much more indiscriminately, and where, as in travelling, little things are of great significance, frequently much more to the purpose. The tourist may be sure that in nine cases out of ten it is not that on which he has bestowed most care and pains which proves most interesting to the reader.

Again, there is an advantage in the very nature of a book of travels peculiarly favourable to a woman's feelings – the almost total absence of responsibility. It is merely the editorship of her own journal, undertaken for the amusement of her children, or the improvement of a younger sister; or the building of a school; for it is a remarkable fact that ladies never publish their tours to please themselves. In short, she can hardly be said to stand committed as an authoress. If she send forth a lively and graceful work, the world will soon tell her it is a pity she is not one; otherwise, the blame falls on her materials.

But though the lady tourist has her modesty thus far screened and sheltered, it is equally certain that there is no department of writing through which her own individual character is more visible. We form a clearer idea of the writer of the most unpretending book of travels than we do of her who gives us the most striking work of imagination. The under current of personality, however little obtruded to sight, is sure to be genuine. The opinions she expresses on the simplest occasions are those which guide her on the greatest; the habits she displays, however interrupted by her irregular movements, are those contracted in her regular life: hence the most interesting result, in our mind, to be gathered from an examination of this class of literature. We see our countrywoman, in these books, unconsciously in the main, but fully portrayed. We see her with her national courage and her national reserve, with her sound head and her tender heart, with the independent freedom of her actions and the decorous restraint of her manners, with her high intellectual acquirements and her simplicity of tastes, with the early attained maturity of her good sense and the long-continued freshness of her youth. We see her nice, scrupulous, delicate, beyond all others of her sex, yet simple, practical, useful, as none but herself understands to be; versed in the humblest in-door duty, excelling in the hardiest out-door exercise; equally fitted for ease or exertion; enthusiastic for nature; keen for adventure; devoted to her children, her flowers, her poor; petting a great Newfoundland dog, loving a horse, and delighting in the sea. In short, we see her the finest production of the finest country upon earth – man's best companion, whether in the travels over this world or the voyage through this life; but only to be understood or deserved by the Englishman, and rather too good even for him.

It is true, and perhaps as well for our pride, that many a reverse to this picture occurs; but even in the worst cases it is rather an affectation, exaggeration, or caricature of the national female character, than any direct departure from it. There are some lady tourists who are over delicate or over adventurous – over enthusiastic or over humdrum – over simple or over wise; but where is she, whatever may be the difference of talent or taste, who ventures to bring forward an infidel opinion or a questionable moral? . . .

To revert, therefore, to the object of our search – while regarding these unstudied and unpretending works as some of the truest channels for the study of the Englishwoman, they cannot be strictly taken as a test of comparison between her and the lady of other countries. Whether as travellers, or writers of travels, the foreign lady can in no way be measured against her. The only just point of comparison is why the one does travel, and the other does not. And, upon the first view of the matter, the impediments would seem to be all on the side of our own countrywoman. Her home is proverbially the most domestic – her manners the most reserved – her comforts the most indispensable. Nevertheless, it is precisely because home, manners, and comforts are what they are, that the Englishwoman excels all others in the art of travelling. It is those very habits of order and regularity which make her domestic, – it is that very exclusiveness of family life which makes her reserved, – it is the very nature of the comforts, to her so indispensable, – it is all that best fits her to live in her own country, that also best fits her to visit others. Where is the foreign lady who combines the four cardinal virtues of travelling – activity, punctuality, courage, and independence – like the Englishwoman? – where is she whose habits fit her for that most exclusive of all companionships, the travelling *tête-à-tête* with a husband for months together? Where is she whose comforts are nine-tenths of them comprised under the head of fresh air and plenty of water, like the Englishwoman's? . . .

The truth is that no foreign nation possesses that same class of women from which the great body of our female tourists are drafted. They have not the same well-read, solid thinking, – early rising – sketch-loving – light-footed – trim-waisted – straw-hatted specimen of women; educated with the refinement of the highest classes, and with the usefulness of the lowest; all-sufficient companion to her husband, and all-sufficient lady's maid to herself – they have her not. Of course in the numbers that flit annually from our coasts, from one motive or other, every shade and, grade is to be found, from the highest *blasée* fashionable, with every faculty of intelligent interest fast closed, to the lowest Biddy Fudge, with every pore of vulgar wonder wide open; the absurdities committed by our countrymen and women under the name of travel are highly significant of the national folly, extravagance, and eccentricity; but the *taste* for travel from which these abuses spring – the *art* of it in which the English so excel – we are inclined to attribute to a something still more conspicuous and honourable in the national life – to nothing less than the *domesticity* of the English character. Who can witness the innumerable family parties which annually take their excursions abroad – the husbands and wives – brothers and sisters – parents and children, – all enjoying the novel scenes, but chiefly because they are enjoying them together? Who can see the joint delight with which these expeditions are planned, the kindly feelings and habits they develop, the joint pleasure with which they are remembered – without recognising a proof of exclusive domestic cohesion which no other people display? What, too, is the secret of that facility with which the Englishman adapts himself to a residence in any remote corner of the world? – why do we so often find him settled happily among scenes and people utterly uncongenial in climate and habit? Simply because he takes his *home* with him; and has more within it and wants less beyond it than any other man in the world.

❊ ❊ ❊ ❊

In times like these the luxury of travel, like every other that fashion recommends, or that money can purchase, will necessarily be shared in by many utterly unfitted to profit by it. Nevertheless, while we lament much desecration of beautiful scenes and hallowed sites, let us turn to the brighter side of the question, and rejoice that the long continuation of peace, the gradual removal of prejudices, the strength of the British character, and the faith in British honesty, have not only made way for the foot of our country-man through countries hardly accessible before, but also for that of the tender and delicate companion, whose participation in his foreign pleasures his home habits have made indispensable to him. We are aware that much more might have been said about the high endowments of mind and great proficiency of attainment which many of these lady tourists display; but we fear no reproach for having brought forward their domestic virtues as the truest foundation for their powers of travelling, and the reflex of their own personal characters as the highest attraction in their books of travel. It is not for any endowments of intellect, either natural or acquired, that we care to prove the Englishwoman's superiority over all her foreign sisters, but for that soundness of principle and healthiness of heart, without which the most brilliant of women's books, like the most brilliant woman herself, never fails to leave the sense of something wanted – a something better than all she has besides.

---

17. Caroline Clive
from *Diary*

June 29th.
At Mr. Lockhart's we met the Author of *Eothen*, Mr. Kinglake, a pale and light-complexioned man, quite silent all dinner time, flirted with by Lady Gordon by whom he sat and with whom he talked in the evening. One expects to see him all polished steel and cut diamonds. Sir Alexander and Lady Duff Gordon, the latter gorgeous in deep rows and berthes of guipure with carbuncle clasps. Her hair was in a net of yellow beads behind and looked as if it was all in a mess so she covered it with the first trumpery she could find. A handsome woman, but wears no stays, and her bosom, as Archer says, falls down to her stomach. . . .

And now comes Mrs. Norton, the finest specimen of human nature I have yet seen in the world. She is like the heroine of an improbable novel uniting perfections which it is wholly unreasonable to think can reside in one woman – perfect beauty, eyes with long eye-lashes on both lids, the lower touching her cheek, a mouth that opens in a way like ideal mouths, hair in rolls and folds which one sees in pictures but not in hair held by iron hair-pins, lovely skin and shape, a flowing, glowing, silk gown and cashmere shawl edged with gold. She sang, and that was with a rich sweet voice giving wonderful expression to the words, unlike any singer except a heroine. Then her poetry is of first-rate excellence, her manners good, gentle, but animated upon due occasion. In short, a woman so gifted by nature that one has no right to say a word against her.

1846

18. Charlotte Brontë
The Teacher's Monologue

THE room is quiet, thoughts alone
People its mute tranquillity;
The yoke put off, the long task done, –
I am, as it is bliss to be,
Still and untroubled. Now, I see,
For the first time, how soft the day
O'er waveless water, stirless tree,
Silent and sunny, wings its way.
Now, as I watch that distant hill,
So faint, so blue, so far removed,
Sweet dreams of home my heart may fill,
That home where I am known and loved:
It lies beyond; yon azure brow
Parts me from all Earth holds for me;
And, morn and eve, my yearnings flow
Thitherward tending, changelessly.
My happiest hours, aye! all the time,
I love to keep in memory,
Lapsed among moors, ere life's first prime
Decayed to dark anxiety.

Sometimes, I think a narrow heart
Makes me thus mourn those far away,
And keeps my love so far apart
From friends and friendships of to-day;
Sometimes, I think 'tis but a dream
I treasure up so jealously,
All the sweet thoughts I live on seem

To vanish into vacancy:
And then, this strange, coarse world around
Seems all that's palpable and true;
And every sight, and every sound,
Combines my spirit to subdue
To aching grief, so void and lone
Is Life and Earth – so worse than vain,
The hopes that, in my own heart sown,
And cherished by such sun and rain
As Joy and transient Sorrow shed,
Have ripened to a harvest there:
Alas! methinks I hear it said,
'Thy golden sheaves are empty air.'

A quiet song, to solace me
    When sleep refused to come;
A strain to chase despondency,
    When sorrowful for home.
In vain I try; I cannot sing;
    All feels so cold and dead;
No wild distress, no gushing spring
    Of tears in anguish shed;

But all the impatient gloom of one
    Who waits a distant day,
When, some great task of suffering done,
    Repose shall toil repay.
For youth departs, and pleasure flies,
    And life consumes away,
And youth's rejoicing ardour dies
    Beneath this drear delay;

And Patience, weary with her yoke,
    Is yielding to despair,
And Health's elastic spring is broke
    Beneath the strain of care.
Life will be gone ere I have lived;
    Where now is Life's first prime?
I've worked and studied, longed and grieved,
    Through all that rosy time.

To toil, to think, to long, to grieve, –
   Is such my future fate?
The morn was dreary, must the eve
   Be also desolate?
Well, such a life at least makes Death
   A welcome, wished-for friend;
Then, aid me, Reason, Patience, Faith,
   To suffer to the end!

All fades away; my very home
I think will soon be desolate;
I hear, at times, a warning come
Of bitter partings at its gate;
And, if I should return and see
The hearth-fire quenched, the vacant chair;
And hear it whispered mournfully,
That farewells have been spoken there,
What shall I do, and whither turn?
Where look for peace? When cease to mourn?

❋ ❋ ❋ ❋

'Tis not the air I wished to play,
   The strain I wished to sing;
My wilful spirit slipped away
   And struck another string.
I neither wanted smile nor tear,
   Bright joy nor bitter woe,
But just a song that sweet and dear,
   Though haply sad, might flow.

19. Emily Brontë
Remembrance

COLD in the earth – and the deep snow piled above thee,
Far, far, removed, cold in the dreary grave!
Have I forgot, my only Love, to love thee,
Severed at last by Time's all-severing wave?

Now, when alone, do my thoughts no longer hover
Over the mountains, on that northern shore,
Resting their wings where heath and fern-leaves cover
Thy noble heart for ever, ever more?

Cold in the earth – and fifteen wild Decembers,
From those brown hills, have melted into spring:
Faithful, indeed, is the spirit that remembers
After such years of change and suffering!

Sweet Love of youth, forgive, if I forget thee,
While the world's tide is bearing me along;
Other desires and other hopes beset me,
Hopes which obscure, but cannot do thee wrong!

No later light has lightened up my heaven,
No second morn has ever shone for me;
All my life's bliss from thy dear life was given,
All my life's bliss is in the grave with thee.

But, when the days of golden dreams had perished,
And even Despair was powerless to destroy;
Then did I learn how existence could be cherished,
Strengthened, and fed without the aid of joy.

Then did I check the tears of useless passion –
Weaned my young soul from yearning after thine;
Sternly denied its burning wish to hasten
Down to that tomb already more than mine.

And, even yet, I dare not let it languish,
Dare not indulge in memory's rapturous pain;
Once drinking deep of that divinest anguish,
How could I seek the empty world again?

1847

20. Sara Coleridge
from *Review of Tennyson, 'The Princess'*

The inquiry what period of a man's life is best fitted for the production of *great* poems – that is, poems on a comprehensive plan – is not precisely the same as the question: at what part of man's life does the poetic faculty attain perfection. The poetic feeling and power may be in its prime long before the poet has begun his most extensive work; for that will include a good deal besides poetry or the mere poetical element; whatever treasure of the imagination may have been laid up at an early period, such a poem will not be produced till multifarious materials have been collected from teaching and experience; but will form a channel into which streams from various periods of life will run. Some, indeed maintain that there is no such distinct poetical faculty as our argument supposes. . . .

We still hold that poetic genius is as truly a distinct gift as a mathematical, a pictorial, or a musical genius – though it is more central than any other, is dependent for its capacity on the scale of the intellect, and takes its colouring from the individual temper and affections. We hold that the poetic power in its essence, the pure poetic spirit, is as distinct an element in the microcosm of the soul, as fire in the system of nature – as distinct a principle as electricity; that it may be described generally as the power of beholding and presenting objects to the mind in pleasurable forms, and corresponds to the beautiful as science to truth, religion and morals to spirituality and goodness. The object of the sublime poetry of the Bible is doubtless to convey truth, not to excite pleasure; but the object of the *form* in which it conveys divine truths was doubtless pleasure; it raises us above the senses by means of them.

We further believe that this peculiar power of using and addressing the imagination common to all men, this power of beholding and bodying forth in pleasurable forms, and of presenting the loveliest and 'happiest attitude of things,' has a special connexion with physical temperament, and is peculiarly stimulated by that condition of body which belongs to youth when it is adult rather than adolescent, or what is called, in reference to corporeal advantages, the prime of life. It will be generally admitted that a youthful vividness of sensation, which the predominance of the reflective and speculative faculties tends to suppress, with the sense of novelty and freshness in all objects with which the mind converses, promotes imaginative energy. Poetic power prolongs youth for the poet, even while his head is prematurely grey; but, perhaps, it is only from impressions carried forward by memory and association of ideas, that any man is able to write poetically in the autumn and winter of his age. Some appear to suppose that every true poet, so he retains a sound mind in a sound body, may continue producing as long as he lives, and the better the older he grows, because as he grows older he becomes wiser and abler. We are rather inclined to believe that the poetic principle has, in each individual to whom it belongs, a certain quantity from the first; that it runs a certain course or cycle and is then exhausted; and that, as many a plant, when its flower has budded, bloomed, and perished, remains erect and flourishing, full of leafy-honours, with stem stronger and foliage more affluent than when it was in full blow, so is it with the intellect of man, of which poetry is the soft and fragrant blossom; a green old age it may well have, but only in anomalous cases a florid one. And as the blooming of a plant may be hastened or retarded by circumstances, so the expansion of poetic growths after they have come into the bud, and even the formation of the bud itself, may be kept back and reserved without being destroyed.

❀ ❀ ❀ ❀

Coleridge . . . though elsewhere he shows himself the 'thoughtful poet, eloquent for truth,' yet in the 'Circassian Love Chaunt,' 'Love,' and 'Kubla Khan,' he set the example of that style of poetry, afterwards extended so far in the hands of Shelley, which describes moods and feelings interpreted by sense rather than thoughts and actions, which interchanges the attributes of the external and internal worlds, now investing the human spirit with a drapery of the forms and colours of nature, now informing nature with the sensations and emotions of man. By comparing the 'Skylark' of Shelley with Mr. Wordsworth's two poems on the same bird, the reader will perceive the characteristic difference which we desire to point out; in the elder example, though outward nature is presented and the senses are called in aid of the poet, yet moral thinking forms the centre of the piece; in the later, vivid painting, fine expression, and the melody of verse are devoted to the illustration of natural feeling, which, though modified by its coexistence with the spiritual and rational, has its seat in a lower part of the soul. Shelley's 'Sensitive Plant' may be cited as a representative of this class of productions. He indeed had ambitious aims; he described the actions and passions of men, and sought to recommend, by the attractions of his splendid verse, the visions of an active but not perfectly sane intellect. Still it was in poetry of the former character that he had the most success; the

men and women in the 'Revolt of Islam' have scarce more life in them than
the snow figures with which, in Southey's beautiful fiction, the father of
Leila peopled her solitude; they are all of the Frankenstein brood; the
story is incongruous and unnatural, and the philosophy, being, as we
hold it, most bewildered, and at best like sweet bells out of tune, never
formed an effective alliance with his poetry; while that which was true in
his spirit, the poetic power, the mirror of the beautiful, seems to be ever
winning him away from the chimeras which an impatient and too resisting
spirit engendered in his understanding. . . .

Tennyson . . . has acquired greater popularity than his predecessor; the
admiration of Shelley is almost confined to poets or students of poetry,
who find in his works interesting studies of the poetical aspect of things;
but the brilliant odes and songs of the living writer arrest the attention of
those who cannot go far in a pure poetic atmosphere; his ballads and idylls
delight numbers who wish but to find in any poem they take in hand a
moral lesson or a tale of the heart, in an ornate and compendious form; his
gayer movement and lighter touch please many who would be scared by
the grave impetuosity of Shelley. Mr. Tennyson, however, stands on higher
ground than has just been indicated as the main ground of his *popularity*;
he has imagination which the true lovers of poetry can alone fully feel,
and a command of diction finer and deeper than is needed for any but
their satisfaction; he excels Shelley in liveliness and variety, in the power
of portraying ideal personages, enduing them with life and bringing out
their characteristics in easy and delightful narrative; he has hardly equalled
his predecessor, in the opinion of that writer's admirers, in force of imagination and clearness of expression, and, with respect to sustained dignity
and refinement, he certainly falls below him. It is high praise to say that he
has sometimes equalled him in the music of verse. The power of music in
Shelley's Spenserian stanza, which in its full rich ringing melody appears
to combine the sound of flutes and soft recorders with that of liquid
musical glasses, has been surpassed by no poet of the present age. In the
art of numbers, however, Mr. Tennyson cannot be held equal to Shelley;
he is often successful in the adaptation of metres and 'modulation of words
and cadences to the swell and fall of the feelings expressed;' but at other
times his irregular measures are devoid of harmony, and mock the eye with
the show of a fine varied lyrical movement, while the ear can make nothing
of them or nothing to the purpose.

1848

21. Elizabeth Rigby, Lady Eastlake
from *Review of 'Jane Eyre'*

The character and events, though some of them masterly in conception, are coined expressly for the purpose of bringing out great effects. The hero and heroine are beings both so singularly unattractive that the reader feels they can have no vocation in the novel but to be brought together; and they do things which, though not impossible, lie utterly beyond the bounds of probability. . . .

It is a very remarkable book: we have no remembrance of another combining such genuine power with such horrid taste. Both together have equally assisted to gain the great popularity it has enjoyed; for in these days of extravagant adoration of all that bears the stamp of novelty and originality, sheer rudeness and vulgarity have come in for a most mistaken worship.

* * * *

Combined with great materials for power and feeling, the reader may trace gross inconsistencies and improbabilities, and chief and foremost that highest moral offence a novel writer can commit, that of making an unworthy character interesting in the eyes of the reader. Mr Rochester is a man who deliberately and secretly seeks to violate the laws both of God and man, and yet we will be bound half our lady readers are enchanted with him for a model of generosity and honour. We would have thought that such a hero had had no chance, in the purer taste of the present day; but the popularity of Jane Eyre is a proof how deeply the love for illegitimate romance is implanted in our nature. Not that the author is strictly responsible for this. Mr. Rochester's character is tolerably consistent. He is made as coarse and as brutal as can in all conscience be required to keep our sympathies at a distance. In point of literary consistency the hero is at all events impugnable, though we cannot say as much for the heroine.

As to Jane's character – there is none of that harmonious unity about it which made little Becky so grateful a subject of analysis – nor are the discrepancies of that kind which have their excuse and their response in our nature. The inconsistencies of Jane's character lie mainly not in her own imperfections, though of course she has her share, but in the author's. There is that confusion in the relations between cause and effect, which is not so much untrue to human nature as to human art. The error in Jane

Eyre is, not that her character is this or that, but that she is made one thing in the eyes of her imaginary companions, and another in that of the actual reader. There is a perpetual disparity between the account she herself gives of the effect she produces, and the means shown us by which she brings that effect about. We hear nothing but self-eulogiums on the perfect tact and wondrous penetration with which she is gifted, and yet almost every word she utters offends us, not only with the absence of these qualities, but with the positive contrasts of them, in either her pedantry, stupidity, or gross vulgarity. She is one of those ladies who put us in the unpleasant predicament of undervaluing their very virtues for dislike of the person in whom they are represented. One feels provoked as Jane Eyre stands before us – for in the wonderful reality of her thoughts and descriptions, she seems accountable for all done in her name – with principles you must approve in the main, and yet with language and manners that offend you in every particular. Even in that *chef-d'œuvre* of brilliant retrospective sketching, the description of her early life, it is the childhood and not the child that interests you. The little Jane, with her sharp eyes and dogmatic speeches, is a being you neither could fondle nor love. There is a hardness in her infantine earnestness, and a spiteful precocity in her reasoning, which repulses all our sympathy. One sees that she is of a nature to dwell upon and treasure up every slight and unkindness, real or fancied, and such natures we know are surer than any others to meet with plenty of this sort of thing. As the child, so also the woman – an uninteresting, sententious, pedantic thing; with no experience of the world, and yet with no simplicity or freshness in its stead.

❀ ❀ ❀ ❀

We have said that this was the picture of a natural heart. This, to our view, is the great and crying mischief of the book. Jane Eyre is throughout the personification of an unregenerate and undisciplined spirit, the more dangerous to exhibit from that prestige of principle and self-control which is liable to dazzle the eye too much for it to observe the inefficient and unsound foundation on which it rests. It is true Jane does right, and exerts great moral strength, but it is the strength of a mere heathen mind which is a law unto itself. No Christian grace is perceptible upon her. She has inherited in fullest measure the worst sin of our fallen nature – the sin of pride. Jane Eyre is proud, and therefore she is ungrateful too. It pleased God to make her an orphan, friendless, and penniless – yet she thanks nobody, and least of all Him, for the food and raiment, the friends, companions, and instructors of her helpless youth – for the care and education vouchsafed to her till she was capable in mind as fitted in years to provide for herself. On the contrary, she looks upon all that has been done for her not only as her undoubted right, but as falling far short of it. The doctrine of humility is not more foreign to her mind than it is repudiated by her heart. It is by her own talents, virtues, and courage that she is made to attain the summit of human happiness, and, as far as Jane Eyre's own statement is concerned, no one would think that she owed anything either to God above or to man below. She flees from Mr. Rochester, and has not a being to turn to. Why was this? . . . Jane had lived . . . for eight years with 110 girls and fifteen teachers. Why had she formed no friendships among them? Other orphans have left the same and similar institutions, furnished with friends for life, and puzzled with homes to choose from. How comes it that Jane had acquired neither? Among that number of associates there were surely some exceptions to what she so presumptuously stigmatises as 'the society of inferior minds.' Of course it suited the author's end to represent the heroine as utterly destitute of the common means of assitance, in order to exhibit both her trials and her powers of self-support – the whole book rests on this assumption – but it is one which, under the circumstances, is very unnatural and very unjust.

Altogether the auto-biography of Jane Eyre is pre-eminently an anti-Christian composition. There is throughout it a murmuring against the comforts of the rich and against the privations of the poor, which, as far as each individual is concerned, is a murmuring against God's appoint-ment – there is a proud and perpetual assertion of the rights of man, for which we find no authority either in God's word or in God's providence – there is that pervading tone of ungodly discontent which is at once the most prominent and the most subtle evil which the law and the pulpit, which all civilised society in fact has at the present day to contend with. We do not hesitate to say that the tone of mind and thought which has overthrown authority and violated every code human and divine abroad, and fostered Chartism and rebellion at home, is the same which has also written Jane Eyre.

Still we say again this is a very remarkable book. We are painfully alive to the moral, religious, and literary deficiences of the picture, and such passages of beauty and power as we have quoted cannot redeem it, but it is impossible not to be spellbound with the freedom of the touch. It would be mere hackneyed courtesy to call it 'fine writing.' It bears no impress of being written at all, but is poured out rather in the heat and hurry of an instinct, which flows ungovernably on its object, indifferent by what means it reaches it, and unconscious too. As regards the author's chief object, how-ever, it is a failure – that, namely, of making a plain, odd woman, destitute of all the conventional features of feminine attraction, interesting in our sight. We deny that he has succeeded in this. Jane Eyre, in spite of some grand things about her, is a being totally uncongenial to our feelings from beginning to end. We acknowledge her firmness – we respect her determination – we feel for her struggles; but, for all that, and setting aside higher considerations, the impression she leaves on our mind is that of a decidedly vulgar-minded woman – one whom we should not care for as an acquaintance, whom we should not seek as a friend, whom we should not desire for a relation, and whom we should scrupulously avoid for a governess.

There seem to have arisen in the novel-reading world some doubts as to who really wrote this book; and various rumours, more or less romantic, have been current in Mayfair, the metropolis of gossip, as to the authorship. . . .Whoever it be, it is a person who, with great mental powers, combines a total ignorance of the habits of society, a great coarseness of taste, and a heathenish doctrine of religion. And as these characteristics appear more or less in the writings of all three, Currer, Acton, and Ellis alike, for their poems differ less in degree of power than in kind, we are ready to accept the fact of their identity or of their relationship with equal satisfaction. At all events there can be no interest attached to the writer of 'Wuthering Heights' – a novel succeeding 'Jane Eyre,' and purporting to be written by Ellis Bell – unless it were for the sake of more individual reprobation. For though there is a decided family likeness between the two, yet the aspect of the Jane and Rochester animals in their native state, as Catherine and Heathfield, is too odiously and abominably pagan to be palatable even to the most vitiated class of English readers. With all the unscrupulousness of the French school of novels it combines that repulsive vulgarity in the choice of its vice which supplies its own antidote. The question of authorship, therefore, can deserve a moment's curiosity only as far as 'Jane Eyre' is concerned, and though we cannot pronounce that it appertains to a real Mr. Currer Bell and to no other, yet that it appertains to a man, and not, as many assert, to a woman, we are strongly inclined to affirm. Without entering into the question whether the power of the writing be above her, or the vulgarity below her, there are, we believe, minutiæ of circumstantial evidence which at once acquit the feminine hand. No woman – a lady friend, whom we are always happy to consult, assures us – makes mistakes in her own *métier* – no woman *trusses game* and garnishes dessert-dishes with the same hands, or talks of so doing in the same breath. Above all, no woman attires another in such fancy dresses as Jane's ladies assume – Miss Ingram coming down, irresistible, 'in a *morning* robe of sky-blue crape, a gauze azure scarf twisted in her hair!!' No lady, we understand, when suddenly roused in the night, would think of hurrying on '*a frock.*' They have garments more convenient for such occasions, and more becoming too. This evidence seems incontrovertible. Even granting that these incongruities were purposely assumed, for the sake of disguising the female pen, there is nothing gained; for if we ascribe the book to a woman at all, we have no alternative but to ascribe it to one who has, for some sufficient reason, long forfeited the society of her own sex.

And if by no woman, it is certainly also by no artist. The Thackeray eye has had no part there. There is not more disparity between the art of drawing Jane assumes and her evident total ignorance of its first principles, than between the report she gives of her own character and the conclusions we form for ourselves. Not but what, in another sense, the author may be classed as an artist of very high grade. Let him describe the simplest things in nature – a rainy landscape, a cloudy sky, or a bare moorside, and he shows the hand of a master; but the moment he talks of the art itself, it is obvious that he is a complete ignoramus.

We cannot help feeling that this work must be far from beneficial to that class of ladies whose cause it affects to advocate. Jane Eyre is not precisely the mouthpiece one would select to plead the cause of governesses, and it is therefore the greater pity that she has chosen it: for there is none we are convinced which, at the present time, more deserves and demands an earnest and judicious befriending. If these times puzzle us how to meet the claims and wants of the lower classes of our dependants, they puzzle and shame us too in the case of that highest dependant of all, the governess – who is not only entitled to our gratitude and respect by her position, but, in nine cases out of ten, by the circumstances which reduced her to it. For the case of the governess is so much the harder than that of any other class of the community, in that they are not only quite as liable to all the vicissitudes of life, but are absolutely supplied by them. There may be, and are, exceptions to this rule, but the real definition of a governess, in the English sense, is a being who is our equal in birth, manners, and education, but our inferior in wordly wealth. Take a lady, in every meaning of the word, born and bred, and let her father pass through the gazette, and she wants nothing more to suit our highest *beau idéal* of a guide and instructress to our children. We need the imprudencies, extravagancies, mistakes, or crimes of a certain number of fathers, to sow that seed from which we reap the harvest of governesses. There is no other class which so cruelly requires its members to be, in birth, mind, and manners, above their station, in order to fit them for their station. From this peculiarity in their very qualifications for office result all the peculiar and most painful anomalies of their professional existence. The line which severs the governess from her employers is not one which will take care of itself, as in the case of a servant. If she sits at table she does not shock you – if she opens her mouth she does not distress you – her appearance and manners are likely to be as good as your own – her education rather better; there is nothing upon the face of the thing to stamp her as having been called to a different state of life from that in which it has pleased God to place you; and therefore the distinction has to be kept up by a fictitious barrier which presses with cruel weight upon the mental strength or constitutional vanity of a woman. People talk of the prevailing vanity of governesses, and we grant it in one sense fully – but how should it not be so? If a governess have a grain of vanity in her composition, it is sought and probed for by every species of slight and mortification, intentional or not, till it starts into unnatural life beneath the irritation. She must be a saint, or no woman at all, who can rise above those perpetual little dropping-water trials to which the self-love of an averagely-placed governess is exposed. That fearful fact that the lunatic asylums of this country are supplied with a larger proportion of their inmates from the ranks of young governesses than from any other class of life, is a sufficient proof how seldom she can. But it is not her vanity which sends her there, but her *wounded* vanity – the distinction is great – and wounded vanity, as all medical men will tell us, is the rock on which most minds go to pieces.

Man cannot live by the head alone, far less woman. A governess has no equals, and therefore can have no sympathy. She is a burden and restraint in society, as all must be who are placed ostensibly at the same table and yet are forbidden to help themselves or to be helped to the same viands. She is a bore to almost any gentleman, as a tabooed woman, to whom he is interdicted from granting the usual privileges of the sex, and yet who is perpetually crossing his path. She is a bore to most ladies by the same rule, and a reproach too – for her dull, fagging, bread-and-water life is perpetually putting their pampered listlessness to shame, The servants invariably detest her, for she is a dependant like themselves, and yet, for all that, as much their superior in other respects as the family they both serve. Her pupils may love her, and she may take the deepest interest in them, but they cannot be her friends. She must, to all intents and purposes, live alone, or she transgresses that invisible but rigid line which alone establishes the distance between herself and her employers.

1849

22. Elizabeth Gaskell
from *The Last Generation in England*

The town in which I once resided is situated in a district inhabited by large landed proprietors of very old family. The daughters of these families, if unmarried, retired to live in — on their annuities, and gave the ton to the society there; stately ladies they were, remembering etiquette and precedence in every occurrence of life, and having their genealogy at their tongue's end. Then there were the widows of the cadets of these same families; also poor, and also proud, but I think more genial and less given to recounting their pedigrees than the former. Then came the professional men and their wives; who were more wealthy than the ladies I have named, but who always treated them with deference and respect, sometimes even amounting to obsequiousness; for was there not 'my brother, Sir John—,' and 'my uncle, Mr.—, of —,' to give employment and patronage to the doctor or the attorney? A grade lower came a class of single or widow ladies; and again it was possible, not to say probable, that their pecuniary circumstances were in better condition than those of the aristocratic dames, who nevertheless refused to meet in general society the *ci-devant* housekeepers, or widows of stewards, who had been employed by their fathers and brothers, they would occasionally condescend to ask 'Mason,' or 'that good Bentley,' to a private tea drinking, at which I doubt not much gossip relating to former days at the hall would pass; but that was patronage; to associate with them at another person's house, would have been an acknowledgement of equality.

Below again came the shopkeepers, who dared to be original; who gave comfortable suppers after the very early dinners of that day, not checked by the honourable Mr. D—'s precedent of a seven o'clock tea on the most elegant and economical principles, and a supperless turn-out at nine. There were the usual respectable and disrespectable poor; and hanging on the outskirts of society were a set of young men, ready for mischief and brutality, and every now and then dropping off the pit's brink into crime. The habits of this class (about forty years ago) were much such as those of the Mohawks a century before. They would stop ladies returning from the card-parties, which were the staple gaiety of the place, and who were only attended by a maidservant bearing a lantern, and whip them; literally whip them as you whip a little child; until administering such chastisement to a good, precise old lady of high family, 'my brother, the magistrate,' came forward and put down such proceedings with a high hand.

Certainly there was more individuality of character in those days than now; no one even in a little town of two thousand inhabitants would now be found to drive out with a carriage full of dogs; each dressed in the male or female fashion of the day, as the case might be; each dog provided with a pair of house-shoes, for which his carriage boots were changed on his return. No old lady would be so oblivious of 'Mrs. Grundy's' existence now as to dare to invest her favourite cow, after its unlucky fall into a lime-pit, in flannel waistcoat and drawers, in which the said cow paraded the streets of — to the day of its death.

There were many regulations which were strictly attended to in the society of —, and which probably checked more manifestations of eccentricity. Before a certain hour in the morning calls were never paid, nor yet after a certain hour in the afternoon; the consequence was that everybody was out, calling on everybody at the same time, for it was *de rigueur* that morning calls should be returned within three days; and accordingly, making due allowance for our proportion of rain in England, every fine morning was given up to this employment. A quarter of an hour was the limit of a morning call.

Before the appointed hour of reception, I fancy the employment of many of the ladies was fitting up their laces and muslins (which, for the information of all those whom it may concern, were never ironed, but carefully stretched, and pinned, thread by thread, with most Lilliputian pieces, on a board covered with flannel). Most of these scions of quality had many pounds' worth of valuable laces descended to them from mothers and grandmothers, which must be 'got up' by no hands, as you may guess, but those of Fairly Fair. Indeed when muslin and net were a guinea a yard, this was not to be wondered at. The lace was washed in buttermilk, which gave rise to an odd little circumstance. One lady left her lace, basted up, in some not very sour buttermilk; and unluckily the cat lapped it up, lace and all (one would have thought the lace would have choked her, but so it was); the lace was too valuable to be lost, so a small dose of tartar emetic was administered to the poor cat; the lace returned to view was carefully darned, and decked the good old lady's best cap for many a year after; and many a time did she tell the story, gracefully bridling up in a prim sort of way, and giving a little cough, as if preliminary to a rather improper story. The first sentence of it was always, I remember, 'I do not think you can guess where the lace on my cap has been ;' dropping her voice, 'in pussy's inside, my dear!'

The dinner hour was three o'clock in all houses of any pretension to gentility; and a very late hour it was considered to be. Soon after four one or two inveterate card-players might be seen in calash and pattens, picking their way along the streets to the house where the party of the evening was to be held. As soon as they arrived and had unpacked themselves, an operation of a good half-hour's duration in the dining-parlour, they were ushered into the drawing-room, where, unless in the very height of summer, it was considered a delicate attention to have the shutters closed, the curtains drawn, and the candles lighted. The card-tables were set out, each with two new packs of cards, for which it was customary to pay by each person placing a shilling under one of the candlesticks.

The ladies settled down to Preference, and allowed of no interruption; even the tea-trays were placed on the middle of the card-tables, and tea hastily gulped down with a few remarks on the good or ill fortune of the evening. New arrivals were greeted with nods in the intervals of the game; and as people entered the room, they were pounced upon by the lady of the house to form another table. Cards were a business in those days, not a recreation. Their very names were to be treated with reverence. Some one came to — from a place where flippancy was in fashion; he called the knave 'Jack,' and everybody looked grave, and voted him vulgar; but when he was overheard calling Preference – the decorous, highly-respectable game of Preference, – Pref., why, what course remained for us but to cut him, and cut him we did.

About half-past eight, notices of servants having arrived for their respective mistresses were given: the games were concluded, accounts settled, a few parting squibs and crackers let off at careless unlucky partners, and the party separated. By ten o'clock all— was in bed and asleep. I have made no mention of gentlemen at these parties, because if ever there was an Amazonian town in England it was—. Eleven widows of respectability at one time kept house there; besides spinsters innumerable. The doctor preferred his arm-chair and slippers to the forms of society, such as I have described, and so did the attorney, who was besides not insensible to the charms of a hot supper. Indeed, I suppose it was because of the small incomes of the more aristocratic portion of our little society not sufficing both for style and luxury, but it was a fact, that as gentility decreased good living increased in proportion. We had the honour and glory of looking at old plate and delicate china at the *comme il faut* tea-parties, but the slices of bread and butter were like wafers, and the sugar for coffee was rather of the brownest, still there was much gracious kindness among our *haute volée*. In those times, good Mr. Rigmarole, carriages were carriages, and there were not the infinite variety of broughams, droskys, &c., &c., down to a wheelbarrow, which now make locomotion easy; nor yet were there

cars and cabs and flys ready for hire in our little town. A post-chaise was
the only conveyance besides *the* sedan-chair, of which more anon. So the
widow of an earl's son, who possessed a proper old-fashioned coach and
pair, would on rainy nights, send her carriage, the only private carriage of
——, round the town, picking up all the dowagers and invalids, and conveying them dry and safe to and from their evening engagement. The various
other ladies who, in virtue of their relations holding manors and maintaining game-keepers, had frequent presents, during the season, of partridges,
pheasants, &c., &c., would daintily carve off the tid-bits, and putting them
carefully into a hot basin, bid Betty or Molly cover it up quickly, and carry
it to Mrs. or Miss So-and-so, whose appetite was but weakly and who
required dainties to tempt it which she could not afford to purchase.

These poorer ladies had also their parties in turn; they were too proud
to accept invitations if they might not return them, although various and
amusing were their innocent make-shifts and imitations. To give you only
one instance, I remember a card-party at one of these good ladies' lodgings; where, when tea-time arrived, the ladies sitting on the sofa had to be
displaced for a minute, in order that the tea-trays, (plates of cake, bread
and butter, and all,) might be extricated from their concealment under the
valances of the couch.

You may imagine the subjects of the conversation amongst these ladies;
cards, servants, relations, pedigrees, and last and best, much mutual interest
about the poor of the town, to whom they were one and all kind and inde-
fatigable benefactresses; cooking, sewing for, advising, doctoring, doing
everything but educating them. One or two old ladies dwelt on the glories
of former days; when — boasted of two earl's daughters as residents.
Though it must be sixty years since they died, there are traces of their
characters yet lingering about the place. Proud, precise, and generous;
bitter tories were they. Their sister had married a General, more distinguished for a successful comedy, than for his mode of conducting the war
in America; and, consequently, his sisters-in-law held the name of
Washington in deep abhorrence. I can fancy the way in which they must
have spoken of him, from the shudder of abomination with which their
devoted admirers spoke years afterwards of 'that man Washington.' Lady
Jane was moreover a benefactress to ——. Before her day, the pavement of
the footpath was composed of loose round stones, placed so far apart that
a delicate ankle might receive a severe wrench from slipping between;
but she left a sum of money in her will to make and keep in repair a flag
pavement, on condition that it should only be broad enough for one to
walk abreast, in order 'to put a stop to the indecent custom coming into
vogue, of ladies linking with gentlemen; linking being the old-fashioned

word for walking arm-in-arm. Lady Jane also left her sedan and money to pay the bearers for the use of the ladies of —, who were frequently like Adam and Eve in the weather-glass in consequence, the first arrival at a party having to commence the order of returning when the last lady was only just entering upon the gaieties of the evening.

The old ladies were living hoards of family tradition and old custom. One of them, a Shropshire woman, had been to school in London about the middle of the last century. The journey from Shropshire took her a week. At the school to which she was sent, besides fine work of innumerable descriptions, pastry, and the art of confectionary were taught to those whose parents desired it. The dancing-master gave his pupils instructions in the art of using a fan properly. Although an only child, she had never sat down in her parents' presence without leave until she was married; and spoke with infinite disgust of the modern familiarity with which children treated their parents. 'In my days,' said she, 'when we wrote to our fathers and mothers, we began "Honoured Sir," or "Honoured Madam," none of your "Dear Mamas," or "Dear Papas" would have been permitted; and we ruled off our margin before beginning our letters, instead of cramming writing into every corner of the paper; and when we ended our letters we asked our parents' blessing if we were writing to them; and if we wrote to a friend we were content to "remain your affectionate friend," instead of hunting up some new-fangled expression, such as "your attached, your loving," &c. Fanny, my dear! I got a letter to-day signed "Yours cordially," like a dram-shop! what will this world come to?' Then she would tell how a gentleman having asked her to dance in her youth, never thought of such familiarity as offering her his arm to conduct her to her place, but taking up the flap of his silk-lined coat, he placed it over his open palm, and on it the lady daintily rested the tips of her fingers. To be sure, my dear old lady once confessed to a story neither so pretty nor so proper, namely, that one of the amusements of her youth was 'measuring noses' with some gentlemen, – not an uncommon thing in those days; and, as lips lie below noses, such measurements frequently ended in kisses. At her house there was a little silver basket strainer, and once remarking on this, she showed me a silver saucer pierced through with holes, and told me it was a relic of the times when tea was first introduced into England; after it had been infused and the beverage drank, the leaves were taken out of the teapot and placed on this strainer, and then eaten by those who liked with sugar and butter, 'and very good they were,' she added. Another relic which she possessed was an old receipt-book, dating back to the middle of the sixteenth century. Our grandmothers must have been strong-headed women, for there were numerous receipts for 'ladies' beverages,' &c., generally beginning with 'Take a gallon of brandy, or any other spirit.' The puddings, too, were no light matters: one receipt, which I copied for the curiosity of the thing, begins with, 'Take thirty eggs, two quarts of cream,' &c. These brobdignagian puddings she explained by saying that the afternoon meal, before the introduction of tea, generally consisted of cakes and cold puddings, together with a glass of what we should now call liqueur, but which was then denominated bitters.

The same old lady advocated strongly the manner in which marriages were formerly often brought about. A young man went up to London to study for the bar, to become a merchant, or what not, and arrived at middle age without having thought about matrimony; when, finding himself rich and desirous of being married, he would frequently write to some college friend, or to the clergyman of his native place, asking him to recommend a wife; whereupon the friend would send a list of suitable ladies; the bachelor would make his selection, and empower his friend to wait upon the parents of the chosen one, who accepted or refused without much consultation of their daughter's wishes; often the first intelligence she had of the affair was by being told by her mother to adorn herself in her best, as the gentleman her parents proposed for her husband was expected by the night-coach to supper.

'And very happy marriages they turned out, my dear – very,' my venerable informant would add, sighing. I always suspected that her own had been of this description.

23. Geraldine Jewsbury
from *Religious Faith and Modern Scepticism*

There is a movement in the religious world of our own day, to which none can close their eyes – of which none can prophesy the result: it has been brooding for a long time, but the tempest has at last broken, and in the confusion of the elements there is neither light nor darkness.

It is quite useless for those who seek to direct the consciences of men to fall back upon their old dogmas about reason and faith, and endeavour to put down the insurrection by appeals to orthodox tradition mingled with unsympathising contempt for the "obstinate questionings " by which the hearts of men are besieged. Christianity was not instituted as we have it, ready made to our hands by dogmatic authority, but by the fierce conflict of opinions and beliefs, and different modes of interpretation of the mystery of our being, and by the subtle metaphysical exercise of all the faculties of that generation of wonderful men whom we now call "*fathers*," but who were in their day men – mortal struggling men – whose *theology* had to be painfully wrestled for, and conquered from the realms of doubt: they had no "*authority*," no traditionary standard of belief or knowledge to appeal to; they had to fight like men, and compel order from the breaking up and vanishing away of that which had been the law of old.

It is vain for those who consider themselves as representatives of the orthodox Christianity of the present day, to look down upon such as are struggling in this movement as if they were a parcel of arrogant and superficial schoolboys who ought to allow themselves to be put down by the frown of their master, and should stand abashed by sneers at their youth and incompetence.

The battle of modern opinion has begun in earnest and cannot now be stopped – it must be fought out manfully to the end. Horrible convulsions have arisen heretofore out of the struggles which have taken place in the world's history between the old order of things, which had become rather the objects of traditional reverence than of vital influence on the emergencies of daily life – and the stirrings of newly-awakened insight to discern a still "better covenant," of which the "former things were but the shadow" – but of which they were also the forerunners. These have been times of "battle and confused noise" – in which many have been trampled down and fallen not to rise again: still the *result* has always been a step gained in the progress of humanity; a clearer faith, and a deeper insight into the realities which were dimly shadowed forth under the former dispensation; "a closer walk with God," unimpeded by the cumbrous machinery by which in the former age they strove to draw nigh unto Him.

Right or wrong, the fact is indubitable that the whole of the civilized world is in a state of ferment, of *transition*, passing from one mode of religious belief and social manifestation to another; new combinations of the social and religious elements are arising whilst others are disappearing.

The Protestant Christian, to whom the "BIBLE" is one entire and perfect chrysolite, who regards it as verbally inspired, and who reveres every sentence with mystic reverence as if it had fallen down from Heaven, suffers quite as much as the Jew of old when he sees the cold-blooded impartiality with which its claims to inspiration are examined, and the indifference with which the doctrines of his religion are laid bare by "discovering the foundation unto the neck," – the cold sceptical distillation to which the "waters of life" are subjected through the modern critical alembic; he feels tempted to cry with Micah, "Ye have taken away my gods, and what have I more?"

The destinies of man and of humanity are in the bosom of God.

Humanity has never yet been abandoned in its course, and it will not be abandoned now. History, which is the magnificent biography of humanity, relates the successive life of mankind and of the world; it is the perpetually renewed hymn of creation; that which already has been, has come out of shadows and darkness like those which shroud the PRESENT, but "the darkness and the light to HIM are both alike."

To look to the facts of the PAST for guidance is only to attempt to imitate *results* which have passed away from the huge kaleidescope of human affairs. Men are engrossed by the PRESENT, and yet they have no reverence for it. They look mysteriously to the PAST for instruction, as if the PAST had alone been sanctified; as if the *present*, with all its unresolved perplexities, were not equally sacred, were not equally the dispensation of Him whose children we are, as much as those were who have gone before.

One reason for our instinctive faith in the past is, that it at at least held together, and has become a FACT, and we cling to it as long as we can.

The PRESENT is crumbling beneath our feet at every step, and we are borne resistlessly on towards the FUTURE – that unknown and ineffable condition which stands like some terrible apparition, into the shadow of which we cannot choose but enter. We must meet it like men, and learn from the PAST the faith, and hope, and religious spirit, which inspired the *preux chevaliers* of old when they went on their way to encounter demons and enchanted forests. They felt courageous, because they believed themselves to be in the presence and under the shield of God himself; and this faith is not taken away from us, for "HE is the same yesterday, to-day, and for ever."

The minor distinctions of sects and creeds are every day being merged into the two broad distinctions of Catholicism and Protestantism; which are both pushed to the extreme assertion of their respective principles.

To the camp of Catholicism, which is the essential type of Christianity – a church which makes itself strong in the traditions of its descent, and keeps itself immoveably at anchor upon the past, as a stereotyped revelation of the will of God to man – to this camp all those repair who desire a VISIBLE CHURCH; a supreme authority and rule of faith in matters of religion, and which professes to offer a final resting-place to the weary seeker after religious peace. The one condition of his everlasting rest is the surrender of his own vague aspirations, and his own private judgment, to the rules and decisions of "the church." No matter what may be the minor shades of doctrine, the varying extent to which liberty of private judgment may be conceded, "under certain necessary limitations." All these subordinate distinctions are but *mediatised princes*, their dominions fall and determine to the claims of the Catholic church – the one great body which unites all the essential features of a visible church, into whose keeping have been committed the "oracles of God."

The assertion of the right of private judgment in matters of religious belief is the distinctive element of Protestantism. To its ranks belong all who insist upon perfect freedom of inquiry in matters of religion, unfettered by any foregone conclusions; those who repudiate tradition, and recognise no absolute tribunal with authority to decide upon debated points of theology; the different bands or sects which have dotted the face of Christendom for three hundred years, each of which has erected its own peculiar barrier to preserve its respective flock from either straying into the wilds of scepticism, or from being encroached upon by neighbouring sects, each holding some form of "unsound doctrine," the only common ground on which they can cordially meet being repudiation of the claims of Rome to their allegiance. Every day these arbitrary defences are breaking down, and Protestantism is asserting more and more distinctly its essential element – the right of private judgment, pushed to its ultimate and logical conclusion. All intermediate resting-places are being swept away, the ground is clearing for a great battle, from which will result a great modification of the existing form of things, social, moral, and political.

It is not minute points of historical criticism – shades of discrepancy in the circumstantial narratives of the evangelists that move the interest of modern sceptics. The hearts of men are intent on deeper things than these. A ponderous dissertation on the miracles, either in proof or in disproof of them, would be left to fall by the weight of its own gravitation; the heart of the question does not lie *there*. Men are becoming every day more anxious to discover and possess themselves of the spiritual secret lodged in the forms of doctrine which have been preached to them; they desire earnestly to hear, not what they now believe to be correct according to the most orthodox letter of tradition, but what they must DO in order to develop all that God made them capable of being and doing. A religious spirit is abroad amongst men; and though they may at present speak with a "stammering tongue," and excite the scornful upbraidings of those whose form of "sound words" has never been perplexed, still the spirit that is promised to all who seek will guide them into truth.

✳ ✳ ✳ ✳

Thomas Carlyle, in his '*Sartor Resartus*,' was the first who recognised in print the fact, that a man may be at once religious of heart and sceptical of doctrine. He was the first man in England who dared to declare that a sincere *doubt* was as much entitled to respect as a sincere *belief*. He treated with *respect* certain conditions of heart which had hitherto been met with grave reprobation, controverted by special pleading, and opposed by foregone conclusions, meeting on all sides nothing but grave official dis- approval. Many are they who owe him a life-long debt of gratitude, for reviving a spirit of religious reverence in hearts which had ceased to recog- nise religious dogmas, and whose souls were like those plants which die down to their roots in winter, showing no life or vegetation above the surface.

Those who had turned sick and disgusted from the "sweets of religion" and the "search after happiness," found strength and refreshing, as from a fountain of living water, in the cold stern stoicism of his words.

"Say to all manner of happiness, 'I can do without thee.
"With *renunciation* life begins."

These words have been like a revelation of light to many.

The spirit of manhood within them was awakened, they were relieved from the obligation to "beat the air" in a baffled struggle after "happiness;" they were delivered from the disgrace of failure, which more or less attaches itself to unsuccessful efforts.

Carlyle, has certainly dispersed the remains of reverence for theological orthodoxy, but he has raised the moral tone of the age, and awakened a noble spirit of strength and courage amongst the young men of the present generation, which far transcends anything they will actually shew to the world. The influence he has had on the *manliness* of the age cannot be sufficiently estimated.

It is true that he gives no prescriptive rule of life, but he is, as it were, the voice of the trumpet inciting to the battle and induing men with the resolution "to do with all their might" whatever they may find appointed.

❈ ❈ ❈ ❈

We are passing through a solemn moment – men of all sects and religions, however they may be opposed to each other in doctrines – men of every creed and men of no creed at all, are nevertheless of one accord in believing that some great change is at hand; they are "as men who watch for the day;" they look for some fresh dispensation which will reconcile the confusion and contradiction in which the world is lying, and which shall combine in a new creation the social elements which are now struggling in a disorganized chaos, and which shall realize the "new heaven and the new earth" which Christians have been taught to expect from the beginning of Christianity. There is one aspiration throughout the world in which all men join – "The Millennium" of the Christians and the *Utopia* of the Socialist is expressed in the same word – and that word is "UNITY."

The state of things in the civilized world looks terrible enough. The PAST and the FUTURE stand face to face; and the actual PRESENT is crushed in the fearful collision between the old and the new. The shadow of the future lies at this moment on every element of social life; and every object seems to be invested with the strange unearthly light which covers nature during an eclipse. There is no place *behind* us to which we may return for refuge; the present crumbles beneath us at every step. We are reminded of a scene we once witnessed, and which we can never forget. We were standing beside the death-bed of a friend in his last moments – he was delirious; and in this state he related aloud as to some invisible being, the events of his past life – the caresses of his mother, the occurrences of his childhood, his *liaisons* with women – he went rapidly over all the chief points of his life down to his last illness, without being in the least conscious of his actual state.

The convulsive movements of nations, and, as it would seem, of, all mankind, resemble the wandering fancies of a dying man, who can feel no strong faith in the life he is entering upon, by reason of the disorganization which is already begun. Nations, like dying men, toss themselves in despair, desiring LIFE at all costs. Whatever hopes one may entertain of the future destinies of mankind, we cannot witness these terrible convulsions without hiding our face to weep. We repeat with trembling lips the "*dies iræ*," even though the end of the funeral mass be

"Lux perpetua luceat ei."

Men and nations alike, we are in the hands of God, and we must say with Job, "though he slay us yet will we trust in him." This seems to us at present the only utterance we can make; our religion is resolved back into this. We shall do well to *realize* it, and walk in the faith of it, not as a mere figure of speech, but as a truth, which will not fail even if we "walk through the valley of the shadow of death."

---

24. Eliza Cook
from *Our Women Servants*

THE women employed as domestic servants constitute by far the most numerous class of workwomen in the kingdom. The field of female employment is exceedingly restricted in all directions, save this; and, accordingly, the number of women who are under the necessity of thus earning their bread, is very large, being considerably upwards of one million. We need not say how much the domestic comfort and well-being of families are influenced by this class. Servants are constantly about us in our homes; the cleanliness, order, and economy of households are dependent on them; and they have in their power the thousand little atoms of which the sum total of domestic happiness is composed. Their moral and social condition re-acts powerfully on those who employ them, and with whom they live in immediate contact. Especially are the manners and morals of children confided to their care affected by their example; for the servant is very often the model of the child during the early years of life, when the mind is most susceptible of impressions. They are about us in health and sickness; in sorrow and festivity; ministering to our wants, our comforts, and our luxuries.

Notwithstanding the acknowledged importance of this class, and the necessity which exists for making the condition of domestic servants one of as much comfort and satisfaction to themselves as possible, it must be admitted, that the actual condition of the great majority of them is exceedingly unsatisfactory, and stands greatly in need of amendment. Their position is such, however, that no law can be devised for their relief, as in the case of the women employed in mines and factories. No Act of Parliament can enter into the home, and determine the relations of employer and domestic servant there. Any amelioration which is possible, can only be effected through the agency of an improved public opinion, which is generally very slow in its operation. We admit that, in many families, servants are treated with the consideration due to them; and where this is the case, their position is one of much comfort, which re-acts beneficially on the comfort of the families themselves. But we regret to say, that these are the exceptions rather than the rule.

The ordinary relation between mistress and servant, is that of an employer who buys service, and a woman who sells it. The bond which unites them, is money-wages. There is little or no sympathy in the relationship, although they are members of the same family. The mistress treats the woman she hires, merely as a servant; the servant regards the woman she serves, merely as an employer. To the servant is allotted generally the least comfortable part of the house to live in – in large towns often a cellar-kitchen by day, and attic by night. A distinction is often made in their food, which the servant cannot help contrasting with the dainty feeding of her employers. Servants must have no visitors, or "followers," as they are called; and are thus required to shut themselves out from companionship and friendly intercourse. They endure a confinement to the house from day to day, and from week to week. Ebullitions of laughter or gay snatches of song, are obnoxious to peremptory prohibition. If the servant goes out on an errand, she "must not loiter away her time.' If she is spoken roughly to, and scolded, even if wrongfully, she must not "answer," but must "know her place." She must bear patiently all sorts of caprices and querulousness. If a kindness is vouchsafed, it is done as if from an superior to an inferior being, and servility is expected in return. In short, the servant is treated, in far too many cases, as but a "necessary evil;" and it is not attempted to be concealed from her that she is so treated. It is too often forgotten that servants have such possessions as feelings, affections, and sympathies; and what wonder need there be, if under such treatment, their better nature should be perverted, and their character become cunning, treacherous, wasteful, careless, and often vicious. This is only what their employers have contributed to make them. Amidst the numerous books of "confessions" made now a-days, we should like to see one containing the real confessions of a domestic servant; giving her general opinion of her several mistresses; her feelings respecting her own conduct, and its reward – her sorrows, and anxiety often so recklessly caused. What a revelation it would be; and how much it would help us to a true understanding of the relations existing between mistress and servant!

It is admitted that domestic servants belong to the poorest and least instructed classes of the community. They are generally the daughters of peasants, artisans, and labourers; and a large proportion of them have not had the benefit of any school education whatever in their early years. Their domestic education has necessarily been of a very imperfect kind; they have grown up in a rude and uncultivated state, and are in this condition transferred to a "place," where they are expected to do everything well; and where, if they fail, they are treated with censure and harsh words. Nothing is done to improve their education; if they learn anything, they must pick it up the best way they can. The policy the most general is, not to lead, but to drive them; and scolding is employed as the goad. Very often, too, their moral culture is not improved by what they see and hear about them. They are ordered to say "not at home" at the door, even when the mistress sits in the next room, within hearing. They dare not venture on espostulation in such a case; this would be deemed a stretch of insolence and audacity. The gossip and scandal which they hear poured out at dining tables does not improve them either; nor the importance which they see attached to dress, equipage, and cookery. They thus insensibly acquire notions, especially in rich families, which lead to vanity, ostentation, and folly, often ending in vice; and, if they marry and return to their own early sphere of life, they carry with them perverted ideas respecting dress, diet, and labour, and often a disregard of economy which is fruitful of much suffering. Generally speaking, we find the best servants, and the most comfortable, in families of moderate income and regular habits. There they are personally known to the master and mistress, and their good feelings are oftener called forth than in families of the higher circles, where servants are as little sympathized with as if they were beings of another race.

It is among the poorer order of the middle-class that we find the most hard-worked, probably, of all human beings, the maids-of-all-work. It would be difficult for any one, who has not been a maid-of-all-work, to picture the hardships of this life, especially where there is a large family, or a house full of lodgers. Up first in the morning, and on foot last at night. In the dark morning she kindles the fires, cleans the boots, and tidies the rooms, before the family are astir. She has no time to tidy herself, for she is engaged during the whole day in the preparation of the family meals, in answering the door, in cleaning up, in putting by, in going errands, and in the thousand indescribable little details of house-work; sometimes running up and down stairs from twenty to thirty times in the course of the day. She must always be at command; she has no leisure, not a minute which she can call her own; all her time is sold to her employer, and the whole of it is demanded. After a life of this sort, the maid-of-all-work finds herself at advanced years without savings, for she is not taught to take care of what she earns, and, with a constitution so broken up, that it is fit only for the workhouse or the lunatic asylum. "We find, on inquiry," said Prince Albert, at the meeting of the Servants' Provident Institution the other day, "that in the metropolis, the greater part of the inmates of the workhouses are domestic servants." . . .

There is, we fear, much in the condition of domestic servants that is unavoidable, and we do not see clearly how it is to be altogether remedied. As we have said, no LAW can touch it. Any amelioration that is possible, must be carried into effect by individual employers; and it is, therefore, our anxious desire to promote among such a more kindly and considerate regard for their servants. The comfort of all families would be greatly promoted thereby. So long as the only bond which unites mistress and servant is money-wages, so long will servants be dull, sulky, self-seeking, and alienated. Every human being has a right to be treated with respect and kindness, whatever the station of life they fill. We must exhibit kind and considerate conduct, in order to beget the affections of others, and obtain their hearty and reasonable service. Employ a contrary course, treat them with distrust and suspicion, be always scolding and complaining at them, and they will distrust, fear, and, perhaps, hate and despise you; and the result will be, a constant carking, discontent, and misery in the midst of the family where such conduct is pursued.

Woman, in whatever station she be placed, is entitled to respect as woman; she is, moreover, entitled to the respect which is due to her as an immortal being. Unless where this truth has entered the minds of the employers of women, we fear the amelioration of the servants employed by them must be regarded as, in a great measure, hopeless. Where this truth is felt, the mistress will then be ready to acknowledge, in the relation which exists between her servant and herself, a social tie, imposing certain duties and affections growing out of their common sympathies as human beings, and the positions they respectively fill, and from the obligation of which no circumstances can release them. We rejoice to believe, that already there are many true-hearted mistresses impenetrated with this truth, and who act accordingly in their households; who are charitable enough to believe, that a broken tea-cup was an accident, and do not punish it as if it were an act of premeditated malice; who are considerate enough to admit, that the best of us are not without faults, the most careful not without moments of carelessness, and that servants may share this common failing without undue punishment. Such mistresses have generally good servants, servants who do their duty cheerfully, if not faultlessly. They are not perpetual declaimers against ingratitude, because, if they sometimes meet with it (and they must meet with it, so long as human nature is imperfect) they know that the fault was not in the kindness, but, most probably, in the harshness of some prior employer, who corrupted the servant's nature. To us the wonder is, on viewing the numerous temptations thrown in servants' way, and the indifference to their interests which is so commonly displayed, not that their good feelings are so often stifled, but that we find among them so many excellent and virtuous characters. . . .

Besides the means which it is so desirable to adopt, for the improvement of the domestic condition of servants, much also might be done to improve their moral state, and to secure for them that competency in old age, which their protracted and valuable services in our families so justly entitle them to. An excellent movement in this direction has already commenced, in which we rejoice to perceive, from the report of the recent meeting of the Servants' Provident and Benevolent Institution, at the Hanover Square Rooms, our enlightened King Consort, Prince Albert, has taken a part, which does him great honour. The institution referred to proposes to enable servants to purchase annuities for their old age, by the deposit of small instalments, at stated periods. A home for servants, when out of place, is a part of the scheme; and also a registry for servants in want of situations.

When the fact, stated by Prince Albert at the above meeting, is considered, that "in the metropolis, the greater part of the inmates of the workhouses are domestic servants," and when we reflect further on the danger, and, too often, the ruin and infamy which befall young women, who are suddenly cast loose upon the temptations of city life, without a home to turn to for shelter, we cannot praise too highly the philanthropic scheme of the Servants' Provident and Benevolent Institution, nor too cordially co-operate in the promotion of its success.

1850

25. Charlotte Brontë
Preface to *Wuthering Heights*

I HAVE just read over 'Wuthering Heights,' and, for the first time, have obtained a clear glimpse of what are termed (and, perhaps, really are) its faults; have gained a definite notion of how it appears to other people – to strangers who knew nothing of the author; who are unacquainted with the locality where the scenes of the story are laid; to whom the inhabitants, the customs, the natural characteristics of the outlying hills and hamlets in the West-Riding of Yorkshire are things alien and unfamiliar.

To all such 'Wuthering Heights' must appear a rude and strange production. The wild moors of the north of England can for them have no interest; the language, the manners, the very dwellings and house hold customs of the scattered inhabitants of those districts, must be to such readers in a great measure unintelligible, and – where intelligible – repulsive. Men and women who, perhaps, naturally very calm, and with feelings moderate in degree, and little marked in kind, have been trained from their cradle to observe the utmost evenness of manner and guardedness of language, will hardly know what to make of the rough, strong utterance, the harshly manifested passions, the unbridled aversions, and headlong partialities of unlettered moorland hinds and rugged moorland squires, who have grown up untaught and unchecked, except by mentors as harsh as themselves. A large class of readers, likewise, will suffer greatly from the introduction into the pages of this work of words printed with all their letters, which it has become the custom to represent by the initial and final letter only – a blank line filling the interval. I may as well say at once that, for this circumstance, it is out of my power to apologize; deeming it, myself, a rational plan to write words at full length. The practice of hinting by single letters those expletives with which profane and violent persons are wont to garnish their discourse, strikes me as a proceeding which, however well meant, is weak and futile. I cannot tell what good it does – what feeling it spares – what horror it conceals.

With regard to the rusticity of 'Wuthering Heights,' I admit the charge, for I feel the quality. It is rustic all through. It is moorish, and wild, and knotty as a root of heath. Nor was it natural that it should be otherwise; the author being herself a native and nursling of the moors. Doubtless, had her lot been cast in a town, her writings, if she had written at all, would have possessed another character. Even had chance or taste led her to choose a similar subject, she would have treated it otherwise. Had Ellis Bell been a lady or a gentleman accustomed to what is called 'the world,' her view of a remote and unreclaimed region, as well as of the dwellers therein, would have differed greatly from that actually taken by the homebred country girl. Doubtless it would have been wider – more comprehensive: whether it would have been more original or more truthful is not so certain. As far as the scenery and locality are concerned, it could scarcely have been so sympathetic: Ellis Bell did not describe as one whose eye and taste alone found pleasure in the prospect; her native hills were far more to her than a spectacle; they were what she lived in, and by, as much as the wild birds, their tenants, or as the heather, their produce. Her descriptions, then, of natural scenery, are what they should be, and all they should be.

Where delineation of human character is concerned, the case is different. I am bound to avow that she had scarcely more practical knowledge of the peasantry amongst whom she lived, than a nun has of the country people who sometimes pass her convent gates. My sister's disposition was not naturally gregarious; circumstances favoured and fostered her tendency to seclusion; except to go to church or take a walk on the hills, she rarely crossed the threshold of home. Though her feeling for the people round was benevolent, intercourse with them she never sought; nor, with very few exceptions, ever experienced. And yet she knew them: knew their ways, their language, their family histories; she could hear of them with interest, and talk of them with detail, minute, graphic, and accurate; but *with* them, she rarely exchanged a word. Hence it ensued that what her mind had gathered of the real concerning them, was too exclusively confined to those tragic and terrible traits of which, in listening to the secret annals of every rude vicinage, the memory is sometimes compelled to receive the impress. Her imagination, which was a spirit more sombre than sunny, more powerful than sportive, found in such traits material whence it wrought creations like Heathcliff, like Earnshaw, like Catherine. Having formed these beings, she did not know what she had done. If the auditor of her work when read in manuscript, shuddered under the grinding influence of natures so relentless and implacable, of spirits so lost and fallen; if it was complained that the mere hearing of certain vivid and fearful scenes banished sleep by night, and disturbed mental peace by day, Ellis Bell would wonder what was meant, and suspect the complainant of affectation. Had she but lived, her mind would of itself have grown like a strong tree, loftier, straighter, wider-spreading, and its matured fruits would have attained a mellower ripeness and sunnier bloom; but on that mind time and experience alone could work: to the influence of other intellects, it was not amenable.

Having avowed that over much of 'Wuthering Heights' there broods 'a horror of great darkness;' that, in its storm-heated and electrical atmosphere, we seem at times to breathe lightning, let me point to those spots where clouded daylight and the eclipsed sun still attest their existence. For a specimen of true benevolence and homely fidelity, look at the character of Nelly Dean; for an example of constancy and tenderness, remark that of Edgar Linton. (Some people will think these qualities do not shine so well incarnate in a man as they would do in a woman, but Ellis Bell could never be brought to comprehend this notion: nothing moved her more than any insinuation that the faithfulness and clemency, the long-suffering and loving-kindness which are esteemed virtues in the daughters of Eve, become foibles in the sons of Adam. She held that mercy and forgiveness are the divinest attributes of the Great Being who made both man and woman, and that what clothes the Godhead in glory, can disgrace no form of feeble humanity.) There is a dry saturnine humour in the delineation of old Joseph, and some glimpses of grace and gaiety animate the younger Catherine. Nor is even the first heroine of the name destitute of a certain strange beauty in her fierceness, or of honesty in the midst of perverted passion and passionate perversity.

Heathcliff, indeed, stands unredeemed; never once swerving in his arrow-straight course to perdition, from the time when 'the little black-haired, swarthy thing, as dark as if it came from the Devil,' was first unrolled out of the bundle and set on its feet in the farm-house kitchen, to the hour when Nelly Dean found the grim, stalwart corpse laid on its back in the panel-enclosed bed, with wide-gazing eyes that seemed 'to sneer at her attempt to close them, and parted lips and sharp white teeth that sneered too.'

Heathcliff betrays one solitary human feeling, and that is *not* his love for Catherine; which is a sentiment fierce and inhuman: a passion such as might boil and glow in the bad essence of some evil genius; a fire that might form the tormented centre – the ever-suffering soul of a magnate of the infernal world: and by its quenchless and ceaseless ravage effect the execution of the decree which dooms him to carry Hell with him wherever he wanders. No; the single link that connects Heathcliff with humanity is his rudely confessed regard for Hareton Earnshaw – the young man whom he has ruined; and then his half-implied esteem for Nelly Dean. These solitary traits omitted, we should say he was child neither of Lascar nor gipsy, but a man's shape animated by demon life – a Ghoul – an Afreet.

Whether it is right or advisable to create beings like Heathcliff, I do not know: I scarcely think it is. But this I know; the writer who possesses the creative gift owns something of which he is not always master – something that at times strangely wills and works for itself. He may lay down rules and devise principles, and to rules and principles it will perhaps for years lie in subjection; and then, haply without any warning of revolt, there comes a time when it will no longer consent 'to harrow the vallies, or be bound with a band in the furrow' – when it 'laughs at the multitude of the city, and regards not the crying of the driver' – when, refusing absolutely to make ropes out of sea-sand any longer, it sets to work on statue-hewing, and you have a Pluto or a Jove, a Tisiphone or a Psyche, a Mermaid or a Madonna, as Fate or Inspiration direct. Be the work grim or glorious, dread or divine, you have little choice left but quiescent adoption. As for you – the nominal artist – your share in it has been to work passively under dictates you neither delivered nor could question – that would not be uttered at your prayer, nor suppressed nor changed at your caprice. If the result be attractive, the World will praise you, who little deserve praise; if it be repulsive, the same World will blame you, who almost as little deserve blame.

'Wuthering Heights' was hewn in a wild workshop, with simple tools, out of homely materials. The statuary found a granite block on a solitary moor: gazing thereon, he saw how from the crag might be elicited a head, savage, swart, sinister; a form moulded with at least one element of grandeur – power. He wrought with a rude chisel, and from no model but the vision of his mediations. With time and labour, the crag took human shape; and there it stands colossal, dark, and frowning, half statue, half rock: in the former sense, terrible and goblin-like; in the latter, almost beautiful, for its colouring is of mellow grey, and moorland moss clothes it; and heath, with its blooming bells and balmy fragrance, grows faithfully close to the giant's foot.

26. Elizabeth Barrett Browning
Sonnets from the Portuguese, XIV

IF thou must love me, let it be for nought
Except for love's sake only. Do not say
'I love her for her smile . . . her look . . . her way
Of speaking gently, . . . for a trick of thought
That falls in well with mine, and certes brought
A sense of pleasant ease on such a day' –
For these things in themselves, Belovèd, may
Be changed, or change for thee, – and love, so wrought,
May be unwrought so. Neither love me for
Thine own dear pity's wiping my cheeks dry, –
A creature might forget to weep who bore
Thy comfort long, and lose thy love thereby.
But love me for love's sake, that evermore
Thou mayst love on through love's eternity.

1854

27. Barbara Bodichon
from *Laws Concerning Women*

Philosophical thinkers have generally come to the conclusion that the tendency of progress is gradually to dispense with law, – that is to say, as each individual man becomes unto himself a law, less external restraint is necessary. And certainly the most urgently needed reforms are simple erasures from the statute book. Women, more than any other members of the community, suffer from over-legislation.

A woman of twenty-one becomes an independent human creature, capable of holding and administering property to any amount; or, if she can earn money, she may appropriate her earnings freely to any purpose she thinks good. Her father has no power over her or her property. But if she unites herself to a man, the law immediately steps in, and she finds herself legislated for, and her condition of life suddenly and entirely changed. Whatever age she may be of, she is again considered as an infant, – she is again under "*reasonable restraint*," – she loses her separate existence, and is merged in that of her husband. . . .

Truly . . . she has no legal right to any property; not even her clothes, books, and household goods are her own, and any money which she earns can be robbed from her legally by her husband, nay, even after the commencement of a treaty of marriage she cannot dispose of her own property without the knowledge of her betrothed. If she should do so, it is deemed a fraud in law and can be set aside after marriage as an injury to her husband.

It is always said, even by those who support the existing law, that it is in fact never acted upon by men of good feeling. That is true; but the very admission condemns the law, and it is not right that the good feeling of men should be all that a woman can look to for simple justice.

There is now a large and increasing class of women who gain their own livelihood, and the abolition of the laws which give husbands this unjust power is most urgently needed.

Rich men and fathers might still make what settlements they pleased, and appoint trustees for the protection of minors and such women as needed protection; but we imagine it well proved that the principle of protection is wrong, and that the education of freedom and responsibility will enable women to take better care of themselves and others too than can be insured to them by any legal precautions.

Upon women of the labouring classes the difficulty of keeping and using their own earnings presses most hardly. In that rank of life where the support of the family depends often on the joint earnings of husband and wife, it is indeed cruel that the earnings of both should be in the hands of one, and not even in the hands of that one who has naturally the strongest desire to promote the welfare of the children.

All who are familiar with the working classes know how much suffering and privation is caused by the exercise of this *right* by drunken and bad men. It is true that men are legally bound to support their wives and children, but this does not compensate women for the loss of their moral right to their own property and earnings, nor for the loss of the mental development and independence of character gained by the possession and thoughtful appropriation of money; nor, it must be remembered, can the claim to support be enforced on the part of the wife unless she appeals to a court of law. Alas, how much will not a woman endure before she will publicly plead for a maintenance!

Why, we ask, should there be this difference between the married and unmarried condition of women? And why does marriage make so little legal difference to men, and such a mighty legal difference to women?

❋ ❋ ❋ ❋

Is there not evidence in our English laws of old opinions relating to women which are passing away with the old state of things which engendered them? In the early times, when women were obliged by the violent state of society to be always under the guardianship of father, brother, or husband, these laws might be necessary; but in our peaceful times, such guardianship is proved to be superfluous by the fact of the secure, honourable, and independent position of single women who are sufficiently protected by the sanctuary of civilization.

Since all the unmarried women in England are supported either by their own exertions or by the exertions or bequests of their fathers and relations, there is no reason why upon marriage they should be thrown upon the pecuniary resources of their husbands, except in so far as the claims of a third party – children – may lessen the wife's power of earning money, at the same time that it increases her expenses. Of course a woman may, and often does, by acting as housekeeper and manager of her husband's concerns, earn a maintenance and a right to share in his property, independent of any children which may come of the marriage. But it is evident that daughters ought to have some sure provision – either a means of gaining their own bread, or property – as it is most undesirable that they should look upon marriage as a means of livelihood.

Fathers seldom feel inclined to trust their daughters' fortunes in the power of a husband, and, in the appointment of trustees, partially elude the law by a legal device. Also, the much abused Court of Chancery tries to palliate the Common Law, and recognizes a separate interest between husband and wife, and allows the wife alone to file a bill to recover and protect her property, and trustees are not necessary if there has been an agreement.

Why should not these legal devices be done away with, by the simple abolition of a law which we have outgrown?

We do not say that these laws of property are the only unjust laws concerning women to be found in the short summary which we have given, but they form a simple, tangible, and not offensive point of attack.

---

28. Caroline Norton
from *English Laws for Women in the Nineteenth Century*

To publish comments on my own case for the sake of obtaining sympathy; to prove merely that my husband has been unjust, and my fate a hard one, would be a very poor and barren ambition. I aspire to a different object. I desire to prove, not my suffering or his injustice, but that the present law of England cannot prevent any such suffering, or control any such injustice. I write in the hope that the law may be amended; and that those who are at present so ill-provided as to have only "Truth and Justice" on their side, may hereafter have the benefit of "Law and Lawyers."

I know all that can be said on my interference with such a subject; all the prejudice and contempt with which men will receive arguments from a woman, and a woman personally interested. But it is of more importance that the law should be altered, than that I should be approved. Many a woman may live to thank Heaven that I had courage and energy left, to attempt the task: and, since no one can foretell the future, even men may pause ere they fling down my pamphlet with masculine scorn; for a day may come, – however improbable, – to some one of my readers, when he would give his right hand, for the sake of sister, daughter, or friend, that the law *were* in such a condition as to afford a chance of justice; without the pain of a protracted struggle, or the disgrace of a public brawl. What I write, is written in no spirit of rebellion; it puts forward no absurd claim of equality; it is simply an appeal for protection. Such protection, in degree, as is accorded to servants, to apprentices, to the sailor on the high seas, to all whom the law admits to be in a subordinate and helpless position. Such protection, in degree, as has lately been extended to women in the lower classes, by the more stringent laws enacted in their behalf. . . .

For the shallower rebuke, that mine is an exceptional case; that the law need scarcely be disturbed to meet a solitary instance of tyranny; there is a ready and reasonable answer. *All* cases requiring legal interference, are exceptional cases; and it will scarcely be argued that a balance must first be struck in numbers, and instances of wrong be reckoned by the dozen or the gross, before justice will condescend to weigh the scales. But it does not follow that mine is a solitary example of injustice, because it may possibly happen, from a combination of peculiar circumstances, to be the instance which shall call attention to the state of the law. Hundreds of women are suffering at this moment, whose cases are not less hard, but more obscure: and it consists with all experience, that although wrong and oppression may be repeated till they become almost of daily occurrence, they strike at last on some heart that revolts instead of enduring; or are witnessed by men whose indignant sympathy works out reform and redress. In either case, oppression is brought to a halt not by a multitude of instances, but by some single example; which example may be neither more nor less important than others, though it be made the argument and opportunity of change.

❋ ❋ ❋ ❋

Mr Norton has lately spoken (in the fabulous histories he has given to the public through the medium of the newspapers) of the profound and patient attachment he entertained for me previous to our union. I do most solemnly declare that at the time he first demanded me of my mother in marriage, I had not exchanged six sentences with him on any subject whatever. Mr Norton was brother to Lord Grantley; and the governess to whose care I was confided, happening to be sister to Lord Grantley's agent, the female members of the Norton family, from courtesy to this lady, invited her and such of her pupils as she chose to accompany her, to Lord Grantley's house. A sister of Mr Norton's, an eccentric person who affected masculine habits and played a little on the violin, amused herself with my early verses and my love of music, and took more notice of me than of my companions. The occasions on which I saw this lady were not frequent; and still more rare were the occasions on which I had also seen her brother; it was therefore with a feeling of mere astonishment, that I received from my governess the intelligence that she thought it right to refuse me the indulgence of accompanying her again to Lord Grantley's till she had heard from my mother; as Mr Norton had professed his intention of asking me in marriage. This lady is still living, and can answer for the exact truth of my statement.

Almost the first step Mr Norton took, after he had made my mother's acquaintance, was to beg her interest with a member of the royal family, whose good word with the Chancellor Eldon was to procure him a small legal appointment; and from the day we were married he never ceased impressing upon me, that as I brought him no present fortune (my portion being only payable on my mother's death), I was bound to use every effort with the political friends of my grandfather, to get him lucrative promotion in his profession. I found this more difficult than I expected. The memory of Mr Sheridan among the Whig party, was not held in that affection which in my inexperience I had fancied; and if it had been, I do not know that it would have been a sufficient plea for serving Mr Norton, who could put forward no personal claims for employment. I did, however, what my husband requested. I besieged, with variously worded letters of importunity, the friends whom I knew as the great names linked with the career of my grandfather; and while waiting the result of the petitions I had sown on so wide a field, I turned my literary ability to account, by selling the copyright of my first poem to Messrs Ebers of Bond street. It is not without a certain degree of romantic pride that I look back and know that the first expenses of my son's life were defrayed from the price of that first creation of my brain; and before that child was two years old, I had procured for my husband, – (for the husband who has lately overwhelmed me, my sons, and his dead patron with slander, rather than yield a miserable annuity) – a place worth a thousand a year, the arduous duty of which consisted in attending three days in the week, for five hours, to hear causes tried in the simplest forms of law. From that day to the present, my husband has always considered that I ought to assist *him* – instead of his supporting *me*. The dependance upon my literary efforts for all extra resources, runs, as a matter of course, through all the letters I received from him during our union. The names of my publishers occur as if they were Mr Norton's bankers. If Murray of Albemarle street will not accept a poem, – if Bull of Holles street does not continue a magazine, – if Heath does not offer the editorship of an Annual, – if Saunders and Otley do not buy the *MS.* of a novel, – if Colburn's agreement is not satisfactory and sufficient, – if Power delays payment for a set of ballads, – if, in short, the *Wife* has no earnings to produce, the *Husband* professes himself to be "quite at a loss to know" how the next difficulty of payment is to be got over. On one occasion, when I had been employed to write words to Spanish music, by an officer of some distinction, and was extremely loth to express to this gentleman the opinion Mr Norton wished conveyed to him, – namely, that payment was too long delayed, – Mr Norton himself undertook the task of dunning him, for the stipulated sum by which *he* was to profit. I worked hard, and was proud of my success. I brought to my many tasks all the energy which youth, high spirits, ambition, good health, and the triumph of usefulness could inspire, joined to a wish for literary fame, so eager, that I sometimes look back and wonder if I was punished for it by unenviable and additional notoriety.

I rejoiced, then, at finding, – woman though I was, – a career in which *I* could earn that which my husband's profession had never brought him. Out of our stormy quarrels I rose undiscouraged, and worked again to help him and forward the interests of my children. I have sat up all night, – even at times when I have had a young infant to nurse, – to finish tasks for some publisher. I made in one year a sum of 1,400*l.* by my pen; and I have a letter from Mr Norton's own brother, proving that even when we were on terms of estrangement, I still provided, without grudging, money that was to be spent on his pleasures.

❀ ❀ ❀ ❀

The treatment that I received as a Wife, would be incredible if, fortunately (or unfortunately), there were not witnesses who can prove it on oath. We had been married but a few weeks when I found that a part of my lot was that which generally belongs to a lower sphere – and that, when angry, Mr Norton resorted to personal violence.

After our honeymoon, we lived for a short time in chambers Mr Norton had occupied as a bachelor; in Garden Court, Temple; and, on the first occasion of dispute, after some high and violent words, he flung the ink-stand, and most of the law-books, which might have served a better purpose, at the head of his bride. We had no servants, only an old woman, who had taken care of these chambers for some years, and who offered me the acceptable consolation, that her master was not "sober", – and would regret it "by-and-bye."

After this happy beginning I accompanied my husband to Scotland. We had been married about two months, when, one evening, after we had all withdrawn to our apartments, we were discussing some opinion he had expressed; I said, (very uncivilly,) that "I thought I had never heard so silly or ridiculous a conclusion." This remark was punished by a sudden and violent kick; the blow reached my side; it caused great pain for many days, and being afraid to remain with him, I sat up the whole night in another apartment.

Four or five months afterwards, when we were settled in London, we had returned home from a ball; I had then no personal dispute with Mr Norton, but he indulged in bitter and coarse remarks respecting a young relative of mine, who, though married, continued to dance, – a practice, Mr Norton said, no husband ought to permit. I defended the lady spoken of, and then stood silently looking out of the window at the quiet light of dawn, by way of contrast. Mr Norton desired I would "cease my contem-plations," and retire to rest, as he had already done; and this mandate producing no result, he suddenly sprang from the bed, seized me by the nape of the neck, and dashed me down on the floor. The sound of my fall woke my sister and brother-in-law, who slept in a room below, and they ran up to my door. Mr Norton locked it, and stood over me, declaring no one should enter. I could not speak, – I only moaned. My brother-in-law burst the door open, and carried me down stairs. I had a swelling on my head for many days afterward, and the shock made my sister exceedingly ill.

On another occasion, when I was writing to my mother, Mr Norton (who was sipping spirits and water, while he smoked his cigar) said he was sure "from the expression of my countenance," that I was "complaining." I answered that "I seldom could do anything else." Irritated by the reply, Mr Norton said I should not write at all, and tore the letter up. I took another sheet of paper, and recommenced. After watching and smoking for a few minutes, he rose, took one of the allumettes I had placed for his cigar, lit it, poured some of the spirits that stood by him over my writing book and, in a moment, set the whole in a blaze. But Mr Norton vouchsafed no other notice of my alarm, than that it would "teach me not to brave him."

On another occasion, some time before the birth of my youngest son, I being at breakfast, and my eldest child playing about the room, Mr Norton entered; he desired me to rise and leave the place I was sitting in, as it faced the park, and it amused him to see the people pass by. I demurred, and said I was not well, and that he should have come down earlier if he had any fancy or choice about places. We had no other word of dispute. Mr Norton then deliberately took the tea-kettle, and set it down upon my hand; I started up from the pain, and was both burnt and scalded. I ran up to the nursery, and the nurse got the surgeon who lived next door to come in and dress my hand, which remained bound up and useless for days. When this was over, I enquired where Mr Norton was? and received for reply, that after I had been hurt, he had simply desired the servant to "brush the crumbs away," in the place he had desired me to yield; had then sat down there and breakfasted; and had since gone out – without one word of apology or enquiry.

About the same period, a dispute having arisen after dinner, I said I really was weary of my life with the perpetual wranglings; that I had a great deal to do, and would sit no longer with him, but go to the drawing-room and write for a Periodical, of which I then had the editorship; that I only asked him to stay where he was, and smoke there, instead of upstairs. He answered, that the house was his, – not mine, – that he should sit in what room he pleased; and that I should find I could not carry things with such a high hand as I desired to do. I left him; called my maid, desired her to bring her work and remain in the room, as I did not feel well, and locking the door of the drawing-room for further security, prepared to write. Mr Norton came and demanded admittance. I refused, and said I was undress-ing. After repeating his demand, and saying, if the door was not instantly opened he would break it open, he was as good as his word. He forced in the door, forcing away the framework with it, and rushed forward. He stopped short on seeing my maid, and desired her instantly to leave the room. I said she must stay, for I was afraid of being left alone with him. Mr Norton then gave way to the most frantic rage, blew out the candles, flung the furniture about, and seized my maid to turn her out of the room by force. I clung to her, and being extremely frightened, and naturally at that time less strong than usual, I became very faint, and some of the other servants entering, Mr Norton desisted. He then lighted a taper, examined the door, asked where the carpenter lived, and left the room. I thought the worst was over; but I was mistaken. Mr Norton returned almost immediately, and seizing me, forced me out of the room and down on the stairs. I really feared for my life; I shrieked for help, and said I was sure Mr Norton was "gone mad." The man-servant held back his arm while he was struggling with the maid, who was terrified to death, – and at length, assisted by the servants, I retired once again to the nursery, and slept with the nurse; leaving Mr Norton master of the room he had broken into, and my literary tasks and the furniture scattered over the ground.

I intended to have left my home in the morning; but when morning came, I was too ill. I saw no more of Mr Norton till the evening of that day. I was sitting with my two little children in the same room. He did not speak to me, – he spoke to one of the children and went away again. I had written to my brother to state all that had occurred. I said that for the sake of those children and the one unborn, I should be loth to part from my husband; that I bore him no ill-will, but that unless he would undertake to be "gentlemanlike" in his conduct towards me, I must leave him. My brother forwarded a copy of my statement to my husband, – told him there could be but one opinion of his cruel and violent assault, and that unless he received, within twenty-four hours, a written expression of contrition and promises for the future, he would expose Mr Norton. To that letter I owe the miserable satisfaction of holding, under Mr Norton's own handwriting, proof of every circumstance of this scene; for he undertook to justify himself to my brother; he admitted all the facts; he admitted that I had withdrawn to write for my publishers, and had told him so, but said he broke open the door "on principle; thinking it necessary, as a husband, to resist such extravagant and disrespectful proceedings" as locking him out of any room in the house. That he blew out the candles to prevent my maid remaining and working in the apartment; and that I had not seemed at all angry when I left him in the dining-room. Recently, Mr Norton has spoken of this scene in one of his letters to the 'Times' newspaper, as a "frivolous quarrel." I leave to others to determine what the notions of general conduct towards a woman were likely to be, in the person whose idea of "frivolous" disputes are thus exemplified. My brother's interference availed, however, for that time. Mr Norton apologised, adjured me to pardon him, and wrote triumphantly to my brother to say that we "were all right".

✿ ✿ ✿ ✿

I said nothing should prevent my going to my brother; that it was Mr Norton's own fault he was not on terms with my family; that the doctor had ordered change of air for the elder child, who was recovering from scarlatina; and that I should give my servants orders to refuse Miss Vaughan admittance to my house, as she laboured always for mischief, in spite of my patience with her. We parted angrily – Mr Norton to dine with the chief magistrate, Sir Frederic Roe, and I to dine with Lady Mary Fox. We spent the evening together at a party at Lord Harrington's, and returned home together. The dispute was then renewed, whether under the circumstances I should go to my brother's. Mr Norton's last words were – "Well, the children shall not, that I have determined;" and as he entered the house he desired the servants to unpack the carriage (which had been prepared for starting), and take the children's things out, for that they were not going. He then went up to the nursery, and repeated the order to the nurse. It was admitted at the trial that the sole observation I made on this occasion, when the nurse asked me "what she was to do?" was, that "Mr Norton's orders must be obeyed." I neither braved him with useless words, nor complained. I waited till the morning, and then went to my sister's, to consult with her what was to be done.

While I was with my sister, my children were kidnapped and taken possession of by Miss Vaughan, as I doubt not had been agreed upon the day before. The man-servant came to my sister, and said "something was going wrong at home;" that the children, with their things, had been put into a hackney-coach and taken away, he did not know where. I had the children traced to Miss Vaughan's house, and followed them. Anything like the bitter insolence of this woman – who thought she had baffled and conquered me for life – I never experienced. She gave vent to the most violent and indecent answers to my reproaches, and said that if I troubled her further she would give me into the hands of the police. I left her, and went alone to my brother's house in the country. I wished him to return immediately to town with me; and so far from having intended, previous to this outrage, to leave my home, or having made any preparation whatever for such an event, I left everything that belonged to me (even my wearing apparel) in Mr Norton's house; and he, who afterwards advertised me as a run-away, thought it so probable that I should reappear next day with my brother, that he gave this order in writing to the man-servant, dated the morning after my departure:–

"In case Mrs Norton or her brother should return to town, and call at Storey's Gate, this is my written authority to you, to refuse admittance, and to open the house-door only with the chain across."

                                                              "G.C. Norton."

It was thought best that I should *not* return, and I therefore escaped the disgraceful reception with the chain across the door of my home, which my husband had prepared for me. I wrote to Mr Norton's mother, to inform her of what had occurred, and to say that I must part from him; and Mr Norton, on his side, requested Lord Harrington to write to my family to say he would part from me, – but make no provision for me, – nor suffer me to have my children. I did not, at first, know that a mother had no legal claim to her children, and I answered by defying this injustice. My mother, my brother, and my brother-in-law, also wrote to Lord Harrington, explaining to him the truth, and disclosing to him, – with very severe comments on Mr Norton's character, – the circumstances of our former disputes. Lord Harrington communicated to Mr Norton the substance of these replies (which contained proofs, extracted from Mr Norton's own letters), and told him that I utterly refused to accede to his terms. Mr Norton then said he would not part from me quietly, but endeavour publicly to disgrace me, that he had put the affair in the hands of lawyers, pledged himself not to interfere, and was not allowed to mention what they thought of doing; that my family had conspired against him, and they should maintain me; that he was occupied with enquiries into my conduct towards my male acquaintance in general, and would "try for a divorce," if a case could be made out.

✳ ✳ ✳ ✳

After the trial was over, I consulted whether a divorce "by reason of cruelty" might not be pleaded for me; and I laid before my lawyers the many instances of violence, injustice, and ill-usage, of which the trial was but the crowning example. I was then told that no divorce *I* could obtain would break my marriage; that I could not plead cruelty *which I had forgiven*; that by returning to Mr Norton I had "*condoned*" all I complained of. I learnt, too, the *law* as to my children – that the right was with the father; that neither my innocence nor his guilt could alter it; that not even his giving them into the hands of a mistress, would give me any claim to their custody. The eldest was but six years old, the second four, the youngest two and a half, when we were parted. I wrote, therefore, and *petitioned* the father and husband in whose power I was, for leave to see them – for leave to keep them, until they were a little older. Mr Norton's answer was, that I should not have them; that if I wanted to see them, I might have an interview with them at the chambers of his attorney. . . .

Eventually, the children were permitted to come to my brother's house; Mr Norton expressly limiting the time of their stay to one half-hour, and sending them with two of the women who had been witnesses on the trial, who stated that their "orders" were to remain in the room with me. I was not allowed to see even my baby of two years old without these "*witnesses*."

What I suffered on my children's account, none will ever know or measure. "The heart knoweth its own bitterness," and God knew mine! The days and nights of tears and anguish, that grew into the struggle of years – it is even *now* a pain to me to look back upon: even *now*, the hot agony of resentment and grief rises in my mind, when I think of the needless tyranny I endured in this respect. Mr Norton held my children as hostages; he felt that while he had them, he still had a power over me that nothing could control. Baffled in the matter of the trial and damages, he still had the power to do more than punish – to torture – the wife who had been so anxious to part from him. I never saw them; I seldom knew where they were. Once, when I wrote to ask after them in illness, my letter to the nurse (which contained no syllable of offence, or, beyond the subject of my inquiry) was turned inside out, and franked back to me. Miss Vaughan was dead, and I appealed to my mother-in-law (with whom I heard my husband meant to place them), entreating her to refuse to take them; which she promised to do, and heard me with tears of sympathy. But my husband's sister, Lady Menzies, decided differently: to her, on payment of so much a head, my three children were consigned; and removed to Scotland, where neither their father nor I could be with them. There, with one whom I knew to be haughty and intemperate, those children were left, who had hitherto been so gently and tenderly treated, and the eldest of whom was delicate in health, sensitive in disposition, and just recovering from illness. The first step she made in their education, was to flog this very child (a child of six years old) for merely receiving and reading a letter from me (I being in England and he in Scotland), to "impress on his memory" that he was not to receive letters from me. Having occasion to correct one still younger, she stripped it naked, tied it to the bed-post, and chastised it with a riding-whip. She was a fit sister and colleague to Mr Norton; and I have lived to see the day when *her* disputes for money, with her own sons, have come to Scotch law-pleading; as Mr Norton has brought to English law-pleading the like disputes with us.

These boys having been the gleam of happiness and compensation in my home; it was not to be supposed that I would give them up without a struggle, because it was so "written in the bond" of English law. Ceaselessly, restlessly, perseveringly, I strove; and, fortunately for me, other cases of hardship had already drawn attention to the necessity of some reform on this subject; especially the case of a Mrs Greenhill, in which Serjeant Talfourd (now Sir Thomas Noon Talfourd) had been professionally concerned. A new "Infant Custody Bill" was brought forward by the learned Serjeant; and passed, after a struggle of three years, by a majority of four to one. . . .

His cruel carelessness was afterwards proved, on a most miserable occasion. My youngest child, then a boy of eight years old, left without care or overlooking, rode out with a brother but little older than himself, was thrown, carried to the house of a country neighbor, and died there of lock jaw, consequent on the accident. Mr Norton allowed the child to lie ill for a week, – indeed to be at death's door, – before he sent to inform me. Sir Fitzroy and Lady Kelly were staying with Mr Norton in the country. Lady Kelly (who was an utter stranger to me) met me at the railway station. I said – "I am here, – is my boy better?" "No," she said – "he is not better, – he is dead." And I found, instead of my child, a corpse already coffined.

Mr Norton asked my forgiveness then, as he had asked it often before; he sent his elder child to plead for him, – for well he knew what my children were to me; he humbled himself, and grieved for an hour, till he changed into pity the horror and repugnance I had expressed at the idea of seeing him, – and then he buried our child, and forgot both his sorrow and his penitence.

1855

29. George Eliot
from *Margaret Fuller and Mary Wollstonecraft*

It is interesting to compare [Margaret Fuller's *Woman in the Nineteenth Century*] published in its earliest form in 1843, with a work on the position of woman, written between sixty and seventy years ago – we mean Mary Wollstonecraft's *Rights of Woman*. The latter work was not continued beyond the first volume; but so far as this carries the subject, the comparison, at least in relation to strong sense and loftiness of moral tone, is not at all disadvantageous to the woman of the last century. There is in some quarters a vague prejudice against the *Rights of Woman* as in some way or other a reprehensible book, but readers who go to it with this impression will be surprised to find it eminently serious, severely moral, and withal rather heavy – the true reason, perhaps, that no edition has been published since 1796, and that it is now rather scarce. There are several points of resemblance, as well as of striking difference, between the two books. A strong understanding is present in both; but Margaret Fuller's mind was like some regions of her own American continent, where you are constantly stepping from the sunny 'clearings' into the mysterious twilight of the tangled forest – she often passes in one breath from forcible reasoning to dreamy vagueness; moreover, her unusually varied culture gives her great command of illustration. Mary Wollstonecraft, on the other hand, is nothing if not rational; she has no erudition, and her grave pages are lit up by no ray of fancy. In both writers we discern, under the brave bearing of a strong and truthful nature, the beating of a loving woman's heart, which teaches them not to undervalue the smallest offices of domestic care or kindliness. But Margaret Fuller, with all her passionate sensibility, is more of the literary woman, who would not have been satisfied without intellectual production; Mary Wollstonecraft, we imagine, wrote not at all for writing's sake, but from the pressure of other motives. So far as the difference of date allows, there is a striking coincidence in their trains of thought; indeed, every important idea in the *Rights of Woman*, except the combination of home education with a common day-school for boys and girls, reappears in Margaret Fuller's essay.

One point on which they both write forcibly is the fact that, while men have a horror of such faculty or culture in the other sex as tends to place it on a level with their own, they are really in a state of subjection to ignorant and feeble-minded women. . . .

There is a notion commonly entertained among men that an instructed woman, capable of having opinions, is likely to prove an impracticable yoke-fellow, always pulling one way when her husband wants to go the other, oracular in tone, and prone to give curtain lectures on metaphysics. But surely, so far as obstinacy is concerned, your unreasoning animal is the most unmanageable of creatures, where you are not allowed to settle the question by a cudgel, a whip and bridle, or even a string to the leg. For our own parts, we see no consistent or commodious medium between the old plan of corporal discipline and that thorough education of women which will make them rational beings in the highest sense of the word. Wherever weakness is not harshly controlled it must *govern*, as you may see when a strong man holds a little child by the hand, how he is pulled hither and thither, and wearied in his walk by his submission to the whims and feeble movements of his companion. A really cultured woman, like a really cultured man, will be ready to yield in trifles. So far as we see, there is no indissoluble connexion between infirmity of logic and infirmity of will, and a woman quite innocent of an opinion in philosophy, is as likely as not to have an indomitable opinion about the kitchen. As to airs of superiority, no woman ever had them in consequence of true culture, but only because her culture was shallow or unreal, only as a result of what Mrs Malaprop well calls 'the ineffectual qualities in a woman' – mere acquisitions carried about, and not knowledge thoroughly assimilated so as to enter into the growth of the character. . . .

Men pay a heavy price for their reluctance to encourage self-help and independent resources in women. The precious meridian years of many a man of genius have to be spent in the toil of routine, that an 'establishment' may be kept up for a woman who can understand none of his secret yearnings, who is fit for nothing but to sit in her drawing-room like a doll-Madonna in her shrine. No matter. Anything is more endurable than to change our established formulæ about women, or to run the risk of looking up to our wives instead of looking down on them. *Sit divus, dummodo non sit vivus* (let him be a god, provided he be not living), said the Roman magnates of Romulus; and so men say of women, let them be idols, useless absorbents of precious things, provided we are not obliged to admit them to be strictly fellow-beings, to be treated, one and all, with justice and sober reverence.

On one side we hear that woman's position can never be improved until women themselves are better; and, on the other, that women can never become better until their position is improved – until the laws are made more just, and a wider field opened to feminine activity. But we constantly hear the same difficulty stated about the human race in general. There is a perpetual action and reaction between individuals and institutions; we must try and mend both by little and little – the only way in which human things can be mended. Unfortunately, many over-zealous champions of women assert their actual equality with men – nay, even their moral supe-riority to men – as a ground for their release from oppressive laws and restrictions. They lose strength immensely by this false position. If it were true, then there would be a case in which slavery and ignorance nourished virtue, and so far we should have an argument for the continuance of bondage. But we want freedom and culture for woman, because subjection and ignorance have debased her, and with her, Man.

––––––

30. Margaret Oliphant
from *Modern Novelists*

GREATNESS is always comparative: there are few things so hard to adjust as the sliding-scale of fame. We remember once looking over a book of autographs, which impressed us with an acute perception of this principle. As we turned over the fair and precious leaves, we lighted upon name after name, unknown to us as to a savage. What were these? They were famous names – scraps of notes and hoarded signatures from the great Professor this, and the great Mr that, gentlemen who wrote F.R.S., and a score of

other initial letters against their names, and were ranked among the remarkable people of their generation. Yet we – we say it with humiliation –
knew them not, and we flatter ourselves that we were not inferior in this
particular to the mass of the literature-loving public. They were great, but
only in their own sphere. How many spheres are there entertaining each
its own company of magnates? How few who attain the universal recognition,
and are great in the sight of all men! There is not a parish or a county in
the three kingdoms without its eminent person – not an art or a science
but has its established oligarchy; and the great philosopher, who maps the
sky like any familiar ocean, is not more emphatically distinguished among
his fellows than is some individual workman in the manufactory from
which came his great telescope – so true is it, in spite of the infinite diversity
of individual constitution, that we have but a series of endless repetitions
in the social economy of human nature. Nor is it much easier to define
greatness than to limit the number of those for whom it is claimed. In the
generation which has just passed, are there not two or three grand names
of unquestionable magnitude and influence, the secret of whose power
we cannot discover in anything they have left behind them? In fact, all that
we can do when we descend from that highest platform whose occupants
are visible to the whole world, and universally acknowledged, is to reconcile the claims of the lesser and narrower eminences, by permitting every
individual of them to be great "in his way."

   And there is no sphere in which it is so necessary to exercise this toler-
ation as among the great army of novelists who minister to our pleasures.
In no other department of literature is the field so crowded; in few others
do success and failure depend so entirely upon the gifts of the artist. A
biography, however indifferently executed, must always have something
real in it. History may be intolerably heavy – may be partial, or disin-
genuous, or flippant, but still it is impossible to remove fact and significance
altogether from its pages. Fiction, on the other hand, has no such foundation to build upon, and it depends entirely on the individual powers of its
professors, whether it is merely a lying legend of impossible people, or a
broad and noble picture of real things and real men. To balance this, it is
also true that few people are without their bit of insight, of whatever kind
it may be, and that the greater portion of those who have the power of
speech, the trick of composition, have really seen or known something
which their neighbours would be the better for hearing. So far as it professes to represent this great crowded world, and the broad lights and
shadows of universal life, with all its depths and heights, its wonders and
mysteries, there are but few successful artists in fiction, and these few are
of universal fame; but there remains many a byway and corner, many a

nook of secret seclusion, and homes of kindly charity, which genius which
is not the highest, and minds of a lower range and scantier experience, may
well be content to embellish and illustrate. Nor does it seldom happen that
a storyteller of this second rank finds a straight road and a speedy entrance
to the natural heart which has but admired and wondered at the master
minstrel's loftier tale.

Place aux dames! how does it happen that the cowardice of womankind
is a fact so clearly established, and that so little notice is ever taken of the
desperate temerity of this half of the creation? . . .

Where philosophic magnates fear to tread, and bodies of divinity
approach with trembling, the fair novelist flies at a gallop. Her warfare, it
is true, is after the manner of women: there is a rush, a flash, a shriek, and
the combatant comes forth from the melée trembling with delight and terror; but the sudden daring of her attack puts bravery to shame. This, which
is the age of so many things – of enlightenment, of science, of progress – is
quite as distinctly the age of female novelists; and women, who rarely or
never find their way to the loftiest class, have a natural right and claim to
rank foremost in the second. The vexed questions of social morality, the
grand problems of human experience, are seldom so summarily discussed
and settled as in the novels of this day which are written by women; and,
though we have little reason to complain of the first group of experienced
novelists who lead our lists, we tremble to encounter the sweeping judgments and wonderful theories of the very strange world revealed to us in
the books of many of the younger sisterhood.

❀ ❀ ❀ ❀

Ten years ago we professed an orthodox system of novel-making. Our
lovers were humble and devoted – our ladies were beautiful, and might be
capricious if it pleased them; and we held it a very proper and most laudable
arrangement that Jacob should serve seven years for Rachel, and recorded
it as one of the articles of our creed; and that the only true-love worth
having was that reverent, knightly, chivalrous true-love which consecrated
all womankind, and served one with fervour and enthusiasm. Such was
our ideal, and such our system, in the old halcyon days of novel-writing;
when suddenly there stole upon the scene, without either flourish of
trumpets or public proclamation, a little fierce incendiary, doomed to turn
the world of fancy upside down. She stole upon the scene – pale, small,
by no means beautiful – something of a genius, something of a vixen – a
dangerous little person, inimical to the peace of society. After we became
acquainted with herself, we were introduced to her lover. Such a lover! – a
vast, burly, sensual Englishman, one of those Hogarth men, whose power

consists in some singular animal force of life and character, which it is impossible to describe or analyse. Such a wooing! – the lover is rude, brutal, cruel. The little woman fights against him with courage and spirit – begins to find the excitement and relish of a new life in this struggle – begins to think of her antagonist all day long – falls into fierce love and jealousy – betrays herself – is tantalised and slighted, to prove her devotion – and then suddenly seized upon and taken possession of, with love several degrees fiercer than her own. Then comes the catastrophe which prevents this extraordinary love from running smooth. Our heroine runs away to save herself – falls in with another man almost as singular as her first love – and very nearly suffers herself to be reduced to marry this unloved and unloving wooer; but, escaping that risk, finally discovers that the obstacle is removed which stood between her and her former tyrant, and rushes back straightway to be graciously accepted by the blind and weakened Rochester. Such was the impetuous little spirit which dashed into our well-ordered world, broke its boundaries, and defied its principles – and the most alarming revolution of modern times has followed the invasion of *Jane Eyre*.

It is not to be wondered at that speculation should run wild about this remarkable production. Sober people, with a sober respect for womankind, and not sufficient penetration to perceive that the grossness of the book was such grossness as only could be perpetrated by a woman, contested indignantly the sex of the writer. The established authorities brought forth proofs in the form of incorrect costume, and errors in dress. Nobody perceived that it was the new generation nailing its colours to its mast. No one would understand that this furious love-making was but a wild declaration of the "Rights of Woman" in a new aspect. The old-fashioned deference and respect – the old-fashioned wooing – what were they but so many proofs of the inferior position of the woman, to whom the man condescended with the gracious courtliness of his loftier elevation! The honours paid to her in society – the pretty fictions of politeness, they were all degrading tokens of her subjection, if she were but sufficiently enlightened to see their true meaning. The man who presumed to treat her with reverence was one who insulted her pretensions; while the lover who struggled with her, as he would have struggled with another man, only adding, a certain amount of contemptuous brutality, which no man would tolerate, was the only one who truly recognised her claims of equality. "A fair field and no favour," screams the representative of womanhood. "Let him take me captive, seize upon me, overpower me if he is the better man – let us fight it out, my weapons against his weapons, and see which is the strongest. You poor fellow, do you not see how you are insulting and humiliating that Rachel, for whom you serve seven years? Let her feel she is your equal – make her your lawful spoil by your bow and by your spear. The cause of the strong hand for ever – and let us   fight it out!" Whereupon our heroine rushes into the field, makes desperate sorties out of her Sebastopol, blazes abroad her ammunition into the skies, commits herself beyond redemption, and finally permits herself to be ignominiously captured, and seized upon with a ferocious appropriation which is very much unlike the noble and grand sentiment which we used to call love.

Yes, it is but a mere vulgar boiling over of the political cauldron, which tosses your French monarch into chaos, and makes a new one in his stead. Here is your true revolution. France is but one of the Western Powers; woman is the half of the world. Talk of a balance of power which may be adjusted by taking a Crimea, or fighting a dozen battles – here is a battle which must always be going forward – a balance of power only to be decided by single combat, deadly and uncompromising, where the combatants, so far from being guided by the old punctilios of the duello, make no secret of their ferocity, but throw sly javelins at each other, instead of shaking hands before they begin. Do you think that young lady is an angelic being, young gentleman? Do you compare her to roses and lilies, and stars and sunbeams, in your deluded imagination? Do you think you would like to "deck and crown your head with bays," . . . all for the greater glory to her, when she found you "serve her evermore"? Unhappy youth! She is a fair gladiator – she is not an angel. In her secret heart she longs to rush upon you, and try a grapple with you, to prove her strength and her equality. She has no patience with your flowery emblems. Why should *she* be like a rose or a lily any more than yourself? Are these beautiful weaklings the only types you can find of *her*? And this new Bellona steps forth in armour, throws down her glove, and defies you – to conquer her if you can. Do you like it, gentle lover? – would you rather break her head and win, or leave her alone and love her? The alternative is quite distinct and unmistakable – only do not insult her with your respect and humility, for this is something more than she can bear.

These are the doctrines, startling and original, propounded by Jane Eyre; and they are not Jane Eyre's opinions only, as we may guess from the host of followers or imitators who have copied them. There is a degree of refined indelicacy possible to a woman, which no man can reach. Her very ignorance of evil seems to give a certain piquancy and relish to her attempts to realise it. She gives a runaway, far-off glimpse – a strange improper situation, and whenever she has succeeded in raising a sufficient amount of excitement to make it possible that something very wrong might follow, she prevents the wrong by a bold *coup*, and runs off in delight.

There are some conversations between Rochester and Jane Eyre which no *man* could have dared to give – which only could have been given by the overboldness of innocence and ignorance trying to imagine what it never could understand, and which are as womanish as they are unwomanly.

When all this is said, *Jane Eyre* remains one of the most remarkable works of modern times – as remarkable as *Villette*, and more perfect. We know no one else who has such grasp of persons and places, and a perfect command of the changes of the atmosphere, and the looks of a country under rain or wind. There is no fiction in these wonderful scenes of hers. The Yorkshire dales, the north-country moor, the streets of Brussels, are illusions equally complete. Who does not know Madame Beck's house, white and square and lofty, with its level rows of windows, its green shutters, and the sun that beams upon its blinds, and on the sultry pavement before the door? How French is Paul Emmanuel and all his accessories! How English is Lucy Snowe! We feel no art in these remarkable books. What we feel is a force which makes everything real – a motion which is irresistible. We are swept on in the current, and never draw breath till the tale is ended. Afterwards we may disapprove at our leisure, but it is certain that we have not a moment's pause to be critical till we come to the end.

❋ ❋ ❋ ❋

Since writing the above, we have heard of an event which will give to some of its comments an air of harsh and untimely criticism. The author of *Jane Eyre*, the most distinguished female writer of her time, has ended her labours, and exchanged these fretting shows of things for the realities which last for ever. To associate bodily weakness or waning life with the name of this remarkable woman, did not occur to us; nor can we think of cancelling now what we have said; but we repeat again over her grave, the great admiration with which we have always regarded her wonderful powers. No one in her time has grasped with such extraordinary force the scenes and circumstances through which her story moved; no one has thrown as strong an individual life into place and locality. Her passionate and fearless nature, her wild, warm heart, are transfused into the magic world she has created – a world which no one can enter without yielding to the irresistible fascination of her personal influence. Perhaps no other writer of her time has impressed her mark so clearly on contemporary literature, or drawn so many followers into her own peculiar path; and she leaves no one behind worthy to take the pre-eminent and leading place of the author of *Jane Eyre*.

31. Jane Carlyle
Budget of a Femme Incomprise

I don't choose to *speak* again on the *money question*! The 'replies' from the Noble Lord are unfair and unkind, and little to the purpose. When you tell me 'I pester your life out about money,' that 'your soul is sick with hearing about it,' that 'I had better make the money I have serve,' 'at all rates, hang it, let you alone of it' – all that I call perfectly unfair, the reverse of kind, and tending to nothing but disagreement. If I were greedy, or extravagant, or a bad manager, you would be justified in 'staving me off' with loud words; but you cannot say *that* of me (whatever else) – cannot *think* it of me. At least, I am sure that I never 'asked for more' from you or anyone, not even from my own mother, in all my life, and that through six-and-twenty years I have kept house for you at more or less cost according to given circumstances, but always on less than it costs the generality of people living in the same style. What I should have expected you to say rather would have been: 'My dear, you *must* be dreadfully hampered in your finances, and dreadfully anxious and unhappy about it, and quite desperate of *making it do*, since *you* are "asking for more." Make me understand the case, then. I can and will help you out of that *sordid* suffering at least, either by giving you more, if that be found prudent to do, or by reducing our wants to within the present means.' That is the sort of thing you would have said had you been a perfect man; so I suppose you are not a perfect man. Then, instead of crying in my bed half the night after, I would have explained my budget to you in peace and confidence. But now I am driven to explain it on paper 'in a state of mind;' *driven*, for I cannot, it is not in my nature to live 'entangled in the details,' and I *will not*. I would sooner hang myself, though 'pestering you about money' is also more repugnant to me than you dream of.

You don't understand why the allowance which sufficed in former years no longer suffices. That is what I would explain to the Noble Lord if he would but – what shall I say? – *keep his temper*.

The beginning of my embarrassments, it will not surprise the Noble Lord to learn, since it has also been 'the beginning of' almost every human ill to himself, was *the repairing of the house*. There was a destruction, an *irregularity*, an *incessant recurrence of small incidental expenses*, during all that period, or *two* periods, through which I found myself in September gone a year, *ten* pounds behind, instead of having some pounds saved up towards the winter's coals. I could have worked round 'out of that,' however, in course of time, if habits of *unpinched* housekeeping had not been long taken to by *you* as well as myself, and if new unavoidable, or not-to-be

avoided, *current* expenses had not followed close on those incidental ones.
I will show the Noble Lord, with his permission, what the new current
expenses *are*, and to what they amount per annum. (Hear, hear! and cries
of 'Be brief!')

1. We have a servant of 'higher grade' than we ever ventured on before;
more expensive in money. Anne's wages are 16 pounds a year; Fanny's were
13. Most of the others had 12; and Anne never dreams of being other than
well fed. The others *scrambled* for their living out of ours. Her regular meat
dinner at one o'clock, regular allowance of butter, &c., adds at least three
pounds a year to the *year's* bills. But she plagues us with no fits of illness
nor of *drunkenness*, no *warnings* nor complainings. She does perfectly
what she is *paid* and *fed* to do. I see houses not so well kept with 'cook,'
'housemaid,' and 'manservant' (Question!). Anne is the last item I should
vote for retrenching in. I may set her down, however, at six additional
pounds.

2. We have now gas and water 'laid on,' both producing admirable
results. But betwixt 'water laid on' at one pound, sixteen shillings per
annum, with *shilling* to turncock, and water carried at fourpence a week,
there is a yearly difference of 19 shillings and four pence; and betwixt *gas*
all the year round and a few sixpenny boxes of lights in the winter the
difference may be computed at *fifteen shillings*. These two excellent innov-
ations, then, increase the yearly expenditure by one pound fourteen
shillings and four pence – a trifle to speak of; but you, my Lord, born and
bred in thrifty Scotland, must know well the proverb, 'Every little mak's a
mickle.'

3. We are higher *taxed*. Within the last eighteen months there has been
added to the Lighting, Pavement, and Improvement Rate ten shillings
yearly, to the Poor Rate one pound, to the sewer rate ten shillings; and now
the doubled Income Tax makes a difference of 5*l*. 16*s*. 8*d*. yearly, which
sums, added together, amount to a difference of 7*l*. 16*s*. 8*d*. yearly, on taxes
which already amounted to 17*l*. 12*s*. 8*d*. There need be no reflections for
want of taxes.

4. Provisions of all sorts are higher priced than in former years. Four
shillings a week for bread, instead of two shillings and sixpence, makes at
the year's end a difference of 3*l*. 18*s*. Butter has kept all the year round 2*d*.
a pound dearer than I ever knew it. On the quantity we use – two pounds
and a half per week 'quite reg'lar' – there is a difference of 21*s*. 8*d*. by the
year. Butcher's meat is a penny a pound dearer. At the rate of a pound and
a half a day, *bones* included – no exorbitant allowance for three people –
the difference on that at the year's end would be 2*l*. 5*s*. 6*d*. Coals, which
had been for some years at 21*s*. per ton, cost this year 26*s*., last year 29*s*.,

bought judiciously, too. If I had had to pay 50*s*. a ton for them, as some housewives had to, God knows what would have become of me. (Passionate cries of 'Question! Question!') We burn, or used to burn – I am afraid they are going faster this winter – twelve tons, one year with another. Candles are *riz*: composites a shilling a pound, instead of 10*d*.; dips 8 pence, instead of 5*d*. or 6*d*. Of the former we burn three pounds in nine days – the greater part of the year you sit so late – and of dips two pounds a fortnight on the average of the whole year. Bacon is 2*d*. a pound dearer; soap ditto; potatoes, at the cheapest, a penny a pound, instead of three pounds for 2*d*. We use three pounds of potatoes in two days' meals. Who could imagine that at the year's end that makes a difference of 15*s*. 2*d*. on one's mere potatoes? Compute all this, and you will find that the difference on *provisions* cannot be under twelve pounds in the year.

5. What I should blush to state if I were not *at bay*, so to speak: ever since we have been in London *you* have, in the handsomest manner, paid the winter's butter with *your own money*, though it was not in the bond. And this gentlemanlike proceeding on your part, till the butter became uneatable, was a good two pounds saved me.

Add up these differences:–

		£	*s.*	*d.*
1.	Rise on servant	6	0	0
2.	Rise on light and water.	1	14	0
3.	On taxes	7	16	8
4.	On provisions	12	0	0
5.	Cessation of butter . . .	2	0	0
	You will find a total of	£29	10	8

My calculation will be found quite correct, though I am not strong in arithmetic. I have *thochtered* all this well in my head, and *indignation* makes a sort of arithmetic, as well as verses. Do you finally understand why the allowance which sufficed formerly no longer suffices, and pity my difficulties instead of being angry at them?

The only thing you *can* reproach me with, *if you like*, is that fifteen months ago, when I found myself already in debt, and everything *rising* on me, I did not fall at once to *pinching* and *muddling*, as when we didn't know where the next money was to come from, instead of 'lashing down' at the accustomed rate: nay, expanding into a 'regular servant.' But you are to recollect that when I first complained to you of the *prices*, you said, quite good-naturedly, 'Then you are coming to bankruptcy, are you? Not going to be able *to go on*, you think? Well, then, we must come to your assistance, poor *crittur*. You mustn't be made a bankrupt of.' So I kept my mind easy, and retrenched in nothing, relying on the promised 'assistance.' But when 'Oh! it was lang o' coming, lang o' coming,' my arrears taking every quarter a more alarming, cypher, what could I do but put you in mind? Once, twice, at the third speaking, what you were pleasantly calling 'a great heap of money' – 15*l*. – was – what shall I say? – flung to me. Far from *leaving anything* to meet the increased demand of another nine months, this sum did not clear me of debt, not by five pounds. But from time to time encouraging *words* fell from the Noble Lord. 'No, you cannot pay the double Income Tax; clearly, I must pay that for you.' And again: 'I will burn as many coals as I like; if you can't pay for them somebody must!' All resulting, however, thus far in *'Don't you wish you may get it?'* Decidedly I should have needed to be more than mortal, or else 'a born daughter of Chaos,' to have gone on without attempt made at ascertaining what *coming to my assistance* meant: whether it meant 15*l*. without a blessing once for all; and if so, what retrenchments were to be permitted.

You asked me at last money row, with withering sarcasm, 'had I the slightest idea what amount of money would *satisfy me*. Was I wanting 50*l*. more; or forty, or thirty? Was there any conceivable sum of money that could put an end to my eternal botheration?' I will answer the question as if it had been asked practically and kindly.

Yes. I have the strongest idea what amount of money would '*satisfy*' me. I have computed it often enough as I lay awake at nights. Indeed, when I can't sleep now it is my 'difficulties' I think about more than my sins, till they become 'a real mental awgony in my own inside.' The above-named sum, 29*l*., divided into quarterly payments, would *satisfy* me (with a certain parsimony about little things, somewhat less might do), I engaging my word of a gentlewoman to *give back* at the year's end whatever portion thereof any diminution of the demand on me might enable me to save.

I am not so unpractical, however, as to ask for the whole 29*l*. without thought or care where it is to come from. I have settled all that (Derisive laughter, and Hear, hear!), so that nine pounds only will have to be disbursed by you over and above your long-accustomed disbursements (Hear, hear!). You anticipate, perhaps, some draft on your waste-paper basket. No, my Lord, it has never been my habit to interfere with your ways of making money, or the rate which you make it at; and if I never did it in early years, most unlikely I should do it *now*. My bill of ways and means has nothing to do with making money, only with disposing of the money made. (Bravo! hear!)

1. Ever since my mother's death you have allowed me for old Mary Mills 3*l*. yearly. She needs them no more. *Continue these three pounds for the house.*

2. Through the same long term of years you have made *me* the handsomest Christmas and birthday presents; and when I had purposely disgusted you from *buying me things*, you gave me at the New Year 5*l*. Oh I know the meaning of that 5*l*. quite well. *Give me nothing*; neither money nor money's worth. I would have it so anyhow, and continue the 5*l*. for the house.

3. Ever since we came to London you have paid some 2*l*., I guess, for *butter*, now become uneatable. Continue that 2*l*. for the house; and we have already *ten* pounds which you can't miss, not having been used to them.

4. My allowance of 25*l*. is a very liberal one; has enabled me to spend freely for myself; and I don't deny there is a pleasure in that when there is no household crisis; but with an appalling deficit in the house exchequer, it is not only no pleasure but an impossibility. I can keep up my dignity and my wardrobe on a less sum – on 15*l*. a year. A silk dress, 'a splendid dressing-gown,' 'a milliner's bonnet' the less; what signifies that at my age? Nothing. Besides, I have had so many 'gowns' given me that they may serve for two or three years. By then, God knows if I shall be needing *gowns* at all. So deduct 10*l*. from my personal allowance; and continue that for the house.

But why not transfer it *privately* from my own purse to the house one, and ask only for 19*l*.? It would have sounded more modest – *figured* better. Just because 'that sort of thing' don't please me. I have tried it and found it a bad *go*: a virtue *not* its own reward! I am for every herring to hang by its own head, every purse to stand on its own bottom. It would worry me to be thought rolling in the wealth of 25*l*., when I was cleverly making 15*l*. do, and investing 10*l*. in coals and taxes. Mrs.—— is up to that sort of self-sacrifice thing, and to finding compensation in the sympathy of many friends, and in smouldering discontent. I am up to neither the magnanimity nor the compensation, but I am quite up to laying down 10*l*. of my allowance in a straightforward recognised way, without standing on my toes to it either. And what is more, I am determined upon it, *will not* accept more than 15*l*. in the present state of affairs.

There only remains to disclose the actual state of the exchequer. It is empty as a drum. (Sensation.) If I consider twenty-nine more pounds indispensable – things remaining as they are – for the coming year, beginning the 22nd of March, it is just because I have found it so in the year that is gone; and I commenced that, as I have already stated, with 10*l*. of arrears. You assisted me with 15*l*., and I have assisted myself with 10*l*., five last August, which I took from the Savings Bank, and the five you gave me at New Year, which I threw into the coal account. Don't suppose – 'if thou's i' the habit of supposing' – that I tell you this in the *un*devout imagination of being *repaid*. By all that's sacred for me – *the memory of my father and mother* – what else can an irreligious creature like me swear by? I would not take back that money if you *offered* it with the best grace, and had picked it up in the street. I tell it you simply that you may see I am not so dreadfully greedy as you have appeared to think me latterly. Setting *my* 10*l*. then against the original arrears, with 15*l*. in assistance from *you*, it would follow, from my own computation, that I should need 14*l*. more to clear off arrears on the weekly bills and carry me on, paying my way until 22nd of March, next quarter-day. (Cries of Shame! and Turn her out!) I say only '*should need.*' Your money is of course yours, to do as you will with, and I *would like* to again 'walk the causeway' carrying my head as high – as – Mr. A., the upholsterer, owing no man anything, and *dearly I would like* to 'at all rates let YOU alone of it,' if I knew who else had any business with my housekeeping, or to whom else I could properly address myself for the moment; as what with that expensive, most ill-timed dressing-gown, and *my* cheap ill-timed chiffonnier, and my half-year's bills to Rhind and Catchpole, I have only what will serve me till June comes round.

If I was a man, I might fling the gauntlet to Society, join with a few brave fellows, and 'rob a diligence.' But my sex 'kind o' debars from that.' Mercy! to think there are women – your friend Lady A., for example ('*Rumeurs!*' Sensation) – I say for *example*; who spend not merely the additamental pounds I must make such pother about, but *four times my whole income* in the *ball* of one night, and none the worse for it, nor anyone the better. It is – what shall I say? – 'curious,' upon my honour. But just in the same manner Mrs. Freeman might say: 'To think there are women – Mrs. Carlyle, for example – who spend 3*l*. 14*s*. 6*d*. on one dressing-gown, and I with just *two loaves* and eighteen pence from the parish, to live on by the week.' There is no bottom to such reflections. The only thing one is perfectly sure of is 'it will come all to the same ultimately,' and I can't say I'll regret the loss of myself, for one. – I add no more, but remain, dear Sir, your obedient humble servant.

JANE WELSH CARLYLE.

1856

32. George Eliot
from *Silly Novels by Lady Novelists*

SILLY novels by Lady Novelists are a genus with many species, determined by the particular quality of silliness that predominates in them – the frothy, the prosy, the pious, or the pedantic. But it is a mixture of all these – a composite order of feminine fatuity, that produces the largest class of such novels, which we shall distinguish as the *mind-and-millinery* species. The heroine is usually an heiress, probably a peeress in her own right, with perhaps a vicious baronet, an amiable duke, and an irresistible younger son of a marquis as lovers in the foreground, a clergyman and a poet sighing for her in the middle distance, and a crowd of undefined adorers dimly indicated beyond. Her eyes and her wit are both dazzling; her nose and her morals are alike free from any tendency to irregularity; she has a superb *contralto* and a superb intellect; she is perfectly well-dressed and perfectly religious; she dances like a sylph, and reads the Bible in the original tongues. Or it may be that the heroine is not an heiress – that rank and wealth are the only things in which she is deficient; but she infallibly gets into high society, she has the triumph of refusing many matches and securing the best, and she wears some family jewels or other as a sort of crown of righteousness at the end. Rakish men either bite their lips in impotent confusion at her repartees, or are touched to penitence by her reproofs, which, on appropriate occasions, rise to a lofty strain of rhetoric; indeed, there is a general propensity in her to make speeches, and to rhapsodize at some length when she retires to her bedroom. In her recorded conversations she is amazingly eloquent, and in her unrecorded conversations, amazingly witty. She is understood to have a depth of insight that looks through and through the shallow theories of philosophers, and her superior instincts are a sort of dial by which men have only to set their clocks and watches, and all will go well. The men play a very subordinate part by her side. You are consoled now and then by a hint that they have affairs, which keeps you in mind that the working-day business of the world is somehow being carried on, but ostensibly the final cause of their existence is that they may accompany the heroine on her 'starring' expedition through life. They see her at a ball, and are dazzled; at a flower-show, and they are fascinated; on a riding excursion, and they are witched by her noble horsemanship; at church, and they are awed by the sweet solemnity of her demeanour. She is the ideal woman in feelings, faculties, and flounces. For all this, she as often as not marries the wrong person to begin with, and she suffers terribly from the plots and intrigues of the vicious baronet; but even death has a soft place in his heart for such a paragon, and remedies all mistakes for her just at the right moment. The vicious baronet is sure to be killed in a duel, and the tedious husband dies in his bed, requesting his wife, as a particular favour to him, to marry the man she loves best, and having already dispatched a note to the lover informing him of the comfortable arrangement. Before matters arrive at this desirable issue our feelings are tried by seeing the noble, lovely, and gifted heroine pass through many *mauvais moments*, but we have the satisfaction of knowing that her sorrows are wept into embroidered pocket-handker-chiefs, that her fainting form reclines on the very best upholstery, and that whatever vicissitudes she may undergo, from being dashed out of her carriage to having her head shaved in a fever, she comes out of them all with a complexion more blooming and locks more redundant than ever.

We may remark, by the way, that we have been relieved from a serious scruple by discovering that silly novels by lady novelists rarely introduce us into any other than very lofty and fashionable society. We had imagined that destitute women turned novelists, as they turned governesses, because they had no other 'lady-like' means of getting their bread. On this suppo-sition, vacillating syntax and improbable incident had a certain pathos for us, like the extremely supererogatory pincushions and ill-devised night-caps that are offered for sale by a blind man. We felt the commodity to be a nuisance, but we were glad to think that the money went to relieve the necessitous, and we pictured to ourselves lonely women struggling for a maintenance, or wives and daughters devoting themselves to the production of 'copy' out of pure heroism, – perhaps to pay their husband's debts, or to purchase luxuries for a sick father. Under these impressions we shrank from criticizing a lady's novel: her English might be faulty, but, we said to ourselves, her motives are irreproachable; her imagination may be unin-ventive, but her patience is untiring. Empty writing was excused by an empty stomach, and twaddle was consecrated by tears. But no! This theory of ours, like many other pretty theories, has had to give way before obser-vation. Women's silly novels, we are now convinced, are written under totally different circumstances. The fair writers have evidently never talked to a tradesman except from a carriage window; they have no notion of the working classes except as 'dependants'; they think five hundred pounds a year a miserable pittance; Belgravia and 'baronial halls' are their primary truths; and they have no idea of feeling interest in any man who is not at least a great landed proprietor, if not a prime minister. It is clear that they write in elegant boudoirs, with violet-coloured ink and a ruby pen; that they must be entirely indifferent to publishers' accounts, and inexperienced in every form of poverty except poverty of brains. It is true that we are constantly struck with the want of verisimilitude in their representations of the high society in which they seem to live; but then they betray no closer acquaintance with any other form of life. If their peers and peeresses are improbable, their literary men, tradespeople, and cottagers are impossible; and their intellect seems to have the peculiar impartiality of reproducing both what they *have* seen and heard, and what they have *not* seen and heard, with equal unfaithfulness.

❋ ❋ ❋ ❋

Writers of the mind-and-millinery school are remarkably unanimous in their choice of diction. In their novels, there is usually a lady or gentleman who is more or less of a upas tree: the lover has a manly breast; minds are redolent of various things; hearts are hollow; events are utilized; friends are consigned to the tomb; infancy is an engaging period; the sun is a luminary that goes to his western couch, or gathers the rain-drops into his refulgent bosom; life is a melancholy boon; Albion and Scotia are conversational epithets. There is a striking resemblance, too, in the character of their moral comments, such, for instance, as that 'It is a fact, no less true than melancholy, that all people, more or less, richer or poorer, are swayed by bad example'; that 'Books, however trivial, contain some subjects from which useful information may be drawn'; that 'Vice can too often borrow the language of virtue'; that 'Merit and nobility of nature must exist, to be accepted, for clamour and pretension cannot impose upon those too well read in human nature to be easily deceived'; and that, 'In order to forgive, we must have been injured'. There is, doubtless, a class of readers to whom these remarks appear peculiarly pointed and pungent; for we often find them doubly and trebly scored with the pencil, and delicate hands giving in their determined adhesion to these hardy novelties by a distinct *très vrai*, emphasized by many notes of exclamation. The colloquial style of these novels is often marked by much ingenious inversion, and a careful avoidance of such cheap phraseology as can be heard every day. Angry young gentlemen exclaim – ''Tis ever thus, methinks'; and in the half hour before dinner a young lady informs her next neighbour that the first day she read Shakespeare she 'stole away into the park, and beneath the shadow of the greenwood tree, devoured with rapture the inspired page of the great magician'. But the most remarkable efforts of the mind-and-millinery writers lie in their philosophic reflections. The authoress of 'Laura Gay', for example, having married her hero and heroine, improves the event by observing that 'if those sceptics, whose eyes have so long gazed on matter that they can no longer see aught else in man, could once enter with heart and soul into such bliss as this, they would come to say that the soul of man and the polypus are not of common origin, or of the same texture'. Lady novelists, it appears, can see something else besides matter; they are not limited to phenomena, but can relieve their eyesight by occasional glimpses of the *noumenon*, and are, therefore, naturally better able than any one else to confound sceptics, even of that remarkable, but to us unknown school, which maintains that the soul of man is of the same texture as the polypus.

The most pitiable of all silly novels by lady novelists are what we may call the *oracular* species – novels intended to expound the writer's religious, philosophical, or moral theories. There seems to be a notion abroad among women, rather akin to the superstition that the speech and actions of idiots are inspired, and that the human being most entirely exhausted of common sense is the fittest vehicle of revelation. To judge from their writings, there are certain ladies who think that an amazing ignorance, both of science and of life, is the best possible qualification for forming an opinion on the knottiest moral and speculative questions. Apparently, their recipe for solving all such difficulties is something like this: – Take a woman's head, stuff it with a smattering of philosophy and literature chopped small, and with false notions of society baked hard, let it hang over a desk a few hours every day, and serve up hot in feeble English, when not required. You will rarely meet with a lady novelist of the oracular class who is diffident of her ability to decide on theological questions, – who has any suspicion that she is not capable of discriminating with the nicest accuracy between the good and evil in all church parties, – who does not see precisely how it is that men have gone wrong hitherto, – and pity philosophers in general that they have not had the opportunity of consulting her. Great writers, who have modestly contented themselves with putting their experience into fiction, and have thought it quite a sufficient task to exhibit men and things as they are, she sighs over as deplorably deficient in the application of their powers. 'They have solved no great questions' – and she is ready to remedy their omission by setting before you a complete theory of life and manual of divinity, in a love story.

❋ ❋ ❋ ❋

'Be not a baker if your head be made of butter,' says a homely proverb, which, being interpreted, may mean, let no woman rush into print who is not prepared for the consequences. We are aware that our remarks are in a very different tone from that of the reviewers who, with a perennial recurrence of precisely similar emotions, only paralleled, we imagine, in the experience of monthly nurses, tell one lady novelist after another that they 'hail' her productions 'with delight'. We are aware that the ladies at whom our criticism is pointed are accustomed to be told, in the choicest phraseology of puffery, that their pictures of life are brilliant, their characters well-drawn, their style fascinating, and their sentiments lofty. But if they are inclined to resent our plainness of speech, we ask them to reflect for a moment on the chary praise, and often captious blame, which their panegyrists give to writers whose works are on the way to become classics. No sooner does a woman show that she has genius or effective talent, than she receives the tribute of being moderately praised and severely criticized. By a peculiar thermometric adjustment, when a woman's talent is at zero, journalistic approbation is at the boiling pitch; when she attains mediocrity, it is already at no more than summer heat; and if ever she reaches excellence, critical enthusiasm drops to the freezing point. Harriet Martineau, Currer Bell, and Mrs Gaskell have been treated as cavalierly as if they had been men. And every critic who forms a high estimate of the share women may ultimately take in literature, will, on principle, abstain from any exceptional indulgence towards the productions of literary women. For it must be plain to every one who looks impartially and extensively into feminine literature, that its greatest deficiencies are due hardly more to the want of intellectual power than to the want of those moral qualities that contribute to literary excellence – patient diligence, a sense of the responsibility involved in publication, and an appreciation of the sacredness of the writer's art. In the majority of women's books you see that kind of facility which springs from the absence of any high standard; that fertility in imbecile combination or feeble imitation which a little self-criticism would check and reduce to barrenness just as with a total want of musical ear people will sing out of tune, while a degree more melodic sensibility would suffice to render them silent. The foolish vanity of wishing to appear in print, instead of being counterbalanced by any consciousness of the intellectual or moral derogation implied in futile authorship, seems to be encouraged by the extremely false impression that to write *at all* is a proof of superiority in a woman. On this ground, we believe that the average intellect of women is unfairly represented by the mass of feminine literature, and that while the few women who write well are very far above the ordinary intellectual level of their sex, the many women who write ill are very far below it. So that, after all, the severer critics are fulfilling a chivalrous duty in depriving the mere fact of feminine authorship of any false prestige which may give it a delusive attraction, and in recommending women of mediocre faculties – as at least a negative service they can render their sex – to abstain from writing.

The standing apology for women who become writers without any special qualification is, that society shuts them out from other spheres of occupation. Society is a very culpable entity, and has to answer for the manufacture of many unwholesome commodities, from bad pickles to bad poetry. But society, like 'matter', and Her Majesty's Government, and other lofty abstractions, has its share of excessive blame as well as excessive praise. Where there is one woman who writes from necessity, we believe there are three women who write from vanity; and, besides, there is something so antiseptic in the mere healthy fact of working for one's bread, that the most trashy and rotten kind of feminine literature is not likely to have been produced under such circumstances. 'In all labour there is profit'; but ladies' silly novels, we imagine, are less the result of labour than of busy idleness.

Happily, we are not dependent on argument to prove that Fiction is a department of literature in which women can, after their kind, fully equal men. A cluster of great names, both living and dead, rush to our memories in evidence that women can produce novels not only fine, but among the very finest; – novels, too, that have a precious speciality, lying quite apart from masculine aptitudes and experience. No educational restrictions can shut women out from the materials of fiction, and there is no species of art which is so free from rigid requirements. Like crystalline masses, it may take any form, and yet be beautiful; we have only to pour in the right elements – genuine observation, humour, and passion. But it is precisely this absence of rigid requirement which constitutes the fatal seduction of novel-writing to incompetent women. Ladies are not wont to be very grossly deceived as to their power of playing on the piano; here certain positive difficulties of execution have to be conquered, and incompetence inevitably breaks down. Every art which has its absolute *technique* is, to a certain extent, guarded from the intrusions of mere left-handed imbecility. But in novel-writing there are no barriers for incapacity to stumble against, no external criteria to prevent a writer from mistaking foolish facility for mastery. And so we have again and again the old story of La Fontaine's ass, who puts his nose to the flute, and, finding that he elicits some sound, exclaims, 'Moi, aussi, je joue de la flute'; – a fable which we commend, at parting, to the consideration of any feminine reader who is in danger of adding to the number of 'silly novels by lady novelists'.

1857

33. Elizabeth Gaskell
from *The Life of Charlotte Brontë*

Mr Brontë wished to make his children hardy, and indifferent to the pleasures of eating and dress. In the latter he succeeded, as far as regarded his
daughters; but he went at his object with unsparing earnestness of purpose.
Mrs Brontës nurse told me that one day when the children had been out
on the moors, and rain had come on, she thought their feet would be wet,
and accordingly she rummaged out some coloured boots which had been
given to them by a friend – the Mr Morgan, who married 'Cousin Jane,'
she believes. These little pairs she ranged round the kitchen fire to warm;
but, when the children came back, the boots were nowhere to be found;
only a very strong odour of burnt leather was perceived. Mr Brontë had
come in and seen them; they were too gay and luxurious for his children,
and would foster a love of dress; so he had put them into the fire. He
spared nothing that offended his antique simplicity. Long before this,
some one had given Mrs Brontë a silk gown; either the make, the colour,
or the material, was not according to his notions of consistent propriety,
and Mrs Brontë in consequence never wore it. But, for all that, she kept
it treasured up in her drawers, which were generally locked. One day,
however, while in the kitchen, she remembered that she had left the key in
her drawer, and, hearing Mr Brontë upstairs, she augured some ill to her
dress, and, running up in haste, she found it cut into shreds.

His strong, passionate, Irish nature was, in general, compressed down
with resolute stoicism; but it was there notwithstanding all his philosophic
calm and dignity of demeanour. He did not speak when he was annoyed
or displeased, but worked off his volcanic wrath by firing pistols out of the
back-door in rapid succession. Mrs Brontë, lying in bed up-stairs, would
hear the quick explosions, and know that something had gone wrong; but
her sweet nature thought invariably of the bright side, and she would say,
'Ought I not to be thankful that he never gave me an angry word?' Now
and then his anger took a different form, but still was speechless. Once he
got the hearthrug, and stuffing it up the grate, deliberately set it on fire, and
remained in the room in spite of the stench, until it had smouldered and
shrivelled away into uselessness. Another time he took some chairs and
sawed away at the backs till they were reduced to the condition of stools.

❀ ❀ ❀ ❀

THIS is perhaps a fitting time to give some personal description of Miss

Brontë. In 1831, she was a quiet, thoughtful girl of nearly fifteen years of age, very small in figure – 'stunted' was the word she applied to herself, – but as her limbs and head were in just proportion to the slight, fragile body, no word in ever so slight a degree suggestive of deformity could properly be applied to her; with soft, thick, brown hair, and peculiar eyes, of which I find it difficult to give a description, as they appeared to me in her later life. They were large, and well shaped; their colour a reddish brown; but if the iris was closely examined, it appeared to be composed of a great variety of tints. The usual expression was of quiet, listening intelligence; but now and then, on some just occasion for vivid interest or wholesome indignation, a light would shine out, as if some spiritual lamp had been kindled, which glowed behind those expressive orbs. I never saw the like in any other human creature. As for the rest of her features, they were plain, large, and ill set; but, unless you began to catalogue them, you were hardly aware of the fact, for the eyes and power of the countenance overbalanced every physical defect; the crooked mouth and the large nose were forgotten, and the whole face arrested the attention, and presently attracted all those whom she herself would have cared to attract. Her hands and feet were the smallest I ever saw; when one of the former was placed in mine, it was like the soft touch of a bird in the middle of my palm. The delicate long fingers had a peculiar fineness of sensation, which was one reason why all her handiwork, of whatever kind – writing, sewing, knitting – was so clear in its minuteness. She was remarkably neat in her whole personal attire; but she was dainty as to the fit of her shoes and gloves.

❋ ❋ ❋ ❋

The feeling, which in Charlotte partook of something of the nature of an affection, was, with Emily, more of a passion. Some one speaking of her to me, in a careless kind of strength of expression, said 'she never showed regard to any human creature; all her love was reserved for animals.' The helplessness of an animal was its passport to Charlotte's heart; the fierce, wild, intractability of its nature was what often recommended it to Emily. Speaking of her dead sister, the former told me that from her many traits in Shirley's character were taken; her way of sitting on the rug reading, with her arm round her rough bull-dog's neck; her calling to a strange dog, running past, with hanging head and lolling tongue, to give it a merciful draught of water, its maddened snap at her, her nobly stern presence of mind going right into the kitchen, and taking up one of Tabby's red-hot Italian irons to sear the bitten place, and telling no one, till the danger was well-nigh over, for fear of the terrors that might beset their weaker minds. All this, looked upon as a well-invented fiction in 'Shirley,' was written

down by Charlotte with streaming eyes; it was the literal true account of
what Emily had done. The same tawny bulldog (with his 'strangled whistle'),
called 'Tartar' in 'Shirley,' was 'Keeper' in Haworth parsonage; a gift to
Emily. With the gift came the warning. Keeper was faithful to the depths of
his nature as long as he was with friends; but he who struck him with a
stick or whip, roused the relentless nature of the brute, who flew at his
throat forthwith, and held him there till one or the other was at the point
of death. Now Keeper's household fault was this. He loved to steal up-stairs,
and stretch his square, tawny limbs, on the comfortable beds, covered over
with delicate white counterpanes. But the cleanliness of the parsonage
arrangements was perfect; and this habit of Keeper's was so objectionable,
that Emily, in reply to Tabby's remonstrances, declared that, if he was
found again transgressing, she herself, in defiance of warning and his
well-known ferocity of nature, would beat him so severely that he would
never offend again. In the gathering dusk of an autumn evening, Tabby
came, half triumphantly, half tremblingly, but in great wrath, to tell Emily
that Keeper was lying on the best bed, in drowsy voluptuousness.
Charlotte saw Emily's whitening face, and set mouth, but dared not speak
to interfere; no one dared when Emily's eyes glowed in that manner out of
the paleness of her face, and when her lips were so compressed into
stone. She went up-stairs, and Tabby and Charlotte stood in the gloomy
passage below, full of the dark shadows of coming night. Down-stairs came
Emily, dragging after her the unwilling Keeper, his hind legs set in a heavy
attitude of resistance, held by the 'scuft of his neck,' but growling low
and savagely all the time. The watchers would fain have spoken, but durst
not, for fear of taking off Emily's attention, and causing her to avert her
head for a moment from the enraged brute. She let him go, planted in a
dark corner at the bottom of the stairs; no time was there to fetch stick or
rod, for fear of the strangling clutch at her throat – her bare clenched fist
struck against his red fierce eyes, before he had time to make his spring,
and, in the language of the turf, she 'punished him' till his eyes were
swelled up, and the half-blind, stupified beast was led to his accustomed
lair, to have his swelled head fomented and cared for by the very Emily
herself. The generous dog owed her no grudge; he loved her dearly ever
after; he walked first among the mourners to her funeral; he slept moaning
for nights at the door of her empty room, and never, so to speak, rejoiced,
dog fashion, after her death. He, in his turn, was mourned over by the
surviving sister. Let us somehow hope, in half Red Indian creed, that he
follows Emily now; and, when he rests, sleeps on some soft white bed of
dreams, unpunished when he awakens to the life of the land of shadows.

✳ ✳ ✳ ✳

I may as well complete here the narrative of the outward events of Branwell Brontë's life. A few months later (I have the exact date, but, for obvious reasons, withhold it) the invalid husband of the woman with whom he had intrigued, died. Branwell had been looking forward to this event with guilty hope. After her husband's death, his paramour would be free; strange as it seems, the young man still loved her passionately, and now he imagined the time was come when they might look forwards to being married, and might live together without reproach or blame. She had offered to elope with him; she had written to him perpetually; she had sent him money – twenty pounds at a time; he remembered the criminal advances she had made; she had braved shame, and her children's menaced disclosures, for his sake; he thought she must love him; he little knew how bad a depraved woman can be. Her husband had made a will, in which what property he left to her was bequeathed solely on the condition that she should never see Branwell Brontë again. At the very time when the will was read, she did not know but that he might be on his way to her, having heard of her husband's death. She despatched a servant in hot haste to Haworth. He stopped at the Black Bull, and a messenger was sent up to the parsonage for Branwell. He came down to the little inn, and was shut up with the man for some time. Then the groom came out, paid his bill, mounted his horse, and was off. Branwell remained in the room alone. More than an hour elapsed before sign or sound was heard; then, those outside heard a noise like the bleating of a calf, and, on opening the door, he was found in a kind of fit, succeeding to the stupor of grief which he had fallen into on hearing that he was forbidden by his paramour ever to see her again, as, if he did, she would forfeit her fortune. Let her live and flourish! He died, his pockets filled with her letters, which he had carried perpetually about his person, in order that he might read them as often as he wished. He lies dead; and his doom is only known to God's mercy. When I think of him, I change my cry to heaven. Let her live and repent! That same mercy is infinite.

For the last three years of Branwell's life, he took opium habitually, by way of stunning conscience; he drank, moreover, whenever he could get the opportunity. The reader may say that I have mentioned his tendency to intemperance long before. It is true; but it did not become habitual, as far as I can learn, until after the commencement of his guilty intimacy with the woman of whom I have been speaking. If I am mistaken on this point, her taste must have been as depraved as her principles. He took opium, because it made him forget for a time more effectually than drink, and, besides, it was more portable. In procuring it he showed all the cunning of the opium-eater. He would steal out while the family were at church – to which he had professed himself too ill to go – and manage to cajole the village druggist out of a lump; or, it might be, the carrier had unsuspiciously brought him some in a packet from a distance. For some time before his death he had attacks of delirium tremens of the most frightful character; he slept in his father's room, and he would sometimes declare that either he or his father should be dead before morning. The trembling sisters, sick with fright, would implore their father not to expose himself to this danger but Mr. Brontë is no timid man, and perhaps he felt that he could possibly influence his son to some self–restraint, more by showing trust in him than by showing fear. The sisters often listened for the report of a pistol in the dead of the night, till watchful eye and hearkening ear grew heavy and dull with the perpetual strain upon their nerves. In the mornings young Brontë would saunter out, saying, with a drunkard's incontinence of speech, 'The poor old man and I have had a terrible night of it; he does his best – the poor old man! but it's all over with me;' (whimpering) 'it's *her* fault, *her* fault.'

❊ ❊ ❊ ❊

The sisters had kept the knowledge of their literary ventures from their father, fearing to increase their own anxieties and disappointment by witnessing his; for he took an acute interest in all that befell his children, and his own tendency had been towards literature in the days when he was young and hopeful. It was true he did not much manifest his feelings in words; he would have thought that he was prepared for disappointment as the lot of man, and that he could have met it with stoicism; but words are poor and tardy interpreters of feelings to those who love one another, and his daughters knew how he would have borne ill-success worse for them than for himself. So they did not tell him what they were undertaking. He says now that he suspected it all along, but his suspicions could take no exact form, as all he was certain of was, that his children were perpetually writing – and not writing letters. We have seen how the communications from their publishers were received 'under cover to Miss Brontë.' Once, Charlotte told me, they overheard the postman meeting Mr Brontë, as the latter was leaving the house, and inquiring from the parson where one Currer Bell could be living, to which Mr Brontë replied that there was no such person in the parish. . . .

Now, however, when the demand for the work had assured success to 'Jane Eyre,' her sisters urged Charlotte to tell their father of its publication. She accordingly went into his study one afternoon after his early dinner, carrying with her a copy of the book, and one or two reviews, taking care to include a notice adverse to it.

She informed me that something like the following conversation took place between her and him. (I wrote down her words the day after I heard them; and I am pretty sure they are quite accurate.)

'Papa, I've been writing a book.'

'Have you, my dear?'

'Yes, and I want you to read it.'

'I am afraid it will try my eyes too much.'

'But it is not in manuscript: it is printed.'

'My dear! you've never thought of the expense it will be! It will be almost sure to be a loss, for how can you get a book sold? No one knows you or your name.'

'But, papa, I don't think it will be a loss; no more will you, if you will just let me read you a review or two, and tell you more about it.'

So she sat down and read some of the reviews to her father; and then, giving him the copy of 'Jane Eyre' that she intended for him, she left him to read it. When he came into tea, he said, 'Girls, do you know Charlotte has been writing a book, and it is much better than likely?'

* * * *

But Emily was growing rapidly worse. I remember Miss Brontë's shiver at recalling the pang she felt when, after having searched in the little hollows and sheltered crevices of the moors for a lingering spray of heather – just one spray, however withered – to take in to Emily, she saw that the flower was not recognised by the dim and indifferent eyes. Yet, to the last, Emily adhered tenaciously to her habits of independence She would suffer no one to assist her. Any effort to do so roused the old stern spirit. One Tuesday morning, in December, she arose and dressed herself as usual, making many a pause, but doing everything for herself, and even endeavouring to take up her employment of sewing: the servants looked on, and knew what the catching, rattling breath, and the glazing of the eye too surely foretold; but she kept at her work; and Charlotte and Anne, though full of unspeakable dread, had still the faintest spark of hope. On that morning Charlotte wrote thus, – probably in the very presence of her dying sister:

'*Tuesday*.

'I should have written to you before, if I had had one word of hope to say; but I have not. She grows daily weaker. The physician's opinion was expressed too obscurely to be of use. He sent some medicine, which she would not take. Moments so dark as these I have never known. I pray for God's support to us all. Hitherto He has granted it.'

The morning drew on to noon. Emily was worse: she could only whisper in gasps. Now, when it was too late, she said to Charlotte, 'If you will send for a doctor, I will see him now.' About two o'clock she died.

1859

34. Geraldine Jewsbury
from *Review of 'Adam Bede'*

The works of true genius seem the most natural things in the world, – so right, that one cannot imagine them different, – so exactly what is needed, that they come as matters of course like daily bread or sunshine. There is always a matter-of-fact solidity in a work of high genius; it never goes contrary to those laws of gravitation which "keep the stars of Heaven from going wrong." In fine, the more true genius there is in a man's work, of whatsoever kind it be, the less it has of startling, unequal or spasmodic; it partakes of the mysterious quietness of Nature. To write a novel does not (in these days especially) sound as though it were any great result; but when genius takes the shape of a novel, then it seems as though that form of manifestation had a truth and fascination all its own. 'Adam Bede' is a novel of the highest class. Full of quiet power, without exaggeration and without any strain after effect, it produces a deep impression on the reader, which remains long after the book is closed. It is as though he had made acquaintance with real human beings: the story is not a story, but a true account of a place and people who have really lived; indeed, some of them may even be living yet, though they will be rather old, but that everything happened as here set down we have no doubt in the world. The duty of a critic is in the present instance almost superseded by the reader. 'Adam Bede' is a book to be accepted, not criticized. The character of Adam is finely done; he is a man as well as the first hero in the story. . . .

There is, too, the secret of the substantial worth of England, the secret of her strength; it is not the number of men and women with brilliant reputation and lyrically recognized name and fame, that makes the enduring prosperity of a nation, but it lies in the amount of worth that is *un*recognized, that remains dumb and unconscious of itself, not clever, but with a certain honest stupidity that understands nothing but doing its best and doing its work without shirking any portion of it. Hetty Sorel, the heroine, is drawn with a cunning and delicate hand; her beauty, her folly, her vanity, her heartlessness, are shaded with a subtle skill that is little less than wonderful: the very truthfulness with which she is indicated keeps the reader from hating her; the author forces the reader to look at her through something of the same medium with which she regards herself: it is a gentle extension of the self-love with which we all soften ourselves and our actions to our own conscience, and that is the great secret of charity. "To see oursels as ithers see us" would be apt to make all but the very strong minded bitter and angry; but if others could only see us as we ourselves really are and intend to be, there would not be so many harsh and sarcastic observations sent out to the world like ugly photographs, the likeness of what we appear to our neighbours: a gently softened picture would be nearer the truth. The Author of 'Adam Bede' has the gift of charity in perfection, without any lack of discernment. Arthur Doricthorne, the young squire, is not quite equal to the complex skill with which Hester is drawn, but it is a true picture. The interview between Arthur and Adam at the hermitage after the trial is wonderful for its reality and truth. All the characters in the book are individuals. Mrs. Pozsus with her sharp incisive sayings is a jewel: she deserves to call Sancho Panza cousin for her similes and comparisons. She never opens her mouth without dropping pearls and diamonds, which would endow a dozen diners-out with good things for a twelvemonth; describing Mr. Craik, the Scotch gardener, she says, "For my part, I think he is welly like a cock as thinks the sun's rose o' purpose to hear him crow." Lisbeth Bede, Adam's poor old mother, is excellent, with her affection and querulousness. The whimsical way in which she mixes up things without connexion, except their chance association in her own thoughts, is pathetic in its unreasonableness; her disparagement of the daughter-in-law she anticipates, her motherly jealousy and matronly dignity are touching; and no reader can withhold his sympathy from the distressing vision of having "to look on belike while she uses the blue-edged platters an' breaks 'em mayhap, tho' there's n'er bin one broke; my old man and me bought 'em at the fair twenty year come next Whissuntide." Dinah Morris, the fair young preacher, half Methodist, half Quaker, is charming, and her sermon and prayers have real genius in them. We do not give our readers any outline of the story, because we will not dull the edge of the interest with which they will read it for themselves. The story is as good as the characters are well drawn. One or two incidents are too melodramatic and traditional, as, for instance, the arrival of Arthur Doricthorne with the reprieve at the latest moment, and the whole scene of proceeding to execution, gives the reader a shock that is decidedly painful; the brutal facts are not softened to fit them for their place in a work of Art, nor are they handled with the skill which the author shows in all the rest of the work; nevertheless, it is very seldom we are called on to deal with a book in which there is so little to qualify our praise.

~——~

1860

35. Florence Nightingale
from *Cassandra*

The intercourse of man and woman – how frivolous, how unworthy it is! Can we call *that* the true vocation of woman – her high career? Look round at the marriages which you know. The true marriage – that noble union, by which a man and woman become together the one perfect being – probably does not exist at present upon earth.

It is not surprising that husbands and wives seem so little part of one another. It is surprising that there is so much love as there is. For there is no food for it. What does it live upon – what nourishes it? Husbands and wives never seem to have anything to say to one another. What do they talk about? Not about any great religious, social, political questions or feelings. They talk about who shall come to dinner, who is to live in this lodge and who in that, about the improvement of the place, or when they shall go to London. If there are children, they form a common subject of some nourishment. But, even then, the case is oftenest thus, – the husband is to think of how they are to get on in life; the wife of bringing them up at home.

But any real communion between husband and wife – any descending into the depths of their being, and drawing out thence what they find and comparing it – do we ever dream of such a thing? Yes, we may dream of it during the season of 'passion'; but we shall not find it afterwards. We even *expect* it to go off, and lay our account that it will. If the husband has, by chance, gone into the depths of *his* being, and found anything there unorthodox, he, oftenest, conceals it carefully from his wife, – he is afraid of 'unsettling her opinions'.

What is the mystery of passion, spiritually speaking? For there *is* a passion of the Spirit. *Blind* passion, as it has most truly been called, seems to come on in man without his exactly knowing why, without his *at all* knowing why for *this* person rather than for *that*, and (whether it has been satisfied or unsatisfied) to go off again after a while, as it came, also without his knowing why.

The woman's passion is generally more lasting.

It is possible that this difference may be, because there is really more in man than in woman. There is nothing in her for him to have this intimate communion *with*. He cannot impart to her his religious beliefs, if he have any, because she would be 'shocked'. Religious men are and must be heretics now – for we must not pray, except in a 'form' of words, made beforehand – or think of God but with a pre-arranged idea.

With the man's political ideas, if they extend beyond the merest party politics, she has no sympathy.

His social ideas, if they are 'advanced', she will probably denounce without knowing why, as savouring of 'socialism' (a convenient word, which covers a multitude of new ideas and offences). For woman is 'by birth a Tory', – has been often said – by education a 'Tory', we mean.

Woman has nothing but her affections, – and this makes her at once more loving and less loved.

But is it surprising that there should be so little real marriage, when we think what the process is which leads to marriage?

Under the eyes of an always present mother and sisters (of whom even the most refined and intellectual cannot abstain from a jest upon the subject, who think it is their *duty* to be anxious, to watch every germ and bud of it) the acquaintance begins. It is fed – upon what? – the gossip of art, musical and pictorial, the party politics of the day, the chit chat of society, and people marry or sometimes they don't marry, discouraged by the impossibility of knowing any more of one another than this will furnish.

They prefer to marry in *thought*, to hold imaginary conversations with one another in idea, rather than, on such a flimsy pretext of communion, to take the chance (*certainty* it cannot be) of having more to say to one another in marriage.

Men and women meet now *to be idle*. Is it extraordinary that they do not know each other, and that, in their mutual ignorance, they form no surer friendships? Did they meet to *do* something together, then indeed they might form some real tie.

But, as it is, *they* are not there, it is only a mask which is there – a mouth-piece of ready-made sentences about the 'topics of the day'; and then people rail against men for choosing a woman 'for her face' – why, what else do they see?

It is very well to say 'be prudent, be careful, try to know each other'. But how are you to know each other?

Unless a woman has lost all pride, how is it possible for her, under the eyes of all her family, to indulge in long exclusive conversations with a man? 'Such a thing' must not take place till after her 'engagement'. And how is she to make an engagement, if 'such a thing' has not taken place?

Besides, young women at home have so little to occupy and to interest them – they have so little reason for *not* quitting their home, that a young and independent man cannot look at a girl without giving rise to 'expectations', if not on her own part, on that of her family. Happy he, if he is not said to have been 'trifling with her feelings', or 'disappointing her hopes'! Under these circumstances, how can a man, who has any pride or any principle, become acquainted with a woman in such a manner as to *justify* them in marrying?

There are four ways in which people marry. First, accident or relationship has thrown them together in their childhood, and acquaintance has grown up naturally and unconsciously. Accordingly, in novels, it is generally cousins who marry; and *now* it seems the only natural thing – the only possible way of making an intimacy. And yet, we know that intermarriage between relations is in direct contravention of the laws of nature for the well-being of the race; witness the Quakers, the Spanish grandees, the royal races, the secluded valleys of mountainous countries, where madness, degeneration of race, defective organization and cretinism flourish and multiply.

The second way, and by far the most general, in which people marry, is this. A woman, thoroughly uninterested at home, and having formed a slight acquaintance with some accidental person, accepts him, if he 'falls in love' with her, as it is technically called, and takes the chance. Hence the vulgar expression of marriage being a lottery, which it most truly is, for that the *right* two should come together has as many chances against it as there are blanks in any lottery.

The third way is, that some person is found sufficiently independent, sufficiently careless of the opinions of others, or sufficiently without modesty to speculate thus: 'It is worth while that I should become acquainted with so and so. I do not care what his or her opinion of me is, if, *after* having become acquainted, to do which can bear no other construction in people's eyes than a desire of marriage, I retreat'. But there is this to be said, that it is doubtful whether, under this unnatural tension, which, to all susceptible characters, such a disregard of the opinions which they care for must be, a healthy or a natural feeling can grow up.

And now they are married – that is to say, two people have received the licence of a man in a white surplice. But they are no more man and wife for that than Louis XIV and the Infanta of Spain, married by proxy, were man and wife. The woman who has sold herself for an establishment, in what is she superior to those we may not name?

Lastly, in a few rare, very rare, cases, such as circumstances, always pro-vided in novels, but seldom to be met with in real life, present – whether the accident of parents' neglect, or of parents' unusual skill and wisdom, or of having no parents at all, which is generally the case in novels – or mar-rying out of the person's rank of life, by which the usual restraints are removed, and there is room and play left for attraction – or extraordinary events, isolation, misfortunes, which many wish for, even though their imaginations be not tainted by romance-reading; such alternatives as these give food and space for the development of character and mutual sympathies.

But a girl, if she has any pride, is so ashamed of having any thing she wishes to say out of the hearing of her own family, she thinks it must be something so very wrong, that it is ten to one, if she have the opportunity of saying it, that she will not.

And yet she is spending her life, perhaps, in dreaming of accidental means of unrestrained communion.

And then it is thought pretty to say that 'Women have no passion'. If passion is excitement in the daily social intercourse with men, women think about marriage much more than men do; it is the only event of their lives. It ought to be a sacred event, but surely not the only event in a woman's life, as it is now. Many women spend their lives in asking men to marry them, in a refined way. Yet it is true that women are seldom in love. How can they be?

———

1861

36. Isabella Beeton
from *The Book of Household Management*

AS WITH THE COMMANDER OF AN ARMY, or the leader of any enterprise, so it is with the mistress of a house. Her spirit will be seen through the whole establishment; and just in proportion as she performs her duties intelligently and thoroughly, so will her domestics follow in her path. Of all those acquirements, which more particularly belong to the feminine character, there are none which take a higher rank, in our estimation, than such as enter into a knowledge of household duties; for on these are per-petually dependent the happiness, comfort, and well-being of a family.

❀ ❀ ❀ ❀

DUTIES OF THE MAID-OF-ALL-WORK

THE general servant, or maid-of-all-work, is perhaps the only one of her class deserving of commiseration: her life is a solitary one, and in, some places, her work is never done. She is also subject to rougher treatment than either the house or kitchen-maid, especially in her earlier career: she starts in life, probably a girl of thirteen, with some small tradesman's wife as her mistress, just a step above her in the social scale; and although the class contains among them many excellent, kind-hearted women, it also contains some very rough specimens of the feminine gender, and to some of these it occasionally falls to give our maid-of-all-work her first lessons in her multifarious occupations: the mistress's commands are the measure of the maid-of-all-work's duties. By the time she has become a tolerable servant, she is probably engaged in some respectable tradesman's house, where she has to rise with the lark, for she has to do in her own person all the work which in larger establishments is performed by cook, kitchen-maid, and housemaid, and occasionally the part of a footman's duty, which consists in carrying messages.

The general servant's duties commence by opening the shutters (and windows, if the weather permits) of all the lower apartments in the house; she should then brush up her kitchen-range, light the fire, clear away the ashes, clean the hearth, and polish with a leather the bright parts of the range, doing all as rapidly and as vigorously as possible, that no more time be wasted than is necessary. After putting on the kettle, she should then proceed to the dining-room or parlour to get it in order for breakfast. She should first roll up the rug, take up the fender, shake and fold up the tablecloth, then sweep the room, carrying the dirt towards the fireplace; a coarse cloth should then be laid down over the carpet, and she should proceed to clean the grate, having all her utensils close to her. When the grate is finished, the ashes cleared away, the hearth cleaned, and the fender put back in its place, she must dust the furniture, not omitting the legs of the tables and chairs; and if there are any ornaments or things on the sideboard, she must not dust round them, but lift them up on to another place, dust well where they have been standing, and then replace the things. Nothing annoys a particular mistress so much as to find, when she comes down stairs, different articles of furniture looking as if they had never been dusted. If the servant is at all methodical, and gets into a habit of *doing* a room in a certain way, she will scarcely ever leave her duties neglected. After the rug is put down, the table-cloth arranged, and every-thing in order, she should lay the cloth for breakfast, and then shut the dining-room door.

The hall must now be swept, the mats shaken, the door-step cleaned, and any brass knockers or handles polished up with the leather. If the family breakfast very early, the tidying of the hall must then be deferred till after that meal. After cleaning the boots that are absolutely required, the servant should now wash her hands and face, put on a clean white apron, and be ready for her mistress when she comes down stairs. In families where there is much work to do before breakfast, the master of the house frequently has two pairs of boots in wear, so that they may be properly cleaned when the servant has more time to do them, in the daytime. This arrangement is, perhaps, scarcely necessary in the summer-time, when there are no grates to clean every morning; but in the dark days of winter it is only kind and thoughtful to lighten a servant-of-all-work's duties as much as possible.

She will now carry the urn into the dining-room, where her mistress will make the tea or coffee, and sometimes will boil the eggs, to insure them being done to her liking. In the mean time the servant cooks, if required, the bacon, kidneys, fish, &c.; – if cold meat is to be served, she must always send it to table on a clean dish, and nicely garnished with tufts of parsley, if this is obtainable.

After she has had her own breakfast, and whilst the family are finishing theirs, she should go upstairs into the bedrooms, open all the windows, strip the clothes off the beds, and leave them to air whilst she is clearing away the breakfast things. She should then take up the crumbs in a dustpan from under the table, put the chairs in their places, and sweep up the hearth.

The breakfast things washed up, the kitchen should be tidied, so that it may be neat when her mistress comes in to give the orders for the day: after receiving these orders, the servant should go upstairs again, with a jug of boiling water, the slop-pail, and two cloths. After emptying the slops, and scalding the vessels with the boiling water, and wiping them thoroughly dry, she should wipe the top of the wash-table and arrange it all in order. She then proceeds to make the beds, in which occupation she is generally assisted by the mistress, or, if she have any daughters, by one of them. Before commencing to make the bed, the servant should put on a large bed-apron, kept for this purpose only, which should be made very wide, to button round the waist and meet behind, while it should be made as long as the dress. By adopting this plan, the blacks and dirt on servants' dresses (which at all times it is impossible to help) will not rub off on to the bed-clothes, mattresses, and bed furniture. When the beds are made, the rooms should be dusted, the stairs lightly swept down, hall furniture, closets, &c., dusted. The lady of the house, where there is but one servant kept, frequently takes charge of the drawing-room herself, that is to say, dusting it; the servant sweeping, cleaning windows, looking-glasses, grates, and rough work of that sort. If there are many ornaments and knick-knacks about the room, it is certainly better for the mistress to dust these herself, as a maid-of-all-work's hands are not always in a condition to handle delicate ornaments.

Now she has gone the rounds of the house and seen that all is in order, the servant goes to her kitchen to see about the cooking of the dinner, in which very often her mistress will assist her. She should put on a coarse apron with a bib to do her dirty work in, which may be easily replaced by a white one if required.

Half an hour before dinner is ready, she should lay the cloth, that everything may be in readiness when she is dishing up the dinner, and take all into the dining-room that is likely to be required, in the way of knives, forks, spoons, bread, salt, water, &c. &c. By exercising a little forethought, much confusion and trouble may be saved both to mistress and servant, by getting everything ready for the dinner in good time.

After taking in the dinner, when every one is seated, she removes the covers, hands the plates round, and pours out the beer; and should be careful to hand everything on the left side of the person she is waiting on.

We need scarcely say that a maid-of-all-work cannot stay in the dining-room during the whole of dinner-time, as she must dish up her pudding, or whatever is served after the first course. When she sees every one helped, she should leave the room to make her preparations for the next course; and anything that is required, such as bread, &c., people may assist themselves to in the absence of the servant.

When the dinner things are cleared away, the servant should sweep up the crumbs in the dining-room, sweep the hearth, and lightly dust the furniture, then sit down to her own dinner.

After this, she washes up and puts away the dinner things, sweeps the kitchen, dusts and tidies it, and puts on the kettle for tea. She should now, before dressing herself for the afternoon, clean her knives, boots, and shoes, and do any other dirty work in the scullery that may be necessary. . . .

When the servant is dressed, she takes in the tea, and after tea turns down the beds, sees that the water-jugs and bottles are full, closes the windows, and draws down the blinds. If the weather is very warm, these are usually left open until the last thing at night, to cool the rooms.

The routine of a general servant's duties depends upon the kind of situation she occupies; but a systematic maid-of-all-work should so contrive to divide her work, that every day in the week may have its proper share. By this means she is able to keep the house clean with less fatigue to herself than if she left all the cleaning to do at the end of the week. Supposing there are five bedrooms in the house, two sitting-rooms, kitchen, scullery, and the usual domestic offices: – on Monday she should thoroughly clean the drawing-room; on Tuesday, two of the bedrooms; on Wednesday, two more; on Thursday, the other bedroom and stairs; on Friday morning she should sweep the dining-room very thoroughly, clean the hall, and in the afternoon her kitchen tins and bright utensils. By arranging her work in this manner, no undue proportion will fall to Saturday's share, and she will then have this day for cleaning plate, cleaning her kitchen, and arranging everything in nice order. The regular work must, of course, be performed in the usual manner, as we have endeavoured to describe.

Before retiring to bed, she will do well to clean up glasses, plates, &c. which have been used for the evening meal, and prepare for her morning's work by placing her wood near the fire, on the hob, to dry, taking care there is no danger of it igniting, before she leaves the kitchen for the night. Before retiring, she will have to lock and bolt the doors, unless the master undertakes this office himself.

If the washing, or even a portion of it, is done at home, it will be impossible for the maid-of-all-work to do her household duties thoroughly, during the time it is about, unless she have some assistance. Usually, if all the washing is done at home, the mistress hires some one to assist at the wash-tub, and sees to little matters herself, in the way of dusting, clearing away breakfast things, folding, starching, and ironing the fine things. With a little management much can be accomplished, provided the mistress be industrious, energetic, and willing to lend a helping hand. Let washing-week be not the excuse for having everything in a muddle; and although "things" cannot be cleaned so thoroughly, and so much time spent upon them, as ordinarily, yet the house may be kept tidy and clear from litter without a great deal of exertion either on the part of the mistress or servant. . . .

A bustling and active girl will always find time to do a little needlework for herself, if she lives with consistent and reasonable people. In the summer evenings she should manage to sit down for two or three hours, and for a short time in the afternoon in leisure days. A general servant's duties are so multifarious, that unless she be quick and active, she will not be able to accomplish this. To discharge these various duties properly is a difficult task, and sometimes a thankless office; but it must be remembered that a good maid-of-all-work will make a good servant in any capacity, and may be safely taken not only without fear of failure, but with every probability of giving satisfaction to her employer.

❀ ❀ ❀ ❀

Briefly to conclude what we have to say of suffocation, let us treat of *Lightning*. When a person has been struck by lightning, there is a general paleness of the whole body, with the exception of the part struck, which is often blackened, or even scorched. – *Treatment*. Same as for drowning. It is not, however, of much use; for when death takes place at all, it is generally instantaneous.

CURE FOR THE TOOTHACHE. – Take a piece of sheet zinc, about the size of a sixpence, and a piece of silver, say a shilling; place them together, and hold the defective tooth between them or contiguous to them; in a few minutes the pain will be gone, as if by magic. The zinc and silver, acting as a galvanic battery, will produce on the nerves of the tooth sufficient electricity to establish a current, and consequently to relieve the pain. Or smoke a pipe of tobacco and caraway-seeds.

37. Adelaide Procter
A Woman's Last Word

WELL – the links are broken,
    All is past;
This farewell, when spoken,
    Is the last.
I have tried and striven
    All in vain;
Such bonds must be riven,
    Spite of pain,
And never, never, never
    Knit again.

So I tell you plainly
    It must be:
I shall try, not vainly,
    To be free;
Truer, happier chances
    Wait me yet,
While you, through fresh fancies
    Can forget; –
And life has nobler uses
    Than Regret.

All past words retracing,
  One by one,
Does not help effacing
  What is done.
Let it be. Oh, stronger
  Links can break!
Had we dreamed still longer
  We could wake, –
Yet let us part in kindness
  For Love's sake.

Bitterness and sorrow
  Will at last,
In some bright to-morrow,
  Heal their past;
But future hearts will never
  Be as true
As mine was – is ever,
  Dear, for you . . .
Then must we part, when loving
  As we do?

1862

38. Queen Victoria
from *Diary*

Balmoral, Thursday, August 21, 1862.

AT eleven o'clock started off in the little pony-chair (drawn by the *Corriemulzie* pony, and led by Brown), Bertie, who had come over from *Birkhall*, on foot, the two girls on ponies, and the two little boys, who joined us later, for *Craig Lowrigan*; and I actually drove in the little carriage to the very top, turning off from the path and following the track where the carts had gone. Grant and Duncan pushed the carriage behind. Sweet Baby (Beatrice) we found at the top. The view was so fine, the day so bright, and the heather so beautifully pink – but no pleasure, no joy! all dead!

And here at the top is the foundation of the cairn – forty feet wide – to be erected to my precious Albert which will be seen all down the valley. I and my poor six orphans all placed stones on it; and our initials, as well as those of the three absent ones, are to be carved on stones all round it. I felt very shaky and nervous.

It is to be thirty-five feet high, and the following inscription to be placed on it: –

TO THE BELOVED MEMORY

OF

ALBERT, THE GREAT AND GOOD
PRINCE CONSORT,

RAISED BY HIS BROKEN-HEARTED WIDOW,

VICTORIA R.

AUGUST 21, 1862.

"He being made perfect in a short time fulfilled a long time;
For his soul pleased the Lord,
Therefore hastened He to take him
Away from among the wicked."
                                    Wisdom of Solomon, iv. 13, 14.

Walked down to where the rough road is, and this first short attempt at walking in the heather shook me and tired me much.

39. Christina Rossetti
Song

WHEN I am dead, my dearest,
    Sing no sad songs for me;
Plant thou no roses at my head,
    Nor shady cypress tree:
Be the green grass above me
    With showers and dewdrops wet;

And if thou wilt, remember,
And if thou wilt, forget.

I shall not see the shadows,
I shall not feel the rain;
I shall not hear the nightingale
Sing on, as if in pain:
And dreaming through the twilight
That doth not rise nor set,
Haply I may remember,
And haply may forget.

1863

40. Hannah Cullwick
from *Diary*

Sunday 31 May.

Clean'd 3 pairs o' boots & lit the fires. Did my hair & wash'd in the scullery. Laid the cloth & took the breakfast up. Clean'd away & wash'd up after. Clean'd the knives & made the kitchen fire up. Put the meat to roast. When dinner was over & I'd put the supper ready & clean'd the hearth & all that I got ready & went to Massa. Reach'd him earlyish & we had a nice evening. We petted a bit & then I put my jacket on, & Massa thought I was jolly & fat & he told me to see if I could lift *him* & I laugh'd & said, 'Of course I can.' I lifted him easy & carried him, & then he lifted me & said I was *heavy* – I am 11 stone & Massa's 13 lbs heavier than me. I got his dinner & clean'd away after & wash'd up. Made cigarettes & then petted & I told Massa things what had happened at Brighton & so he told me not to forget to put them things down what I'd bin telling him. So what I can remember I will, as there's room in this sheet & it's end o' the month.

❀ ❀ ❀ ❀

Massa met me at the top of Chancery Lane today – walk'd down on the other side & sign'd to me to go in at the other gate. But the gentleman wouldn't let me through 'cause I wouldn't say who I was going to see, so I told him he could leave it alone, 'cause he made me cross, speaking like that. I am thirty years old this month – must be quite a woman now, though I don't feel any different than I ever did except in feeling lower in heart I think, for I've bin a servant now 20 years or more. Always the lowest kind, but I think different about it now a good deal than I did ten years ago 'fore I knew Massa. He has taught me, though it's been difficult to learn thoroughly, the beauty in being nothing but a common drudge & to bear being despised by others what don't have to work the same way. I have hardly ever met wi' a *servant* yet who wasn't ashamed o' dirty work & who wouldn't be glad to get out of it for something they think is *better*, but *I* wouldn't get out of it if I could, nor change from being Massa's slave for anything else I know of. I've bin a slave now 9 years & worn the chains & padlocks 6 years – I don't hide 'em now from Mary for she saw 'em every night at Brighton this time.

❀ ❀ ❀ ❀

Wednesday 14 October.
Clean'd 3 pair o' boots & lit the fires. Swept the steps & shook the mats. Got our breakfast & wash'd up after. Clean'd the knives & made the fire up & got dinner. Clean'd away after & got ready to go to Massa. Reach'd him 'fore 5 & we had a nice evening together. I told M. I was sorry about that Sunday & he talk'd about it a little & then I was good again, & so Massa told me to black my face like it was that night I clean'd after the coalmen. So I did, & got the dinner & clean'd the boots & wash'd up the things & Massa's feet with it black, & M. seem'd pleas'd wi' it so but said my hands wasn't looking so thick & red as they did the Sunday when he read them verses to me. They was rhymes in the country talk & some o' the words I know'd how to speak better than Massa even. While I made the cigars I sat 'tween his knees & heard Massa read some verses he'd made up for me. They was very nice & all just as I should o' said if I could o' made 'em, for they was wrote as if I was saying it, & I'd to kiss Massa at all the best parts – about going up the chimney & that. When the cigars was done I put coals on & had a little petting, for I'd wash'd the black of my face in the water I wash'd the feet in, & at $^1/_2$ past 9 Massa walk'd wi' me up the lane & saw me get in an omnibus. I got home by $^1/_2$ past ten & to bed.

Friday 16 October.
Got up & open'd the shutters. Got our breakfast over & wash'd up. Made the fire up & got dinner. Clean'd away & begun to scrub the tins & covers – Master Charley said I look'd like a milkmaid only blacker. Sarah took the boys to Bromley & Mary went out so Fred & me was alone. I work'd

till eight o'clock & then had supper. Clean'd away & then to bed at ten o'clock. I'd a capital chance to go up the chimney, so I lock'd up & waited till ½ past ten till the grate was cool enough & then I took the carpets up & got the tub o' water ready to wash me in. Moved the fender & swept ashes up. Stripp'd myself quite naked & put a pair of old boots on & tied an old duster over my hair & then I got up into the chimney with a brush. There was a lot o' soot & it was soft & warm. Before I swept I pull'd the duster over my eyes & mouth, & I sat on the beam that goes across the middle & cross'd my legs along it & I was quite safe & comfortable & out o' sight. I swept lots o' soot down & it come all over me & I sat there for ten minutes or more, & when I'd swept all round & as far as I could reach I come down, & I lay on the hearth in the soot a minute or two thinking, & I wish'd rather that Massa could see me. I black'd my face over & then got the looking glass & look'd at myself & I was certainly a fright & hideous all over, at least I should o' seem'd so to anybody but Massa. I set on & wash'd myself after, & I'd hard work to get the black off & was obliged to leave my shoulders for Massa to finish. I got the tub emptied & to bed before twelve.

---

41. Christina Rossetti
L. E. L.

'Whose heart was breaking for a little love.'
E. B. BROWNING

DOWNSTAIRS I laugh, I sport and jest with all:
  But in my solitary room above
I turn my face in silence to the wall;
  My heart is breaking for a little love.
    Tho' winter frosts are done,
    And birds pair every one,
And leaves peep out, for springtide is begun.

I feel no spring, while spring is wellnigh blown,
  I find no nest, while nests are in the grove:
Woe's me for mine own heart that dwells alone,
  My heart that breaketh for a little love.
    While golden in the sun
    Rivulets rise and run,
While lilies bud, for springtide is begun.

All love, are loved, save only I; their hearts
　　Beat warm with love and joy, beat full thereof:
They cannot guess, who play the pleasant parts,
　　My heart is breaking for a little love.
　　　　While beehives wake and whirr,
　　　　And rabbit thins his fur,
In living spring that sets the world astir.

I deck myself with silks and jewelry,
　　I plume myself like any mated dove:
They praise my rustling show, and never see
　　My heart is breaking for a little love.
　　　　While sprouts green lavender
　　　　With rosemary and myrrh,
For in quick spring the sap is all astir.

Perhaps some saints in glory guess the truth,
　　Perhaps some angels read it as they move,
And cry one to another full of ruth,
　　'Her heart is breaking for a little love.'
　　　　Tho' other things have birth,
　　　　And leap and sing for mirth,
When springtime wakes and clothes and feeds the earth.

Yet saith a saint: 'Take patience for thy scathe';
　　Yet saith an angel: 'Wait, for thou shalt prove
True best is last, true life is born of death,
　　O thou, heart-broken for a little love
　　　　Then love shall fill thy girth,
　　　　And love make fat thy dearth,
When new spring builds new heaven and clean new earth.'

———

42. Julia Kavanagh
from *Jane Austen*

THE writings of women are betrayed by their merits as well as by their
faults. If weakness and vagueness often characterize them, they also possess
when excellent, or simply good, three great redeeming qualities, which
have frequently betrayed anonymous female writers. These qualities are:

Delicacy, Tenderness, and Sympathy. We do not know if there exists, for instance, a novel of any merit written by a woman, which fails in one of these three attributes. Delicacy is the most common – delicacy in its broadest sense, not in its conventional meaning. Where that fails, which is a rare case, one of the other qualities assuredly steps in. Aphra Behn had no delicacy of intellect or of heart, but she had sympathy. Perhaps only a woman could have written "Oroonoko," as only another woman could have written "Uncle Tom's Cabin" two hundred years later. Man has the sense of injustice, but woman has essentially pity for suffering and sorrow. Her side is the vanquished side, amongst men or nations, and when she violates that law of her nature she rarely fails to exceed man in cruelty and revenge.

Delicacy was the great attribute of the writer under our notice. Mademoiselle de Scudéry alone equalled Miss Austen in delicacy, with this difference, however, that one applied hers to thought, feeling, and intellectual speculation, and that the other turned hers to the broader and more living field of character and human nature. The method, too, was as different as the application. One analyzed, the other painted.

Miss Austen, however, though she adopted the pictorial method, is not an effective writer. Her stories are moderately interesting – her heroes and heroines are not such as to charm away our hearts, or to fascinate our judgment; but never has character been displayed in such delicate variety as in her tales; never have commonplace men and women been invested with so much reality. She cannot be said to have created or invented; Jane Austen had an infinitely rarer gift – she saw.

Not without cause did the faith and superstition of our forefathers invest with veneration and awe that mysterious word – a seer. The poet, the painter, are no more – they see. To see well is one of the greatest, and strange, too, of the rarest attributes of the mind. Commonplace people see little or nothing. Beauty and truth escape their dull perceptions. Character does not exist for them; for them life is no story – Nature no wonderful poem.

That great gift Miss Austen possessed, not in its fulness, for her range of vision was limited, but in all its keenness. The grand, the heroic, the generous, the devoted, escaped her, or, at least, were beyond her power; but the simply good, the dull, the lively, the mean, the coarse, the selfish, the frivolous, she saw and painted with a touch so fine that we often do not perceive its severity. Yet inexorable it is, for it is true. To this rare power Miss Austen added another equally rare – she knew where to stop. Two qualities are required to write a good book: to know what to say and what to withhold. She had the latter gift, one which is rarely appreciated: it seems so natural not to say more than is needed! In this respect she must have exercised great judgment, or possessed great tact, since her very qualities are those that lead to minuteness. Mademoiselle de Scudéry's prolixity was the result of a delicate and subtle mind, and that prolixity ruined her, for it made her well-nigh unreadable. Her fame decreased with time; steady progress has marked that of Jane Austen. In vain every year sees the birth of works of fiction that prove her deficiencies. She has remained unequalled in her own region – a wide one, the region of commonplace.

Persons who care to think on literary subjects, as well as to enjoy literature, must often be struck with the want of truth which tragedy and comedy display, whether on the stage or in fiction. There is nothing so unlike life as either. Life as we see it around us is not cast in sorrow or in mirth – it is not all stately or ridiculous – but a strange compound in which commonplace acts a far more striking part than heroic events or comic incidents. This middle region Jane Austen painted with a master-hand. Great calamities, heroic sorrows, adventures, and all that hangs upon them, she left to more gifted or to more ambitious painters. Neither did she trench on that other world of fiction where satire, ridicule, and exaggerated character are needed. She was satisfied with life and society, as she saw them around her, without endless sorrows, without great passions or unbecoming follies, and especially without exaggeration. Her men and women are neither very good nor very bad; nothing singular or very dramatic falls to their lot; they move in the circle of friends and home, and the slight incidents of their life are not worked up to gloomy interest, in order to suit the purposes of a tale. Indeed, if Miss Austen's merit, and it is a great one, is to have painted simply and naturally such people as we meet with daily, her fault is to have subdued life and its feelings into even more than their own tameness. The stillness of her books is not natural, and never, whilst love and death endure, will human lives flow so calmly as in her pages.

The impression life produced on Miss Austen was peculiar. She seems to have been struck especially with its small vanities and small falsehoods, equally remote from the ridiculous or the tragic. She refused to build herself, or to help to build for others, any romantic ideal of love, virtue, or sorrow. . . . Her irony, though gentle, was a fault, and the parent of much coldness. She learned to check it, but she never conquered it entirely.

❋ ❋ ❋ ❋

Wonderful, indeed, is the power that out of materials so slender, out of characters so imperfectly marked, could fashion a story. This is her great, her prevailing merit, and yet, it cannot be denied, it is one that injures her with many readers. It seems so natural that she should have told things and painted people as they are, so natural and so easy, that we are apt to forget the performance in the sense of its reality. The literary taste of the majority is always tinged with coarseness; it loves exaggeration, and slights the modesty of truth.

Another of Miss Austen's excellencies is also a disadvantage. She does not paint or analyze her characters; they speak for themselves. Her people have never those set sayings or phrases which we may refer to the author, and of which we may think, how clever! They talk as people talk in the world, and quietly betray their inner being in their folly, falsehood, or assumption. . . .

But it was natural that powers so great should fail somewhere, and there were some things which Miss Austen could not do. She could not speak the language of any strong feeling, even though that feeling were ridiculous and unjust. . . .

The delicate mind that could evolve, so shrewdly, foolishness from its deepest recesses, was powerless when strong feelings had to be summoned. They heard her, but did not obey the call.

This want of certain important faculties is the only defect, or rather causes the only defect, of Miss Austen's works: that everything is told in the same tone. An elopement, a death, seduction, are related as placidly as a dinner or ball, but with much less spirit. As she is, however, we must take her, and what her extraordinary powers wanted in extent, they made up in depth. In her own range, and admitting her cold views of life to be true, she is faultless, or almost faultless. By choosing to be all but perfect, she sometimes became monotonous, but rarely. The value of light and shade, as a means of success, she discarded. Strong contrasts, bold flights, she shunned. To be true, to show Life in its everyday aspect, was her ambition. To hope to make so much out of so little showed no common confidence in her own powers, and more than common daring. Of the thousands who take up a pen to write a story meant to amuse, how many are there who can, or who dare, be true, like Jane Austen?

---

43. Frances Anne Kemble
from *Journal of a Residence on a Georgian Plantation*

I walked down the settlement towards the infirmary or hospital, calling in at one or two of the houses along the row. These cabins consist of one room about twelve feet by fifteen, with a couple of closets smaller and closer than the state-rooms of a ship, divided off from the main room and each other by rough wooden partitions in which the inhabitants sleep. They have almost all of them a rude bedstead, with the grey moss of the forests for mattress, and filthy, pestilential-looking blankets, for covering. Two families (sometimes eight and ten in number) reside in one of these huts, which are mere wooden frames pinned, as it were, to the earth by a brick chimney outside, whose enormous aperture within pours down a flood of air, but little counteracted by the miserable spark of fire, which hardly sends an attenuated thread of lingering smoke up its huge throat. A wide ditch runs immediately at the back of these dwellings, which is filled and emptied daily by the tide. Attached to each hovel is a small scrap of ground for a garden, which, however, is for the most part untended and uncultivated. Such of these dwellings as I visited to-day were filthy and wretched in the extreme, and exhibited that most deplorable consequence of ignorance and an abject condition, the inability of the inhabitants to secure and improve even such pitiful comfort as might yet be achieved by them. Instead of the order, neatness, and ingenuity which might convert even these miserable hovels into tolerable residences, there was the careless, reckless, filthy indolence which even the brutes do not exhibit in their lairs and nests, and which seemed incapable of applying to the uses of existence the few miserable means of comfort yet within their reach. Firewood and shavings lay littered about the floors, while the half-naked children were cowering round two or three smouldering cinders. The moss with which the chinks and crannies of their ill-protecting dwellings might have been stuffed, was trailing in dirt and dust about the ground, while the back-door of the huts, opening upon a most unsightly ditch, was left wide open for the fowls and ducks, which they are allowed to raise, to travel in and out, increasing the filth of the cabin, by what they brought and left in every direction. In the midst of the floor, or squatting round the cold hearth, would be four or five little children from four to ten years old, the latter all with babies in their arms, the care of the infants being taken from the mothers (who are driven afield as soon as they recover from child labour), and devolved upon these poor little nurses, as they are called, whose business it is to watch the infant, and carry it to its mother whenever it may require nourishment. To these hardly human little beings, I addressed my remonstrances about the filth, cold, and unnecessary wretchedness of their room, bidding the elder boys and girls kindle up the fire, sweep the floor, and expel the poultry. For a long time my very words seemed unintelligible to them, till when I began to sweep and make up the fire, &c., they first fell to laughing, and then imitating me. The encrustations of dirt on their hands, feet, and faces, were my next object of attack, and the stupid negro practice (by the bye, but a short time since nearly universal in enlightened

Europe), of keeping the babies with their feet bare, and their heads, already well capped by nature with their woolly hair, wrapped in half-a-dozen hot filthy coverings. Thus I travelled down the 'street,' in every dwelling endeavouring to awaken a new perception, that of cleanliness, sighing, as I went, over the futility of my own exertions, for how can slaves be improved? Nathless, thought I, let what can be done; for it may be, that, the two being incompatible, improvement may yet expel slavery – and so it might, and surely would, if, instead of beginning at the end, I could but begin at the beginning of my task. If the mind and soul were awakened, instead of mere physical good attempted, the physical good would result, and the great curse vanish away; but my hands are tied fast, and this corner of the work is all that I may do. Yet it cannot be but, from my words and actions, some revelations should reach these poor people; and going in and out amongst them perpetually, I shall teach, and they learn involuntarily a thousand things of deepest import. They must learn, and who can tell the fruit of that knowledge alone, that there are beings in the world, even with skins of a different colour from their own, who have sympathy for their misfortunes, love for their virtues, and respect for their common nature – but oh! my heart is full almost to bursting, as I walk among these most poor creatures.

The infirmary is a large two-storey building, terminating the broad orange-planted space between the two rows of houses which form the first settlement; it is built of white washed wood, and contains four large-sized rooms. But how shall I describe to you the spectacle which was presented to me, on my entering the first of these? But half the casements, of which there were six, were glazed, and these were obscured with dirt, almost as much as the other windowless ones were darkened by the dingy shutters, which the shivering inmates had fastened to, in order to protect themselves from the cold. In the enormous chimney glimmered the powerless embers of a few sticks of wood, round which, however, as many of the sick women as could approach, were cowering; some on wooden settles, most of them on the ground, excluding those who were too ill to rise; and these last poor wretches lay prostrate on the floor, without bed, mattress, or pillow, buried in tattered and filthy blankets, which, huddled round them as they lay strewed about, left hardly space to move upon the floor. And here, in their hour of sickness and suffering, lay those whose health and strength are spent in unrequited labour for us – those who, perhaps even yesterday, were being urged on to their unpaid task – those whose husbands, fathers, brothers and sons, were even at that hour sweating over the earth, whose produce was to buy for us all the luxuries which health can revel in, all the comforts which can alleviate sickness. I stood in the midst of them, perfectly unable to speak, the tears pouring from my eyes at this sad spectacle of their misery, myself and my emotion alike strange and incomprehensible to them. Here lay women expecting every hour the terrors and agonies of child-birth, others who had just brought their doomed offspring into the world, others who were groaning over the anguish and bitter disappointment of miscarriages – here lay some burning with fever, others chilled with cold and aching with rheumatism, upon the hard cold ground, the draughts and dampness of the atmosphere increasing their sufferings, and dirt, noise, and stench, and every aggravation of which sickness is capable, combined in their condition – here they lay like brute beasts, absorbed in physical suffering; unvisited by any of those Divine influences which may ennoble the dispensations of pain and illness, forsaken, as it seemed to me, of all good; and yet, O God, Thou surely hadst not forsaken them! Now, pray take notice, that this is the hospital of an estate, where the owners are supposed to be humane, the overseer efficient and kind, and the negroes remarkably well cared for and comfortable. As soon as I recovered from my dismay, I addressed old Rose, the midwife, who had charge of this room, bidding her open the shutters of such windows as were glazed, and let in the light. I next proceeded to make up the fire, but upon my lifting a log for that purpose, there was one universal outcry of horror, and old Rose, attempting to snatch it from me, exclaimed, 'Let alone, missis – let be – what for you lift wood – you have nigger enough, missis, to do it!' I hereupon had to explain to them my view of the purposes for which hands and arms were appended to our bodies, and forthwith began making Rose tidy up the miserable apartment, removing all the filth and rubbish from the floor that could be removed, folding up in piles the blankets of the patients who were not using them, and placing, in rather more sheltered and comfortable positions, those who were unable to rise. It was all that I could do, and having enforced upon them all my earnest desire that they should keep their room swept, and as tidy as possible, I passed on to the other room on the ground floor, and to the two above, one of which is appropriated to the use of the men who are ill. They were all in the same deplorable condition, the upper rooms being rather the more miserable, inasmuch as none of the windows were glazed at all, and they had, therefore, only the alternative of utter darkness, or killing draughts of air, from the unsheltered casements. In all, filth, disorder and misery abounded; the floor was the only bed, and scanty begrimed rags of blankets the only covering. I left this refuge for Mr.——'s sick dependants, with my clothes covered with dust, and full of vermin, and with a heart heavy enough, as you will well believe.

❋ ❋ ❋ ❋

We have, as a sort of under nursemaid and assistant of my dear M——, whose white complexion, as I wrote you, occasioned such indignation to my southern fellow-travellers, and such extreme perplexity to the poor slaves on our arrival here, a much more orthodox servant for these parts, a young woman named Psyche, but commonly called Sack, not a very graceful abbreviation of the divine heathen appellation: she cannot be much over twenty, has a very pretty figure, a graceful gentle deportment, and a face which, but for its colour (she is a dingy mulatto), would be pretty, and is extremely pleasing, from the perfect sweetness of its expression; she is always serious, not to say sad and silent, and has altogether an air of melancholy and timidity, that has frequently struck me very much, and would have made me think some special anxiety or sorrow must occasion it, but that God knows the whole condition of these wretched people naturally produces such a deportment, and there is no necessity to seek for special or peculiar causes to account for it. Just in proportion as I have found the slaves on this plantation intelligent and advanced beyond the general brutish level of the majority, I have observed this pathetic expression of countenance in them, a mixture of sadness and fear, the involuntary exhibition of the two feelings, which I suppose must be the predominant experience of their whole lives, regret and apprehension, not the less heavy, either of them, for being, in some degree, vague and indefinite – a sense of incalculable past loss and injury, and a dread of incalculable future loss and injury.

I have never questioned Psyche as to her sadness, because, in the first place, as I tell you, it appears to me most natural, and is observable in all the slaves, whose superior natural or acquired intelligence allows of their filling situations of trust or service about the house and family; and, though I cannot and will not refuse to hear any and every tale of suffering which these unfortunates bring to me, I am anxious to spare both myself and them the pain of vain appeals to me for redress and help, which, alas! it is too often utterly out of my power to give them. It is useless, and indeed worse than useless, that they should see my impotent indignation and unavailing pity, and hear expressions of compassion for them, and horror at their condition, which might only prove incentives to a hopeless resistance on their part to a system, under the hideous weight of whose oppression any individual or partial revolt must be annihilated and ground into the dust. Therefore, as I tell you, I asked Psyche no questions, but, to my great astonishment, the other day M—— asked me if I knew to whom Psyche belonged, as the poor woman had enquired of her with much hesitation and anguish if she could tell her who owned her and her children. She has two nice little children under six years old, whom she keeps as clean and tidy, and who are sad and as silent, as herself. My astonishment at this question was, as you will readily believe, not small, and I forthwith sought out Psyche for an explanation. She was thrown into extreme perturbation at finding that her question had been referred to me, and it was some time before I could sufficiently reassure her to be able to comprehend, in the midst of her reiterated entreaties for pardon, and hopes that she had not offended me, that she did not know herself who owned her. She was, at one time, the property of Mr. K——, the former overseer, of whom I have already spoken to you, and who has just been paying Mr.—— a visit. He, like several of his predecessors in the management, has contrived to make a fortune upon it (though it yearly decreases in value to the owners, but this is the inevitable course of things in the southern states), and has purchased a plantation of his own in Alabama, I believe, or one of the southwestern states. Whether she still belonged to Mr. K—— or not she did not know, and entreated me if she did to endeavour to persuade Mr.—— to buy her. Now, you must know that this poor woman is the wife of one of Mr. B——'s slaves, a fine, intelligent, active, excellent young man, whose whole family are among some of the very best specimens of character and capacity on the estate. I was so astonished at the (to me) extraordinary state of things revealed by poor Sack's petition, that I could only tell her that I had supposed all the negroes on the plantation were Mr.——'s property, but that I would certainly enquire, and find out for her if I could to whom she belonged, and if I could, endeavour to get Mr.—— to purchase her, if she really was not his.

Now, E——, just conceive for one moment the state of mind of this woman, believing herself to belong to a man who, in a few days, was going down to one of those abhorred and dreaded south-western states, and who would then compel her, with her poor little children, to leave her husband and the only home she had ever known, and all the ties of affection, relationship, and association of her former life, to follow him thither, in all human probability never again to behold any living creature that she had seen before; and this was so completely a matter of course that it was not even thought necessary to apprise her positively of the fact, and the only thing that interposed between her and this most miserable fate was the faint hope that Mr.—— *might have* purchased her and her children. But if he had, if this great deliverance had been vouchsafed to her, the knowledge of it was not thought necessary; and with this deadly dread at her heart she was living day after day, waiting upon me and seeing me, with my husband beside me, and my children in my arms in blessed security, safe from all separation but the one reserved in God's great providence for all His creatures. Do you think I wondered any more at the woe-begone expression of her countenance, or do you think it was easy for me to restrain within prudent and proper limits the expression of my feelings at such a state of things? And she had gone on from day to day enduring this agony, till I suppose its own intolerable pressure and M——'s sweet countenance and gentle sympathising voice and manner had constrained her to lay down this great burden of sorrow at our feet. I did not see Mr.—— until the evening; but in the meantime, meeting Mr. O——, the overseer, with whom, as I believe I have already told you, we are living here, I asked him about Psyche, and who was her proprietor, when to my infinite surprise he told me that *he* had bought her and her children from Mr. K——, who had offered them to him, saying that they would be rather troublesome to him than otherwise down where he was going; 'and so,' said Mr. O——, 'as I had no objection to investing a little money that way, I bought them.' With a heart much lightened I flew to tell poor Psyche the news, so that at any rate she might be relieved from the dread of any immediate separation from her husband. You can imagine better than I can tell you what her sensations were; but she still renewed her prayer that I would, if possible, induce Mr.—— to purchase her, and I promised to do so.

Early the next morning, while I was still dressing, I was suddenly startled by hearing voices in loud tones in Mr.——'s dressing-room, which adjoins my bedroom, and the noise increasing until there was an absolute cry of despair uttered by some man. I could restrain myself no longer, but opened the door of communication, and saw Joe, the young man, poor Psyche's husband, raving almost in a state of frenzy, and in a voice broken with sobs and almost inarticulate with passion, reiterating his determination never to leave this plantation, never to go to Alabama, never to leave his old father and mother, his poor wife and children, and dashing his hat, which he was wringing like a cloth in his hands, upon the ground, he declared he would kill himself if he was compelled to follow Mr. K——. I glanced from the poor wretch to Mr.——, who was standing, leaning against a table with his arms folded, occasionally uttering a few words of counsel to his slave to be quiet and not fret, and not make a fuss about what there was no help for. I retreated immediately from the horrid scene, breathless with surprise and dismay, and stood for some time in my own room, with my heart and temples throbbing to such a degree that I could hardly support myself. As soon as I recovered myself I again sought Mr. O—— , and enquired of him if he knew the cause of poor Joe's distress. He then told me that Mr.——, who is highly pleased with Mr. K——'s past administration of his property, wished, on his departure for his newly-acquired slave plantation, to give him some token of his satisfaction, and *had made him a present* of the man Joe, who had just received the intelligence that he was to go down to

Alabama with his new owner the next day, leaving father, mother, wife, and children behind. You will not wonder that the man required a little judicious soothing, under such circumstances, and you will also, I hope, admire the humanity of the sale of his wife and children by the owner who was going to take him to Alabama, because *they* would be incumbrances rather than otherwise down there. If Mr. K—— did not do this after he knew that the man was his, then Mr.—— gave him to be carried down to the South after his wife and children were sold to remain in Georgia. I do not know which was the real transaction, for I have not had the heart to ask; but you will easily imagine which of the two cases I prefer believing.

When I saw Mr.—— after this most wretched story became known to me in all its details, I appealed to him for his own soul's sake not to commit so great a cruelty. Poor Joe's agony while remonstrating with his master was hardly greater than mine while arguing with him upon this bitter piece of inhumanity – how I cried, and how I adjured, and how all my sense of justice and of mercy and of pity for the poor wretch, and of wretchedness at finding myself implicated in such a state of things, broke in torrents of words from my lips and tears from my eyes! God knows such a sorrow at seeing anyone I belonged to commit such an act was indeed a new and terrible experience to me, and it seemed to me that I was imploring Mr.—— to save himself, more than to spare these wretches. He gave me no answer whatever, and I have since thought that the intemperate vehemence of my entreaties and expostulations perhaps deserved that he should leave me as he did without one single word of reply; and miserable enough I remained. Towards evening, as I was sitting alone, my children having gone to bed, Mr. O—— came into the room. I had but one subject in my mind; I had not been able to eat for it. I could hardly sit still for the nervous distress which every thought of these poor people filled me with. As he sat down looking over some accounts, I said to him, 'Have you seen Joe this afternoon, Mr. O——?' (I give you our conversation as it took place.) 'Yes, ma'am; he is a great deal happier than he was this morning.' 'Why, how is that?' asked I eagerly. 'Oh, he is not going to Alabama. Mr. K—— heard that he had kicked up a fuss about it (being in despair at being torn from one's wife and children is called *kicking up a fuss*; this is a sample of overseer appreciation of human feelings), and said that if the fellow wasn't willing to go with him, he did not wish to be bothered with any niggers down there who were to be troublesome, so he might stay behind.' 'And does Psyche know this?' 'Yes, ma'am, I suppose so.' I drew a long breath; and whereas my needle had stumbled through the stuff I was sewing for an hour before, as if my fingers could not guide it, the regularity and rapidity of its evolutions were now quite edifying. The man was for the present safe, and I remained silently pondering his deliverance and the whole proceeding, and the conduct of everyone engaged in it, and above all Mr,——'s share in the transaction, and I think for the first time almost a sense of horrible personal responsibility and implication took hold of my mind, and I felt the weight of an unimagined guilt upon my conscience; and yet God knows this feeling of self-condemnation is very gratuitous on my part, since when I married Mr.—— I knew nothing of these dreadful possessions of his, and even if I had, I should have been much puzzled to have formed any idea of the state of things in which I now find myself plunged, together with those whose well-doing is as vital to me almost as my own.

With these agreeable reflections I went to bed. Mr.—— said not a word to me upon the subject of these poor people all the next day, and in the meantime I became very impatient of this reserve on his part, because I was dying to prefer my request that he would purchase Pysche and her children, and so prevent any future separation between her and her husband, as I supposed he would not again attempt to make a present of Joe, at least to anyone who did not wish to be *bothered* with his wife and children. In the evening I was again with Mr. O—— alone in the strange bare wooden-walled sort of shanty which is our sitting-room, and revolving in my mind the means of rescuing Psyche from her miserable suspense, a long chain of all my possessions, in the shape of bracelets, necklaces, brooches, ear-rings, &c., wound in glittering procession through my brain, with many hypo-thetical calculations of the value of each separate ornament, and the very doubtful probability of the amount of the whole being equal to the price of this poor creature and her children; and then the great power and privilege I had foregone of earning money by my own labour occurred to me; and I think, for the first time in my life, my past profession assumed an aspect that arrested my thoughts most seriously. For the last four years of my life that preceded my marriage, I literally coined money; and never until this moment, I think, did I reflect on the great means of good, to myself and others, that I so gladly agreed to give up for ever, for a maintenance by the unpaid labour of slaves – people toiling not only unpaid, but under the bitter conditions the bare contemplation of which was then wringing my heart. You will not wonder that, when in the midst of such cogitations I suddenly accosted Mr. O——, it was to this effect. 'Mr. O——, I have a par-ticular favour to beg of you. Promise me that you will never sell Psyche and her children without first letting me know of your intention to do so, and giving me the option of buying them.' Mr. O—— is a remarkably deliberate man, and squints, so that, when he has taken a little time in directing his eyes to you, you are still unpleasantly unaware of any result in which you are concerned; he laid down a book he was reading, and directed his head and one of his eyes towards me and answered, 'Dear me, ma'am, I am very sorry – I have sold them.' My work fell down on the ground, and my mouth opened wide, but I could utter no sound, I was so dismayed and surprised; and he deliberately proceeded: 'I didn't know, ma'am, you see, at all, that you entertained any idea of making an investment of that nature; for I'm sure, if I had, I would willingly have sold the woman to you; but I sold her and her children this morning to Mr.——.' My dear E——, though —— had resented my unmeasured upbraidings, you see they had not been without some good effect, and though he had, perhaps justly, punished my violent outbreak of indignation about the miserable scene I witnessed by not telling me of his humane purpose, he had bought these poor creatures, and so, I trust, secured them from any such misery in future. I jumped up and left Mr. O—— still speaking, and ran to find Mr.——, to thank him for what he had done, and with that will now bid you good bye. Think, E——, how it fares with slaves on plantations where there is no crazy Englishwoman to weep and entreat and implore and upbraid for them, and no master willing to listen to such appeals.

❀ ❀ ❀ ❀

I had my usual evening reception, and, among other pleasant incidents of plantation life, heard the following agreeable anecdote from a woman named Sophy, who came to beg for some rice. In asking her about her husband and children, she said she had never had any husband, that she had had two children by a white man of the name of Walker, who was employed at the mill on the rice island; she was in the hospital after the birth of the second child she bore this man, and at the same time two women, Judy and Sylla, of whose children Mr. K—— was the father, were recovering from their confinements. It was not a month since any of them had been delivered, when Mrs. K—— came to the hospital, had them all three severely flogged, a process which *she* personally superintended, and then sent them to Five Pound – the swamp Botany Bay of the plantation, of which I have told you – with further orders to the drivers to flog them every day for a week. Now, E——, if I make you sick with these disgusting stories, I cannot help it – they are the life itself here; hitherto I have thought these details intolerable enough, but this apparition of a female fiend in the middle of this hell I confess adds an element of cruelty which seems to me to surpass all the rest. Jealousy is not an uncommon quality in the feminine temperament; and just conceive the fate of these unfortunate women between the passions of their masters and mistresses, each alike armed with power to oppress and torture them. Sophy went on to say that

Isaac was her son by driver Morris, who had forced her while she was in her miserable exile at Five Pound. Almost beyond my patience with this string of detestable details, I exclaimed – foolishly enough, heaven knows – 'Ah, but don't you know, did nobody ever tell or teach any of you, that it is a sin to live with men who are not your husbands?' Alas, E——, what could the poor creature answer but what she did, seizing me at the same time vehemently by the wrist: 'Oh yes, missis, we know – we know all about dat well enough; but we do anything to get our poor flesh some rest from de whip; when he made me follow him into de bush, what use me tell him no? he have strength to make me.' I have written down the woman's words; I wish I could write down the voice and look of abject misery with which they were spoken. Now, you will observe that the story was not told to me as a complaint; it was a thing long past and over, of which she only spoke in the natural course of accounting for her children to me. I make no comment; what need, or can I add, to such stories? But how is such a state of things to endure? – and again, how is it to end? While I was pondering, as it seemed to me, at the very bottom of the Slough of Despond, on this miserable creature's story, another woman came in (Tema), carrying in her arms a child the image of the mulatto Bran; she came to beg for flannel. I asked her who was her husband. She said she was not married. Her child is the child of bricklayer Temple, who has a wife at the rice island By this time, what do you think of the moralities, as well as the amenities, of slave life? These are the conditions which can only be known to one who lives among them; flagrant acts of cruelty may be rare, but this ineffable state of utter degradation, this really *beastly* existence, is the normal condition of these men and women, and of that no one seems to take heed, nor have I ever heard it described so as to form any adequate conception of it, till I found myself plunged into it; – where and how is one to begin the cleansing of this horrid pestilential immondezzio of an existence? . . .

I must tell you that I have been delighted, surprised, and the very least perplexed, by the sudden petition on the part of our young waiter, Aleck, that I will teach him to read. He is a very intelligent lad of about sixteen, and preferred his request with an urgent humility that was very touching. I told him I would think about it. I mean to do it. I will do it, – and yet, it is simply breaking the laws of the government under which I am living. Unrighteous laws are made to be broken, – *perhaps*, – but then, you see, I am a woman, and Mr.—— stands between me and the penalty. If I were a man, I would do that and many a thing besides, and doubtless should be shot some fine day from behind a tree by some good neighbour, who would do the community a service by quietly getting rid of a mischievous incendiary; and I promise you in such a case no questions would be asked, and my lessons would come to a speedy and silent end; but teaching slaves to read is a fineable offence, and I am *femme couverte*, and my fines must be paid by my legal owner, and the first offence of the sort is heavily fined, and the second more heavily fined, and for the third, one is sent to prison.

44. Frances Anne Kemble
On the Stage

THINGS dramatic and things theatrical are often confounded together in the minds of English people, who, being for the most part neither the one nor the other, speak and write of them as if they were identical, instead of, as they are, so dissimilar that they are nearly opposite.

That which is dramatic in human nature is the passionate emotional humorous element, the simplest portion of our composition, after our mere instincts, to which it is closely allied, and this has no relation whatever, beyond its momentary excitement and gratification, to that which imitates it, and is its theatrical reproduction; the dramatic is the *real*, of which the theatrical is the *false*.

Both nations and individuals in whom the dramatic temperament strongly preponderates are rather remarkable for a certain vivid simplicity of nature, which produces sincerity and vehemence of emotion and expression, but is entirely without the *consciousness* which is never absent from the theatrical element.

Children are always dramatic, but only theatrical when they become aware that they are objects of admiring attention; in which case the assuming and dissembling capacity of *acting* develops itself comically and sadly enough in them.

The Italians, nationally and individually, are dramatic; the French, on the contrary, theatrical; we English of the present day are neither the one nor the other, though our possession of the noblest dramatic literature in the world proves how deeply at one time our national character was imbued with elements which are now so latent as almost to be of doubtful existence; while, on the other hand, our American progeny are, as a nation, devoid of the dramatic element, and have a considerable infusion of that which is theatrical, delighting, like the Athenians of old, in processions, shows, speeches, oratory, demonstrations, celebrations, and declarations, and such displays of public and private sentiment as would be repugnant to English taste and feeling; to which theatrical tendency, and the morbid love of excitement which is akin to it, I attribute the fact that Americans, both nationally and individually, are capable of a certain sympathy with the French character, in which we are wanting.

The combination of the power of representing passion and emotion with that of imagining or conceiving it, that is, of the theatrical talent with the dramatic temperament, is essential to make a good actor; their combination in the highest possible degree alone makes a great one.

There is a specific comprehension of effect and the means of producing it which, in some persons, is a distinct capacity, and this forms what actors call the study of their profession; and in this, which is the alloy necessary to make theatrical that which is only dramatic, lies the heart of their mystery and the snare of their craft in more ways than one: and this, the actor's *business*, goes sometimes absolutely against the dramatic temperament, which is nevertheless essential to it.

Every day lessens the frequency of this specific combination among ourselves, for the dramatic temperament, always exceptional in England, is becoming daily more so under the various adverse influences of a state of civilization and society which fosters a genuine dislike to exhibitions of emotion, and a cynical disbelief in the reality of it, both necessarily repressing, first, its expression, and next, its existence. On the other hand, greater intellectual cultivation and a purer and more elevated taste are unfavourable to the existence of the true theatrical spirit; and English actors of the present day are of the public, by being "nothing if not critical," and are not of their craft, having literally ceased to know "what belongs to a frippery." They have lost for the most part alike the dramatic emotional temperament and the scenic science of mere effect, and our stage is and must be supplied, if supplied at all, by persons less sophisticated and less civilized. The plays brought out and revived at our theatres of late years bear doleful witness to this. We have in them archæology, ethnology, history, geography, botany (even to the curiosity of ascertaining the Danish wild-flowers that Ophelia might twist with her mad straws), and upholstery; everything, in short, but acting, which it seems we cannot have.

When Mrs. Siddons, in her spectacles and mob-cap, read *Macbeth* or *King John*, it was one of the grandest dramatic achievements that could be imagined, with the least possible admixture of the theatrical element; the representation of the *Duke's Motto*, with all its resources of scenic effect, is a striking and interesting theatrical entertainment, with hardly an admixture of that which is truly dramatic.

Garrick was, I suppose, the most perfect actor that our stage has ever produced, equalling in tragedy and comedy the greatest performers of both; but while his dramatic organization enabled him to represent with exquisite power and pathos the principal characters of Shakespeare's noblest plays, his theatrical taste induced him to garble, desecrate, and disfigure the masterpieces of which he was so fine an interpreter, in order to produce or enhance those peculiar effects which constitute the chief merit and principal attraction of all theatrical exhibitions.

Mrs. Siddons could lay no claim to versatility – it was not in her nature; she was without mobility of mind, countenance, or manner; and her dramatic organization was in that respect inferior to Garrick's; but out of a family of twenty-eight persons, all of whom made the stage their vocation, she alone pre-eminently combined the qualities requisite to make a great theatrical performer in the highest degree.

Another member of that family – a foreigner by birth, and endowed with the most powerful and vivid dramatic organization – possessed in so small a degree the faculty of the stage, that the parts which she represented successfully were few in number, and though among them there were some dramatic *creations* of extraordinary originality and beauty, she never rose to the highest rank in her profession, nor could claim in any sense the title of a great theatrical artist. – This was my mother. And I suppose no member of that large histrionic family was endowed to the same degree with the natural dramatic temperament. The truth of her intonation, accent, and emphasis, made her common speech as good as a play to hear, (oh, how much better than some we *do* hear!) and whereas I have seen the Shakespeare of my father, and the Shakespeare and Milton of Mrs. Siddons, with every emphatic word underlined and accentuated, lest they should omit the right inflection in delivering the lines, my mother could no more have needed such notes whereby to speak *true* than she would a candle to have walked by at noonday. She was an incomparable critic; and though the intrepid sincerity of her nature made her strictures sometimes more accurate than acceptable, they were inestimable for the fine tact for truth, which made her instinctively reject in nature and art whatever sinned against it.

I do not know whether I shall be considered competent to pass a judgement on myself in this matter, but I think I am. Inheriting from my father a theatrical descent of two generations and my mother's vivid and versatile organization, the stage itself, though it became from the force of circumstances my career, was, partly from my nature and partly from my education, so repugnant to me, that I failed to accomplish any result at all worthy of my many advantages. I imagine I disappointed alike those who did and those who did not think me endowed with the talent of my family, and incurred, towards the very close of my theatrical career, the severe verdict from one of the masters of the stage of the present day, that I was "ignorant of the first rudiments of my profession."

In my father and mother I have had frequent opportunities of observing in most marked contrast the rapid intuitive perception of the dramatic instinct in an organization where it preponderated, and the laborious process of logical argument by which the same result, on a given question, was reached by a mind of different constitution (my father's), and reached with much doubt and hesitation, caused by the very application of analytical reasoning. The slow mental process *might* with time have achieved a right result in all such cases; but the dramatic instinct, aided by a fine organization, was unerring; and this leads me to observe, that there is no reason whatever to expect that fine actors shall be necessarily profound commentators on the parts that they sustain most successfully, but rather the contrary.

I trust I shall not be found wanting in due respect for the greatness that is gone from us, if I say that Mrs. Siddons' analysis of the part of "Lady Macbeth" was to be found *alone* in her representation of it – of the magnificence of which the "essay" she has left upon the character gives not the faintest idea.

If that great actress had possessed the order of mind capable of conceiving and producing a philosophical analysis of any of the wonderful poetical creations which she so wonderfully embodied, she would surely never have been able to embody them as she did. For to whom are all things given? and to whom were ever given, in such abundant measure, consenting and harmonious endowments of mind and body for the peculiar labour of her life?

The dramatic faculty, as I have said, lies in a power of apprehension quicker than the disintegrating process of critical analysis, and when it is powerful, and the organization fine, as with Mrs. Siddons, perception rather than reflection reaches the aim proposed; and the persons endowed with this specific gift will hardly unite with it the mental qualifications of philosophers and metaphysicians; no better proof of which can be adduced than Mrs. Siddons herself, whose performances were, in the strict sense of the word, excellent, while the two treatises she has left upon the characters of "Queen Constance" and "Lady Macbeth" – two of her finest parts – are feeble and superficial. Kean, who possessed, beyond all actors whom I have seen, tragic inspiration, could very hardly, I should think, have given a satisfactory reason for any one of the great effects which he produced. Of Mdlle. Rachel, whose impersonations fulfilled to me the idea of perfect works of art of their kind, I have heard, from one who knew her well, that her intellectual processes were limited to the consideration of the most purely mechanical part of her vocation; and Pasta, the great lyric tragedian, who, Mrs. Siddons said, was capable of giving her lessons, replied to the observation, "Vous avez dû beaucoup étudier l'antique," "Je l'ai beaucoup senti." The reflective and analytical quality has little to do with the complex process of acting, and is alike remote from what is dramatic and what is theatrical.

There is something anomalous in that which we call the dramatic art that has often arrested my attention and exercised my thoughts; the special gift and sole industry of so many of my kindred, and the only labour of my own life, it has been a subject of constant and curious speculation with me, combining as it does elements at once so congenial and so antagonistic to my nature.

Its most original process, that is, the conception of the character to be represented, is a mere reception of the creation of another mind – and its mechanical part, that is, the representation of the character thus apprehended, has no reference to the intrinsic, poetical, or dramatic merit of the original creation, but merely to the accuracy and power of the actor's perception of it; thus the character of "Lady Macbeth" is as majestic, awful, and poetical, whether it be worthily filled by its pre-eminent representative, Mrs. Siddons, or unworthily by the most incompetent of ignorant provincial tragedy queens.

This same dramatic art has neither fixed rules, specific principles, indispensable rudiments, nor fundamental laws; it has no basis in positive science, as music, painting, sculpture, and architecture have; and differs from them all, in that the mere appearance of spontaneity, which is an acknowledged assumption, is its chief merit. And yet –

> This younger of the sister arts,
> Where all their charms combine –

requires in its professors the imagination of the poet, the ear of the musician, the eye of the painter and sculptor, and over and above these a faculty peculiar to itself, inasmuch as the actor personally fulfils and embodies his conception; his own voice is his cunningly modulated instrument; his own face the canvas whereon he portrays the various expressions of his passion; his own frame the mould in which he casts the images of beauty and majesty that fill his brain; and whereas the painter and sculptor may select, of all possible attitudes, occupations, and expressions, the most favourable to the beautiful effect they desire to produce, and fix, and bid it so remain fixed for ever, the actor must live and move through a temporary existence of poetry and passion, and preserve throughout its duration that ideal grace and dignity, of which the canvas and the marble give but a silent and motionless image. And yet it is an art that requires no study worthy of the name: it creates nothing – it perpetuates nothing; to its professors, whose personal qualifications form half their merit, is justly given the need of personal admiration, and the reward of contemporaneous popularity is well bestowed on those whose labour consists in exciting momentary emotion. Their most persevering and successful efforts can only benefit, by a passionate pleasure of at most a few years' duration, the play-going public of their own immediate day, and they are fitly recompensed with money and applause, to whom may not justly belong the rapture of creation, the glory of patient and protracted toil, and the love and honour of grateful posterity.

———

1864

45. Margaret Oliphant
from *Autobiography*

I did not know when I wrote the last words that I was coming to lay my sweetest hope, my brightest anticipations for the future, with my darling, in her father's grave. Oh this terrible, fatal, miserable Rome! I came here rich and happy, with my blooming daughter, my dear bright child, whose smiles and brightness everybody noticed, and who was sweet as a little mother to her brothers. There was not an omen of evil in any way. Our leaving of home, our journey, our life here, have all been among the brightest passages of my life; and my Maggie looked the healthiest and happiest of all the children, and ailed nothing and feared nothing, – nor I for her.

Four short days made all the difference, and now here I am with my boys thrown back again out of the light into the darkness, into the valley of the shadow of death. My dearest love never knew nor imagined that she was dying; no shadow of dread ever came upon her sweet spirit. She got into heaven without knowing it, and God have pity upon me, who have thus parted with the sweetest companion, on whom unconsciously, more than on any other hope of life, I have been calculating. I feared from the first moment her illness began, and yet I had a kind of underlying conviction that God would not take my ewe-lamb, my woman-child from me.

The hardest moment in my present sad life is the morning, when I must wake up and begin the dreary world again. I can sleep during the night, and I sleep as long as I can; but when it is no longer possible, when the light can no longer be gainsaid, and life is going on everywhere, then I, too, rise up to bear my burden. How different it used to be ! When I was a girl I remember the feeling I had when the fresh morning light came round. Whatever grief there had been the night before, the new day triumphed over it. Things must be better than one thought, must be well, in a world which woke up to that new light, to the sweet dews and sweet air which renewed one's soul. Now I am thankful for the night and the darkness, and shudder to see the light and the day returning.

The Principal calls "In Memorian" an embodiment of the spirit of this age, which he says does not know what to think, yet thinks and wonders and stops itself, and thinks again; which believes and does not believe, and *perhaps*, I think, carries the human yearning and longing farther than it was ever carried before. Perhaps my own thoughts are much of the same kind. I try to realise heaven to myself, and I cannot do it. The more I think of it, the less I am able to feel that those who have left us can start up at once into a heartless beatitude without caring for our sorrow. Do they sleep until the great day? Or does time so cease for them that it seems but a matter of hours and minutes till we meet again? God who is Love cannot give immortality and annihilate affection; that surely, at least, we must take for granted – as sure as they live they live to love us. Human nature in the flesh cannot be more faithful, more tender, than the purified human soul in heaven. Where, then, are they, those who have gone before us? Some people say around us, still knowing all that occupies us; but that is an idea I cannot entertain either. It would not be happiness but pain to be beside those we love yet unable to communicate with them, unable to make ourselves known.

❀ ❀ ❀ ❀

The world is changed, and my life is darkened; and all that I can do is to take desperate hold of this one certainty, that God cannot have done it without reason.

1867

46. Ellen Johnston
from *Autobiography*

[M]y father was James Johnston, second eldest son of James Johnston, canvas-weaver, Lochee, Dundee, where he learned the trade of a stone-mason. After which he removed to Glasgow, where he became acquainted with my mother, Mary Bilsland, second daughter of James Bilsland, residing in Muslin Street, and then well known as the Bridgeton Dyer.

I do not remember hearing my father's age, but my mother at the time of her marriage was only eighteen years old. I was the first and only child of their union, and was born in the Muir Wynd, Hamilton, in 183–, my father at the time being employed as a mason extending the northern wing of the Duke of Hamilton's Palace.

When the Duke was informed that my father was a poet, he familiarly used to call him Lord Byron, and, as I have been told, his Grace also used to take special notice of me when an infant in my mother's arms, as she almost daily walked around his domain.

When I was about seven months old my father's contract at Hamilton Palace was finished, and being of an active disposition, somewhat ambitious, proud, and independent, with some literary and scientific attainments, with a strong desire to become a teacher and publish a volume of his poet-ical works, he resolved to emigrate, engaged a passage to America for my mother and himself, and got all things ready for the voyage.

But when all the relatives and friends had assembled at the Broomielaw to give the farewell kiss and shake of the hand before going on board, my mother determined not to proceed, pressed me fondly to her bosom, exclaiming – 'I cannot, will not go, my child would die on the way ;' and taking an affectionate farewell with my father, he proceeded on the voyage, and my mother fled from the scene and returned to her father's house, where she remained for some years, and supported herself by dressmaking and millinery.

✷ ✷ ✷ ✷

In the course of time my mother received some information of my father's death in America, and again married a power-loom tenter when I was about eight years of age, till which time I may truly say that the only heart-felt sorrow I experienced was the loss of 'Dainty Davie', but, alas! shortly after my mother's second marriage I was dragged, against my own will and the earnest pleadings and remonstrance of my maternal grandfather, from his then happy home to my stepfather's abode, next land to the Cross Keys Tavern, London Road.

HOW I BECAME THE FACTORY GIRL.

About two months after my mother's marriage my stepfather having got work in a factory in Bishop Street, Anderston, they removed to North Street, where I spent the two last years of young life's sweet liberty – as it was during that time I found my way to Kelvin Grove, and there spent many happy hours in innocent mirth and glee – but 'time changes a' things.' My stepfather could not bear to see me longer basking in the sunshine of freedom, and therefore took me into the factory where he worked to learn power-loom weaving when about eleven years of age, from which time I became a factory girl; but no language can paint the suffering which I afterwards endured from my tormentor. . . .

Before I was thirteen years of age I had read many of Sir Walter Scott's novels, and fancied I was a heroine of the modern style. I was a self-taught scholar, gifted with a considerable amount of natural knowledge for one of my years, for I had only been nine months at school when I could read the English language and Scottish dialect with almost any classic scholar; I had also read 'Wilson's Tales of the Border;' so that by reading so many love adventures my brain was fired with wild imaginations, and therefore resolved to bear with my own fate, and in the end gain a great victory. . . .

By this time my mother had removed from Anderston to a shop in Tradeston, and my stepfather and myself worked in West Street Factory. When one morning early, in the month of June, I absconded from their house as the fox flies from the hunters' hounds, to the Paisley Canal, into which I was about submerging myself to end my sufferings and sorrow, when I thought I heard like the voice of him I had fixed my girlish love upon. I started and paused for a few moments, and the love of young life again prevailed over that of self-destruction, and I fled from the scene as the half-past five morning factory bells were ringing, towards the house of a poor woman in Rose Street, Hutchesontown, where, after giving her my beautiful earrings to pawn, I was made welcome, and on Monday morning following got work in Brown & M'Nee's factory, Commercial Road. I did not, however, remain long in my new lodgings, for on the Tuesday evening, while threading my way among the crowd at the shows, near the foot of Saltmarket, and busy dreaming of the time when I would be an actress, I was laid hold of by my mother's eldest brother, who after questioning me as to where I had been, and what I was doing, without receiving any satisfaction to his interrogations, compelled me to go with him to my mother, who first questioned me as to the cause of absconding, and then beat me till I felt as if my brain were on fire; but still I kept the secret in my own bosom. But had I only foreseen the wretched misery I was heaping upon my own head – had I heard the dreadful constructions the world was putting on my movements – had I seen the shroud of shame and sorrow I was weaving around myself, I should then have disclosed the mystery of my life, but I remained silent and kept my mother and friends in ignorance of the cause which first disturbed my peace and made me run away from her house for safety and protection.

However, I consented to stay again with my mother for a time, and resolved to avoid my tormentor as much as possible.

❄ ❄ ❄ ❄

Dear reader, should your curiosity have been awakened to ask in what form fate had then so hardly dealt with the hapless 'Factory Girl,' this is my answer: – I was falsely accused by those who knew me as a fallen woman, while I was as innocent of the charge as the unborn babe. Oh! how hard to be blamed when the heart is spotless and the conscience clear. For years I submitted to this wrong, resolving to hold my false detractors at defiance.

While struggling under those misrepresentations, my first love also deserted me, but another soon after offered me his heart – without the form of legal protection – and in a thoughtless moment I accepted him as my friend and protector, but, to use the words of a departed poet –

> When lovely woman stoops to folly,
> And finds too late that men betray,
> What can sooth her melancholy,
> What can wash her guilt away?
>
> The only art her guilt to cover,
> To hide her shame from every eye,
> To wring repentance from her lover,
> And sting his bosom, is to die.'

I did not, however, feel inclined to die when I could no longer conceal what the world falsely calls a woman's shame. No, on the other hand, I never loved life more dearly and longed for the hour when I would have something to love me – and my wish was realised by becoming the mother of a lovely daughter on the 14th of September, 1852.

No doubt every feeling mother thinks her own child lovely, but mine was surpassing so, and I felt as if I could begin all my past sorrows again if

Heaven would only spare me my lovely babe to cheer my bleeding heart, for I never felt bound to earth till then; and as year succeeded year, 'My Mary Achin' grew like the wild daisy – fresh and fair – on the mountain side.

As my circumstances in life changed, I placed my daughter under my mother's care when duty called me forth to turn the poetic gift that nature had given me to a useful and profitable account, for which purpose I commenced with vigorous zeal to write my poetical pieces, and sent them to the weekly newspapers for insertion, until I became extensively known and popular. As an instance, in 1854 the Glasgow Examiner published a song of mine, entitled 'Lord Raglan's Address to the Allied Armies,' which made my name popular throughout Great Britain and Ireland; but as my fame spread my health began to fail, so that I could not work any longer in a factory.

My stepfather was unable longer to work, and my mother was also rendered a suffering object; my child was then but an infant under three years of age, and I, who had been the only support of the family, was informed by my medical adviser that, unless I took a change of air, I would not live three months.

❈ ❈ ❈ ❈

New scenes and systems made a great change in my natures. I became cheerful, and sought the society of mirthmakers, so that few would have taken me for the former moving monument of melancholy. I had again resumed work at Galbraith's factory, and all went on well. 'My bonnie Mary Auchinvole' was growing prettier every day and I was growing strong; peace and good-will reigned in our household, the past seemed forgiven and forgotten, and the 'Factory Girl' was a topic of the day for her poetical productions in the public press, but the shadow of death was hovering behind all this gladsome sunshine.

My mother had been an invalid for several years, and, to add to her sorrow, a letter had come from her supposed dead husband, my father, in America, after an absence of twenty years, inquiring for his wife and child; on learning their fate he became maddened with remorse, and, according to report, drank a death-draught from a cup in his own hand; and my mother, after becoming aware of the mystery of my life, closed her weary pilgrimage on earth on 25th May, 1861. Thus I was left without a friend, and disappointed of a future promised home and pleasure which I was not destined to enjoy, I therefore made up my mind to go to Dundee, where my father's sister resided, whose favourite I was when a child.

❈ ❈ ❈ ❈

[P]eace and pleasure [were] restored to my bosom again, by obtaining work at the Chapelshade Factory, at the east end of Dundee, where I have been working for the last three years and a-half to a true friend. I had not been long in my present situation when I fortunately became a reader of the 'Penny Post,' and shortly afterwards contributed some pieces to the 'Poet's Corner,' which seemed to cast a mystic spell over many of its readers whose numerous letters reached me from various districts, highly applauding my contributions, and offering me their sympathy, friendship, and love; while others, inspired by the muses, responded to me through the same popular medium some of whose productions will be found, along with my own in the present volume.

47. Ellen Johnston
A Mother's Love

I love thee, I love thee, and life will depart
Ere thy mother forgets thee, sweet child of her heart;
Yea, death's shadow only my memory can dim,
For thou'rt dearer than life to me – Mary Achin.

I love thee, I love thee, and six years hath now fled
Since first on my bosom I pillow'd thy head;
Since I first did behold thee in sorrow and sin
Thou sweet offspring of false love – my Mary Achin.

I love thee, I love thee, and twelve months hath now past,
My sweet child, since I gazed on thy fairy form last;
And our parting brought sorrow, known only to Him
Who can see through the heart's depths – my Mary Achin.

I love thee, I love thee, thy beauty and youth
Are spotless and pure as the fountain of truth;
Thou'rt my star in the night, till daybreak begin,
And my sunshine by noontide – my Mary Achin.

I love thee, I love thee, wherever I go
Thou'rt shrined in my bosom in joy or in woe
A murmuring music my fancy doth win,
'Tis the voice of my darling – Mary Achin.

I love thee, I love thee, is ever my lay,
I sing it by night and I sing it by day,
Its chorus swells forth like the stern patriot's hymn,
Thrice hallowed with visions of Mary Achin.

I love thee, I love thee, though now far away
Thour't nearer and dearer to me every day;
Would they give me a choice – a nation to win –
I would not exchange with my Mary Achin.

1868

48. Eliza Lynn Linton
from *La Femme Passée*

Without doubt it is a time of trial to all women, more or less painful according to individual disposition, when they first begin to grow old and lose their good looks. Youth and beauty make up so much of their personal value, so much of their natural *raison d'être*, that when these are gone many feel as if their whole career was at an end, and as if nothing was left to them now that they are no longer young enough to be loved as girls are loved, or pretty enough to be admired as once they were admired. For women of a certain position have so little wholesome occupation, and so little ambition for anything, save indeed that miserable thing called "getting on in society," that they cannot change their way of life with advancing years; they do not attempt to find interest in things outside themselves, and independent of the mere personal attractiveness which in youth constituted their whole pleasure of existence. This is essentially the case with fashionable women, who have staked their all on appearance, and to whom good looks are of more account than noble deeds; and, accordingly, the struggle to remain young is a frantic one with them, and as degrading as it is frantic. With the ideal woman of middle age – that pleasant woman, with her happy face and softened manner, who unites the charms of both epochs, retaining the ready responsiveness of youth while adding the wider sympathies of experience – with her there has never been any such struggle to make herself an anachronism. Consequently she remains beautiful to the last, far more beautiful than all the pastes and washes in Madame Rachel's shop could make her . . . What she has lost in outside material charm – in that mere *beauté du diable* of youth – she has gained in character and expression; and, not attempting to simulate the attractiveness of a girl, she keeps what nature gave her – the attractiveness of middle age. And as every epoch has its own beauty, if women would but learn that truth, she is as beautiful now as a matron of fifty, because in harmony with her years, and because her beauty has been carried on from matter to spirit, as she was when a maiden of sixteen. This is the ideal woman of middle age, met with even yet at times in society – the woman whom all men respect, whom all women envy, and wonder how she does it, and whom all the young adore, and wish they had for an elder sister or an aunt. And the secret of it all lies in truth, in love, in purity, and in unselfishness.

Standing far in front of this sweet and wholesome idealization is *la femme passée* of to-day – the reality as we meet with it at balls and fêtes and afternoon at homes, ever foremost in the mad chase after pleasure, for which alone she seems to think she has been sent into the world. Dressed in the extreme of youthful fashion, her thinning hair dyed and crimped and fired till it is more red-brown tow than hair, her flaccid cheeks ruddled, her throat whitened, her bust displayed with unflinching generosity, as if beauty was to be measured by cubic inches, her lustreless eyes blackened round the lids, to give the semblance of limpidity to the tarnished whites – perhaps the pupil dilated by belladonna, or perhaps a false and fatal brilliancy for the moment given by opium, or by eau de cologne, of which she has a store in her carriage, and drinks as she passes from ball to ball; no kindly drapery of lace or gauze to conceal the breadth of her robust maturity, or to soften the dreadful shadows of her leanness – there she stands, the wretched creature who will not consent to grow old, and who will still affect to be like a fresh coquettish girl when she is nothing but *la femme passée – la femme passée et ridicule* into the bargain. There is not a folly for which even the thoughtlessness of youth is but a poor excuse into which she, in all the plenitude of her abundant experience, does not plunge. Wife and mother as she may be, she flirts and makes love as if an honourable issue was as open to her as to her daughter, or as if she did not know to what end flirting and making love lead in all ages. If we watch the career of such a woman, we see how, by slow but very sure degrees, she is obliged to lower the standard of her adorers, and to take up at last with men of inferior social position, who are content to buy her patronage by their devotion. To the best men of her own class she can give nothing that they value; so she barters with snobs who go into the transaction with their eyes open, and take the whole affair as a matter of exchange, and *quid pro quo* rigidly exacted. Or she does really dazzle some very young and low-born man who is weak as well as ambitious, and who thinks the fugitive regard of a middle-aged woman of high rank something to be proud of and boasted about. That she is as old as his own mother – at this moment selling tapes behind a village counter or gathering up the eggs in a country farm – tells nothing against the association with him; and the woman who began her career of flirtation with the son of a duke ends it with the son of a shopkeeper, having between these two terms spanned all the several degrees of degradation which lie between giving and buying. She cannot help herself; for it is part of the insignia of her artificial youth to have the reputation of a love affair, or the pretence of one, if even the reality is a mere delusion. When such a woman as this is one of the matrons, and consequently one of the leaders in society, what can we expect from the girls? What worse example could be given to the young? . . .

What good in life does this kind of woman do? All her time is taken up, first in trying to make herself look twenty or thirty years younger than she is, and then in trying to make others believe the same; and she has neither thought nor energy to spare from this, to her, far more important work than is feeding the hungry or nursing the sick, rescuing the fallen or soothing the sorrowful.

—◆—

49. Josephine Butler
from *The Education and Employment of Women*

THE economical position of women is one of those subjects on which there exists a "conspiracy of silence." While most people, perhaps, imagine that nearly all women marry and are supported by their husbands, those who know better how women live, or die, have rarely anything to say on the subject. Such social problems as this are certainly painful; they may or may not be insoluble; they must not be ignored.

The phrase "to become a governess" is sometimes used as if it were a satisfactory outlet for any unsupported woman above the rank of housemaid. When we see advertisements in the newspapers, offering "a comfortable home," with no salary, as a sufficient reward for accomplishments of the most varied character, we sometimes wonder at the audacity of employers; but when we learn that such an advertisement, offering the situation of nursery governess, *unpaid*, was answered by *three hundred women*, our surprise has in it something of despair.

The truth is, that the facts of the society have changed more rapidly than its conventions. Formerly muscles did the business of the world, and the weak were protected by the strong; now brains do the business of the world, and the weak are protected by law. The industrial disabilities of women, unavoidable under the earlier *régime*, have become cruel under the later. There is neither the old necessity of shelter, nor the old certainty of support. . . .

In the first place . . . it appears that marriage, as a means of subsistence (to say nothing of the indecorum of looking forward to it in this light) is exceedingly precarious in two ways. The proportion of wives to widows and spinsters in 1861 was just about three to two, while of these wives themselves nearly one in four was occupied in other than domestic duties, either as her husband's coadjutor, as in farm-houses or shops, or, of necessity, as his substitute in cases of his desertion, or helplessness, or vice. In the second place, the number of widows and spinsters supporting themselves, which in 1851 was two millions, has increased in 1861 to more than two millions and a half. The rapidity of the increase of this class is painfully significant. Two and a half millions of Englishwomen without husbands, and working for their own subsistence! This is not an accident, it is a new order of things. Of the three and a half millions of women – wives, widows, and spinsters – engaged in other than domestic occupations, it is probable that scarcely a thousand make, without capital, and by their own exertions, one hundred pounds a year. The best paid are housekeepers in large establishments, a few finishing governesses, and professed cooks. 43,964 women are returned as outdoor agricultural labourers – a fact worthy of remembrance when it is said that women are too weak to serve in haberdashers' shops. Women, refused admission to such shops on the pretext that they are not strong enough to lift bales of goods, have been afterwards traced to the occupations of dock porters and coal-heavers. In practice the employments of women are not deterrnined by their lightness, but by their low pay. One newspaper still scoffs at the desire of women to be self-supporting: but starvation is a sufficient answer to sneers. As a favourable symptom of the last few years, I may add that 1,822 women are returned as employed by the Post-office. 213 women are returned as telegraph-clerks. It is instructive to note the way in which the salary of these women telegraph-clerks has fallen. When the telegraph companies were first formed, the pay of a female clerk was eight shillings a week, to be increased by a shilling yearly, until it reached fourteen shillings a week. So great, however, has been the competition of women for these situations, that the pay has been reduced to five shillings a week, a sum on which a woman can scarcely live unassisted. In France the women telegraph-clerks have met with a worse fate. The government took the management of the telegraphs, and dismissed the women, because they had no votes to bestow on the government candidates. The exclusion of women from the suffrage has been called a harmless injustice; but there is no injustice from which is not liable to become an injury.

At present the principal employments open to women are teaching, domestic service, and sewing. I come to consider the remuneration of the highest profession open to women.

In 1861 there were 80,017 female teachers in England, of whom the majority were governesses in private families. It is difficult to ascertain the average salary of governesses, because the Governesses' Institutions in London and Manchester, which are the chief sources of information on the subject, refuse to register the applications of governesses who accept salaries less than £25 a year. The number of this lowest class may be guessed from the fact that for a situation as nursery governess, with a salary of £20 a year, advertised in a newspaper, there were five hundred applicants; as I have already stated, three hundred applied for a similar place with no salary at all. To return to the higher class. The register of the last six months at the Manchester Governesses' Institution shows an entry of –

54 governesses who asked for £30 and under, per annum.
20   ″   ″   ″   ″ £40   ″   ″   ″   ″
19   ″   ″   ″   ″ £50   ″   ″   ″   ″
17   ″   ″   ″   ″ £60   ″   ″   ″   ″
10   ″   ″   ″   ″ £70 and upwards.

These sums, it must be remembered, are expressions of what governesses wish to receive. Taking nursery governesses into the account, and remembering that the above statistics refer only to the higher ranks of the profession, it is probably not too much to say that from 0 to £50 a year is the salary of nine governesses in ten. Situations offering more than £50 are the prizes of the profession, but are generally such as to compel a serious outlay on dress and personal expenditure. It is difficult to imagine how the majority of governesses manage to scramble through life, when we remember that their position involves several journeys in the year, that they must sometimes provide for themselves during holiday seasons, and that they must always dress as ladies. Miserable must be their means of providing of old age or sickness, to say nothing of the claims of affection or of charity throughout life, or the means required for self-culture.

Probably there are few portions of society in which more of silent suffering and misery is endured than among female teachers, and in the class which supplies them. Charitable people who have opened little "Homes" for decayed governesses can tell histories of struggling lives and crushed hopes which it saddens one to hear. The reports of Bethlehem Hospital and other lunatic asylums prove that not a few poor governesses find their way thither. Some are found in Penitentiaries among the fallen. Inquiry shows that insufficient food while out of situations, added to the mental trials of an unloved and isolated being, have driven some of these governesses to opium or to strong drink, until, penniless and degraded, they have sought a refuge among penitents where there was nothing to pay. "Her funds are exhausted, and she earnestly seeks a re-engagement", words such as these taken from an advertisement in *Times*, headed – "To the benevolent," are no unfrequent symptom of a deep and wide distress. Some determined women there are who have devoted to self-culture as much of their pittance as could be spared from the barest needs of life, and of whom it is known that, night after night when they went to bed, they have tied a band around their waist to keep down the gnawings of hunger. One such I know who has risen by her force of character to almost as high a place as it is at present possible for a *woman* to occupy in the educational world, but who is not yet free from the sufferings entailed by years of mental anxiety and bodily privations. An insufficiency of the necessaries of life is not the bitterest complaint of many of these sufferers, who by their lives protest that man does not live by bread alone. "Worse than the bodily privations or pains" (I quote the words of one of them) "are these *aches and pangs of ignorance*, this unquenched thirst for knowledge, these unassisted and disappointed efforts to obtain it, this sight of bread enough and to spare, but locked away from *us*, this depressing sense of a miserable waste of powers bestowed on us by God, and which we know we could have used for the lessening of evil and the increase of the happiness of our fellow-creatures."

The desire for education which is widely felt by English women, and which has begun to find its expression in many practical ways, is a desire which springs from no conceit of cleverness, from no ambition of the prizes of intellectual success, as is sometimes falsely imagined, but from the conviction that for many women to get knowledge is the only way to get bread, and still more from that instinctive craving for light which in many is stronger than the craving for bread. "Amongst the wealthier classes," – I give the words of one who has much knowledge of that of which she speaks – "women are better provided for materially, though even here they are often left to the mercy of the chances of life, indulged and petted whilst fortune smiles, left helpless to face the storm of adverse circumstances; but here, more often than elsewhere, one meets with those sad, dreary lives, that have always seemed to me amongst the worst permitted evils of earth, –

> A wall so blank
> My shadow I thank
> For sometimes falling there

is true of many a life. Even sharp misfortune is sometimes a blessing in a life of this sort; something to do, and leave to do it. I do not say that any possible education, any freedom of career, any higher training of faculty, would spare *all* this waste; some part of it is of that sad mystery of life which we cannot explain, and for the unveiling of which we can only wait and pray. But I am quite sure that much of it is altogether needless, and comes from the shutting up in artificial channels of those good gifts of God which are meant to flow forth freely and bless the world. If I could only tell, as I have felt in my own life, and in the lives of other women whom I have loved, how wearily one strains the eyes for light, which often comes not at all! . . .

For the amelioration of the condition of female teachers two things are necessary: the first is to raise the intellectual status of qualified teachers, and to accord a juster social recognition to their profession; the second is, to find other occupations for those who are unfit to teach, and only take to teaching because they can do nothing else.

❀ ❀ ❀ ❀

There are two classes of advocates of the improvement of the education and condition of women The one class urge everything from the domestic point of view. They argue in favour of all which is likely to make women better mothers, or better companions for men, but they seem incapable of judging of a woman as a human being by herself, and superstitiously afraid of anything which might strengthen her to stand alone, prepared, single-handed, to serve her God and her country. When it is urged upon them that the women who do and must stand alone are counted by millions, they are perplexed, but only fall back on expressions of a fear lest a masculine race of women should be produced, if we admit any theories respecting them apart from conjugal and maternal relationships.

On the other hand, there are advocates who speak with some slight contempt of maternity; in whose advocacy there appears to me little evidence of depth of thought, or tenderness, or wisdom, and which bespeaks a dry, hard, unimaginative conception of human life. They appear to have no higher ideal for a woman than that of a *man* who has been "tripos'ed," and is going to "get on in the world," either in the way of making money or acquiring fame. They speak of women as if it were a compliment to them, or in any way true, to say that they are like men. Now it appears to me that both these sets of advocates have failed to see something which is very true, and that their ears are deaf to some of the subtle harmonies which exist in God's creation – harmonies sometimes evolved from discords – and which we are much hindered from hearing by the noise of the world, and by our own discordant utterances.

The first class of advocates do not know how strong Nature is, how true she is for the most part, and how deeply the maternal character is rooted in almost all women, married or unmarried: they are not, therefore, likely to see that when a better education is secured to women, when permission is granted them not only to win bread for themselves, but to use for the good of society, every gift bestowed on them by God, we may expect to find, (as certainly we shall find,) that they will become the *more* and not the *less* womanly. Every good quality, every virtue which we regard as distinctively feminine, will, under conditions of greater freedom, develop more freely, like plants brought out into the light from a cellar in which they languished, dwarfed and blanched, without sun or air. The woman is strong in almost every woman; and it may be called an infidelity against God and against the truth of nature to suppose that the removal of unjust restrictions, and room given to breathe freely, and to do her work in life without depression and without bitterness, will cause her to cast off her nature. It will always be in her nature to foster, to cherish, to take the part of the weak, to train, to guide, to have a care for individuals, to discern the small seeds of a great future, to warm and cherish those seeds into fulness of life. "I serve," will always be one of her favourite mottos, even should the utmost freedom be accorded her in the choice of vocation; for she, more readily perhaps than men do, recognises the wisdom and majesty of Him who said – "I am among you as he that serveth."

❋ ❋ ❋ ❋

The second kind of advocacy of the rights of women, of which I spoke, may be said to be simply a reaction against the first. It is chiefly held by a few women of superior intellect who feel keenly the disadvantages of their class, their feebleness, through want of education, against public opinion, which is taken advantage of by base people, their inability, through want of representation, to defend their weaker members, and the dwarfing of the faculties of the ablest and best among them. These women have associated little with men, or at best, know very little of their inner life, and do not therefore see as clearly as they see their own loss, the equal loss that it is to men, and the injury it involves to their characters, to live dissociated from women: they therefore look forth from their isolation with something of an excusable envy on the freer and happier lot, which includes, they believe, a greater power to do good, and imagine that the only hope for themselves is to push into the ranks of men, to demand the same education, the same opportunities, in order that they may compete with them on their own ground. They have lost the conception of the noblest development possible for both men and women, for assuredly that which men, for the most part, aim at, is not the noblest, and yet that is what such women appear to wish to imitate; they have lost sight of the truth, too, that men and women were made equal indeed, but not alike, and were meant to supplement one another, and that in so doing, – each supplying force which the other lacks, – they are attracted with a far greater amount of impulse to a common centre. . . .

The above misconception, like many other errors, results from men and women living so dissociated as they do in our country; hence comes also all that reserve, and incapacity for understanding each other which has existed between the sexes for so many generations, those false notions about women which are entertained in society, and great injury to the work, and happiness, and dignity of man and woman alike: for it may be truly said that many of the most serious evils in England are but the bitter and various fruit of the sacrilegious disjoining of the which God had joined together, the disunion of men and women, theoretically and practically, in all the graver work of life.

❋ ❋ ❋ ❋

To conclude this part of my subject, although I grant that too much stress cannot be laid upon the improvement of the education of women who will be actually the mothers of a future generation, yet I wish, on the one hand, that persons who only look at it from this point of view would take more into account the valuable service our country might command if it but understood the truth about the condition and feelings of its unmarried women, and that a more generous trust were felt in the strength of woman's nature, and the probable direction of its development when granted more expansion, while on the other hand I should like to see a truer conception of the highest possibilities for women than is implied in the attempt to imitate men, and a deeper reverence for the God of nature, whose wisdom is more manifested in variety than in uniformity. It cannot be denied that a just cause has sometimes been advocated by women in a spirit of bitterness. Energy impeded in one direction, will burst forth in another; hence the defiant and sometimes grotesque expression which the lives and acts of some few women have been of the injustice done to them by society. This will cease, and while it lasts, it ought to excite our pity rather than our anger. It must be remembered that it is but a symptom of a long endured servitude, a protest against a state of things which we hope will give place to a better. It is folly to regard it as the natural fruit of that of which we have scarcely seen the beginning. Acts of violence on the part of a long oppressed nation are not the offspring of dawning liberties, but of a doomed tyranny. Again, no important reform can be carried without a measure of attendant confusion. Evil agencies are the most vigilant for destruction at the beginning of a great and good work, and many lives have to be consumed in its inauguration. Any evils which may at first attend a social reform ought not to alarm us: they are transient; they are but the breakers on the bar which must be crossed before we launch into deep waters, but the "noise and dust of the wagon which brings the harvest home."

1869

50. Josephine Butler
from *An Appeal . . . on . . . Prostitution*

It is reported by witnesses from Paris that fresh relays of healthy women have to be continually drafted in from the provinces. . . . And the history of every Continental town where this system prevails, shows a constant increase in the number of prostitutes from year to year, this increase being out of all proportion to any increase in the population in general; it is a gulf into which women are flung by thousands, but which never closes. Such are the effects which inevitably follow the introduction of a "*system*" by which the souls and bodies of tens of thousands of women are deliberately, and under the direction of the government, sacrificed to a supposed necessity.

While the public acknowledgement of such a supposed necessity is deeply degrading to men, both as an avowal that they are utterly and hopelessly the slaves of their own passions, and as an incentive to increased immorality, it is utterly destructive to the hopes of all good women for a purer and better state of society. The happiness and character of all virtuous women throughout the land must eventually suffer from the consequences of such measures, while upon the poor women, on whom the proposed Law takes immediate effect, there falls a blight and a destruction more complete than anything they can in its absence experience – heavy as their punishment in any case is.

The women who are terrified to submission again and again to the ordeal which this law requires them to submit to, are reduced by it to the character of wild beasts, in whom every trace of womanhood, and all hope of recovery are deadened and crushed out; not only does the horrible ordeal to which they are subjected destroy the last trace of the natural womanly instinct which is always a formulation upon which to build the hope of reformation, but, as a little knowledge of human nature teaches us, and all experience proves to us, the last lingering light of conscience is extinguished in them by the direct official sanction, which, under this law they cannot but believe they possess for the practice of their vocation.

Further, the proposed measures, politically considered, are without precedent in the history of our country in their tyranny, and their defiance of all which has ever been considered by Englishmen as *justice*. If you will study the provisions of the Acts of 1866 and 1869, and the evidence given last Session before the select committee of the House of Commons, you will see how distinctly the introduction of such a law tends to the creation of a bureaucracy in England, which would be intolerable to a free people. It resembles the Spanish Inquisition in its system of paid spies, and the admission of anonymous whispers as evidence not to be rebutted. Contrary to the entire spirit of English Law, the whole burden of proof is thrown not upon the accuser, but upon the accused; there is a complete absence of all fair and open court – to say nothing of jury; and the accused, in this case, are the weakest, the most helpless, and most friendless of the community.

By this Law a crime has been *created* in order that it may be severely punished; but observe, that has been ruled to be a crime in women which is not to be considered a crime in men. There are profligate men who are spreading disease everywhere, but the law does not take effect on *these*.

I have said that a crime has been created – which is to be severely punished. The alternative for every woman accused is either to appear before the Magistrates, or to submit to a torture which to any woman with a spark of feeling left in her is worse than death. Refusing to submit to the torture she is imprisoned. There is no escape from the one penalty or the other. An innocent woman who is accused may escape the torture, but she cannot escape the appearance before the Magistrates, and that very appearance means ruin to the character and prospects of a poor and virtuous woman. The torture to which these poor fallen women (to whom, if there be an acknowledged *necessity* on the side of men for their existence, the State ought to be grateful and tender) are subjected by this Law, has no parallel except in the darkest and foulest forms of persecution practised on helpless women in the cruelest ages of history. This and none other is the character of the inquisition imposed by this Law, albeit it is advocated and practiced in the name of humanity. Insensibility engendered by custom, and ignorance of the nature of women alone can account for the fact that men should be found to practice such horrors in the name of humanity. It is sometimes said that to *these* women it is no torture. Perhaps it is to women rather than to men that they *confess* the shame, and the anguish. I will only say, from a large and intimate experience of women of this pitiable class, that I never found one among them, except those very few who are degraded so far as to be beyond the pale of human nature, who did not shrink with horror from that torture, and who would not rather endure any amount of bodily pain than that which is so intolerable to womanhood, violence done to the deepest and the most indelible instincts of her nature. How, then, must the better and more tender, – the very young, the still womanly among them, regard it? It is a solemn question, whether it be lawful for the State to inflict torture of so cruel and indecent a nature upon any of its subjects for *any given end whatsoever*, or for *any crime that can be named* – to say nothing of the lawfulness of the infliction of such torture for a crime which it treats as a crime *only* in one sex, and *only* among the *poor* of that sex – *i.e.* the crime of incontinence.

❀ ❀ ❀

Some of the appeals made to us on behalf of the innocent who suffer, amaze one by their impudence. I must be excused for making use of so harsh a word, but I can call it nothing else. These appeals assume that the only remedy for this slaughter of the innocent is the making safe for married men the path of the fornicator. They continually speak as though there were but two sets of persons to be considered – fallen and conta-gious women on the one hand, and pure women and children on the other. It is curious to observe how they ignore in their arguments the existence of that intermediate class, who convey contagion from the one to the other. Certain persons resent, as if it were an indelicacy, any allusion to that most important link, the adulterous husbands and fathers who are dispensing disease and death in their families. Yet to a truth-loving mind the question must occur, "would not the abstinence from fornication on the part of these husbands and fathers be at least as direct a mode of hindering disease as that of reducing a vast proportion of the female population to a condition worse than that of the lower animals for their convenience?"

But, it is objected, it is not for married men chiefly that this safe provision
needs to be made, but for youths who will afterwards be married, and there
is an affecting case in point always ready for citation, of some young man
upon whom life-long suffering has been entailed by a single lapse of his
youth, and not only on himself but on his wife and children. We, mothers
of England, are not less concerned for our sons than for our daughters.
Assuredly we do not fail in compassion towards anyone upon whom retri-
bution falls so heavily: and undoubtedly the penalty for a single offence in
a man is sometimes very heavy; in the case of a woman it is invariably
overpoweringly heavy. Such a case as this is one which is continually cited
as an argument appealing at once to our reason and our compassion for
the establishment of these public regulations. But let us look at the matter
a little more closely, and see whether it is wholly compassionate either to
the erring or the innocent to set this Act into operation. Does it not occur
to those who use this argument that under the operation of this Act such
lapses among young men, who would afterwards be married, would be
somewhat more frequent, nay that they would become so much more
frequent as altogether to counterbalance the advantages said to be gained
by the one-sided expedient which we deprecate. We know what human
nature is, and the very prevalence of this terrible disease proves a state
of morality among men which warrants us in saying that the moment the
double restraint is withdrawn, the moral and physical, by means of the
recognition by Government on the one hand of the veniality or necessity
of such offences, and by the supposed removal of a material risk, young
men in England will plunge into vice as freely as they do in countries
which have adopted this system. I have dwelt at some length on this part
of the subject, but I beg to be excused for doing so, since the testimony
which pours in from foreign countries, while I write, is of such weight and
significance that I cannot but feel that the advocates of the measure at
home have failed to look at this part of the matter calmly, and with a wise
consideration. Before leaving this part of the subject I must say, with shame
and grief, that it is well known to those women whose charity leads them
to seek out their unhappy sisters in their haunts of sin, that these incautious
young men are not in fact the only persons in whose interest this Act
proposes to work; that it is not the young and unmarried alone who support
these abodes of infamy.

51. Margaret Oliphant
from *Review of 'On the Subjection of Women'*

Of all writers on the claims of women, Mr. Mill alone has treated the question on its fundamental principles. The apologists of woman have eluded the first dilemma in many ingenious ways. They have not ventured to go to the fountainhead and begin with the beginning. We have heard much talk about moral superiority and mental equality, but more in the shape of guesses than of argument; and we have had an amount of wild statement on both sides which it is amazing should have been tolerated in any reasonable discussion. Men have gravely informed us that women were incapable of self-government, or of any share in the serious work of the world, notwithstanding the patent facts which we have only to open our eyes and see; and women, with equal gravity and more heat, have endeavoured to impress upon us the belief that they were competent to undertake the work of men, not instead of, but in addition to, their own. We have been told that the one sex is better and that it is worse than the other, that it is full of intuitive wisdom and intuitive folly, that it is stronger, that it is weaker, that it is purer, that it is wickeder. We have been told that most of the harm done in the world has originated with women; and we have been told that all the good comes from their influence and soft example. In the face of such assertions what is the puzzled spectator to do? If we could imagine an intelligent being looking on, who was neither man nor woman, and had no prejudices one way or another, listening to all this babble, yet casting his eyes around him in the world in the exercise of an independent judgment, what should we imagine his real impressions to be?

Looking down from some angelic height he would see a mass of creatures moving about on the face of the earth on that general level of humanity which is the first standing ground of the children of Adam. The chances are that his first look would convey to him an impression of intense similarity, almost uniformity. He would see the two halves of humanity not divided into two armies, but mingled and mixed up together with the most curious absence of primary identity. He would find on the whole that motive of a very similar character actuated the mass; that some were lofty and some petty, some wise and some foolish, some able and some stupid, with wonderfully little distinction of sex. The first glance would reveal this to him in a curiously confusing way, and would probably make the conditions of human life a very bewildering problem. And when those distinctions which do really mark out sex from sex became apparent to him, he would be more puzzled still. He would find many things expedient that are not altogether just. He would find necessities which nature imposed, but which abstract equity turned against. He would find indeed a great troubled confused uncertain world, ruled by anything but logic, not even ruled by justice, in which century after century had over again demonstrated the impossibility not only of perfection in action or agreement in thought, but even of any universal infallible code of right and wrong as applied to the most intimate relations of life.

One can imagine a young and romantic angel putting his inexperienced hand to the work with the idea of bringing light out of darkness, and absolute order from the midst of this confusion. But we fear the chances are that he would soon withdraw in consternation from the difficult task. He would find conflicting claims too fine to be ever discriminated; interests which even the balance of the sanctuary would be unable to weigh and divide; rights and wrongs so involved and complicated that no trenchant steel of keen justice coming down upon them could do other than cut and sever many heartstrings in its descent. We who are not angels but men and women of the nineteenth century, very reluctant to allow that any hardship can exist for which a remedy is impossible, must inevitably find the matter a still more difficult one. And no doubt it is the inherent human consciousness of its supreme difficulties which has so long placed it out of the sphere of discussion. Now, however, when even this barrier is insufficient to restrain the audacity of argument, the question has become one which must be looked in the face; and the more seriously we can do it, and the less trust we put in those picturesque and sentimental pleas which tempt the advocates on both sides, the more likely we shall be to come to some real and satisfactory conclusion.

❄ ❄ ❄ ❄

If the highest claim of woman was, as Mr. Mill declares, that of being a perfectly equal and similar creature, occupying exactly the same ground and possessing the same powers as man, in respect to intellect, character, and endowments, then there could remain no doubt of woman's fundamental inferiority on any reasonable mind. We repeat: if they are precisely the same kind of beings with no differences except those which are physical, then we allow without a moment's hesitation that women are the natural inferiors of men. Equality must embrace the whole being; it cannot be taken as belonging only to a part of it. And woman is confessedly and unmistakeably man's inferior in one part of her being; therefore, unless she is as unmistakeably his superior in another, she can have no claim to consider herself his equal. Now it cannot be asserted for an instant that she is notably his superior in intellect; all that the boldest theoriser ever dreams of asserting is that she is equal with him in that particular, while she is manifestly not equal to him in bodily strength and personal courage. Thus in every way in which we can put the comparison, so long as we examine the two as competitors for one prize, her inferiority is marked and undeniable. If we could say, the woman is weaker, less courageous, incapable of the violent exertion which comes natural to her companion, and which is necessary for the maintenance of life; but at the same time she has a greater power of thought, a much higher grasp of the necessities of the position, a mind which can guide him in his ruder work – we should then be at ease in the contrast and feel that the point of equality had been reached. But this it is altogether out of our power to say. That her intellect is as good as his, is all that we can assert, and even this with hesitation and uncertainty; but then intellect is but one part, and her other powers are not so good as his. Must we therefore conclude that the woman is inferior? Taking Mr. Mill's ground that she is exactly the same kind of creature as the man, we are certainly driven to that conclusion. We cannot get out of it by any expedient of logic. We have no superfluity on one side to put against the want in the other. Equal in one point she is deficient in another, and deficiency means inferiority. With all our desire to make out a flaw, we are obliged to yield before the facts which will allow no comparison. Not being man's superior anyhow, in natural constitution, she cannot be man's equal, let us twist the matter how we will.

But let us turn for one moment to the other view of the question. It is that a woman is a woman, and not a lesser edition of man. The competition in which we are for ever labouring to involve them, has no existence in nature. They are not rivals, nor antagonists. They are two halves of a complete being. The offices they hold in the world are essentially different. There is scarcely any natural standing ground which we can realise on which these two creatures appear as rivals. The very thought is preposterous. Shall the woman challenge the man to a trial of strength? Shall the man pit himself against the woman for delicacy of eye and taste? Shall she plough the heavy fields with him, wading through the new-turned mould, or shall he watch the children with her, patient through the weary vigil? An exchange of place and toil, the man taking the indoor work and the woman the outdoor, in order to prove the futility of their mutual discontent, was a favourite subject with the old ballad-makers; and the witty minstrel is generally very great on the domestic confusion that follows, and gives the wife the best of it. But the fact is that such a rivalry can be nothing but a jest. The two are not rivals, they are not alike. They are different creatures. They are one.

To illustrate this theory we have but to look at the life which they lead

together. Civilisation has a wonderful faculty for altering and confounding
the natural conditions of existence. But in primitive circumstances it is
always the man who is the bestower of material advantages; it is his to give,
to provide for, to labour, to protect. He is the bread-winner – the strength
is his. It is he alone who without intermission can face the outside world,
and force a subsistence out of the reluctant soil or the barren seas. When
the typical pair set out together who are to found all human economies, all
domestic relations, and from whom the new life is to proceed – and every
new pair is but a repetition of the first – nature places them at once with a
certainty beyond theory in their traditional places. The woman has an
office to perform which renders unremitting labour impossible to her. She
is the fountain of life, bound by all the laws of her nature to guard the
sacred seed and bring it forth to crush the serpent's head, and fill the world
with increase and gladness. The man may shirk his work, but hers she
cannot shirk. And in the pride and joy of her special office there mingles
a sacred shame which compels her to intervals of seclusion and avoidance
of the world's gaze. Her life is interrupted, broken up into morsels; now
she can go forth, can work if it be needful, can use in any way that may be
necessary the faculties that God has given her: and anon there comes a
time in which all such labours must be suspended in consideration of
something else which God has given her to do. But the man has no interruptions to his life; his strength is steady without breach or variation. What
partnership is there that can have any analogy with this? Let us suppose
that they laboured together in their Eden a little while, scarcely knowing
which was which in the first sweet unity of being. And then the time came
when he went out alone to labour, and she in her sanctity of weakness
stayed at home. When he returned how could it be otherwise than that
one for whom he had been toiling all day should meet him with offices of
service, with domestic ministrations, with grateful lessening of herself
and magnifying of him? From that moment must not equality have fled to
the winds like all other foolish pretences? The man was out all day toiling,
struggling, meeting the winds and the storm, the sun beating on his head,
the powers of nature resisting him; what could he be but king when he
returned to that first hut or hovel and stretched out his weary limbs by the
new-lighted fire? Service was his due. The food he had earned, must it not
be offered to him, with observances copied afar off from those with which
the gifts of His giving were offered back again to God? The imagination
refuses to believe in, refuses to frame, any other conception. His inferior
– that might or might not be – but his servant, yes – his minister, the natural Second, the born solace and consolation. When we cast our eyes back
to the primeval husband and wife – when we turn to any subsequent pair

who have ever set out upon the world like Adam and Eve, we find the same course of events recurring in infallible sequence. This is fact and nature let theory say what it will. The woman in such a union is in no way called upon to be the man's inferior. She may be intellectually his superior even, and it will not change the course of nature. She will serve him should all the world interfere to prevent her. She will spread his table, and watch his wishes, and give him of his own, with rites of gratitude, with flowers and incense, and a whole liturgy of ministration. Eve would have done it had Mr. Mill been there ever so distinctly, shaking his head at her, and bidding her remember the rules of equality. Equality! what does it mean? Has it any existence as between any two people in intimate relations on the face of the earth? And were it established over and over, were it measureable by line and weight like any tangible material, what place is there for its consideration between the two thus linked and bound together, the one the supplement of the other? Man goes out to his work and labour till the evening. Woman prepares for him, waits for him, serves him at home. So natural is this, that when, as the case may be, it is a woman who is the bread-winner for a household of women, the worker is turned into an impromptu superior on the spot, and served and waited on as the man in other circumstances is waited on and served. It is the hire of the labourer, the reward of the provider, an instinctive law which antedates all legislation, and lies at the very root and beginning of all human affairs.

Thus, though we have declared without hesitation our belief that the law which takes all property and all right from married women is an insult and injustice, equally cruel and unwise, we are ready to grant as frankly that the economical position of man is that of the superior, the first in the natural hierarchy. He it is whose office is to maintain, support, and protect. He may not always be equal to the duties of this office. He may by nature be no more powerful, no more steadfast, no more trustworthy, in fact, than the wife who is recognised as dependent on him. But in his official position he stands first, and has in his favour all the instincts and prejudices of nature. It is vain to assert of a rule which is so universal that it originates in the arbitrary will of the stronger half of the species. We might say on the contrary, with much greater appearance of justice, that it is women who have framed this infallible law. Every observer, whose eyes are open to the common facts about him, will see it re-enacted every day by every bride who crosses the threshold of a new household. Mr. Mill will tell us that this is the result of defective education, and of the long habit of slavery; but let him take the most high-spirited young woman he can find, trained in his own school, and roused to full defence of the theoretical rights of her sex by the enthusiasm of youth and vehement sectarian education, and let her but marry a man she loves, and the philosopher will find the code re-established, it may be secretly, it may be with a sense of guilt and confusion, and even treachery to her own cause, ere she has well taken her place in her new kingdom. She may rule her husband even, yet she will serve him; she may lead him blindfold by right of love, or wit, or superior character, and yet she will minister to him, wait upon him, offer him sacrifices as if she were the commonest daughter of Eve. For were the confusing conditions of our civilisation abolished, along with dowers and laws of property and marriage settlements, would it not be his office to work for her? His it must be to protect her, whatever external dangers come their way; his to toil when Providence forbids her from toiling; his to stand between her and the world, and screen off from her at those moments when nature demands seclusion, the offensive gaze of the crowd. Far be it from us to dwell with prurient sentiment upon the details of that grand function which is the distinguishing work of woman in the world. But any theory of her being which ignores it, or gives it a secondary place, or in any way whatever leaves it out of the calculation, is inevitably a futile theory. Let us imagine even that at other times she may be capable of maintaining her own independence and securing her livelihood apart from the help of man – yet at these times she is not so capable. It is then that his strength which is liable to no interruption asserts its superiority. He has nothing to do which calls him off his day's work, prompts him to seek the covert, puts him aside from ordinary employments. Such a fact makes rivalry utterly impossible. It would be as reasonable to expect that a soldier engaged in a dangerous campaign, and with the necessity upon him of periodically confronting death, and running all the risks of a battle, should at the same time compete with a civilian in some art or handicraft. The comparison is weak, for there is no reason why the soldier should not be in robust health up to the moment of marching, and it is his own life only which is concerned. But the women who are men's wives are bound in most cases to undergo periodically a risk which is as great as that which any individual soldier encounters in a battle. And they have not only to brace their nerves to encounter this danger for themselves, but it is their grand moment of responsibility, when they must vindicate the trust reposed in them by God and the world. Can there be any doubt that this essential element of her life at once and for ever disables a woman from all trial of strength and rude equality with man? Nobody but a fool, we believe, will assert that the burden of this great trust stamps her as inferior. It would be just as reasonable to say that it gave her a superior place in the economy of nature as the possessor of a faculty more utterly essential to the continuance of the race. But there can be no doubt about the fact that it separates her and her work and her office from the office and work of man. The two are not made to contend and compete and run races for the same prize. There is no natural opposition, but on the contrary harmony unbounded in their differences of nature – harmony which can never be attained by two creatures framed on the self-same plan.

* * * *

As for the possession of political power by a married woman in independence of that possessed by her husband, we cannot but feel the idea to run counter to the whole theory of married life. This is not to say that the woman is to take no interest in politics, to form no opinions, to be politically dead. But there is no social justice in giving to two people so closely bound by all the complications of nature as to be, to all intents and purposes one, two voices in the commonwealth. This is as much as to abrogate altogether the family constitution, the first primitive constituency. We have pointed out, we trust with sufficient clearness, the impossibility of woman holding her own as against man in any race of individualities; but when she is united to man, perfecting and being perfected by the conjunction, it is unjust to the rest of the world that this composite being should have two voices in the sway of the world. It is one, not in imagination but in reality, and why should it speak as for two? Nobody who has ever come into collision (being but a solitary individual) with a pair of married persons will fail to see the weight of this. The double being is so strong in its double sense of one interest, so curiously wrapt in its compound adherence to its one opinion, that the single opponent is generally wound to a point of exasperation which no encounter with another solitary would produce. For there can be little doubt that the two will almost invariably agree, whether by better information on one side – and that without doubt the man's – or by stronger feeling on some special point, which may just as likely be the woman's – in which case the effect would be simply that one opinion would obtain two expressions. If, on the contrary, the two disagreed, it would not only introduce a jar into their union, but would be a simple stultification of the family voice and obliteration of its influence. In this, as in so many other things, it seems to us a positive impossibility to sever the two who are one. They have one home, one interest, one place in the world; the one, whenever absent, is represented in an inexpressible but perfectly real way by the other. We cannot explain how it is, but we know that it is. They agree together, whatever may be their differences between themselves, to maintain in almost all ordinary matters a policy of unanimity before the world, knowing well that their one voice thus united is worth far more than it would be divided. Nature thus demonstrates the wisest mode of procedure; for there is no law which forbids a woman in other matters from standing on her own opinion and saying her independent say; and we are not blind enough to believe that she is so intimidated as to be afraid of expressing herself on common subjects. Here, once more, it is not a matter of individual right, but of social necessity and policy, and what we may call the economics of humanity. The two have given up their separate privileges, which is the fundamental question – they have relinquished the right to live where they like, to do what they like, with little less abandonment on one side than the other. And to give one interest two voices, one thought two expressions, would be not to ease but to complicate the workings of government, whether in its higher or in its lower levels.

But when we turn to the consideration of professional education for girls, we feel that we have returned to the general fundamental conditions of women, and can only argue the one question by an appeal to the other. Professional education in man occupies all the season of youth. He has reached his majority at least before he is qualified to put his powers to the test, and exercise the knowledge he has gained. Unless he steps into an exceptional position, reaping the benefit of some one else's labours, the first ten or fifteen years of manhood are spent in a struggle for position more or less hard in proportion to his talents and his character, and his power of awaiting a slow result. Under favourable circumstances, of course, this struggle is not mortal, but it always requires the man's full force, his clearest judgment, and most careful labour. If he is prosperously established in the exercise of his profession at thirty-five, with a clear prospect of gain and social honour, he has done as well as he could possibly hope, and can look forward with tolerable confidence on the career before him. During this early struggle he has to exert all his powers; if he pauses for a moment he knows that it is at the hazard not of losing that moment alone but of sacrificing ten times its value. The road is so uphill that he slides down one step for every three he makes, and is aware that to stop short or turn aside on the way is destruction. A temporary illness sometimes neutralises years of labour: he must be always at his post, pushing on with speed unbroken. Should he fall some one else is ready to jostle him out of the already too crowded way. Such is a very ordinary statement of the usual difficulties which beset the path, say, of a young physician; and the other professions are not less toilsome. Let us see what effect these obstacles would have on the career of the candidate were it a woman and not a man.

The first thing we have to imagine is that the girl's entire youth, its bloom, and softest years should be passed like that of the young man in the steady pursuit of knowledge. At one-and-twenty, by the devotion of all her youth, she is qualified to enter upon the practice of her profession; when lo! there appears at the threshold of life the most natural of all interruptions to a young woman's career, a young husband ready to take upon himself the charge of her fortunes. She is married let us suppose, her education being no bar to the exercise of the primitive duties of her sex; and let us also imagine that she is loth to sacrifice at a stroke the labours of so many years, and that she attempts to combine professional exertions with the duties of a wife. She works for a year, let us say with intermissions, finding it more and more difficult to maintain her place against the lively competition of men who have no divided duty. Then she is stopped short by the inevitable discharge of the primary function of woman. This business over, she resumes again with a heart and attention sorely divided between the claims of the infant she leaves at home and the duties she finds outside. During the interval of her seclusion, however restricted in point of time, every one of her male competitors has made a stride before her. Faltering and discouraged she resumes her laborious way; and if she has the energy of half a dozen men in her single person, if her courage is indomitable, and her determination sublime, she perhaps manages by a strain of mind and body which it would be impossible to continue long, to make up half of the ground she has lost; when lo another interruption comes, and she has to step aside again and bear her feminine burden, and see her competitors, light and unladen, stride past once more. This is the inevitable course, known only too well to every woman who has endeavoured to combine professional exertions with the ordinary duties of a man's wife. Other complications such as we shrink from mentioning, probably come in to take all the elasticity out of a mind so burdened. Her children born amid these cares, and injured before their birth by the undue activity of brain which weakens their mother's physical powers, come into the world feeble or die in her arms, quenching out her courage in the bitterest waves of personal suffering. This is no fancy picture. At every step in her career it becomes less possible for her to maintain the unequal conflict. Her competitors have marched far before her, while she toils and strives midway on the steep ascent. They have gone on without intermission; she has had to stop short again and again in her course. With what sickness of heart, with what a weary hopeless sense of the unattainable, and desperate consciousness of the mistake, she maintains the struggle, only they can tell who have done it, and happily the number is not great. Such is all that a woman has to expect who attempts to combine the work of a man to which she has been trained with the common duties of female life.

On the other hand, let us suppose that she puts aside the profession she has acquired and gives herself up to domesticity and wifehood until the period of childbearing is over, and her special responsibilities so far accomplished. This period cannot be estimated at less than twenty years. It may be considerably shorter; it is sometimes longer; but we are not understating the possibilities if we grant that at forty she may consider herself emancipated from woman's natural disabilities, and may stretch out her hands towards the tools which she put from her all new and shining at one-and-twenty. Will these tools have improved or will they have deteriorated in the meantime? Will her training of twenty years ago come back all fresh to her memory as if it had been but twenty days? Will the world be so good as to stand still in the meantime and keep everything just as it was in the days of her apprenticeship that she may begin again with some chance of success? Alas, no! this is precisely what the world will not do. She will find her fellow-students a hundred miles ahead of her, and their sons ready to tread on her heels and gibe at her old-world principles. She will be of the old school, before she has even begun to put in practice her rusty knowledge. She will feel in herself the painful consciousness of faculties blunted by want of use, and powers numbed by long inaction. If she is a wonderful woman, with the energy of half a dozen men, she will perhaps make a desperate effort and force her way alongside of some plodding bungler whose indolence or stupidity have left him out of the race. This is the best that can befall her if she adopts this second course and waits until she can give to her profession the matured and steady powers of middle age.

There is, however, an alternative open to her. She can take a vow of celibacy. She can throw off altogether the yoke of nature, and fit herself to compete with man by consciously and voluntarily rejecting the life of woman. This is a possibility which is not to be rejected with disdain as out of the question. If all is true that we continually read about the number of women who cannot marry, it is no unfit question for the more resolute souls among them, whether they should not make up their minds that they will not marry, and thus qualify themselves by one severe yet effectual effort for an existence resembling that of man. By this means alone can they procure for themselves fair play in the world, or a reasonable chance of success in any profession. But this is a penalty which perhaps not one of all their male fellow-students would undertake to pay; and it is the most cruel renunciation which can be exacted from a human creature. Thus success in a profession – nay, the mere initiatory possibility of success – requires from a woman not equality with man, but an amount of intellectual and moral superiority over him, which can only be found in the rarest and most isolated cases. To him the prospect of marriage is the strongest incentive to industry and exertion. To her it is simple ruin, so far as her work is concerned. If then she has the magnanimity and self-devotion to cut herself off from all that is popularly considered happiness in life – from all that youth most dreams of, and the heart most cares for – she is free to enter into and pursue, and very likely will succeed in a profession, which men, with all solaces of love and help of companionship, pursue by her side at not half the cost. Perhaps even then, after she has made this sacrifice, she will find that she is the pot of earth making her way among their pots of iron; and that their superior physical powers and bolder temperament will carry them beyond her, notwithstanding the superior devotion she has shown and the price she has paid. But this is the best we can promise her when all is done – to (perhaps) succeed as well, at the cost of everything, as her competitors who go into it with the commonest of motives and at no cost at all.

This is a very serious, very weighty consideration at the outset of a career. Professional education too is very costly, and the parents of young women to whom self-support is necessary are not generally rolling in wealth; can we then wonder at their reluctance to purchase dearly such a training for their daughter, knowing that the expense will most probably be all in vain, and indeed hoping that her first step in actual life will be to render herself incapable of her profession by a happy marriage? We do not for one moment deny that the picture we have just drawn, and the truth of which we are but too certainly aware of, is the very contrary of encouraging to those hapless women who are seeking work to do and know not where to find it. We acknowledge sadly that it is not encouraging, but it is better to face the truth than to ignore it. These things would remain true were all the colleges in Christendom thrown open to-morrow with all their means of instruction to the girl-graduates, who, we are told, thirst for improved education. By all means, we say, let them be thrown open. Let all contemptuous laws that teach fools to sneer at the mother who bore them be erased from our statute-book. Let the women who stand apart from woman's natural existence, be it by choice, be it by necessity, be permitted to assume men's privileges if they choose. And what then, oh daughters of Eve? The most of you will still be wives, will still be mothers all the same, will still lie under nature's own disabilities and be trusted with nature's high responsibilities, and have your work to do, which no man is capable of doing instead of you. Legislation may help the surplus, the exceptional women. If it does really aid them to find a practicable standing ground it will do well; but for the majority, legislation can do little and revolution nothing at all.

1871

52. Hannah Cullwick
from *Diary*

Sunday 1 January.

This is the beginning of another year, & I am still general servant like, to Mrs Henderson at 20 Gloucester Crescent. This month on the 16th I shall o' bin in her service 2 years & a 1/2, & if I live till the 26th o' May when I shall be 38 year old, I shall o' bin in service 30 years & have known Massa 17 years. Now there's such a little boy kept here I've a deal more to do of jobs that's hard, like digging coals & carrying 'em up & the boxes, & high windows & the fanlight over the door to clean & anything as wants strength or height I am sent for or call'd up to do it. All the cabs that's wanted I get, & if the young ladies want fetching or taking anywhere I've to walk with them & carry their cloaks or parcels. I clean all the copper scuttles & dig the coals clean the tins & help to clean the silver & do the washing up if I'm wanted, & carry things up as far as the door for dinner. I clean 4 grates & do the fires & clean the irons, sweep & clean 3 rooms & my attic, the hall & front steps & the flags & area railings & all that in the street. I clean the water closet & privy out & the back yard & the area, the back stairs & the passage, the larder, pantry & boy's room & the kitchen & scullery, all the cupboards downstairs & them in the storeroom. And at the house cleaning I do the walls down from the top to the bottom o' the house & clean all the high paint, & dust the pictures. I get all the meals down stairs & lay the cloth & wait on the boy & the housemaid as much as they want & if it's my work, like changing their plates & washing their knife & fork & that.

Missis never goes away – hardly for a day throughout the year, so as there's no change & no good chance for thorough cleaning. I'm getting more used to the family now so I don't mind them seeing me clean upstairs as much as I used to, but I do like the family to be away for house-cleaning, 'cause one can have so much more time at it & do it more thoroughly & be as black at it as one likes without fear o' bein' seen by the ladies. 'Cause I know they don't like to see a servant look dirty, however black the job is one has to do.

I've two days & two nights' holiday since last October twelve months, & bin to no theatres or Crystal Palace or anything except to Exeter Hall once wi' the young ladies & heard the ragged school children sing. And

I've read nothing but a book call'd Adam Bede, excepting my Bible. I've bin to church every chance I've had when Massa's bin away or when I've not gone to him of a Sunday. It's rather unpleasant to ask leave so I seldom get out of a weekday. I go with notes or parcels, & fetch my beer or for any errands. Yet I get very little outing all together. The most fresh air is washing the front door steps & flags in the street & out at the back door washing the yard. Still, I'm quite content & like service – especially if I could get to Massa more & without having to ask. But that I canna so am obliged to make the best of the time I do have & do as much in it as I can for him.

———

53. Frances Power Cobbe
To Elizabeth Garrett Anderson

The Woman's cause was rising fast
When to the Surgeons' College past
A maid who bore in fingers nice
A banner with the new device
                    Excelsior!

"Try not to pass!" the Dons exclaim,
"M.D. shall grace no woman's name" –
"Bosh!" cried the maid, in accents free,
"To France I'll go for my degree."
                    Excelsior!

The School-Board seat came next in sight,
"Beware the foes of woman's right!"
"Beware the awful husting's fight!"
Such was the moan of many a soul –
A voice replied from top of poll –
                    Excelsior!

In patients' homes she saw the light
Of household fires beam warm and bright;
Lectures on Bones grew wondrous dry,
But still she murmured with a sigh
                    Excelsior!

"Oh, stay!" – a lover cried, – "Oh, rest
Thy much-learned head upon this breast;
Give up ambition! Be my bride!"
– Alas! *no* clarion voice replied
                                    Excelsior!

At end of day, when all is done,
And woman's battle fought and won,
Honour will aye be paid to one
Who erst called foremost in the van
                                    Excelsior!

But not for her that crown so bright,
Which her's had been, of surest right,
Had she still cried, – serene and blest –
"The Virgin throned by the West."
                                    Excelsior!

1872

54. Sophia Jex Blake
from *Medicine as a Profession for Women*

We are told so often that nature and custom have alike decided against the admission of women to the Medical Profession, and that there is in such admission something repugnant to the right order of things, that when we see growing evidences of a different opinion among a minority perhaps, but a minority which already includes many of our most earnest thinkers of both sexes, and increases daily, it surely becomes a duty for all . . . to test these statements by the above principles, and to see how far their truth is supported by evidence.

In the first place, let us take the testimony of Nature in the matter. If we go back to primeval times, and try to imagine the first sickness or the first injury suffered by humanity, does one instinctively feel that it must have been the *man's* business to seek means of healing, to try the virtues of various herbs, or to apply such rude remedies as might occur to one unused to the strange spectacle of human suffering? I think that few would maintain that such ministration would come most naturally to the man, and be instinctively avoided by the woman; indeed, I fancy that the presumption would be rather in the other direction. And what is such ministration but the germ of the future profession of medicine?

Nor, I think, would the inference be different if we appealed to the actual daily experience of domestic life. If a child falls down stairs, and is more or less seriously hurt, is it the father or the mother (where both are without medical training) who is most equal to the emergency, and who applies the needful remedies in the first instance? Or again, in the heart of the country, where no doctor is readily accessible, is it the squire and the parson, or their respective wives, who are usually consulted about the ailments of half the parish? Of course it may be said that such practice is by no means scientific, but merely empirical, and this I readily allow; but that fact in no way affects my argument that women are *naturally* inclined and fitted for medical practice. And if this be so, I do not know who has the right to say that they shall not be allowed to make their work scientific when they desire it, but shall be limited to merely the mechanical details and wearisome routine of nursing, while to men is reserved all intelligent knowledge of disease, and all study of the laws by which health may be preserved or restored.

Again, imagine if you can that the world has reached its present standing point, that society exists as now in every respect but this, – that the art of healing has never been conceived as a separate profession, that no persons have been set apart to receive special education for it, and that in fact empirical "domestic medicine," in the strictest sense, is the only thing of the kind existing. Suppose now that society suddenly awoke to the great want so long unnoticed, that it was recognized by all that a scientific knowledge of the human frame in health and in disease, and a study of the remedies of various kinds which might be employed as curative agents, would greatly lessen human suffering, and that it was therefore resolved at once to set apart some persons who should acquire such knowledge, and devote their lives to using it for the benefit of the rest of the race. In such case, would the natural idea be that members of each sex should be so set apart for the benefit of their own sex respectively, – that men should fit themselves to minister to the maladies of men, and women to those of women, – or that one sex only should undertake the care of the health of all, under all circumstances? For myself, I have no hesitation in saying that the former seems to me the *natural* course, and that to civilized society, if unaccustomed to the idea, the proposal that persons of one sex should in every case be consulted about every disease incident to those of the other, would be very repugnant; nay, that were every other condition of society the same as now, it would probably be held wholly inadmissable. I maintain that not only is there nothing strange or unnatural in the idea that women are the fit physicians for women, and men for men; but on the contrary, that it is only custom and habit which blind society to the extreme strangeness and incongruity of any other notion.

I am indeed far from pretending, as some have done, that it is morally wrong for men to be the medical attendants of women, and that grave mischiefs are the frequent and natural results of their being placed in that position. I believe that these statements not only materially injure the cause they profess to serve, but that they are in themselves false. In my own experience as a medical student, I have had far too much reason to acknowledge the honour and delicacy of feeling habitually shown by the gentlemen of the medical profession, not to protest warmly against any such injurious imputation. I am very sure that in the vast majority of cases, the motives and conduct of medical men in this respect are altogether above question, and that every physician who is also a gentleman is thoroughly able, when consulted by a patient in any case whatever, to remember only the human suffering brought before him and the scientific bearing of its details; for as was said not very long ago by a most eminent London surgeon, "Whoever is not able, in the course of practice, to put the idea of sex out of his mind, is not fit for the medical profession at all." It will, however, occur to most people that the medical man is only one of the parties concerned, and that it is possible that a difficulty which may be of no importance from his scientific standpoint, may yet be very formidable indeed to the far more sensitive and delicately organized feelings of his patient, who has no such armour of proof as his own, and whose very condition of suffering may entail an even exaggerated condition of nervous susceptibility on such points. At any rate, when we hear so many assertions about natural instincts and social propriety, I cannot but assert that their evidence, such as it is, is wholly for, and not against, the cause of women as physicians for their own sex.

❋ ❋ ❋ ❋

Probably the next argument will be that women do not require, and are not fitted to receive, the scientific education needful for a first-rate Physician, and that "for their own sakes" it is not desirable that they should pursue some of the studies indispensably necessary. To this the answer must be, that the wisest thinkers teach us to believe that each human being must be "a law unto himself," and must decide what is and what is not suitable for his needs, what will and what will not contribute to his own development, and fit him best to fulfil the life-work most congenial to his tastes. If women claim that they do need and can appreciate instruction in any or all sciences, I do not know who has the right to deny the assertion. . . .

If it be argued that the study of Natural Science may injure a woman's character, I would answer, in the words of one of the purest-minded women I know, that "if a woman's womanliness is not deep enough in her nature to bear the brunt of any needful education, it is not worth guarding." It is, I think, inconceivable that any one who considers the study of natural science to be but another word for earnest and reverent inquiry into the works of God, and who believes that, in David's words, these are to be "sought out of all them that have pleasure therein," can imagine that any such study can be otherwise than elevating and helpful to the moral, as well to the mental nature of every student who pursues it in a right spirit. In the words of Scripture, "To the pure, all things are pure," and in the phrase of chivalry, "Honi soit qui mal y pense."

It has always struck me as a curious inconsistency, that while almost everybody applauds and respects Miss Nightingale and her followers for their brave disregard of conventionalities on behalf of suffering humanity, and while hardly any one would pretend that there was any want of feminine delicacy in their going among the foulest sights and most painful scenes, to succour, not their own sex, but the other, many people yet profess to be shocked when other women desire to fit themselves to take the medical care of those of their sisters who would gladly welcome their aid. Where is the real difference? If a woman is to be applauded for facing the horrors of an army hospital when she believes that she can there do good work, why is she to be condemned as indelicate when she professes her willingness to go through an ordeal, certainly no greater, to obtain the education necessary for a medical practitioner? Surely work is in no way degraded by being made scientific; it cannot be commendable to obey instructions as a nurse when it would be unseemly to learn the reasons for them as a student, or to give them as a doctor; more especially as the nurse's duties may lead her, as they did in the Crimea, to attend on men with injuries and diseases of all kinds, whereas the woman who practises as a physician would confine her practice to women only. It is indeed hard to see any reason of delicacy, at least, which can be adduced in favour of women as nurses, and against them as physicians.

Their natural capacity for the one sphere or the other is, of course, a wholly different matter, and is, indeed, a thing not to be argued about, but to be tested. If women fail to pass the re-required examinations for the ordinary medical degree, or if, after their entrance into practice, they fail to succeed in it, the whole question is naturally and finally disposed of. But that is not the point now at issue.

That the most thorough and scientific medical education need do no injury to any woman might safely be prophesied, even if the experiment had never been tried; but we have, moreover, the absolute confirmation of experience on the point, as I, for one, will gladly testify from personal acquaintance in America with many women who have made Medicine their profession; having had myself the advantage of studying under one who was characterized, by a medical gentleman known throughout the professional world, as "one of the best physicians in Boston," and who, certainly, was more remarkable for thorough refinement of mind than most women I know, – Dr Lucy Sewall.

Of course there may always be unfortunate exceptions, or rather there will always be those of both sexes who, whatever their profession may be, will be sure to disgrace it; but it is not of them that I speak, nor is it by such individual cases that the supporters of any great movement should be judged.

The next argument usually advanced against the practice of medicine by women is that there is no demand for it; that women, as a rule, have little confidence in their own sex, and had rather be attended by a man. That everybody had rather be attended by a competent physician is no doubt true; that women have hitherto had little experience of competent physicians of their own sex is equally true; nor can it be denied that the education bestowed on most women is not one likely to inspire much confidence. It is probably a fact, that until lately there has been "no de mand" for women doctors, because it does not occur to most people to demand what does not exist; but that very many women have wished that they could be medically attended by those of their own sex I am very sure, and I know of more than one case where ladies have habitually gone through one confinement after another without proper attendance, because the idea of employing a man was so extremely repugnant to them. I have indeed repeatedly found that even doctors, not altogether favourable to the present movement, allow that they consider men rather out of place in midwifery practice; and an eminent American practitioner once remarked to me that he never entered a lady's room to attend her in confinement without wishing to apologize for what he felt to be an intrusion, though a necessary and beneficent intrusion, in one of his sex.

I suppose that the real test of "demand" is not in the opinions expressed by those women who have never even seen a thoroughly educated female physician, but in the practice which flows in to any such physician when her qualifications are clearly satisfactory. In England there are at present but two women legally qualified to practise Medicine, and I understand that already their time is much more fully occupied, and their receipts much greater, than is usually the case with medical men who have been practising for so short a period. Dr Garrett Anderson's Dispensary for poor women is also largely attended, and during the five years which have elapsed since it was opened, more than 40,000 visits have been made to it; 9,000 new patients have been admitted, and 250 midwifery cases have been attended by the midwives attached to the charity, Dr Garrett Anderson being called in when necessary.

❋ ❋ ❋ ❋

There is reason to hope that women doctors may do even more for the health of their own sex in the way of prevention than of cure, and surely this is the very noblest province of the true physician. Already it is being proved with what eagerness women will attend lectures on physiology and hygiene when delivered to them by a woman, though perhaps not one in ten would go to the same course of lectures if given by a medical man. I look forward to the day when a competent knowledge of these subjects shall be as general among women as it now is rare; and when that day arrives, I trust that the "poor health" which is now so sadly common in our sex, and which so frequently comes from sheer ignorance of sanitary laws, will become rather the exception than, as now too often, the rule. I hope that then we shall find far fewer instances of life-long illness entailed on herself by a girl's thoughtless ignorance; I believe we shall see a generation of women far fitter in mind and body to take their share in the work of the world, and that the Registrar will have to record a much lower rate of infantile mortality when mothers themselves have learned to know something at least of the elementary laws of health It has been well said that the noblest end of education is to make the educator no longer necessary; and I, at least, shall think it the highest proof of success if women doctors can in time succeed in so raising the standard of health among their sister women, that but half the present percentage of medical practitioners are required in comparison to the female population.

❋ ❋ ❋ ❋

Is there not one of the English, Scotch, or Irish Universities that will win future laurels by now taking the lead generously, and announcing its willingness to cease, at least, its policy of arbitrary exclusion? Let the authorities, if they please, admit women to study in the ordinary classes with or without any special restrictions (and it is hard to believe that at least the greater part of the lectures could not be attended in common); or let them, if they think needful, bid the women make their own arrangements, and gather their knowledge as they can; with this promise only, that, when acquired, such knowledge shall be duly tested, and, if found worthy, shall receive the Hall-mark of the regular Medical Degree.

Surely this is not too much to ask, and no more is absolutely essential. If, indeed, the assertions so often made about the incapacity of women are true, the result of such examinations (which may be both theoretical and practical, scientific and clinical,) will triumphantly prove the point. If the examinations are left in the hands of competent men, we may be very sure that all unqualified women will be summarily rejected, as indeed it is to be desired that they should be.

If, on the contrary, some women, however few, can, under all existing disadvantages, successfully pass the ordeal, and go forth with the full authority of the degree of Doctor of Medicine, surely all will be glad to welcome their perhaps unexpected success, and bid every such woman, as she sets forth on her mission of healing, a hearty God-speed!

55. Diana Mulock Craik
Only a Woman

She loves with love that cannot tire:
    And if, ah, woe! she loves alone,
Through passionate duty love flames higher,
    As grass grows taller round a stone.
                  Coventry Patmore

So, the truth's out. I'll grasp it like a snake, –
It will not slay me. My heart shall not break
Awhile, if only for the children's sake.

For his too, somewhat. Let him stand unblamed;
None say, he gave me less than honor claimed,
Except – one trifle scarcely worth being named –

The *heart*. That's gone. The corrupt dead might be
As easily raised up, breathing – fair to see,
As he could bring his whole heart back to me.

I never sought him in coquettish sport,
Or courted him as silly maidens court,
And wonder when the longed-for prize falls short.

I only loved him – any woman would:
But shut my love up till he came and sued,
Then poured it o'er his dry life like a flood.

I was so happy I could make him blest!
So happy that I was his first and best,
As he mine – when he took me to his breast.

Ah me! if only then he had been true!
If for one little year, a month or two,
He had given me love for love, as was my due!

Or had he told me, ere the deed was done,
He only raised me to his heart's dear throne –
Poor substitute – because the queen was gone!

O, had he whispered, when his sweetest kiss
Was warm upon my mouth in fancied bliss,
He had kissed another woman even as this, –

It were less bitter! Sometimes I could weep
To be thus cheated, like a child asleep: –
Were not my anguish far too dry and deep.

So I built my house upon another's ground;
Mocked with a heart just caught at the rebound –
A cankered thing that looked so firm and sound.

And when that heart grew colder – colder still,
I, ignorant, tried all duties to fulfil,
Blaming my foolish pain, exacting will,

All – anything but him. It was to be:
The full draught others drink up carelessly
Was made this bitter Tantalus-cup for me.

I say again – he gives me all I claimed,
I and my children never shall be shamed:
He is a just man – he will live unblamed.

Only – O God, O God, to cry for bread,
And get a stone! Daily to lay my head
Upon a bosom where the old love's dead!

Dead? – Fool! It never lived. It only stirred
Galvanic, like an hour-cold corpse. None heard:
So let me bury it without a word.

He'll keep that other woman from my sight.
I know not if her face be foul or bright;
I only know that it was his delight –

As his was mine: I only know he stands
Pale, at the touch of their long-severed hands,
Then to a flickering smile his lips commands,

Lest I should grieve, or jealous anger show.
He need not. When the ship's gone down, I trow,
We little reck whatever wind may blow.

And so my silent moan begins and ends.
No world's laugh or world's taunt, no pity of friends
Or sneer of foes with this my torment blends.

None knows – none heeds. I have a little pride;
Enough to stand up, wife-like, by his side,
With the same smile as when I was a bride.

And I shall take his children to my arms;
They will not miss these fading, worthless charms;
Their kiss – ah, unlike his – all pain disarms.

And haply, as the solemn years go by,
He will think sometimes with regretful sigh,
The other woman was less true than I.

1873

56. Sara Coleridge
from *Recollections of Early Life*

My young life is almost a blank in memory... till the time of my visit to
Allan Bank, when I was six years old. That journey to Grasmere gleams
before me as the shadow of a shade. Some goings on of my stay there I
remember more clearly. Allan Bank is a large house on a hill overlooking
Easedale on one side, and Grasmere on the other. Dorothy, Mr Wordsworth's
only daughter, was at this time very picturesque in her appearance, with
her long, thick, yellow locks, which were never cut, but curled with papers,
a thing which seems much out of keeping with the poetic simplicity of the
household. I remember being asked by my father and Miss Wordsworth,
the poet's sister, if I did not think her very pretty. 'No,' said I, bluntly; for
which I met a rebuff which made me feel as if I was a culprit.

My father's wish it was to have me for a month with him at Grasmere,
where he was domesticated with the Wordsworths. He insisted upon it
that I became rosier and hardier during my absence from mama. She did
not much like to part with me, and I think my father's motive, at bottom,
must have been a wish to fasten my affections on him. I slept with him, and
he would tell me fairy stories when he came to bed at twelve and one
o'clock. I remember his telling me a wild tale, too, in his study, and my
trying to repeat it to the maids afterwards.

I have no doubt there was much enjoyment in my young life at that time,
but some of my recollections are tinged with pain. I think my dear father
was anxious that I should learn to love him and the Wordsworths and their
children, and not cling so exclusively to my mother, and all around me at
home. He was therefore much annoyed when, on my mother's coming to
Allan Bank, I flew to her, and wished not to be separated from her any
more. I remember his shewing displeasure to me, and accusing me of want
of affection. I could not understand why. The young Wordsworths came
in and caressed him. I sat benumbed; for truly nothing does so freeze
affection as the breath of jealousy. The sense that you have done very
wrong, or at least given great offence, you know not how or why – that you
are dunned for some payment of love or feeling which you know not how
to produce or to demonstrate on a sudden, chills the heart, and fills it with
perplexity and bitterness. My father reproached me, and contrasted my
coldness with the childish caresses of the little Wordsworths. I slunk away,

and hid myself in the wood behind the house, and there my friend John, whom at that time I called my future husband, came to seek me.

It was during this stay at Allan Bank that I used to see my father and Mr De Quincey pace up and down the room in conversation. I understood not, nor listened to a word they said, but used to note the handkerchief hanging out of the pocket behind, and long to clutch it. Mr Wordsworth, too, must have been one of the room walkers. How gravely and earnestly used Samuel Taylor Coleridge and William Wordsworth and my uncle Southey also to discuss the affairs of the nation, as if it all came home to their business and bosoms, as if it were their private concern! Men do not canvass these matters now-a-days, I think, quite in the same tone. Domestic concerns absorb their deeper feelings, national ones are treated more as things aloof, the speculative rather than the practical.

My father used to talk to me with much admiration and affection of Sarah Hutchinson, Mrs Wordsworth's sister, who resided partly with the Wordsworths, partly with her own brothers. At this time she used to act as my father's amanuensis. She wrote out great part of the 'Friend' to his dictation. She had fine, long, light brown hair, I think her only beauty, except a fair skin, for her features were plain and contracted, her figure dumpy, and devoid of grace and dignity. She was a plump woman, of little more than five feet. I remember my father talking to me admiringly of her long light locks, and saying how mildly she bore it when the baby pulled them hard in play.

Miss Wordsworth, Mr Wordsworth's sister, of most poetic eye and temper, took a great part with the children. She told us once a pretty story of a primrose, I think, which she spied by the way-side when she went to see me soon after my birth, though that was at Christmas, and how this same primrose was still blooming when she went back to Grasmere.

. . . My father had particular feelings and fancies about dress, as had my uncle Southey and Mr Wordsworth also. He could not abide the scarlet socks which Edith and I wore at one time. I remember going to him when mama had just dressed me in a new stuff frock. He took me up, and set me down again without a caress. I thought he disliked the dress; perhaps he was in an uneasy mood. He much liked everything feminine and domestic, pretty and becoming, but not fine-ladyish. My uncle Southey was all for gay, bright, cheerful colours, and even declared he had a taste for the *grand*, in half jest.

Mr Wordsworth loved all that was rich and picturesque, light and free in clothing. A deep Prussian blue or purple was one of his favourite colours for a silk dress. He wished that white dresses were banished, and that our peasantry wore blue and scarlet and other warm colours, instead of sombre, dingy black, which converts a crowd that might be ornamental in the landscape into a swarm of magnified ants. I remember his saying how much better young girls looked of an evening in bare arms, even if the arms themselves were not very lovely, it gave such a lightness to their general air. I think he was looking at Dora when he said this. White dresses he thought cold, a blot and disharmony in any picture, in door or out of door. My father admired white clothing, because he looked at it in reference to woman, as expressive of her delicacy and purity, not merely as a component part of a general picture.

My father liked my wearing a cap. He thought it looked girlish and domestic. Dora and I must have been a curious contrast, – she with her wild eyes, impetuous movements, and fine, long, floating yellow hair, – I with my timid, large blue eyes, slender form, and little fair delicate face, muffled up in lace border and muslin. But I thought little of looks then; only I fancied Edith S., on first seeing her, most beautiful.

❀ ❀ ❀ ❀

Such are the chief *historical* events of my little life up to nine years of age. But can I in any degree retrace what being I was then, what relation my then being held to my maturer self? Can I draw any useful reflection from my childish experience, or found any useful maxim upon it? What *was* I? In person very slender and delicate, not habitually colourless, but often enough pallid and feeble looking. Strangers used to exclaim about my eyes, and I remember remarks made upon their large size, both by my Uncle Southey and Mr Wordsworth. I suppose the thinness of my face, and the smallness of the other features, with the muffling close cap, increased the apparent size of the eye, for only artists, since I have grown up, speak of my eyes as large and full. They were bluer, too, in my early years than now. My health alternated, as it has done all my life, till the last ten or twelve years, when it has been unchangeably depressed, between delicacy and a very easy, comfortable condition. I remember well that nervous sensitiveness and morbid imaginativeness had set in with me very early. During my Grasmere visit I used to feel frightened at night on account of the darkness. I then was a stranger to the whole host of night-agitators, ghosts, goblins, demons, burglars, elves, and witches. Horrid ghastly tales and ballads, of which crowds afterwards came in my way, had not yet cast their shadows over my mind. And yet I was terrified in the dark, and used to think of lions, the only form of terror which my dark-engendered agitation would take. My next bugbear was the Ghost in Hamlet. Then the picture of Death at Hell Gate in an old edition of Paradise Lost, the delight of my girlhood. Last and worst came my Uncle Southey's ballad horrors, above all the Old Woman of Berkeley. Oh, the agonies I have endured between nine and twelve at night, before mama joined me in bed, in presence of that hideous assemblage of horrors, the horse with eyes of flame! I dare not, even now, rehearse these particulars, for fear of calling up some of the old feeling, which, indeed, I have never in my life been quite free from. What made the matter worse was that, like all other nervous sufferings, it could not be understood by the inexperienced, and consequently subjected the sufferer to ridicule and censure. My Uncle Southey laughed heartily at my agonies. I mean at the cause. He did not enter into the agonies. Even mama scolded me for creeping out of bed after an hour's torture, and stealing down to her in the parlour, saying I could bear the loneliness and the night-fears no longer. But my father understood the case better. He insisted that a lighted candle should be left in my room, in the interval between my retiring to bed and mama's joining me. From that time forth my sufferings ceased. I believe they would have destroyed my health had they continued.

Yet I was a most fearless child by daylight, ever ready to take the difficult mountain-path and outgo my companions' daring in tree-climbing. In those early days we used to spend much of our summer-time in trees, greatly to the horror of some of our London visitors.

---

57. Hannah Cullwick
from *Diary*

Saturday 13 September.

I got up & put my dirty things on. Lighted the fire & swept up. Wash'd me at the sink, where I always do, in the tin bowl, & M. was pleas'd to see me do it. I've no looking glass down here, & as I told M. I'd not seen my face for days. Only yesterday I look'd to see how black I look'd after being out on errands & there was a streak o' black across my nose, & my whole face more or less dusty. And every day I've wore my striped apron & peasant's bonnet & had my dirty cotton frock on, so as I'm surprised that young man shd ask me to go out with him. Massa saw me clean his boots this morning, & I fetch'd the bath downstairs for him to use & brought a basin down, but M. had to wash at the sink. He said that's one part of a servant's life he should not like, & seeing the dirty cloth hanging about, but he suppos'd that was nothing to me. I said no, 'cause I was used to it. Then I laid M.'s breakfast things, & went out to fetch various things in, for M. & for breakfast. I read a chapter out & we knelt down at the kitchen table & had prayers and it was ½ past 11 when I clean'd away & lighted the fire upstairs for M. to sit & see me scrub.

I put my bonnet & apron on & took my pail & things up & begun, & M. told me to kiss him afore I black'd my face. So I did, & then rubb'd my black hand across my face & arms, & when I'd to go down for a fresh [pail] o' water M. said he hoped to see me blacker still when I come back. So downstairs I black'd both my hands & wiped them all over my face & that pleas'd Massa & he said I was blacker even than any o' the pit wenches. And I scour'd round the room changing the water 3 or 4 times, & talking now & then my simple talk, & bits o' French, till about ½ past one he got so sleepy & I was still then, & he went fast off. And I felt tired too, & I lay on the bed waiting for the laundress & *I* went to sleep. At 3 [I] woke M. & he came down & wash'd & dress'd to start away again. I thought I shd feel dull & bad after, but M. kiss'd me so heartily & said such a nice goodbye, & I went out of errands & pass'd it off & went to bed by 9, for it was raining all the evening.

Sunday 14 September.

Altho' Massa has bin & gone away again so sudden I've not felt dull today, nor last night either. Mr Rees (the gentleman on the ground floor) coming while M. was saying goodbye, & Massa of course not wanting to be seen especially in the kitchen, it started both of us. M. was off to get dinner before going to King's Cross, & I up Fetter Lane in the rain to get my errands in. So when I come back to my tea in the kitchen I was at home again, & all was again as afore M. came, only I felt *happier*. How could I help it, after having such a proof of his love – to come from impulse 2 hundred miles just to see me after I had written to him what I didn't think was anything especially nice. But *he* liked it, & in the afternoon couldn't help starting from Wigan, to me, instead of going to his other home – all for *love*. And I was as much pleas'd as I was surprised when I got the telegram soon after six to say he would be here from ten to 11. I'd begun to feel very tired, but all that was gone, & I made haste & made his bedroom quite ready & air'd things. Went out afore I wash'd me for things for his tea, & then I clean'd the kitchen round on my hands & knees & made a nice bright fire & tea things laid & all for my dear lord & master. And it seem'd so much nicer & more homely & cosy somehow, getting the *kitchen* ready for *him*.

Should I have felt *such* pleasure for a common working man? I *might* if I had found a working man as could love as purely & be as Massa is (I mean in everything but his learning) & honour him as much, but that's a difficulty I doubt, the finding such a one. And so when I was young & *did* meet with Massa (whose face I'd seen in the fire) I made my mind up that it was best & safest to be a slave to a *gentleman*, nor wife & equal to any vulgar man, still with the wish & determination to be independent by working in service and without the slightest hope o' been rais'd in rank either in place or by being married. And so at last after all these nearly twenty years, by God's help & Massa's true heart & fervent love to me (more than ever I could dare to hope for from anyone but him, & I always trusted Massa). I am as I am. A servant still, & a very low one, in the eyes o' the world. I can work at ease. I can go out & come in when I please, & I can look as degraded as ever I like without caring how much I'm despised in the Temple, or in Fetter Lane or in the streets.

And with all that I have the inward comfort o' knowing that I am loved & honoured & admired & that I am united in heart & soul as well as married at church to the truest, best, & handsomest man in my eyes that ever was born. No man I ever see, or ever saw, is so lovely. And M. is pleas'd with me & after all this there can be no doubt of our being made for each other. And so may God bless together, & give us both wisdom to live happily always, & health & strength to do the work afore us, & grace that we may never forget who is the giver of all our comforts, & to praise Him more & more. But Massa would not sleep in his own room, but downstairs in the kitchen bedroom with me & we talk'd till two o'clock. And in the morning he noticed how rough my knees are. They feel like a nutmeg grater, so different to his, & M. was so pleas'd to feel 'em 'cause he said, it was such a true sign of being a servant.

I went to St. James's Church this evening & enjoy'd the service very much – such nice quiet singing – and I saw the clergyman who married us, & thought he look'd at me.

---

58. Emily Pfeiffer
Peace to the Odalisque, I

PEACE to the odalisque, the facile slave,
Whose uninvidious love rewards the brave,
Or cherishes the coward; she who yields
Her lord the fief of waste, uncultur'd fields
To perish in non-using; she whose hour
Is measur'd by her beauties' transient flower;

Who lives in him, as he in God, and dies
The death of parasites, no more to rise.
Graceful ephemera! Fair morning dream
   Of the young world! In vain would women's hearts
In love with sacrifice, withstand the stream
   Of human progress; other spheres, new parts
Await them. God be with them in their quest –
Our brave, sad working-women of the west!

1874

59. Bertha Thomas
Latest Intelligence from the Planet Venus

IT may be reckoned among those things not generally known that within
a short time direct telescopic communication, by means of signals, has
been established between the earth and the planet Venus, and that at certain
stations regular interchange of intelligence is now carried on. The results
have hitherto been kept secret, partly, it is said, owing to the disappointment of the astronomers at finding in the new country but a mirror of our
own, with an hereditary constitutional monarchy, two Houses, a civilisation
in about the same stage of advancement as ours, and political and social
institutions generally similar. The single remarkable difference presented
to their notice is one they are loth to reveal, for fear, we believe, of the
family discords it might possibly excite at home, and we are the first to
acquaint our readers with the curious fact that in the planet Venus, though
the present sovereign happens to be a king, all political business, electoral
and parliamentary, is allotted to the women. Women only have the right to
vote or to sit in the House of Commons, and the Upper House is formed
of the eldest daughters of deceased Peers. Politics, therefore, are included
among the usual branches of ladies' education, but except in this respect
their social condition presents no unusual features.

    This monopoly by women of political power is as old as their system of
government, and until a few years ago no one dreamt of complaining or of
questioning its wisdom. But a pamphlet advocating the enfranchisement
of males has lately been published by a clever female agitator, and caused
a considerable stir. It is not pretended that a majority of the sex ask or even

desire the privilege. The plea put forward is abstract justice backed by possible expediency, and, the cry once sounded, arguments are not wanting, petitions flow in, idle men have taken the matter up and find supporters among the younger women, and last night a member of the Government redeemed the pledge made to her constituents last election, to bring forward a bill for removing the electoral disabilities of men. She has no lack of supporters, some sincere, some interested. Her greatest difficulty was in persuading the House to treat the measure seriously. The notion of admitting young cornets, cricketers, and fops of the Dundreary pattern to a share in the legislation, the prospect of Parliamentary benches recruited from the racecourse, the hunting field, and the billiard-room was a picture that proved too much for the gravity of the Commons. A division, however, was insisted upon by the original proposer. At this juncture the leader of the Opposition, a lady as distinguished for her personal attractions as by her intelligence, moderation, common sense, and experience, arose, and made the following forcible speech, which we transcribe for the benefit of all such as it may directly or indirectly, concern:

'Madam, – Before proceeding to state my opinions on this question, or my reasons for holding them, I wish to impress on you a sense of the importance of the measure just brought forward, that it may at least obtain from you the attention it deserves. I must urge you not to allow party or personal motives to blind you to its nature and bearings. The supporters of Male Suffrage are seeking not only to introduce a startling innovation into a system of government that has hitherto worked remarkably well, but in so doing they would tamper with the foundations of society, and in a blind cry for equality and supposititious justice ignore the most elementary laws of nature. The question is not a political, it is a scientific and physiological one. About the equality of the sexes we may go on disputing for ever, but with regard to their identity there can be no manner of doubt. No one has ever ventured to assert it. Each sex has its special sphere – mission – call it what you will, originally assigned to it by nature, appropriated by custom. What now are the special and distinguishing natural characteristics of the male sex? Assuredly muscular strength and development. With less quickness of instinct, flexibility, and patience than women, men are decidedly our superiors in physical power. Look at individuals, men of all classes – mark their capability for, nay their enjoyment of, exertion and exposure. If these do not naturally fall to their lot they find artificial employment for their faculties in violent games and athletic exercises; some indeed go as far as to seek it in the distant hunting grounds and prairies of uncivilised continents. This quality of theirs has its proper outlet in the active professions. To man, therefore, war and navigation, engineering and commerce, agriculture and trade, their perils and toils, their laurels and gains; to man, in short, all those callings in which his peculiar endowment of greater physical force and endurance of physical hardships is a main and necessary element. Those with superior mental gifts will turn to such scientific pursuits as specially demand courage, exposure, and rough labour. It is most essential that their energies should not be diverted from these channels. We should then have bad soldiers, bad ships, bad machines, bad artisans. Government, on the other hand, is no game to be played at by amateurs. The least of its functions claims much honest thought and watchfulness. Either, then, the manly professions will suffer, or else – and this is the worse danger of the two – the suffrage will be carelessly exercised, and the mass of new voters, without leisure to think and judge for themselves, will be swayed by a few wire-pullers, unprincipled adventurers, who, seeking only to feather their own nests, will not hesitate to turn to account the ignorance and preoccupation of the electors.

'Now turn to the woman. Her organisation no less clearly defines her sphere. With finer natural perceptions than man, less ungovernable in her emotions, quicker and clearer in intellect, physically better fitted for sedentary life, more inclined to study and thought, everything seems to qualify her specially for legislation. For the judicious application of general rules to particular cases, peculiar delicacy of instinct is required, and in no capacity have any but women been known to approach the ideal of government – that perfect rule – all-efficient, yet unfelt.

'Take the family as a rough type of the nation. To whom, at home is naturally allotted the government of young children? To the mother. To whom that of the domestic household? To the mistress. Widowers and bachelors are proverbially the slaves and victims of spoilt children and ill-trained servants. In all such home matters the husband defers to his wife, and would as soon expect to have to instruct her in them as she to teach him fortification, boxing, or mechanics. Little time or thought, indeed, has the professional man to spare for household superintendence; how much less for matters requiring such careful study as the government of a nation. The clergyman, wearied with his day's visiting of the sick, teaching or preaching; the doctor after his rounds; the merchant or trades-man overwhelmed with business; what they require when their daily toil is over is rest, relaxation, not to be set down to work out complex social and political problems, to study the arguments for and against the several measures to which members offer to pledge themselves and to form a judgment on the merits of respective candidates. What time or opportunity have they for qualifying themselves to do so? But the wives of these men, on the other hand, have lives comparatively unoccupied, and of physical and intellectual leisure enough and to spare. Here, then, is a commodity; there a demand and a field for it, and this surplus, so to speak, of time, strength, and attention with us has been always applied to the science of government, nor do I see how a happier or more judicious arrangement could have been made.

'I will proceed now to enumerate a few of the dangers to which the enfranchisement of men would inevitably expose us. Male voters will view each political question in a narrow professional light, irrespective of its justice or general expediency. Large proprietors will stand up for the game laws, eldest sons for primogeniture. Publicans, brewers, and railway directors will exercise a baneful, blind, one-sided influence on our counsels. An impartial debate or decision will soon become a thing of the past, fairness sink into the shade, and a majority of direct pecuniary interest turn the scale in all cases.

'Again, the bulk of the national property being in the hands of the men, the openings and temptations to bribery would be enormously increased. Few women have the power, had they the will, to offer bribes sufficient to suborn a constituency, but when millionaires are admitted to the suffrage we may expect to see parliamentary elections bought and sold, and going, like other wares, to the highest bidder.

'But there is a more alarming danger still. The muscular force of the community being male, an opportunity would be afforded for an amount of intimidation it would shock us now even to contemplate. Right has ever been might in our land. Shall we reverse our motto? Shall we, who have ever taken pride in the fact that our counsels are swayed by reason and judgment alone – a fact from which men have benefited at least as much as women – invite the fatal indefensible element of force to enter in and meddle with our elections, and let the hustings become the scene of such struggles and riots as in certain countries where, by a singular distortion of judgment, the management of political affairs is thrust entirely on the men? Supposing that the suffrage were irrespective of sex, and supposing it to happen that the men in a wrong cause were arrayed against and outvoted by the women in a right, would they not, as they could, use force to compel the women to submit? And here we are threatened with a relapse into barbarism from which the present constitution of our State affords so admirable a guarantee. And that something of the sort would ensue I have little doubt. Probably the next step would be to oust women altogether from the legislature – the standard of female education would then decline, and woman would sink lower and lower both in fact and in the estimation of men. Being physically weak, she must always, among the rough and uneducated classes, be especially exposed to ill-treatment. Of this in our country, I am happy to say, there are but rare instances, nevertheless. But there are lands where men monopolise the suffrage, and where a state of things exists among the lower classes – let us hope the upper and civilised orders do not realise it, for their apathy would otherwise be monstrous – which if widely and thoroughly known would be recognised as the darkest page of modern history, something to which a parallel must be sought in the worst days of legalised slavery. Penal laws have utterly failed as a remedy, and it is obvious that they must always do so. What has been our guard against this particular evil? Is it not that point in our social system which raises woman's position, both actually and in the eyes of the men of her class, by entrusting to her functions of general importance, which she is at least as well qualified by nature to fill as man, and which we take care that her education shall fit her for, as a man's, necessarily unequal, semi-professional, and engrossing, can never do? Thus men have an irksome, thankless, exacting, life-long labour taken off their hands, which are left free to work out their fame and fortune; educated women their faculties turned to the best account; while among the lower orders, the artificial superiority conferred on the female sex by its privilege of the suffrage, raising the woman's status in fact and in the eyes of her husband, acts as an effectual check on domestic tyranny of the worst sort, and the nation has the advantage of being governed by that section of the community whose organisation, habits, and condition best enable them to study political science.

'That any wrong is done to men by the existing arrangement, I entirely deny. Most of them are married, and it is so seldom that a wife's political opinions differ materially from her husband's, that the vote of the former may fairly be said to represent both. The effect on the sex itself would be most undesirable. It is a fatal mistake to try to turn men into women, to shut them up indoors, and set them to study blue-books and reports in their intervals of business, to enforce on them an amount of thought, seclusion, and inaction so manifestly uncongenial to their physical constitution, which points so plainly to the field, the deck, the workshop, as the proper theatre for their activity. The best men are those who are most earnest and laborious in their professions, and do not trouble themselves with politics. Already they have sufficient subjects to study – special studies imperatively necessary for their respective occupations. Do not let us put another weight on the shoulders of those who, from the cradle to the grave, have so much less leisure than ourselves for reflection and acquiring political knowledge, or else, let us look no more for calm and judicious elections, but to see candidates supported from the lowest motives, and members returned by a majority of intimidation, bribery, private interest, or at best by chance, all through the ill-advised enfranchisement of an enormous body of muscular indeed, but necessarily prejudiced, ignorant, preoccupied members of society.'

The honourable member here resumed her seat amid loud cheers. On a division being taken, the motion was rejected by an overwhelming majority, and the question of Male Suffrage may be considered shelved for the present in the planet Venus.

1875

60. Isabella Bird
from *The Hawaiian Archipelago*

All the gulches for the first twenty-four miles contain running water. The great Hakalau gulch we crossed early yesterday, has a river with a smooth bed as wide as the Thames at Eton. Some have only small quiet streams, which pass gently through ferny grottoes. Others have fierce strong torrents dashing between abrupt walls of rock, among immense boulders into deep abysses, and cast themselves over precipice after precipice into the ocean. Probably, many of these are the courses of fire torrents, whose jagged masses of *a-a* have since been worn smooth, and channelled into holes by the action of water. A few are crossed on narrow bridges, but the majority are forded, if that quiet conventional term can be applied to the violent flounderings by which the horses bring one through. The transparency deceives them, and however deep the water is, they always try to lift their fore feet out of it, which gives them a disagreeable rolling motion. . . .

We lunched in one glorious valley, and Kaluna made drinking cups which held fully a pint, out of the beautiful leaves of the Arum esculentum. Towards afternoon turbid-looking clouds lowered over the sea, and by the time we reached the worst *pali* of all, the south side of Laupahoehoe, they burst on us in torrents of rain accompanied by strong wind. This terrible precipice takes one entirely by surprise. Kaluna, who rode first, disappeared so suddenly that I thought he had gone over. It is merely a dangerous broken ledge, and besides that it looks as if there were only foothold for a goat, one is dizzied by the sight of the foaming ocean immediately below, and, when we actually reached the bottom, there was only a narrow strip of shingle between the stupendous cliff and the resounding surges, which came up as if bent on destruction. The path by which we descended looked a mere thread on the side of the precipice. I don't know what the word beetling means, but if it means anything bad, I will certainly apply it to that *pali*.

A number of disastrous-looking native houses are clustered under some very tall palms in the open part of the gulch, but it is a most wretched situation; the roar of the surf is deafening, the scanty supply of water is brackish, there are rumours that leprosy is rife, and the people are said to be the poorest on Hawaii. We were warned that we could not spend a night comfortably there, so wet, tired, and stiff, we rode on [an]other six miles to the house of a native called Bola-Bola, where we had been instructed to remain. The rain was heavy and ceaseless, and the trail had become so slippery that our progress was much retarded. It was a most unpropitious-looking evening, and I began to feel the painful stiffness arising from prolonged fatigue in saturated clothes. I indulged in various imaginations as we rode up the long ascent leading to Bola-Bola's, but this time they certainly were not of sofas and tea, and I never aspired to anything beyond drying my clothes by a good fire, for at Hilo some people had shrugged their shoulders, and others had laughed mysteriously at the idea of our sleeping there, and some had said it was one of the worst of native houses.

A single glance was enough. It was a dilapidated frame-house, altogether forlorn, standing unsheltered on a slope of the mountain, with one or two yet more forlorn grass piggeries, which I supposed might be the cook house, and eating-house near it.

A prolonged *har-r-r-rouche* from Kaluna brought out a man with a female horde behind him, all shuffling into clothes as we approached, and we stiffly dismounted from the wet saddles in which we had sat for ten hours, and stiffly hobbled up into the littered verandah, the water dripping from our clothes, and squeezing out of our boots at every step. Inside there was one room about 18 x 14 feet, which looked as if the people had just arrived and had thrown down their goods promiscuously. There were mats on the floor not over clean, and half the room was littered and piled with mats rolled up, boxes, bamboos, saddles, blankets, lassos, cocoanuts, *kalo* roots, bananas, quilts, pans, calabashes, bundles of hard *poi* in *ti* leaves, bones, cats, fowls, clothes. A frightful old woman, looking like a relic of the old heathen days, with bristling grey hair cut short, her body tattooed all over, and no clothing but a ragged blanket huddled round her shoulders; a girl about twelve, with torrents of shining hair, and a piece of bright green calico thrown round her, and two very good-looking young women in rose-coloured chemises, one of them holding a baby, were squatting and lying on the mats, one over another, like a heap of savages.

When the man found that we were going to stay all night he bestirred himself, dragged some of the things to one side and put down a shake-down of *pulu* (the silky covering of the fronds of one species of tree-fern), with a sheet over it, and a gay quilt of orange and red cotton. There was a thin printed muslin curtain to divide off one half of the room, a usual arrangement in native houses. He then helped to unsaddle the horses, and the confusion of the room was increased by a heap of our wet saddles, blankets, and gear. All this time the women lay on the floor and stared at us.

Rheumatism seemed impending, for the air up there was chilly, and I said to Deborah that I must make some change in my dress, and she signed to Kaluna, who sprang at my soaked boots and pulled them off, and my stockings too, with a savage alacrity which left it doubtful for a moment whether he had not also pulled off my feet! I had no means of making any further change except putting on a wrapper over my wet clothes.

Meanwhile the man killed and boiled a fowl, and boiled some sweet potato, and when these untempting viands, and a calabash of *poi* were put before us, we sat round them and [ate]; I with my knife, the others with their fingers. There was some coffee in a dirty bowl. The females had arranged a row of pillows on their mat, and all lay face downwards, with their chins resting upon them, staring at us with their great brown eyes, and talking and laughing incessantly. They had low sensual faces, like some low order of animal. When our meal was over, the man threw them the relics, and they soon picked the bones clean. It surprised me that after such a badly served meal the man brought a bowl of water for our hands, and something intended for a towel.

By this time it was dark, and a stone, deeply hollowed at the top, was produced, containing beef fat and a piece of rag for a wick, which burned with a strong flaring light. The women gathered themselves up and sat round a large calabash of *poi*, conveying the sour paste to their mouths with an inimitable twist of the fingers, laying their heads back and closing their eyes with a look of animal satisfaction. When they had eaten they lay down as before, with their chins on their pillows, and again the row of great brown eyes confronted me. Deborah, Kaluna, and the women talked incessantly in loud shrill voices till Kaluna uttered the word *auwé* with a long groaning intonation, apparently signifying weariness, divested himself of his clothes and laid down on a mat alongside our shake-down, upon which we let down the dividing curtain and wrapped ourselves up as warmly as possible.

I was uneasy about Deborah who had had a cough for some time, and consequently took the outside place under the window which was broken, and presently a large cat jumped through the hole and down upon me, followed by another and another, till five wild cats had effected an entrance, making me a stepping-stone to ulterior proceedings. Had there been a sixth I think I could not have borne the infliction quietly. Strips of jerked beef were hanging from the rafters, and by the light which was still burning I watched the cats climb up stealthily, seize on some of these, descend, and disappear through the window, making me a stepping-stone as before, but with all their craft they let some of the strips fall, which awoke Deborah, and next I saw Kaluna's magnificent eyes peering at us under the curtain. Then the natives got up, and smoked and [ate] more *poi* at intervals, and talked, and Kaluna and Deborah quarrelled, jokingly, about the time of night she told me, and the moon through the rain-clouds occasionally gave us delusive hopes of dawn, and I kept moving my place to get out of the drip from the roof, and so the night passed. I was amused all the time, though I should have preferred sleep to such nocturnal diversions. It was so new, and so odd, to be the only white person among eleven natives in a lonely house, and yet to be as secure from danger and annoyance as in our own home.

* * * *

We breakfasted on fowl, *poi*, and cocoanut milk, in presence of even a larger number of spectators than the night before, one of them a very old man looking savagely picturesque, with a red blanket tied round his waist, leaving his lean chest and arms, which were elaborately tattooed, completely exposed.

The mule had been slightly chafed by the gear, and in my anxiety about a borrowed animal, of which Mr. Austin makes a great joke, I put my saddle-bags on my own mare, in an evil hour, and not only these, but some fine cocoanuts, tied up in a waterproof which had long ago proved its worthlessness. It was a grotesquely miserable picture. The house is not far from the beach, and the surf, beyond which a heavy mist hung, was coming in with such a tremendous sound that we had to shout at the top of our voices in order to be heard. The sides of the great gulch rose like prison walls, cascades which had no existence the previous night hurled themselves from the summit of the cliffs directly into the sea, the rain, which fell in sheets, not drops, covered the ground to the depth of two or three inches, and dripped from the wretched, shivering horses, which stood huddled together with their tails between their legs. My thin flannel suit was wet through even before we mounted. I dispensed with stockings, as I was told that wearing them in rain chills and stiffens the limbs. D., about whom I was anxious, as well as about the mule, had a really waterproof cloak, and I am glad to say has quite lost the cough from which she suffered before our expedition. She does not care about rain any more than I do.

We soon reached the top of the worst and dizziest of all the *palis*, and then splashed on mile after mile, down sliding banks, and along rocky tracks, from which the soil had been completely carried, the rain falling all the time. In some places several feet of soil had been carried away, and we passed through water-rents, the sides of which were as high as our horses' heads, where the ground had been level a few days before. By noon the aspect of things became so bad that I wished we had a white man with us, as I was uneasy about some of the deepest gulches. . . .

We crossed one gulch in which the water was strong, and up to our horses' bodies . . . D. then said that the next gulch was rather a bad one, and that we must not wait for Kaluna, but ride fast, and try to get through it. When we reached the *pali* above it, we heard the roaring of a torrent, and when we descended to its brink it looked truly bad, but D. rode in, and I waited on the margin. She got safely across, but when she was near the opposite side her large horse plunged, slipped, and scrambled in a most unpleasant way, and she screamed something to me which I could not hear. Then I went in, and the brave animal struggled through, with the water up to the top of her back, till she reached the place where D.'s horse had looked so insecure. In another moment she and I rolled backwards into deep water, as if she had slipped from a submerged rock. I saw her fore feet pawing the air, and then only her head was above water. I struck her hard with my spurs, she snorted, clawed, made a desperate struggle, regained her footing, got into shallow water, and landed safely. It was a small but not an agreeable adventure.

We went on again, the track now really dangerous from denudation and slipperiness. The rain came down, if possible, yet more heavily, and coursed fiercely down each *pali* track. Hundreds of cascades leapt from the cliffs, bringing down stones with a sharp rattling sound. We crossed a bridge over one gulch, where the water was thundering down in such volume that it seemed as if it must rend the hard basalt of the *palis*. Then we reached the lofty top of the great Hakalau gulch, the largest of all, with the double river, and the ocean close to the ford. Mingling with the deep reverberations of the surf, I heard the sharp crisp rush of a river, and of "a river that has no bridge."

The dense foliage, and the exigencies of the steep track, which had become very difficult, owing to the washing away of the soil, prevented me from seeing anything till I got down. I found Deborah speaking to a native, who was gesticulating very emphatically, and pointing up the river. The roar was deafening, and the sight terrific. Where there were two shallow streams a week ago, with a house and good-sized piece of ground above their confluence, there was now one spinning, rushing, chafing, foaming river, twice as wide as the Clyde at Glasgow, the land was submerged, and, if I remember correctly, the house only stood above the flood. And, most fearful to look upon, the ocean, in three huge breakers, had come quite in, and its mountains of white surge looked fearfully near the only possible crossing. I entreated D. not to go on. She said we could not go back, that the last gulch was already impassable, that between the two there was no house in which we could sleep, that the river had a good bottom, that the man thought if our horses were strong we could cross now, but not later, &c. In short, she overbore all opposition, and plunged in, calling to me, "spur, spur, all the time."

Just as I went in, I took my knife and cut open the cloak which contained the cocoanuts, one only remaining. Deborah's horse I knew was strong, and shod, but my unshod and untried mare, what of her? My soul and senses literally reeled among the dizzy horrors of the wide, wild tide, but with an effort I regained sense and self-possession, for we were in, and there was no turning. D., ahead, screeched to me what I could not hear; she said afterwards it was "spur, spur, and keep up the river;" the native was shrieking in Hawaiian from the hinder shore, and waving to the right, but the torrents of rain, the crash of the breakers, and the rush and hurry of the river confused both sight and hearing. I saw D.'s great horse carried off his legs, my mare, too, was swimming, and shortly afterwards, between swimming, struggling, and floundering, we reached what had been the junction of the two rivers, where there was foothold, and the water was only up to the seat of the saddles.

Remember, we were both sitting nearly up to our waists in water, and it was only by screaming that our voices were heard above the din, and to return or go on seemed equally perilous. Under these critical circumstances the following colloquy took place, on my side, with teeth chattering, and on hers, with a sudden forgetfulness of English produced by her first sense of the imminent danger we were in.

Self. – "My mare is so tired, and so heavily weighted, we shall be drowned, or I shall."

Deborah (with more reason on her side). – "But can't go back, we no stay here, water higher all minutes, spur horse, think we come through."

Self. – "But if we go on there is broader, deeper water between us and the shore; your husband would not like you to run such a risk."

Deborah. – "Think we get through, if horses give out, we let go; I swim and save you."

Even under these circumstances a gleam of the ludicrous shot through me at the idea of this small fragile being bearing up my weight among the breakers. I attempted to shift my saddle-bags upon her powerful horse, but being full of water and under water, the attempt failed, and as we spoke both our horses were carried off their vantage ground into deep water.

With wilder fury the river rushed by, its waters whirled dizzily, and, in spite of spurring and lifting with the rein, the horses were swept seawards. It was a very fearful sight. I saw Deborah's horse spin round, and thought woefully of the possible fate of the bright young wife, almost a bride; only the horses' heads and our own heads and shoulders were above water; the surf was thundering on our left, and we were drifting towards it "broadside on." When I saw the young girl's face of horror I felt increased presence of mind, and raising my voice to a shriek, and telling her to do as I did, I lifted and turned my mare with the rein, so that her chest and not her side should receive the force of the river, and the brave animal, as if seeing what she should do, struck out desperately. It was a horrible suspense. Were we stemming the torrent, or was it sweeping us back that very short distance which lay between us and the mountainous breakers? I constantly spurred my mare, guiding her slightly to the left, the side grew nearer, and after exhausting struggles, Deborah's horse touched ground, and her voice came faintly towards me like a voice in a dream, still calling "spur, spur." My mare touched ground twice, and was carried off again before she fairly got to land some yards nearer the sea than the bridle track.

When our tired horses were taking breath I felt as if my heart stopped, and I trembled all over, for we had narrowly escaped death. I then put our saddle-bags on Deborah's horse. It was one of the worst and steepest of the *palis* that we had to ascend; but I can't remember anything about the road except that we had to leap some place which we could not cross otherwise. Deborah, then thoroughly alive to a sense of risk, said that there was only one more bad gulch to cross before we reached Onomea, but it was the most dangerous of all, and we could not get across, she feared, but we might go and look at it. I only remember the extreme solitude of the region, and scrambling and sliding down a most precipitous *pali*, hearing a roar like cataract upon cataract, and coming suddenly down upon a sublime and picturesque scene, with only standing room, and that knee-deep in water, between a savage torrent and the cliff. . . .

One huge compressed impetuous torrent, leaping in creamy foam, boiling in creamy eddies, rioting in deep black chasms, roared and thundered over the whole in rapids of the most tempestuous kind, leaping down to the ocean in three grand broad cataracts, the nearest of them not more than forty feet from the crossing. Imagine the Moriston at the Falls, four times as wide and fifty times as furious, walled in by precipices, and with a miniature Niagara above and below, and you have a feeble illustration of it.

Portions of two or three rocks only could be seen, and on one of these, about twelve feet from the shore, a nude native, beautifully tattooed, with a lasso in his hands, was standing nearly up to his knees in foam; and about a third of the way from the other side, another native in deeper water, steadying himself by a pole. A young woman on horseback, whose near relative was dangerously ill at Hilo, was jammed under the cliff, and the men were going to get her across. Deborah, to my dismay, said that if she got safely over we would go too, as these natives were very skilful. I asked if she thought her husband would let her cross, and she said "No." I asked her if she were frightened, and she said "Yes;" but she wished so to get home, and her face was as pale as a brown face can be. I only hope the man will prove worthy of her affectionate devotion.

Here, though people say it is a most perilous gulch, I was not afraid for her life or mine, with the amphibious natives to help us; but I was sorely afraid of being bruised, and scarred, and of breaking the horses' legs, and I said I would not cross, but would sleep among the trees; but the tumult drowned our voices, though the Hawaiians by screeching could make themselves understood. The nearest man then approached the shore, put the lasso round the nose of the woman's horse, and dragged it into the torrent; and it was exciting to see a horse creeping from rock to rock in a cataract with alarming possibilities in every direction. But beasts may well be bold, as they have not "the foreknowledge of death." When the nearest native had got the horse as far as he could, he threw the lasso to the man who was steadying himself with the pole, and urged the horse on. There was a deep chasm between the two into which the animal fell, as he tried to leap from one rock to another. I saw for a moment only a woman's head and shoulders, a horse's head, a commotion of foam, a native tugging at the lasso, and then a violent scramble on to a rock, and a plunging and floundering through deep water to shore.

Then Deborah said she would go, that her horse was a better and stronger one; and the same process was repeated with the same slip into the chasm, only with the variation that for a second she went out of sight altogether. It was a terribly interesting and exciting spectacle with sublime accompaniments. Though I had no fear of absolute danger, yet my mare was tired, and I had made up my mind to remain on that side till the flood abated; but I could not make the natives understand that I wished to turn, and while I was screaming "No, no," and trying to withdraw my stiffened limbs from the stirrups, the noose was put round the mare's nose, and she went in. It was horrible to know that into the chasm as the others went I too must go, and in the mare went with a blind plunge. With violent plunging and struggling she got her fore feet on the rock, but just as she was jumping up to it altogether she slipped back snorting into the hole, and the water went over my eyes. I struck her with my spurs, the men screeched and shouted, the hinder man jumped in, they both tugged at the lasso, and slipping and struggling, the animal gained the rock, and plunged through deep water to shore, the water covering that rock with a rush of foam, being fully two feet deep.

Kaluna came up just after we had crossed, undressed, made his clothes into a bundle, and got over amphibiously, leaping, swimming, and diving, looking like a water-god, with the horse and mule after him. His dexterity was a beautiful sight; but on looking back I wondered how human beings ever devised to cross such a flood. We got over just in time. . . .

We had several more gulches to cross, but none of them were dangerous; and we rode the last seven miles at a great pace, though the mire and water were often up to the horses' knees, and came up to Onomea at full gallop, with spirit and strength enough for riding other twenty miles. Dry clothing, hot baths, and good tea followed delightfully upon our drowning ride. I remained over Sunday at Onomea, and yesterday rode here with a native in heavy rain, and received a warm welcome. Our adventures are a nine days' wonder, and every one says that if we had had a white man or an experienced native with us, we should never have been allowed to attempt the perilous ride. I feel very thankful that we are living to tell of it, and that Deborah is not only not worse but considerably better. . . .

Due honour must be given to the Mexican saddle. Had I been on a side-saddle, and encumbered with a riding-habit, I should have been drowned.

1877

61. Harriet Martineau
from *Autobiography*

I must have been a remarkably religious child, for the only support and pleasure I remember having from a very early age was from that source. . . .

While I was afraid of everybody I saw, I was not in the least afraid of God. Being usually very unhappy, I was constantly longing for heaven, and seriously, and very frequently planning suicide in order to get there. I was sure that suicide would not stand in the way of my getting there. I knew it was considered a crime; but I did not feel it so. I had a devouring passion for justice; – justice, first to my own precious self, and then to other oppressed people. Justice was precisely what was least understood in our house, in regard to servants and children. Now and then I desperately poured out my complaints; but in general I brooded over my injuries, and those of others who dared not speak; and then the temptation to suicide was very strong. No doubt, there was much vindictiveness in it. I gloated over the thought that I would make somebody care about me in some sort of way at last: and, as to my reception in the other world, I felt sure that God could not be very angry with me for making haste to him when nobody else cared for me, and so many people plagued me. One day I went to the kitchen to get the great carving knife, to cut my throat; but the servants were at dinner; and this put it off for that time. By degrees, the design dwindled down into running away. I used to lean out of the window, and look up and down the street, and wonder how far I could go without being caught. I had no doubt at all that if I once got into a farm-house, and wore a woollen petticoat, and milked the cows, I should be safe, and that nobody would inquire about me any more. – It is evident enough that my temper must have been very bad. It seems to me now that it was downright devilish, except for a placability which used to annoy me sadly. My temper might have been early made a thoroughly good one, by the slightest indulgence shown to my natural affections, and any rational dealing with my faults: but I was almost the youngest of a large family, and subject, not only to the rule of severity to which all were liable, but also to the rough and contemptuous treatment of the elder children, who meant no harm, but injured me irreparably. I had no self-respect, and an unbounded need of approbation and affection. My capacity for jealousy was something frightful. When we were little more than infants, Mr. Thomas Watson, son of my father's partner, one day came into the yard, took Rachel up in his arms, gave her some grapes off the vine, and carried her home, across the street, to give her Gay's Fables, bound in red and gold. I stood with a bursting heart, beating my hoop, and hating every body in the world. I always hated Gay's Fables, and for long could not abide a red book. Nobody dreamed of all this; and the 'taking down' system was pursued with me as with the rest, issuing in the assumed doggedness and wilfulness which made me desperately disagreeable during my youth, to every body at home. The least word or tone of kindness melted me instantly, in spite of the strongest predeterminations to be hard and offensive.

❀ ❀ ❀ ❀

We were horribly nervous, the first day we went to school. It was a very large vaulted room, whitewashed, and with a platform for the master and his desk; and below, rows of desks and benches, of wood painted red, and carved all over with idle boys' devices. Some good many boys remained for a time; but the girls had the front row of desks, and could see nothing of the boys but by looking behind them. The thorough way in which the boys did their lessons, however, spread its influence over us, and we worked as heartily as if we had worked together. I remember being some-what oppressed by the length of the first morning, – from nine till twelve, and dreading a similar strain in the afternoon, and twice every day: but in a very few days, I got into all the pleasure of it; and a new state of happiness had fairly set in. I have never since felt more deeply and thoroughly the sense of progression than I now began to do. As far as I remember, we never failed in our lessons, more or less. Our making even a mistake was very rare; and yet we got on fast. This shows how good the teaching must have been. We learned Latin from the old Eton grammar, which I there-fore, and against all reason, cling to, – remembering the repetition-days (Saturdays) when we recited all that Latin, prose and verse, which occupied us four hours. Two other girls, besides Rachel and myself, formed the class; and we certainly attained a capability of enjoying some of the classics, even before the two years were over. Cicero, Virgil, and a little of Horace were our main reading then: and afterwards I took great delight in Tacitus. I believe it was a genuine understanding and pleasure, because I got into the habit of thinking in Latin, and had something of the same pleasure in sending myself to sleep with Latin as with English poetry. Moreover, we stood the test of verse-making, in which I do not remember that we ever got any disgrace, while we certainly obtained, now and then, considerable praise. When Mr. Perry was gone, and we were put under Mr. Banfather, one of the masters at the Grammar School, for Latin, Mr. B. one day took a little book out of his pocket, and translated from it a passage which he desired us to turn into Latin verse. My version was precisely the same as the original, except one word (*annosa* for *antiqua*) and the passage was from the Eneid. Tests like these seem to show that we really were well taught, and that our attainment was sound, as far as it went. Quite as much care was bestowed on our French, the grammar of which we learned thoroughly, while the pronunciation was scarcely so barbarous as in most schools during the war, as there was a French lady engaged for the greater part of the time. . . .

Next to Composition, I think arithmetic was my favourite study. My pleasure in the working of numbers is something inexplicable to me, – as much as any pleasure of sensation. I used to spend my play hours in covering my slate with sums, washing them out, and covering the slate again. The fact is, however, that we had no lessons that were not pleasant. That was the season of my entrance upon an intellectual life. In an intellectual life I found then, as I have found since, refuge from moral suffering, and an always unexhausted spring of moral strength and enjoyment.

❋ ❋ ❋ ❋

My brother James, then my idolized companion, discovered how wretched I was when he left me for his college, after the vacation; and he told me that I must not permit myself to be so miserable. He advised me to take refuge, on each occasion, in a new pursuit; and on that particular occasion, in an attempt at authorship. I said, as usual, that I would if he would: to which he answered that it would never do for him, a young student, to rush into print before the eyes of his tutors; but he desired me to write something that was in my head, and try my chance with it in the 'Monthly Repository,' – the poor little Unitarian periodical. . . .

What James desired, I always did, as of course; and after he had left me to my widowhood soon after six o'clock, one bright September morning, I was at my desk before seven, beginning a letter to the Editor of the 'Monthly Repository,' – that editor being the formidable prime minister of his sect, – Rev. Robert Aspland. I suppose I must tell what that first paper was, though I had much rather not; for I am so heartily ashamed of the whole business as never to have looked at the article since the first flutter of it went off. It was on Female Writers on Practical Divinity. I wrote away, in my abominable scrawl of those days, on foolscap paper, feeling mightily like a fool all the time. I told no one, and carried my expensive packet to the post office myself, to pay the postage. I took the letter V for my signature, – I cannot at all remember why. The time was very near the end of the month: I had no definite expectation that I should ever hear any thing of my paper; and certainly did not suppose it could be in the forthcoming number. That number was sent in before service-time on a Sunday morning. My heart may have been beating when I laid hands on it; but it thumped prodigiously when I saw my article there, and, in the Notices to Correspondents, a request to hear more from V. of Norwich. There is certainly something entirely peculiar in the sensation of seeing oneself in print for the first time: – the lines burn themselves in upon the brain in a way of which black ink is incapable, in any other mode. So I felt that day, when I went about with my secret. – I have said what my eldest brother was to us, – in what reverence we held him. He was just married, and he and his bride asked me to return from chapel with them to tea. After tea he said, 'Come now, we have had plenty of talk; I will read you something ;' and he held out his hand for the new 'Repository.' After glancing at it, he exclaimed, 'They have got a new hand here. Listen.' After a paragraph, he repeated, 'Ah! this is a new hand; they have had nothing so good as this for a long while.' (It would be impossible to convey to any who do not know the 'Monthly Repository' of that day, how very small a compliment this was.) I was silent, of course. At the end of the first column, he exclaimed about the style, looking at me in some wonder at my being as still as a mouse. Next (and well I remember his tone, and thrill to it still) his words were – 'What a fine sentence that is! Why, do you not think so?' I mumbled out, sillily enough, that it did not seem any thing particular. 'Then,' said he, 'you were not listening. I will read it again. There now!' As he still got nothing out of me, he turned round upon me, as we sat side by side on the sofa, with 'Harriet, what is the matter with you? I never knew you so slow to praise any thing before.' I replied, in utter confusion, – 'I never could baffle any body. The truth is, that paper is mine.' He made no reply; read on in silence, and spoke no more till I was on my feet to come away. He then laid his hand on my shoulder, and said gravely (calling me 'dear' for the first time) 'Now, dear, leave it to other women to make shirts and darn stockings; and do you devote yourself to this.' I went home in a sort of dream, so that the squares of the pavement seemed to float before my eyes. That evening made me an authoress.

* * * *

I am, in truth, very thankful for not having married at all. I have never since been tempted, nor have suffered any thing at all in relation to that matter which is held to be all-important to woman, – love and marriage. Nothing, I mean, beyond occasional annoyance, presently disposed of. Every literary woman, no doubt, has plenty of importunity of that sort to deal with; but freedom of mind and coolness of manner dispose of it very easily: and

since the time I have been speaking of, my mind has been wholly free from
all idea of love-affairs. My subsequent literary life in London was clear
from all difficulty and embarrassment, – no doubt because I was evidently
too busy, and too full of interest of other kinds to feel any awkwardness,
– to say nothing of my being then thirty years of age; an age at which, if
ever, a woman is certainly qualified to take care of herself. I can easily conceive how I might have been tempted, – how some deep springs in my
nature might have been touched, then as earlier; but, as a matter of fact,
they never were; and I consider the immunity a great blessing, under the
liabilities of a moral condition such as mine was in the olden time. If I had
had a husband dependent on me for his happiness, the responsibility
would have made me wretched. I had not faith enough in myself to endure
avoidable responsibility. If my husband had *not* depended on me for his
happiness, I should have been jealous. So also with children. The care
would have so overpowered the joy, – the love would have so exceeded the
ordinary chances of life, – the fear on my part would have so impaired the
freedom on theirs, that I rejoice not to have been involved in a relation for
which I was, or believed myself unfit. The veneration in which I hold
domestic life has always shown me that that life was not for those whose
self-respect had been early broken down, or had never grown. Happily,
the majority are free from this disability. Those who suffer under it had
better be as I, – as my observation of married, as well as single life assures
me. When I see what conjugal love is, in the extremely rare cases in which
it is seen in its perfection, I feel that there is a power of attachment in me
that has never been touched. When I am among little children, it frightens
me to think what my idolatry of my own children would have been. But,
through it all, I have ever been thankful to be alone. My strong will, combined with anxiety of conscience, makes me fit only to live alone; and my
taste and liking are for living alone. The older I have grown, the more
serious and irremediable have seemed to me the evils and disadvantages of
married life, as it exists among us at this time: and I am provided with
what it is the bane of single life in ordinary cases to want – substantial,
laborious and serious occupation. My business in life has been to think
and learn, and to speak out with absolute freedom what I have thought and
learned. The freedom is itself a positive and never-failing enjoyment to me,
after the bondage of my early life. My work and I have been fitted to each
other, as is proved by the success of my work and my own happiness in it.
The simplicity and independence of this vocation first suited my infirm
and ill-developed nature, and then sufficed for my needs, together with
family ties and domestic duties, such as I have been blessed with, and as
every woman's heart requires. Thus, I am not only entirely satisfied with

my lot, but think it the very best for me, – under my constitution and circumstances: and I long ago came to the conclusion that, without meddling
with the case of the wives and mothers, I am probably the happiest single
woman in England.

∗ ∗ ∗

Nobody can be further than I am from being satisfied with the condition
of my own sex, under the law and custom of my own country; but I decline
all fellowship and co-operation with women of genius or otherwise
favourable position, who injure the cause by their personal tendencies.
When I see an eloquent writer insinuating to every body who comes across
her that she is the victim of her husband's carelessness and cruelty, while
he never spoke in his own defence: when I see her violating all good taste
by her obtrusiveness in society, and oppressing every body about her by
her epicurean selfishness every day, while raising in print an eloquent cry
on behalf of the oppressed; I feel, to the bottom of my heart, that she is the
worst enemy of the cause she professes to plead. The best friends of that
cause are women who are morally as well as intellectually competent to the
most serious business of life, and who must be clearly seen to speak from
conviction of the truth and not from personal unhappiness. The best
friends of the cause are the happy wives and the busy, cheerful, satisfied
single women, who have no injuries of their own to avenge, and no painful
vacuity or mortification to relieve. The best advocates are yet to come, – in
the persons of women who are obtaining access to real social business,
– the female physicians and other professors in America, the women of
business and the female artists of France; and the hospital administrators,
the nurses, the educators and substantially successful authors of our own
country. Often as I am appealed to to speak, or otherwise assist in the
promotion of the cause of Woman, my answer is always the same: – that
women, like men, can obtain whatever they show themselves fit for. Let
them be educated, – let their powers be cultivated to the extent for which
the means are already provided, and all that is wanted or ought to be
desired will follow of course. Whatever a woman proves herself able to do,
society will be thankful to see her do, – just as if she were a man. If she is
scientific, science will welcome her, as it has welcomed every woman so
qualified. I believe no scientific woman complains of wrongs. If capable of
political thought and action, women will obtain even that. I judge by my
own case. The time has not come which certainly will come when women
who are practically concerned in political life will have a voice in making
the laws which they have to obey; but every woman who can think and
speak wisely, and bring up her children soundly, in regard to the rights and

duties of society, is advancing the time when the interests of women will be represented, as well as those of men. I have no vote at elections, though I am a tax-paying housekeeper and responsible citizen; and I regard the disability as an absurdity, seeing that I have for a long course of years influenced public affairs to an extent not professed or attempted by many men. But I do not see that I could do much good by personal complaints, which always have some suspicion or reality of passion in them. I think the better way is for us all to learn and to try to the utmost what we can do, and thus to win for ourselves the consideration which alone can secure us rational treatment.

❋ ❋ ❋ ❋

When I learned what my state is, it was my wish (as far as I wish anything, which is indeed very slightly and superficially) that my death might take place before long, and by the quicker process: and such is, in an easy sort of way, my wish still. The last is for the sake of my nurse, and of all about me; and the first is mainly because I do not want to deteriorate and get spoiled in the final stage of my life, by ceasing to hear the truth, and the whole truth: and nobody ventures to utter any unpleasant truth to a person with 'a heart-complaint.' I must take my chance for this; and I have a better chance than most, because my nurse and constant companion knows that I do not desire that anybody should 'make things pleasant' because I am ill. I should wish, as she knows, to live under complete and healthy moral conditions to the last, if these can be accommodated, by courage and mutual trust, with the physical conditions. . . . Night after night since I have known that I am mortally ill, I have tried to conceive, with the help of the sensations of my sinking-fits, the act of dying, and its attendant feelings; and thus far I have always gone to sleep in the middle of it. And this is after really knowing something about it; for I have been frequently in extreme danger of immediate death within the last five months, and have felt as if I were dying, and should never draw another breath. Under this close experience, I find death in prospect the simplest thing in the world, – a thing not to be feared or regretted, or to get excited about in any way.

62. Frances Power Cobbe
from *Why Women Desire the Franchise*

Politicians consider that a subject enters an important phase when it becomes publicly recognised as a "Question." During the last five years the proposal to give votes to women has very distinctly grown into the "Question of Female Suffrage." Few of the most sanguine advocates of the cause would have ventured, in 1865, to hope that by the close of 1872, it should stand where it now obviously does in public opinion, or that 355,801 persons should have petitioned in its behalf.

The last Reform Bill, by lowering the franchise for men, has affected the claims of women in several indirect ways. In the first place, by admitting to the exercise of political judgment a class whose education is confessedly of the narrowest, and whose leisure to study politics extremely small, it has virtually silenced for all future time the two favourite arguments against the claims of women; that their understandings are weak, and their time too fully occupied by domestic cares. The most strenuous asserter of the mental and moral inferiority of women cannot urge that the majority of the new voters have more power to understand, or more leisure to attend to, public affairs than even the inferior class of female householders; not to speak of such women as Miss Nightingale and Mrs. Somerville, Miss Martineau and Lady Coutts. . . .

Women are often asked, Why they desire the franchise? Have they not everything already which they can possibly desire: personal liberty, the right to hold property, and an amount of courtesy and chivalrous regard which (it is broadly hinted) they would bitterly regret were they to exchange them for equality of political rights? Why should those epicurean gods, who dwell in the serene empyrean of drawing-rooms descend to meddle with the sordid affairs of humanity? What a pity and a loss it would be to the toiling world could it never look up and behold afar such a spectacle of repose as a true lady now presents! We can easily dispense with more legislators; but what is the world to do without those mild Belgravian mothers, those innocent young "Girls of the Period," those magnificent *grandes dames* who are the glory of our social life?

Let us briefly answer these questions, once for all. We do not believe that one particle of womanly gentleness and dignity, nay, not even the finest flavour of high-bred grace, will be lost when women are permitted to record their votes for representatives in Parliament. We consider the fear that it might be so among the idlest of chimeras. What *will* be lost, we are persuaded, will be a little of the frivolity, a little of the habit of expressing opinions without having conscientiously weighed them, a little of the practice of underhand and unworthy persuasion, which have been hitherto faults fostered in women by their position. Women can lose nothing, and have much to gain by entering a field of nobler interests than has hitherto been open to them. It was deemed well said of the old Roman, that nothing human was alien to him. It will be well when all women learn to feel that none of the wrongs and sins and sufferings of other women can be alien to *them*. The condition of women of the lower orders is beset with hardships; and it is for the very reason that a lady is freed from those heavy trials, that she should exert every power she possesses or can acquire, first to understand, and then, if possible, to remedy them. How these evils are to be lightened; how the burdens of the poor toilers are to be made less intolerable; how wives are to be protected from brutal husbands; how, above all, the ruin of the hapless thousands of lost ones is to be stopped: – how these things are to be done, may need more wisdom than all the men and women in England together may possess. But it is quite certain that if women had heretofore been represented in Parliament, such evils and wrongs would never have reached, unchecked, their present height, and that whenever women are at last represented, some more earnest efforts will be made to arrest them.

But it is not only for the sake of women of the suffering classes that we seek for female influence on politics; nor for that of happier women whose sphere of usefulness might thereby be enlarged, and their lives supplied with nobler interests. We believe that the recognition of the political rights of women, as it will be a signal act of justice on the part of men, so it will also prove an act beneficial to them no less than to us; and that when a generation has passed after the change, it will be said, by all alike, "What did our fathers mean by forbidding women to have a voice in politics? If it were nothing more, their influence must always be the safest ballast to keep steady the Ship of State."

Finally, to sum up our meaning in the most concise terms we can find, we desire that the political franchise be extended to women of full age, possessed of the requisite property qualification, for the following eight reasons –

1. Because the possession of property and the payment of rates being the admitted bases of political rights in England, it is unjust that persons who possess such property, and pay such rates, should be excluded from those rights, unless from the clearest and gravest reasons of public interest. Such interest, however, we believe, requires, not the exclusion, but the admission of women into the franchise.
2. Because the denial of the franchise to qualified women entails on the community a serious loss; namely, that of the legislative influence of a numerous class, whose moral sense is commonly highly developed, and whose physical defencelessness attaches them peculiarly to the cause of justice and public order.

3. Because, under a representative Government, the interests of any non-represented class are confessedly liable to be misunderstood and neglected; and nothing but evidence that the interests of women are carefully weighed and faithfully guarded by the Legislature would nullify the presumptive injustice of denying them representation. Such evidence, however, is not forthcoming; but, on the contrary, experience demonstrates that the gravest interests of women are continually postponed by Parliament to the consideration of trifling questions concerning male electors, and, when introduced into debates, are treated by half the House rather as jests than as measures of serious importance.

4. Because, while the natural and artificial disabilities of women demand in their behalf the special aid and protection of the State, no proposal has ever been made to deal with their perils and difficulties; nor even to relieve them of the smallest portion of the burden of taxation, which they are compelled to bear without sharing the privileges attached thereto.

5. Because women, by the denial to them of the franchise, are placed at a serious disadvantage in competition for numerous offices and employments; especially women of the middle class, whose inability to vote tends extensively to deter landlords interested in politics from accepting them as tenants, even in cases where they have long conducted for their deceased male relatives the business of the farms, shops etc., to whose tenure they seek to succeed.

6. Because the denial of women of the direct exercise of political judgment in the typical act of citizenship, has a generally injurious influence on the minds of men as regards women, leading them to undervalue their opinions on all the graver matters of life, and to treat offences against them with levity, as committed against beings possessed only of inferior rights.

7. Because the denial of the direct exercise of their judgment has a doubly injurious effect upon the minds of women, inclining them to adopt, without conscientious inquiry the opinions which, they are warned, must be always practically inoperative; and beguiling them to exert, through tortuous and ignoble channels, the influence whose open and honest exercise has been refused.

8. Finally, we desire the franchise for women, because, while believing that men and women have different work to do in life, we still hold that, in the choice of political representatives, they have the same task to accomplish; namely, the joint election of a Senate which shall guard with equal care the rights of both sexes, and which shall

embody in its laws that true Justice which shall approve itself not only to the strong, but also the weak.

———

1878

63. Frances Anne Kemble
from *Record of a Girlhood*

We reached Queenstown, on the Niagara river, below the falls, at about twelve o'clock, and had three more miles to drive to reach them. The day was serenely bright and warm, without a cloud in the sky, or a shade in the earth, or a breath in the air. We were in an open carriage, and I felt almost nervously oppressed with the expectation of what we were presently to see. We stopped the carriage occasionally to listen for the giant's roaring, but the sound did not reach us until, within three miles over the thick woods which skirted the river, we saw a vapoury silver cloud rising into the blue sky. It was the spray, the breath of the toiling waters ascending to heaven. When we reached what is called the Niagara House, a large tavern by the roadside, I sprang out of the carriage and ran through the house, down flights of steps cut in the rock, and along a path skirted with low thickets, through the boughs of which I saw the rapids running a race with me, as it seemed, and hardly faster than I did. Then there was a broad, flashing sea of furious foam, a deafening rush and roar, through which I heard Mr. Trelawney, who was following me, shout, "Go on, go on; don't stop!" I reached an open floor of broad, flat rock, over which the water was pouring. Trelawney seized me by the arm, and all but carried me to the very brink; my feet were in the water and on the edge of the precipice, and then I looked down. I could not speak, and I could hardly breathe; I felt as if I had an iron band across my breast. I watched the green, glassy, swollen heaps go plunging down, down, down; each mountainous mass of water, as it reached the dreadful brink, recoiling, as in horror, from the abyss; and after rearing backwards in helpless terror, as it were, hurling itself down to be shattered in the inevitable doom over which eternal clouds of foam and spray spread an impenetrable curtain. The mysterious chasm, with its uproar of voices, seemed like the watery mouth of hell. I looked and listened till the wild excitement of the scene took such possession of me that, but for the strong arm that held me back, I really think I should have let myself slide down into the gulf. It was long before I could utter, and as I began to draw my breath I could only gasp out, "O God! O God!" No words can describe either the scene itself, or its effect upon me.

We stayed three days at Niagara, the greater part of which I spent by the water, under the water, on the water, and more than half in the water. Wherever foot could stand I stood, and wherever foot could go I went. I crept, clung, hung, and waded; I lay upon the rocks, upon the very edge of the boiling cauldron and I stood alone under the huge arch over which the water pours with the whole mass of it, thundering over my rocky ceiling, and falling down before me like an immeasurable curtain, the noonday sun looking like a pale spot, a white wafer, through the dense thickness. Drenched through, and almost blown from my slippery footing by the whirling gusts that rush under the fall, with my feet naked for better safety, grasping the shale broken from the precipice against which I pressed myself, my delight was so intense that I really could hardly bear to come away.

The rock over which the rapids run is already scooped and hollowed out to a great extent by the action of the water; the edge of the precipice, too, is constantly crumbling and breaking off under the spurn of its downward leap. At the very brink the rock is not much more than two feet thick, and when I stood under it and thought of the enormous mass of water rushing over and pouring from it, it did not seem at all improbable that at any moment the roof might give way, the rock break off fifteen or twenty feet, and the whole huge cataract, retreating back, leave a still wider basin for its floods to pour themselves into. . . .

Before I leave off speaking of that wonderful cataract, I must tell you that the impression of awe and terror it produced at first upon me completely wore away, and as I became familiar with it, its dazzling brightness, its soothing voice, its gliding motion, its soft, thick, furry beds of foam, its veils and draperies of floating light, and gleaming, wavering diadems of vivid colours, made it to me the perfection of loveliness and the mere magnificence of beauty. It was certainly not the "familiarity" that "breeds contempt," but more akin to the "perfect love" which "casteth out fear;" and I began at last to understand Mr. Trelawney's saying that the only impression it produced on him was that of perfect repose; but perhaps it takes Niagara to mesmerize him.

64. Frances Power Cobbe
from *Wife Torture in England*

It once happened to me to ask an elderly French gentleman of the most exquisite manners to pay any attention she might need to a charming young lady who was intending to travel by the same train from London to Paris. M. de — wrote such a brilliant little note in reply that I was tempted to preserve it as an autograph; and I observe that, after a profusion of thanks, he assured me he should be 'trop heureux de se mettre au service' of my young friend. Practically, as I afterwards learned, M. de — did make himself quite delightful, till, unluckily, on arriving at Boulogne, it appeared that there was some *imbroglio* about Miss —'s luggage and she was in serious difficulty. Needless to say, on such an occasion the intervention of a French gentleman with a ribbon at his button-hole would have been of the greatest possible service; but to render it M. de — would have been obliged to miss the train to Paris; and this was a sacrifice for which his politeness was by no means prepared. Expressing himself as utterly *au désespoir*, he took his seat, and was whirled away, leaving my poor young friend alone on the platform to fight her battles as best she might with the impracticable officials. The results might have been annoying had not a homely English stranger stepped in and proffered his aid; and, having recovered the missing property, simply lifted his hat and escaped from the lady's expressions of gratitude.

In this little anecdote I think lies a compendium of the experience of hundreds of ladies on their travels. The genuine and self-sacrificing kindness of English and American gentlemen towards women affords almost a ludicrous contrast to the florid politeness, compatible with every degree of selfishness, usually exhibited by men of other European nations. The reflection then is a puzzling one – How does it come to pass that while the better sort of Englishmen are thus exceptionally humane and considerate to women, the men of the lower class of the same nation are proverbial for their unparalleled brutality, till wife-beating, wife-torture, and wife-murder have become the opprobrium of the land? How does it happen (still more strange to note!) that the same generous-hearted gentlemen, who would themselves fly to render succour to a lady in distress, yet read of the beatings, burnings, kickings, and 'cloggings' of poor women well-nigh every morning in their newspapers without once setting their teeth, and saying, 'This must be stopped! We can stand it no longer'?

The paradox truly seems worthy of a little investigation. What reason can be alleged, in the first place, why the male of the human species, and particularly the male of the finest variety of that species, should be the only animal in creation which maltreats its mate, or any female of its own kind?

To get to the bottom of the mystery we must discriminate between assaults of men on other men; assaults of men on women who are not their wives; and assaults of men on their wives. I do not think I err much if I affirm that, in common sentiment, the first of these offences is considerably more heinous than the second – being committed against a more worthy person; and lastly that the assault on a woman who is *not* a man's wife is worse than the assault on a wife by her husband. Towards this last or *minimum* offence a particular kind of indulgence is indeed extended by public opinion. The proceeding seems to be surrounded by a certain halo of jocosity which inclines people to smile whenever they hear of a case of it (terminating anywhere short of actual murder), and causes the mention of the subject to conduce rather than otherwise to the hilarity of a dinner party. The occult fun thus connected with wife-beating forms by no means indeed the least curious part of the subject. Certainly in view of the state of things revealed by our criminal statistics there is something ominous in the circumstances that 'Punch' should have been our national street-drama for more than two centuries. . . .

It is equally remarkable that so much of the enjoyment should concentrate about the thwacking of poor Judy, and the flinging of the baby out of the window. Questioned seriously whether he think that the behaviour of Punch as a citizen and *père de famille* be in itself a good joke, the British gentleman would probably reply that it was not more facetious than watching a carter flogging a horse. But invested with the drollery of a marionette's behaviour, and accompanied by the screeches of the man with the Pan-pipe, the scene is irresistible, and the popularity of the hero rises with every bang he bestows on the wife of his bosom and on the representatives of the law.

The same sort of half-jocular sympathy unquestionably accompanies the whole class of characters of whom Mr Punch is the type. Very good and kindhearted men may be frequently heard speaking of horrid scenes of mutual abuse and violence between husbands and wives, as if they were rather ridiculous than disgusting. The 'Taming of the Shrew' still holds its place as one of the most popular of Shakespeare's comedies. . . . Where is the hidden fan of this and scores of similar allusions, which sound like the cracking of whips over the cowering dogs in a kennel?

I imagine it lies in the sense, so pleasant to the owners of superior physical strength, that after all, if reason and eloquence should fail, there is always an *ultima ratio*, and that that final appeal lies in their hands. The sparring may be all very well for a time, and may be counted entirely satisfactory *if they get the better*. But then, if by any mischance the unaccountably sharp wits of the weaker creature should prove dangerous weapons, there is always the club of brute force ready to hand in the corner. The listener is amused, as in reading a fairy tale, wherein the hero, when apparently completely vanquished, pulls out a talisman given him by an Afreet, and lo! his enemies fall flat on the ground and are turned into rats.

Thus it comes to pass, I suppose, that the abstract idea of a strong man hitting or kicking a weak woman – *per se*, so revolting – has somehow got softened into a jovial kind of domestic lynching, the grosser features of the case being swept out of sight, just as people make endless jests on tipsiness, forgetting how loathsome a thing is a drunkard. A 'jolly companions' chorus seems to accompany both kinds of exploits. This, and the prevalent idea (which I shall analyze by-and-by) that the woman has generally deserved the blows she receives, keep up, I believe, the indifference of the public on the subject.

Probably the sense that they must carry with them a good deal of tacit sympathy on the part of other men has something to do in encouraging wife-beaters, just as the fatal notion of the good fellowship of drink has made thousands of sots. But the immediate causes of the offence of brutal violence are of course very various, and need to be better understood than they commonly are if we would find a remedy for them. First, there are to be considered the class of people and the conditions of life wherein the practice prevails; then the character of the men who beat their wives; next that of the wives who are beaten and kicked; and finally, the possible remedy.

Wife-beating exists in the upper and middle classes rather more, I fear, than is generally recognized; but it rarely extends to anything beyond an occasional blow or two not of a dangerous kind. In his apparently most ungovernable rage, the gentleman or tradesman somehow manages to bear in mind the disgrace he will incur if his outbreak be betrayed by his wife's black eye or broken arm, and he regulates his cuffs or kicks accordingly. The dangerous wife-beater belongs almost exclusively to the artisan and labouring classes. Colliers, 'puddlers', and weavers have long earned for themselves in this matter a bad reputation, and among a long list of cases before me, I reckon shoemakers, stonemasons, butchers, smiths, tailors, a printer, a clerk, a bird-catcher, and a large number of labourers. In the worst districts of London (as I have been informed by one of the most experienced magistrates) four-fifths of the wife-beating cases are among the lowest class of Irish labourers – a fact worthy of more than passing notice, had we time to bestow upon it, seeing that in their own country Irishmen of all classes are proverbially kind and even chivalrous towards women.

❀ ❀ ❀ ❀

I entreat my readers not to turn away and forget this wretched subject. I entreat the gentlemen of England, – the bravest, humanest, and most generous in the world, – not to leave these helpless women to be trampled to death under their very eyes. I entreat English ladies, who, like myself, have never received from the men with whom we associate anything but kindness and consideration, and who are prone to think that the lot of others is smooth and happy as our own, to take to heart the wrongs and agonies of our miserable sisters, and to lift up on their behalf a cry which must make Parliament either hasten to deal with the matter, or renounce for very shame the vain pretence that it takes care of the interests of women.

1879

65. Isabella Bird
from *A Lady's Life in the Rocky Mountains*

Saturday.

The snow began to fall early this morning, and as it is unaccompanied by wind we have the novel spectacle of a smooth white world; still it does not look like anything serious. We have been gradually growing later at night and later in the morning. To-day we did not breakfast till ten. We have been becoming so disgusted with the pickled pork, that we were glad to find it just at an end yesterday, even though we were left without meat, for which in this climate the system craves. You can fancy my surprise, on going into the kitchen, to find a dish of smoking steaks of venison on the table. We ate like famished people, and enjoyed our meal thoroughly. Just before I came the young men had shot an elk, which they intended to sell in Denver, and the grand carcass, with great branching antlers, hung outside the shed. Often while vainly trying to swallow some pickled pork I had looked across to the tantalising animal, but it was not to be thought of. However, this morning, as the young men felt the pinch of hunger even more than I did, and the prospects of packing it to Denver became worse, they decided on cutting into one side, so we shall luxuriate in venison while it lasts. We think that Edwards will surely be up to-night, but unless he brings supplies our case is looking serious. The flour is running low, there is only coffee for one week, and I have only a scanty three ounces of tea left. The baking-powder is nearly at an end. We have agreed to economise by breakfasting very late, and having two meals a day instead of three. The young men went out hunting as usual, and I went out and found Birdie, and on her, brought in four other horses, but the snow balled so badly that I went out and walked across the river on a very passable ice bridge, and got some new views of the unique grandeur of this place. Our evenings are social and pleasant. We finish supper about eight, and make up a huge fire. The men smoke while I write to you. Then we draw near the fire, and I take my endless mending, and we talk or read aloud. Both are very intelligent, and Mr. Buchan has very extended information and a good deal of insight into character. Of course our circumstances, the likelihood of release, the prospects of snow blocking us in and of our supplies holding out, the sick calves, "Jim's" mood, the possible intentions of a man whose footprints we have found and traced for three miles, are all topics that often recur, and few of which can be worn threadbare.

❀ ❀ ❀ ❀

ESTES PARK, *Sunday.*

A TRAPPER passing last night brought us the news that Mr. Nugent is ill; so, after washing up the things after our late breakfast, I rode to his cabin, but I met him in the gulch coming down to see us. He said he had caught cold on the Range, and was suffering from an old arrow wound in the lung. We had a long conversation without adverting to the former one, and he told me some of the present circumstances of his ruined life. It is piteous that a man like him, in the prime of life, should be destitute of home and love, and live a life of darkness in a den with no companions but guilty memories, and a dog which many people think is the nobler animal of the two. I urged him to give up the whisky which at present is his ruin, and his answer had the ring of a sad truth in it: "I cannot, it binds me hand and foot – I cannot give up the only pleasure I have." His ideas of right are the queerest possible. He says that he believes in God, but what he knows or believes of God's law I know not. To resent insult with your revolver, to revenge yourself on those who have injured you, to be true to a comrade and share your last crust with him, to be chivalrous to good women, to be generous and hospitable, and at the last to die game – these are the articles of his creed, and I suppose they are received by men of his stamp. . . .

On returning down the gulch the view was grander than I have ever seen it, the gulch in dark shadow, the Park below lying in intense sunlight, with all the majestic canyons which sweep down upon it in depths of infinite blue gloom, and above, the pearly peaks, dazzling in purity and glorious in form, cleft the turquoise blue of the sky. How shall I ever leave this "land which is very far off"? How *can* I ever leave it? is the real question. We are going on the principle, "Let us eat and drink, for to-morrow we die," and the stores are melting away. The two meals are not an economical plan, for we are so much more hungry that we eat more than when we had three. We had a good deal of sacred music to-day, to make it as like Sunday as possible. The "faint melancholy" of this winter loneliness is very fascinating. How glorious the amber fires of the winter dawns are, and how gloriously to-night the crimson clouds descended just to the mountain-tops and were reflected on the pure surface of the snow! The door of this room looks due north, and as I write the Pole Star blazes, and a cold crescent moon hangs over the ghastliness of Long's Peak.

ESTES PARK, COLORADO, *November.*

We have lost count of time, and can only agree on the fact that the date is somewhere near the end of November. Our life has settled down into serenity, and our singular and enforced partnership is very pleasant. We might be three men living together, but for the unvarying courtesy and consideration which they show to me. Our work goes on like clockwork; the only difficulty which ever arises is that the men do not like me to do anything that they think hard or unsuitable, such as saddling a horse or bringing in water. The days go very fast; it was 3.30 to-day before I knew that it was 1. It is a calm life without worries. The men are so easy to live with; they never fuss, or grumble, or sigh, or make a trouble of anything. It would amuse you to come into our wretched little kitchen before our disgracefully late breakfast, and find Mr. Kavan busy at the stove frying venison, myself washing the supper-dishes, and Mr. Buchan drying them, or both the men busy at the stove while I sweep the floor. Our food is a great object of interest to us, and we are ravenously hungry now that we have only two meals a day. About sundown each goes forth to his "chores" – Mr. K. to chop wood, Mr. B. to haul water, I to wash the milk-pans and water the horses. On Saturday the men shot a deer, and on going for it to-day they found nothing but the hind legs, and following a track which they expected would lead them to a beast's hole, they came quite carelessly upon a large mountain lion, which, however, took itself out of their reach before they were sufficiently recovered from their surprise to fire at it. These lions, which are really a species of puma, are bloodthirsty as well as cowardly. Lately one got into a sheepfold in the canyon of the St. Vrain, and killed thirty sheep, sucking the blood from their throats.

November ?

This has been a day of minor events, as well as a busy one. I was so busy that I never sat down from 10.30 till 1.30. I had washed my one change of raiment, and though I never iron my clothes, I like to bleach them till they are as white as snow, and they were whitening on the line when some furious gusts came down from Long's Peak, against which I could not stand, and when I did get out all my clothes were blown into strips from an inch to four inches in width, literally destroyed! One learns how very little is necessary either for comfort or happiness. I made a four-pound spiced ginger cake, baked some bread, mended my riding dress, cleaned up generally, wrote some letters with the hope that some day they might be posted, and took a magnificent walk, reaching the cabin again in the melancholy glory which now immediately precedes the darkness.

❄ ❄ ❄ ❄

Thanksgiving Day.

The thing dreaded has come at last, a snowstorm, with a north-east wind. It ceased about midnight, but not till it had covered my bed. Then the mercury fell below zero, and everything froze. I melted a tin of water for washing by the fire, but it was hard frozen before I could use it. My hair, which was thoroughly wet with the thawed snow of yesterday, is hard frozen in plaits. The milk and treacle are like rock, the eggs have to be kept on the coolest part of the stove to keep them fluid. Two calves in the shed were frozen to death. Half our floor is deep in snow, and it is so cold that we cannot open the door to shovel it out. The snow began again at eight this morning, very fine and hard. It blows in through the chinks and dusts this letter while I write. Mr. Kavan keeps my ink-bottle close to the fire, and hands it to me every time that I need to dip my pen. We have a huge fire, but cannot raise the temperature above 20°. Ever since I returned the lake has been hard enough to bear a waggon, but to-day it is difficult to keep the water hole open by the constant use of the axe. The snow may either melt or block us in. Our only anxiety is about the supplies. We have tea and coffee enough to last over to-morrow, the sugar is just done, and the flour is getting low. . . .

Mr. Buchan is very far from well, and dreads the prospect of "half rations." All this sounds laughable, but we shall not laugh if we have to look hunger in the face! Now in the evening the snowclouds, which have blotted out all things, are lifting, and the winter scene is wonderful. The mercury is 5° below zero, and the aurora is glorious. In my unchinked room the mercury is 1° below zero. Mr. Buchan can hardly get his breath; the dryness is intense. We spent the afternoon cooking the Thanksgiving dinner. I made a wonderful pudding, for which I had saved eggs and cream for days, and dried and stoned cherries supplied the place of currants. I made a bowl of custard for sauce, which the men said was "splendid;" also a rolled pudding, with molasses; and we had venison steaks and potatoes, but for tea we were obliged to use the tea-leaves of the morning again. I should think that few people in America have enjoyed their Thanksgiving dinner more. We had urged Mr. Nugent to join us, but he refused, almost savagely, which we regretted.

❊ ❊ ❊ ❊

How a cook at home would despise our scanty appliances, with which we turn out luxuries. We have only a cooking-stove, which requires incessant feeding with wood, a kettle, a frying-pan, a six-gallon brass pan, and a bottle for a rolling-pin. The cold has been very severe, but I do not suffer from it even in my insufficient clothing. I take a piece of granite made very hot to bed, draw the blankets over my head, and sleep eight hours, though the snow often covers me. One day of snow, mist, and darkness was rather depressing, and yesterday a hurricane began about five in the morning, and the whole Park was one swirl of drifting snow, like stinging wood smoke. My bed and room were white, and the frost was so intense that water brought in a kettle hot from the fire froze as I poured it into the basin. Then the snow ceased, and a fierce wind blew most of it out of the Park, lifting it from the mountains in such clouds as to make Long's Peak look like a smoking volcano. To-day the sky has resumed its delicious blue, and the Park its unrivalled beauty. I have cleaned all the windows, which, ever since I have been here, I supposed were of discoloured glass, so opaque and dirty they were; and when the men came home from fishing they found a cheerful new world. We had a great deal of sacred music and singing on Sunday. Mr. Buchan asked me if I knew a tune called "America," and began the grand roll of our National Anthem to the words:

> "My country, 'tis of thee,
> Sweet land of liberty," etc.

❊ ❊ ❊ ❊

The mercury is eleven degrees below zero, and I have to keep my ink on the stove to prevent it from freezing. The cold is intense – a clear, brilliant, stimulating cold, so dry that even in my threadbare flannel riding-dress I do not suffer from it. I must now take up my narrative of the nothings which have all the interest of *somethings* to me. We all got up before daybreak on Tuesday, and breakfasted at seven. I have not seen the dawn for some time, with its amber fires deepening into red, and the snow peaks flushing one by one, and it seemed a new miracle. It was a west wind, and we all thought it promised well. I took only two pounds of luggage, some raisins, the mail bag, and an additional blanket under my saddle. I had not been up from the Park at sunrise before, and it was quite glorious, the purple depths of M'Ginn's Gulch, from which at a height of 9,000 feet you look down on the sunlit Park 3,500 feet below, lying in a red haze, with its pearly needle-shaped peaks, framed by mountainsides dark with pines – my glorious, solitary, unique mountain home! The purple sun rose in front. Had I known what made it purple I should certainly have gone no farther. Then clouds, the morning mist as I supposed, lifted themselves up rose-lighted, showing the sun's disc as purple as one of the jars in a chemist's window, and having permitted this glimpse of their king, came down again as a dense mist, the wind chopped round, and the mist began to freeze hard. Soon Birdie and myself were a mass of acicular crystals; it was a true easterly fog. I galloped on, hoping to get through it, unable to see a yard before me; but it thickened, and I was obliged to subside into a jog-trot. As I rode on, about four miles from the cabin, a human figure, looking gigantic like the spectre of the Brocken, with long hair white as snow, appeared close to me, and at the same moment there was the flash of a pistol close to my ear, and I recognised "Mountain Jim" frozen from head to foot, looking a century old with his snowy hair. It was "ugly" altogether certainly, a "desperado's" grim jest, and it was best to accept it as such, though I had just cause for displeasure. He stormed and scolded, dragged me off the pony – for my hands and feet were numb with cold – took the bridle, and went off at a rapid stride, so that I had to run to keep them in sight in the darkness, for we were off the road in a thicket of scrub, looking like white branch-coral, I knew not where. Then we came suddenly on his cabin, and dear old "Ring," white like all else; and the "ruffian" insisted on my going in, and he made a good fire, and heated some coffee, raging all the time. He said everything against my going forward, except that it was dangerous; all he said came true, and here I am safe! Your letters, however, outweighed everything but danger, and I decided on going on, when he said, "I've seen many foolish people, but never one so foolish as you – you haven't a grain of sense. Why, I, an old mountaineer, wouldn't go down to the plains to-day." I told him he could not, though he would like it very much, for that he had turned his horses loose; on which he laughed heartily, and more heartily still at the stories I told him of young Lyman, so that I have still a doubt how much of the dark moods I have lately seen was assumed.

He took me back to the track; and the interview which began with a pistol-shot, ended quite pleasantly. It was an eerie ride, one not to be for-gotten, though there was no danger. I could not recognise any localities. Every tree was silvered, and the fir-tree tufts of needles looked like white chrysanthemums. The snow lay a foot deep in the gulches, with its hard, smooth surface marked by the feet of innumerable birds and beasts. Ice bridges had formed across all the streams, and I crossed them without knowing when. Gulches looked fathomless abysses, with clouds boiling up out of them, and shaggy mountain summits, half seen for a moment through the eddies, as quickly vanished. Everything looked vast and indefinite. Then a huge creation, like one of Doré's phantom illustrations, with much breathing of wings, came sailing towards me in a temporary opening in the mist. As with a strange rustle it passed close over my head, I saw, for the first time, the great mountain eagle, carrying a good-sized beast in his talons. It was a noble vision. Then there were ten miles of metamorphosed gulches – silent, awful – many ice bridges, then a frozen drizzle, and then the wind changed from east to north-east. Birdie was covered with exquisite crystals, and her long mane and the long beard which covers her throat were pure white. I saw that I must give up crossing the mountains to this place by an unknown trail; and I struck the old trail to the St. Vrain, which I had never travelled before, but which I knew to be more legible than the new one. The fog grew darker and thicker, the day colder and windier, the drifts deeper; but Birdie, whose four cunning feet had carried me 600 miles, and who in all difficulties proves her value, never flinched or made a false step, or gave me reason to be sorry that I had come on. I got down to the St. Vrain Canyon in good time, and stopped at a house thirteen miles from Longmount to get oats. I was white from head to foot, and my clothes were frozen stiff. The women gave me the usual invitation, "Put your feet in the oven;" and I got my clothes thawed and dried, and a delicious meal consisting of a basin of cream and bread. They said it would be worse on the plains, for it was an easterly storm; but as I was so used to riding, I could get on, so we started at 2.30. Not far off I met Edwards going up at last to Estes Park, and soon after the snowstorm began in earnest – or rather I entered the storm, which had been going on there for several hours. By that time I had reached the prairie, only eight miles from Longmount, and pushed on. It was simply fearful. It was twilight from the thick snow, and I faced a furious east wind loaded with fine, hard-frozen crystals, which literally made my face bleed. I could only see a very short distance anywhere; the drifts were often two feet deep, and only now and then, through the blinding whirl, I caught a glimpse of snow through which withered sunflowers did not protrude, and then I knew that I was on the track. But reaching a wild place, I lost it, and still cantered on, trusting to the pony's sagacity. It failed for once, for she took me on a lake and we fell through the ice into the water, 100 yards from land, and had a hard fight back again. It grew worse and worse. I had wrapped up my face, but the sharp, hard snow beat on my eyes – the only exposed part – bringing tears into them, which froze and closed up my eyelids at once. You cannot imagine what that was. I had to take off one glove to pick one eye open, for as to the other, the storm beat so savagely against it that I left it frozen, and drew over it the double piece of flannel which protected my face. I could hardly keep the other open by picking the ice from it constantly with my numb fingers, in doing which I got the back of my hand slightly frostbitten. It was truly awful at the time. I often thought, "Suppose I am going south instead of east? Suppose Birdie should fail? Suppose it should grow quite dark?" I was mountaineer enough to shake these fears off and keep up my spirits, but I knew how many had perished on the prairie in similar storms. I calculated that if I did not reach Longmount in half an hour it would be quite dark, and that I should be so frozen or paralysed with cold that I should fall off. Not a quarter of an hour after I had wondered how long I could hold on I saw, to my surprise, close to me, half smothered in snow, the scattered houses and blessed lights of Longmount, and welcome, indeed, its wide, dreary, lifeless, soundless road looked! When I reached the hotel I was so benumbed that I could not get off, and the worthy host lifted me off and carried me in. Not expecting any travellers, they had no fire except in the barroom, so they took me to the stove in their own room, gave me a hot drink and plenty of blankets, and in half an hour I was all right and ready for a ferocious meal. "If there's a traveller on the prairie to-night, God help him!" the host had said to his wife just before I came in.

1880

66. Anne Evans
Outcry

> AWAY with loving! Let it all go by;
> For losing is too grievous,
> And our beloved successively
> Turn cold and leave us!
> What matter whence the cold may come
> Which makes them deaf to us, and blind, and dumb –
> Whether from dark thoughts clouding old regard,

Or from their lodging out in the churchyard?
Friends? We may lose our best
Through some poor jest,
And all our after-days lament the losing!
Besides, there is no choosing
One of them all on whom to reckon
If death should beckon.
O miserable men!
O dreary doom!
Our love's delight is hollow –
Hollow as treachery, hollow as the tomb!
Away, away with loving then,
With hoping and believing;
For what should follow,
But grieving, grieving?

1881

67. Christina Rossetti
Monna Innominata, I

COME back to me, who wait and watch for you: –
　　Or come not yet, for it is over then,
　　And long it is before you come again,
So far between my pleasures are and few.
While, when you come not, what I do I do
　　Thinking 'Now when he comes,' my sweetest 'when':
　　For one man is my world of all the men
This wide world holds; O love, my world is you.
Howbeit, to meet you grows almost a pang
　　Because the pang of parting comes so soon;
　　My hope hangs waning, waxing, like a moon
　　　Between the heavenly days on which we meet:
Ah me, but where are now the songs I sang
　　When life was sweet because you called them sweet?

68. Edith Simcox
from *George Eliot: A Valedictory Article*

In 1854 Miss Evans found what had been wanting to her loving and generous nature since her father's death – some one 'whose life would have
been worse without her.' In return we owe to Mr. Lewes the complete
works of George Eliot, not one of which would have been written or even
planned without the inspiriting influence of his constant encouragement,
his obvious, unfeigned, unforced delight in her powers and success, his
total freedom from – we will not say jealousy – but the least inclination
towards self-comparison: even more might be said, but to say more would
be to quote words which were not written to be published. It is needless
now to guard such statements against the misinterpretation satirised in
Middlemarch, where we read, of Fred's and Mary's authorship, how
Middlemarch satisfied itself 'that there was no need to praise anybody for
writing a book, because it was always done by somebody else.' Mr. Lewes
had written novels, and Miss Evans had translated German books; therefore when George Eliot published stories and Mr. Lewes a *Life of Goethe*,
the critics of the day agreed, with the worthies of Middlemarch, that each
was inspired by the other, and so the work of neither ought to count for
much. But it will not be out of place to acknowledge a further obligation.
It is the snare of versatile and sympathetic natures to feel almost as if they
themselves were convinced by the opinions held by those with whom they
sympathise for reasons they have taken pains to understand. Mrs. Lewes was
conscious of a temptation to agree too readily under such circumstances,
to identify herself as it were dramatically with the views she did not really
share, and she acknowledged a debt of gratitude to Mr. Lewes for his
scrupulous anxiety that she should not be biassed in that way by him.
He was careful to guard her mental independence even against her own
too great readiness to defer to another, even though that other might be
himself.

Such obligations as these can be mentioned; it is scarcely possible,
without intruding on the sanctity of private life, to allude to the perfect
union between those two, which lent half its charm to all worship paid at
the shrine of George Eliot. She herself has spoken somewhere of the
element of almost maternal tenderness in a man's protecting love: this
patient, unwearying care for which no trifles are too small, watched over
her own life; he stood between her and the world, he relieved her from all
those minor cares which chafe and fret the artist's soul; he wrote her
letters (a proceeding for which he would say laughingly her correspondents
were *not* grateful); in a word, he so smoothed the course of her outer life

as to leave all her powers free to do what she alone could do for the world and for the many who looked to her for help and guidance. No doubt this devotion brought its own reward, but we are exacting for our idols and do not care to have even a generous error to condone, and therefore we are glad to know that great as his reward was, it was no greater than was merited by the most faithful perfect love that ever crowned a woman's life. All those who pleased themselves by giving that name to their love and admiration were content to know that their devotion was welcome to the one whose devotion exceeded theirs – their fellow-worshipper, George Henry Lewes, who counted it, I think, for his chief glory to take the lead in this cult. And here let us encounter what has been said or whispered by some who knew that George Eliot was the centre of a throng of ardent worshippers, and doubted perhaps, in Baconian phrase, whether it was possible to love and be wise, or, at all events, to be wise in loving with the unreserved enthusiasm of admiration common to those for whom George Eliot was the one woman in the world, the 'throned lady whose colours they wore between their heart and their armour.' It is not usual for men or women to be called on to justify in words their strongest feelings of personal attachment. These are usually accepted as an ultimate fact, and when we see such feelings subsisting with unwonted strength between two otherwise commonplace individuals, we conclude that they cannot both be wholly commonplace, since one or other must have an exceptional power of loving or inspiring love. In like manner, let us be content to know that if George Eliot was the object of much passionate and romantic worship, it was because her nature was so framed as to subdue to this same result numerous and very diverse characters. Men and women, old friends and new, persons of her own age and of another generation, the married and the single, impulsive lovers and hard-headed philosophers, nay, even some who elsewhere might have passed for cynics, all classes alike yielded to the attractive force of this rare character, in which tenderness and strength were blended together and as it were transfused with something that was all her own – the genius of sweet goodness.

Now, if we admit as to the objective side of a character that its *esse* is *percipi* (and any other view is hard to establish), it follows that George Eliot *was* what she appeared to this band of worshippers. It has been suggested that this worship was a fashion that had to be adopted for the sake of uniformity by all acquaintances; but the conjecture shows how little, after all, was understood of the intense feeling she inspired. The commonplaces of superficial admiration can be picked up and repeated at the call of fashion; but Mrs. Lewes was accustomed to hear, and her worshippers to speak, another language, which cannot be borrowed at will, and, to do her acquaintances justice, few or none of them were rash enough to play the hypocrite before so keen a judge. But another doubt too has been hinted at. The *rôle* of idol is a trying one to play: granted that George Eliot's worshippers had all reason on their side at first, does not so much incense end by becoming in some sort a necessity to its recipient?

In friendship George Eliot had the unconscious exactingness of a full nature. She was intolerant of a vacuum in the mind or character, and she was indifferent to admiration that did not seem to have its root in fundamental agreement with those first principles she held to be most 'necessary to salvation.' Where this sympathy existed, her generous affection was given to a fellow-believer, a fellow-labourer, with singularly little reference to the fact that such full sympathy was never unattended with profound love and reverence for herself as a living witness to the truth and power of the principles thus shared. To love her was a strenuous pleasure, for in spite of the tenderness for all human weakness that was natural to her, and the scrupulous charity of her overt judgments, the fact remained that her natural standard was ruthlessly out of reach, and it was a painful discipline for her friends to feel that she was compelled to lower it to suit their infirmities. The intense humility of her self-appreciation, and the unfeigned readiness with which she would even herself with any sinner who sought her counsel, had the same effect upon those who could compare what she condemned in herself with what she tolerated in them. And at the same time, no doubt, this total absence of self-sufficiency had something to do with the passionate tenderness with which commonplace people dared to cherish their immortal friend.

It is scarcely possible that a sect of fanatics should have developed itself by a spontaneous identical mistake in all parts of the world at once, that enthusiasts with a bent towards unreasonable adoration should have agreed in professing the same feeling for the same object without a common sufficient cause. . . .

It may be said of almost all love that it is deserved by those who are able to inspire it continuously, and reasons neither need nor should be given for such merely private feeling. But many of George Eliot's friends were first attracted to her by admiration for her writings, and though some of these ended by putting even her writings in the second place, the double intercourse with herself and her works was so far intermingled that explanation is possible up to a certain point.

We are conscious in her works of a many-sided sympathy with the various phases of real existence, with its commonest experiences as well as with its finest emotions, together with a keen intelligence of the laws which regulate, and the general truths which bear upon, the best and worst possibilities of human life. In like manner, her character seemed to include every possibility of action and emotion: no human passion was wanting in her nature, there were no blanks or negations; and the marvellous thing was to see how, in this wealth of impulses and desires, there was no crash of internal discord, no painful collisions with other human interests outside; how, in all her life, passions of volcanic strength were harnessed in the service of those nearest her, and so inspired by the permanent instinct of devotion to her kind, that it seemed as if it were by their own choice they spent themselves there only where their force was welcome. Her very being was a protest against the opposing and yet cognate heresies that half the normal human passions must be strangled in the quest of virtue, and that the attainment of virtue is a dull and undesirable end, seeing it implies the sacrifice of most that makes life interesting. She was intolerant of those who find life dull as well as of those who find their fellow-creatures unattractive, and both for the same reason, holding that such indifference was due to the lack of vital energy and generosity in the complainer, since the same world held interests enough for those who had enough impulses and affections of their own whereby to entangle themselves in its affairs. But though she set herself chiefly to preach the worth of common things, the admirableness of obscure good deeds, the value of common lives, and the sacredness of commonplace people in the crisis of the great primitive emotions, though she preached thus to the conviction of her hearers and her readers, there was reserved for her friends another experience, not indeed invalidating the other doctrine, but supplementing it with a truth she did not preach. If ordinary folks, with but mediocre powers of intelligence and attraction, were deserving of affection and respect – even from herself – could any intensity of such feelings transcend what was due to one who rose as far as she did above this margin of mediocrity within which she thought the choicest feelings of our nature might find ample food? To be content with the rest of the world, and to have her to adore *par-dessus le marché*, was a happiness she gave to many, perhaps to some who without her might have remained entangled in the heresies she condemned. And I think the world, in counting what it owes her, should not forget the welcome reminder given by her life, that the level of respectable mediocrity, which we are not suffered to despise, may yet be broken for us by the advent of an ideal nature whose rare powers and yet more rare unselfishness create anew the impressions to which the language of religion owes its birth. . . .

And in this context it may be well to consider the much-debated question whether the general impression left by her writings, the general tendency of her teaching, is melancholy or otherwise. It follows from what has been said that the consolations she had to offer were of a strenuous sort. She came as a very angel of consolation to those persons of sufficiently impartial mind to find comfort in the hint that the world might be less to blame than they were as to those points on which they found themselves in chronic disagreement with it. But she had nothing welcome for those whose idea of consolation is the promise of a *deux ex machinâ* by whose help they may gather grapes of thorns and figs of thistles. She thought that there was much needed doing in the world, and criticism of our neighbours and the natural order might wait at all events until the critic's own character and conduct were free from blame. Imperfect agents might lend a hand in mending what was amiss, it was only unhelpful criticism that stirred her anger; and the observation may have been present to her mind that people usually have a sneaking kindness for their own handiwork, even while it continues to fall short of the desired perfection. One who does not care for china in itself will survey with complacency a neatly mended fracture, and her severity in this direction must have been due to the perception that long orations upon the evils of creation proceed most readily from the lips of those who are otherwise at little pains to lessen the evils. To a friend who once playfully called her optimist she responded, 'I will not answer to the name of optimist, but if you like to invent Meliorist, I will not say you call me out of my name.' She felt so strongly that there was a worse and a better, almost at every turn in every life; and this being so, since it was in the power of human beings again and again to help each other to prefer and reach the better, the continuous passive dwelling upon all the possibilities of evil, whether in resentment or despair, assumed in her eyes the shape of a folly closely verging on crime.

Of course sincere and industrious reformers may suffer from melancholy as well as more cynical pessimists, and to such infirmity she could be tender enough, but in herself or others she gave the name of weakness to the unmotived depression which leads some people to do all their doings sadly. Her own view of the world as a whole was too veracious to be summed up in a phrase. Her mind was a mirror, upon which the truth concerning all human relations was reflected with literal fidelity. What one generalisation can cover so wide a range? You can no more draw one moral lesson from her books than you can from life itself; you may draw a thousand if you will, but merely to read one of her books in an impressionable mood is to see such a portion of the world with her eyes and to share in the multiform influence exercised by the vision. The mind unconsciously becomes attuned to the set of ideas by which all her single perceptions were dominated and explained, and without having drawn a single inference in thought, the reader is lured into the mood which, become permanent in a sweet woman of genius, inspires the writer and the friend we mourn.

69. Constance Naden
The Lady Doctor

SAW ye that spinster gaunt and grey,
Whose aspect stern might well dismay
    A bombardier stout-hearted?
The golden hair, the blooming face,
And all a maiden's tender grace
    Long, long from her have parted.

A Doctor she – her sole delight
To order draughts as black as night,
    Powders, and pills, and lotions;
Her very glance might cast a spell
Transmuting Sherry and Moselle
    To chill and acrid potions.

Yet if some rash presumptuous man
Her early life should dare to scan,
    Strange things he might discover;
For in the bloom of sweet seventeen
She wandered through the meadows green
    To meet a boyish lover.

She did not give him Jesuit's bark,
To brighten up his vital spark,
    Nor ipecacuanha,
Nor chlorodyne, nor camomile,
But blushing looks, and many a smile,
    And kisses sweet as manna.

But ah! the maiden's heart grew cold,
Perhaps she thought the youth too bold,
    Perhaps his views had shocked her;
In anger, scorn, caprice, or pride,

She left her old companion's side
  To be a Lady Doctor.

She threw away the faded flowers,
Gathered amid the woodland bowers,
  Her lover's parting token:
If suffering bodies we relieve,
What need for wounded souls to grieve?
  Why mourn, though hearts be broken?

She cared not, though with frequent moan
He wandered through the woods alone
  Dreaming of past affection:
She valued at the lowest price
Men neither patients for advice
  Nor subjects for dissection.

She studied hard for her degree;
At length the coveted MD
  Was to her name appended;
Joy to that Doctor, young and fair,
With rosy cheeks and golden hair,
  Learning with beauty blended.

Diseases man can scarce endure
A lady's glance may quickly cure,
  E'en though the pains be chronic;
Where'er that maiden bright was seen
Her eye surpassed the best quinine,
  Her smile became a tonic.

But soon, too soon, the hand of care
Sprinkled with snow her golden hair,
  Her face grew worn and jaded;
Forgotten was each maiden wile,
She scarce remembered how to smile,
  Her roses all were faded.

And now, she looks so grim and stern,
We wonder any heart could burn
  For one so uninviting;

No gentle sympathy she shows,
She seems a man in woman's clothes,
    All female graces slighting.

Yet blame her not, for she has known
The woe of living all alone,
    In friendless, dreary sadness;
She longs for what she once disdained,
And sighs to think she might have gained
    A home of love and gladness.

MORAL

Fair maid, if thine unfettered heart
Yearn for some busy, toilsome part,
    Let that engross thee only;
But oh! if bound by love's light chain,
Leave not thy fond and faithful swain
    Disconsolate and lonely.

70. May Probyn
Soapsuds

WITH apple-trees on either hand,
Before the tub I saw her stand, –
The sunlights caught her as I came,
And eddied round her like a flame,
And loud the finches shrilled her name.
Her arms were bare from wrist to shoulder
    For plying, plashing in the water;
So cool her lilac gown did fold her,
    All kilted up to make it shorter,
        Where both her little shoes peeped out,
        And twinkled when she tripped about.
Down in the border, at her feet,
    Mint and marjoram were growing, –
Among her hair, in the ripples sweet,
    One great daisy-moon was blowing, –
And as I came I heard her singing,

Where she stood the clothes a-wringing,
High aloft her round arms flinging,
With the soapsuds drifting, clinging –

   (Oh, the rosemary and rue
   That within her garden grew!)
     Singing –
       Wringing –
    Bare arms flinging –
  All the way I heard her singing –
   "Lovers meet – and lovers part –
   Where's the need to break one's heart?"

Her arms were white as milky curds;
Her speech was like the song of birds;
Her eyes were grey as mountain lakes
Where dream of shadow stirs and breaks.
Her gown was print – her name was Sally –
  Her summer years were barely twenty –
She dropped the soap to glance and dally,
  And then the dimples came in plenty!
I praised her fingers, dripping sweet,
Where warmth and whiteness seemed to meet –
I made her blush, and made her pout,
And watched her wring her linen out.
    Oh, to meet her in the valley,
    Snatch her hand, and call her Sally!
    Oh, to find her on the hill,
    Kiss, and call her Sally still!
    Oh, to clasp her quite alone,
    And call her Sally of one's own!
Thyme and marjoram were sweet,
  All the lavender was blowing –
Through the honeysuckled heat
  Bees were coming, bees were going –
  Half she turned from me unwilling,
  Snow of soapsuds downward spilling, –
  Linnet-like she took to trilling,
  High across the borders shrilling –

   (Oh, the thyme, with flowers half shed,
   Blowing in her garden-bed!)

Trilling –
Shrilling –
Soapsuds spilling –
Merrily she tuned her trilling –
"Lovers meet – and lovers part –
Where's the need to break one's heart?"

I came more near – I called her Sally –
She blushed like bloom in orchard alley;
Her arms she leaned upon the tub –
Forgot to rinse, forgot to rub –

"Lovers meet and part," she said,
"Some to weep, and some to wed;
Yesterday 'twas Colin came,
Kissed me while I cried 'for shame!' –
Next 'tis Lubin, or 'tis you –
Where's the need to make ado?"
"Nay," I said, "not so for me!
Not so I dreamed of love and Sally!"
The leaping dimples seemed to flee,
The flitting rose-leaves seemed to rally,
And she spoke a little slowly,
With a touch of melancholy,
"Colin kissed me yesterday!
If you go – nay, I'll not sorrow!
Drop my hand, and wend your way –
Lubin's sure to come to-morrow!"

Turned I then, and wandered back,
Past the shrivelled bean-pod stack,
Through the grey-green apple-boughs,
And the clover-cropping cows.
Summer thistledowns were flying –
Seemed to me I heard her sighing –
Seemed to hear her half-replying –
Wondered if she could be crying,
Linen all neglected lying –?
Stopped I there, and looked a second –
I but heard the rose-leaves fall;
Had she called, or had she beckoned –!

But she made no sign at all.
I but saw her tripping by,
Where the clothes-line stretched on high,
And stand a-tiptoe 'gainst the sky,
Hanging out the things to dry.

   (Oh, the mint and marigold!
   Oh, the savours manifold!
   Marjoram, and thyme, and tansy,
   Pimpernel, and pink, and pansy –
   All within her garden growing,
      Blowing,
         Growing,
    All a-blowing –
   Oh, the lavender that bloomed,
   And the big brown bees that boomed!)
Still I seemed to hear her sighing,
Hanging out the clothes for drying,
Sending storms of soapsuds flying,
   Half replying,
   Half denying,

Was it song, or was it sighing?
(Oh, the fennel! oh, the rue!
Both within her garden grew –)
"Lovers meet – and lovers part –
Where's the need to break one's heart?

1886

71. E. Nesbit
The Wife of all Ages

I DO not catch these subtle shades of feeling,
   Your fine distinctions are too fine for me;
This meeting, scheming, longing, trembling, dreaming,
   To me mean love, and only love, you see;
In me at least 'tis love, you will admit,
And you the only man who wakens it.

Suppose *I* yearned, and longed, and dreamed, and fluttered,
   What would you say or think, or further, do?
Why should one rule be fit for me to follow,

      While there exists a different law for you?
   If all these fires and fancies came my way,
   Would you believe love was so far away?

   On all these other women – never doubt it –
      'Tis love you lavish, love you promised me!
   What do I care to be the first, or fiftieth?
      It is the *only one* I care to be.
   Dear, I would be your sun, as mine you are,
   Not the most radiant wonder of a star.

   And so, good-bye! Among such sheaves of roses
      You will not miss the flower I take from you;
   Amid the music of so many voices
      You will forget the little songs I knew –
   The foolish tender words I used to say,
   The little common sweets of every day.

   The world, no doubt, has fairest fruits and blossoms
      To give to you: but what, ah! what for me?
   Nay, after all I am your slave and bondmaid,
      And all my world is in my slavery.
   So, as before, I welcome any part
   Which you may choose to give me of your heart.

72. Annie Besant
from *The World and Its Gods*

THERE are many who acknowledge that Christianity has made for the retardation of scientific thought, the hindering of human progress. By thousands of educated men and women, the question I lately asked, "Is Christianity a success?" has been answered in the negative. Face to face with the evidence borne by history, honesty forces from them this one answer. They read of the countless frauds out of which struggled its "historical" books; of its success among the most ignorant and superstitious of an

uninstructed populace; of the horrible crimes of its first imperial support-
er; of the violence, treachery, and bribery by which it won its way through
Europe; of its shocking barbarities towards heretics and unbelievers; of its
crusades and its Inquisition; of its ferocious struggles against each new
truth, and its fawning supple acceptance of each when it had won its way
by agony and martyrdom. Glancing over Europe, they see that to-day the
most backward and the most ignorant countries are those over which
Christianity still rules unchallenged, while those which are in the van of
civilisation are penetrated through and through with all the forms of
scepticism, from moderate doubt of Biblical inspiration up to the most
pronounced and aggressive Atheism. As the result of all this cumulative
evidence, they pronounce Christianity to be a failure. But very many of
them still cling to a belief in "God", whether as a "personal Deity", a "great
First Cause", a "pervading Power" that "makes for righteousness", and is
the Creator, Upholder, Father of all. They think that the world would be
hopeless were it not for God, and that humanity walks the more strongly
for leaning on a divine crutch. I propose to traverse this contention and
to show, by surveying the Gods of the world, that they have been its
hindrances rather than its helpers.

For what is God? He is the black cloud of the Unknown. Vast, stretching
in every direction, brooding over existence from horizon to horizon, such
was God in the childhood of the race. He was huge as its ignorance,
omnipresent as its wonder and its fear. As man has grown in knowledge,
God has diminished in extent. Each acquisition of new truth has lessened
the domain of uncertainty over which he spreads. The telescope has
chased him from his throne beyond the stars; navigation has left him no
"heaven above" towards which prayer can be directed; the understood
forces of nature render him unnecessary; "there is no" longer "need for
such a hypothesis".

That man's belief in God was natural, and indeed inevitable, every
student must admit. Theism is a stage through which the race must pass in
its intellectual evolution. The supernatural, being the unknown portion of
the natural, must needs play a large part in the thoughts of the race as it
begins to study and to question. The Gods believed in will vary as their
creators vary, some cruel, some brutal, some lustful, some noble, some
beautiful, some stately. Men who desire to use God for personal gain will
proclaim cruel Gods who need to be propitiated by sacrifice and gift; on the
other hand, the most poetic and most advanced minds of a semi-civilised
community will body out their best thoughts into God, will picture him as
the realisation of their loftiest ideal, will claim his authority for their most
beneficent legislation.

But while belief in God was inevitable, human progress has consisted in growing out of it. The advanced thought of each generation, the thought which moulded the intellect of the succeeding one, has ever been branded as Atheistic. For every popular God is the fossil of a dead thought, while the fresh living thought bodies itself into a new form, a higher God.

✾ ✾ ✾ ✾

It must not be forgotten that Christianity, the child of the Semitic races, is founded on a human sacrifice. The torture of Christ upon the cross and his death in agony was an expiatory sacrifice to an angry God. A fresh horror is added to the picture in that the sacrifice is that of a son to his own father; there is an exquisite refinement of cruelty in the notion of pleasure being taken by the parent in contemplating the anguish of his own child. The bloodthirsty nature of the Christian God is marked out with terrible distinctness in the epistle to the Hebrews: "By his own blood he entered in once into the holy place, having obtained eternal redemption for us . . .without shedding of blood is no remission . . . once in the end of the world hath he appeared to put away sin by the sacrifice of himself" (Heb. ix., 12, 22, 26). What more could be demanded by Moloch or by Kemosh, than the torture of the victim in the Prætorium and the cruel and prolonged death-agony on Calvary?

The Church founded on a human sacrifice has demanded thousands of such sacrifices during its bloodstained existence. What were the burnings of heretics save burnt offerings to the Christian God, "acts of faith", as they were termed by the pious Spaniards?

Of all the Gods of the world, the Christian Gods have, perhaps, wrought the most harm, and this both because of their genealogy and of the doctrines of the religion which belongs to them. They descend from the Semitic deities, whose bloodthirsty and cruel characters have already been dealt with, and they inherit the qualities of their ancestors. And these qualities appear in the doctrines of the Christian religion. Christians worship the Hebrew Jahveh, with all his hideous cruelties: they believe that this God made a world and peopled it with sentient beings who prey upon each other; that he created a man and woman who he foreknew would become the parents of a fallen race; that he placed them in an environment which would mould them into "sinful" beings; that he gave an arbitrary command, the breach of which was to ruin them, but the wrongness of breaking which they were not to know until they had broken it; that when they had broken it, he cursed them for the act he fore-knew and fore-ordained; that, not content with cursing them, he entailed his curse on their helpless innocent posterity; that the curse for the trifling act of eating some fruit by two people included heavy toil, pain, disease, death in this world, and unending torture in another, for countless millions unborn when their doom was pronounced; that, having brought about a detestable state of things in his own world, he drowned it in a fury, slaying all living beings, save a few whom he kept alive in order that the entail of the curse should not be broken; that the posterity of these selected ones turned out as badly as their fore-runners; that he threatened to burn the world up instead of drowning it again; that he sent his son to become a man, and then, as man, to suffer, to die in agony, that by his pain a few elected from the cursed race might escape the doom of the majority; that these "few chosen" shall be eternally happy, while the myriads of the lost shall suffer the inherited curse. This is the teaching of the Christian religion; these Gods, the Avenger and the Redeemer, are the Gods that the Christians worship. They have also a third, God the Holy Ghost, much overlooked and under-worshipped; and some of them, the great majority, believe in a fourth, a curious composite of incompatible attributes, a virgin and a mother, the creature of God yet his mother. The puzzle becomes yet more complex when we are taught that the son is "begotten of the father before all worlds", but is as old as his begettor; that the son is "conceived by the Holy Ghost", who is therefore presumably his father also; so that in the Trinity we have two fathers of different dates, one "before all worlds", and the other nine months B.C., of the same son, the first father being identical with the son ("I and my father are one"), and the second father being identical with the first father and the common son ("they are not three Gods, but one God") – the family arrangements being so complex that plain men can only gape at them, yet of such vital importance that "he therefore which will be saved must thus think of the Trinity". Think! Belief in the Trinity is the negation of thought.

Out of this chaos has been evolved the superstition and the ignorance of the Christian world. Those who cannot pretend to believe are accursed.

The whole biblical scheme of creation and divine providence is as revolting to morality as is its salvation to intelligence. . . .

Out of this cruelty of nature, and out of the belief in hell, have grown the horrible persecutions which have distinguished Christianity beyond every other creed. What other God can reckon among his victims so many of human kind as can the Christian? . . . The hosts of slain heretics are practically innumerable. The command of Jahveh, "Thou shalt not suffer a witch to live," met with full obedience, and thousands of foolish human beings were burned and drowned and tortured to death for their supposed commerce with the evil one.

If from these judicial murders we turn to religious wars, to the *Cherem* of the Christian Gods, we shall find them as bloody as any of those of the more ancient deities. In the crusades alone the slaughter was horrible . . . Not a God of antiquity can hope to rival the Christian God in the huge roll of his victims.

Nor is bloodshed the only evil which must be ascribed to this terrible deity. The dense darkness of ignorance that shrouded Europe like a pall for centuries; the cruelty with which each effort to gain knowledge was crushed out; the poisoning of education with superstition after some slight education had at length been won; the diseases which scourged Christendom for its filth and its poverty, and were met with prayer instead of with knowledge; the poverty which was blessed by the priests and unshared by the Church; these horrors lie at the feet of the Christian Gods, in awful amount, piled up as offering. . . .

Even now their influence causes misery; broken hearts, marred lives, ruined homes, liberty outraged, honesty punished, slander virulent, hypocrisy wellnigh general, all these still bear witness to the maleficent power of the Christian Gods.

❀ ❀ ❀ ❀

Thus has the world fared at the hands of its Gods: useless bloodshed, needless discord, religious hatreds, delayed progress, all these come from the Gods. All that is hopeful with promise for the future comes from man's unaided efforts, man's strenuous labor. The day is coming, already its dawn is on the mountains of knowledge, when man shall live free in a
WORLD WITHOUT GOD.

1887

73. May Kendall
Woman's Future

COMPLACENT they tell us, hard hearts and derisive,
    In vain is our ardour: in vain are our sighs:
Our intellects, bound by a limit decisive,
    To the level of Homer's may never arise.
We heed not the falsehood, the base innuendo,
    The laws of the universe, these are our friends.

Our talents shall rise in a mighty crescendo,
    We trust Evolution to make us amends!

But ah, when I ask you for food that is mental,
    My sisters, you offer me ices and tea!
You cherish the fleeting, the mere accidental,
    At cost of the True, the Intrinsic, the Free.
Your feelings, compressed in Society's mangle,
    Are vapid and frivolous, pallid and mean.
To slander you love; but you don't care to wrangle:
    You bow to Decorum, and cherish Routine.

Alas, is it woolwork you take for your mission,
    Or Art that your fingers so gaily attack?
Can patchwork atone for the mind's inanition?
    Can the soul, oh my sisters, be fed on a *plaque*?
Is this your vocation? My goal is another,
    And empty and vain is the end you pursue.
In antimacassars the world you may smother;
    But intellect marches o'er them and o'er you.

On Fashion's vagaries your energies strewing,
    Devoting your days to a rug or a screen,
Oh, rouse to a lifework – do something worth doing!
    Invent a new planet, a flying-machine.
Mere charms superficial, mere feminine graces,
    That fade or that flourish, no more you may prize;
But the knowledge of Newton will beam from your faces,
    The soul of a Spencer will shine in your eyes.

ENVOY

Though jealous exclusion may tremble to own us,
    Oh, wait for the time when our brains shall expand!
When once we're enthroned, you shall never dethrone us –
    The poets, the sages, the seers of the land!

1888

74. A. Mary F. Robinson
The Idea

BENEATH this world of stars and flowers
  That rolls in visible deity,
I dream another world is ours
  And is the soul of all we see.

It hath no form, it hath no spirit;
  It is perchance the Eternal Mind;
Beyond the sense that we inherit
  I feel it dim and undefined.

How far below the depth of being,
  How wide beyond the starry bound
It rolls unconscious and unseeing,
  And is as Number or as Sound.

And through the vast fantastic visions
  Of all this actual universe,
It moves unswerved by our decisions,
  And is the play that we rehearse.

———

1889

75. Clementina Black
A Working Woman's Speech

There is perhaps no class of whom the wealthy or the educated know so little as of working women. Everybody in these days knows something of the slums, something of the crofter's cottage and the Irish cabin; but the industrious, independent woman who spends her days working at a skilled trade in a factory crosses our path but seldom, and few of us know anything of her thoughts, her aims, and her struggles.

  For this reason I think the readers of this Review may care to have as exact a report as I can give them of the tale told in my presence by a working woman (who has given me leave to use it) at a meeting of working women. The object of the meeting was the formation in Liverpool of a branch trade-union for female cigar-makers, and the speaker was the secretary of the Nottingham and Leicester Cigar Makers' Union. She is a young married woman, the mother of two children, and her husband is also a cigar-maker, working in the same factory as herself. I will try to tell the story, as nearly as I can, in her own words:–

"Work had been slack for a few weeks, and they had kept on complaining and finding fault about simple little things, and there had been rumours of something horrible going to happen to us, and if ever we said anything it was: 'Ah, it will be worse by-and-by; you wait till by-and-by.' But we never dreamed of a reduction; we thought, you know, perhaps we'd only work two days a week, or something like that. Well, one morning I came in to work, and there was all the others, and they was all a-talking and in a great state, and they said to me: 'Mrs. Briant, have you seen that notice?' and I says, 'No, what notice?' And there was a great paper pasted up as big as that (unfolding a printed balance-sheet of four octavo pages), and it said that, owing to foreign competition – for the Mexican work was just coming in about that time, you remember – Messrs. Robinson and Barnsdale could not afford to pay their cigar-makers what they had done, and there would be a reduction, but it didn't say what. And then it said the sale of cigars had fallen off because the English working men had taken to smoking tobacco in pipes. Well, I was a stranger there, so to speak, for I had not been there above a twelvemonth, and there was women there that had worked there for years and years. And so I said, 'Well, what shall we do?' And they said, 'What can we do?' 'I won't take it,' I said; 'I'll leave sooner. We can go back to London where we came from; but I won't take any reduction.' And then in comes the foreman. 'Now, don't excite yourself, Mrs. Briant,' says he. And I said to him, 'Now, Tommy, just tell us what is the reduction, for you haven't put it up.' And he hadn't been foreman above a matter of a couple of months, and he was one of them that would have gone through fire and water, as they say, for an extra penny of his own. 'Oh,' he said, 'I darsen't tell you, I really darsen't. It's something horrible.' So I said, 'Well, placard it, like you did the other, then.' And he went and got a paper, and stuck it up under the other, and it said it was to be sixpence a hundred. Well, you may think that was a drop! If they had offered a penny or twopence a hundred, there was them as would have sat down to it, – but sixpence! The two-and-threepenny ones to be one-and-nine; and the two shillings, eighteenpence; and the one-and-nine, one-and-three; and right down to the one-and-fourpenny ones, which would only be tenpence a hundred. Why, it meant six or seven shillings a week.

"Well, we all began to talk about it, and I said again I would not take a reduction; and we said what should we do, and then we said we ought to hold a meeting and form a union. And we went and got a gentleman to lend us a room – it was a kind of concert room, close to a public house – and we wrote out bits of notices on papers, we had no handbills nor nothing, and Mr. Beckton, of the men's society, he came over to address the meeting. And so we formed our society, and the men's society gave us our book and rules and contribution cards, just to start. And we chose out a deputation and Mr. Beckton, and Mr. Radcliffe, another member of the society that we had chosen to be our president, were to go too. And Mr. Robinson, the senior partner, never took any part in the business, any way, he was a sort of sleeping partner; it was Mr. Barnsdale managed everything. So we went to Mr. Robinson, who was in his office, and he said to the foreman: 'Are these *my* work-people?' And the foreman said: 'The ladies are, but not the gentlemen.' So he asked them to go away, and said he would settle his business himself with his own work-people, without any one from outside. But Mr. Radcliffe began to talk to him, first one thing and then another, and to turn him round a bit, for you know you have to use a lot of what I may call soft soap. And so at last we came to it, and he showed us a map all marked out with red lines, and he said how trade was so bad, and they wanted to put on a new traveller to go to fresh places and get more orders, and our wages was to go down to pay for that new traveller. And I said (and perhaps you might blame me for having the cheek, but what I thought was, Well, if they make the reduction I can't stay, and he can but turn me away; and it's better one should go than all be reduced, and if they reduce here it will go round all the shops, of course): 'And it's always the workers that it's to fall on, when trade's slack. It's always *them* that's to suffer, and never any one else.' And he said, 'How do you mean that, Mrs. Briant?' And I said, 'It's not your travellers or your foremen that you reduce when trade's bad; no, nor yet your profits – oh, dear no! It's always the cigar-makers that you go to reduce first thing, and yet you can't do without the cigar-maker: it's the cigar-maker that makes your money for you. I know we couldn't do without your capital, but neither could you do without us, and we are always to be the ones to suffer.' And he said, 'I wish I had your tongue, Mrs. Briant.' (Here a roar of laughter, and a burst of applause interrupted.) Well, and then he said, 'Well, but would you rather work only two days a week than take the work lower and have more of it?' And we called out, 'Yes.' Because of course you may take it at a lower price, think-ing to get the price back when work is brisk; but it's a hard matter to get it back, and oftentimes you never do. And besides you may as well play half time, as work full time and make no more for it at the end of the week. And so we all stuck to it, and we all came out, every woman in the place – not one stayed in. And you know if there had been one stayed, perhaps they would not have given in to us, but they all stood together and the firm gave way. And I'm working there now. Well, then we went on with our union, and we had our troubles at first, I can tell you. I think there was nearly every employer in the town tried to fight us one way or the other. I don't think there's a shop in the town that I haven't been on a deputation to.

"But we beat them all except one, and now there is only one shop that isn't a union house – and I'll tell you about that – over a hundred pounds that dispute cost us. That was the dispute at —'s. He was quite a young fellow, not more than two or three-and-twenty, and he had just come into his father's business. A very proud old gentleman Mr. —, his father, was, and he paid a penny or twopence a hundred more than anybody else in the town, just so that he might have the pick of the trade. He had twenty-two working for him, and a better set of women you never saw. They were not all young; some of them had been there for years and years. Well, first he brought them down to the same as other places, and they sat down content with that. But then he began to think he would reduce them lower, and he told one of them he would reduce them all. And she said, 'If you do they'll all go out, that's certain.' And he said, 'Well, I won't reduce them all; I'll reduce five of them, to begin with.' So she told all the others, and they made up their minds that they would hold all together. So when he picked out five and told them they would be reduced, the others all said that they should go out. And he sent for the one that had first stirred up the others, into his private office, and she stayed and talked to him for half an hour. When she came out they said to her, 'Well, Nelly, what did he say to you?' And she said, 'What he said to me is my own business, not yours.' And, do you know, she would not go out when all the other one-and-twenty did. Of course he had told her she should have her price, to keep her, and she stayed, and she's there now. Well, we went on a deputation from the union, and he would not see us; and he said he would have a policeman in to turn us out. And I said to him, 'You'll be wanting a police-man for more than that, at this rate, Mr. —.' And they all came out, and we paid them all dispute pay from the union, all those one-and-twenty girls. But there was that Nelly sitting there at work all the time. And then I heard that he would see me if I would go by myself. And so I got up at five, for it was more than three or four miles from where we lived, and we started out at six, me and my husband. And it were snowing and raining – oh! it were an awful day; it was in November. And those poor girls were on picket there in the snow, walking up and down and telling people there was a strike, to stop them from going in to work. And we saw Mr. — go in, and he came and stood at a window and called all his clerks and even the engineers to see us there in the snow, and to make a mock of us. And the policeman stood watching us on the other side of the street. And there came a young woman to go in to work, and we spoke to her, my husband and me. And then when they saw that, out came two clerks and said to her, 'Come in, come in.' And we begged to her, and I said, 'We'll pay you out of the union more than you'll get from him. Look at those girls walking up and down in the snow, and you'll go in and take their place and take the very bread out of their mouths.' And my husband said, 'For God's sake, don't go in.' And we did not dare so much as to lay our hands on her arm, for the policeman would have taken us up. And the clerks took hold of her two arms and took her in. And we had to ask some of the people living near to let us go in and sit by their fire, and I took off my boots and poured the water out of them, and dried my stockings on my feet. And I cried – I'm not ashamed to tell you so – I had a right-down good cry. And we went to the young woman's husband, her that had gone in, and begged him not to let her go to work. And he said, 'Well, what is she to do? I'm out of work and she's got to keep the two children.' And I said, 'I suppose she's got to keep you too?' And he said, 'Well, partly.' And he told us she had been working at Jackson's, and she'd been discharged, and she must go to work somewhere. Well, we told her we'd gladly pay her out of the union funds till she got work. And he said he'd go and fetch her at dinner-time, and she should not go back. Then we thought perhaps we had been to blame about Jackson's, for we had not tried to get any members there; there were only ten worked there. And when Mr. Jackson heard about the union he offered her to come back to work, and he said he hoped all his girls would join, and they did, all ten of them. But Mr. — got in girls that we would not have in the union, some that he had sent away himself, but he has not got a single union girl. And all the twenty-one got work after a time, and now we haven't got one on the funds. And Mr. — came and applied to us later to send him ten; but we had not got them. And every other shop in the town is a union shop; and if a new woman comes in we tell her she has got to join the union, and if she didn't we would not work with her; but they always do. And so that is the story of how our union was formed, and what we have had to fight through."

This, in substance, and almost in actual words, was the speech to which we all listened; but the voice of the speaker, the turns of tone, the ring of sincerity cannot be given in mere black and white. For myself, as I sat and heard, I felt the same sort of hope and gladness that came to me last summer when I saw the unity, the self-control, and the moderation of the hundreds of match girls who came out on strike from Bryant and May's.

Be the evils around us what they may, there is hope for the country which has among its workers young women of this sort.

76. Michael Field
Long Ago, LIV

ADOWN the Lesbian vales,
When spring first flashes out,
I watch the lovely rout
Of maidens flitting 'mid the honey-bees
For thyme and heath,
Cistus, and trails
Of myrtle-wreath:
They bring me these
My passionate, unsated sense to please.

In turn, to please my maids,
Most deftly will I sing
Of their soft cherishing
In apple-orchards with cool waters by,
Where slumber streams
From quivering shades,
And Cypris seems
To bend and sigh,
Her golden calyx offering amorously.

What praises would be best
Wherewith to crown my girls?
The rose when she unfurls
Her balmy, lighted buds is not so good,
So fresh as they
When on my breast
They lean, and say
All that they would,
Opening their glorious, candid maidenhood.

> To that pure band alone
> I sing of marriage-loves;
> As Aphrodite's doves
> Glance in the sun their colour comes and goes:
> No girls let fall
> Their maiden zone
> At Hymen's call
> Serene as those
> Taught by a poet why sweet Hesper glows.

1890

77. Mona Caird
from *The Morality of Marriage*

Many social and economic changes must take place before *all* women can, without injury to themselves and the race, earn their own living (in the accepted sense of the term), but what is there to prevent a woman having a legal claim to a salary, when she works in her husband's business? There is an ungenerous dislike on the part of many men to the idea of a wife being her own mistress. They do not realise that they are demanding what they have no moral right to demand from any human being when they endow a woman with their name and their "worldly goods." Were it possible for a wife to leave her husband without penalty if the worst came to the worst, that worst, in nine cases out of ten, would never come. One seldom hears of very bad cases of ill-treatment when a woman has private means under her own control. Wives who have begun their married life without such means, and acquired them afterwards, notice that a marked difference is discernible in the husband's attitude towards them. It is the unconscious recognition of the new status.

Dependence, in short, is the curse of our marriages, of our homes and of our children, who are born of women who are not free – not free even to refuse to bear them. What is the proportion of children whose mothers were perfectly willing and able to bring them into the world, willing in a strict sense, apart from all considerations of duty, or fear of unsanctioned sentiment? A true answer to this question would shake down many brave edifices of ignorance and cant which are now flying holiday flags from their battlements.

Nervous exhaustion and many painful forms of ill-health among women are appallingly common, and people try to find round-about explanations for the fact. Do we need explanations? The gardener takes care that his very peach-trees and rose-bushes shall not be weakened by over-production (though to produce is their sole mission); valuable animals are spared in the same way and for the same reason. It is only women for whom there is no mercy. In them the faculties are discouraged and destroyed which lead away from the domestic "sphere" and "duties," the whole nature is sub-jected to hot-house cultivation in such a manner as to drive all the forces into a single channel. Such treatment means over-wrought nerves, over-stimulated instincts, weakened constitution, a low intellectual development, or if otherwise a development at the cost of further physical suffering.

This misdirection of nervous energy creates innumerable miseries, and some of them seem to have become chronic, or hereditary, and from being so common have lost the very name of disease. Yet with these facts before them, people still dare to argue from the present condition and instincts of average women to the eternal mandates of nature regarding them; they still fail to see that to found a theory of society upon special adaptations of structure and impulse which they now find in a long enslaved and abused race, is to found a theory of nature upon artificial and diseased development.

The nervous strain which the civilised woman endures is truly appalling. The savage, to whom the infinite little cares and troubles, responsibilities and anxieties of modern life are unknown, has also the advantage of a far less severe tax on her strength as regards her maternal functions. Nature appears to be kind to her primitive children; their families rarely exceed two or three in number, and the task of bearing and rearing cannot be compared for severity to that of the civilised mother. It is one of the many instances of "cussedness" in nature, that a more protected, well-fed, complex life causes the race to become more prolific, thus increasing the demands upon the nervous energy from every side. People are beginning to feel the danger to the race in all this; but how do they propose to meet it? By trying to hold women back from the full appointed maternal func-tions! One-half of the race is to be rescued at the expense of the other! A highly moral and scientific solution of the difficulty. Highly moral and scientific men have advocated this singular method of averting the danger of race degeneration, so we must conclude that the proposal shares the qualities of its authors. Women, who already are crippled in body and mind by excessive performance of the functions of maternity, are to plunge yet further in the same disastrous direction – to cut off all chance of respite and relief, all hope of the over-taxed system righting itself by more general distribution of energy. The longing and the effort – so striking among the present generation – for a less one-sided, more healthily-balanced life, must be sternly checked. Do we not see that the mother of half-a-dozen children, who struggles to cultivate her faculties, to be an intelligent human being, nearly always breaks down under the burden, or shows very marked intellectual limitations? This naturally scares the scientific imagination, and the decree goes forth: "Cease this unwomanly effort to be intelligent; confine yourself to the useful office which Nature ordains for you. Consider the welfare of the race." At this, however, there are murmurs; a rebellion is brewing.

It is too late to press "Nature" into the service. Women are beginning to aspire to try their own experiments with Nature, ignoring the old worm-eaten sign-posts of their guides, philosophers, and friends. It is idle to attempt to lure them back into their cage, the temper of the age is against it; and although much suffering is caused by the present effort to do the old duties more perfectly than before, while adding to them a vast number of fresh duties, intellectual and social, yet the result in the long run promises to be the creation of a new balance of power, of many varieties of feminine character and aptitude, and, through the consequent influx of new ideals and activities, a social revolution, reaching in its results almost beyond the regions of prophecy. The mad attempt to move backwards against the current would, if successful, be the beginning of a retrogressive evolution, which, one must not forget, is always possible at any stage of history. It is remarkable that even the one function to which a whole sex is asked to devote itself is, under the old order, very badly performed. Among men we have had division of labour; among women such a thing has scarcely existed. We give the heads of our pins into the hands of specialists; the future race may be looked after by unqualified amateurs. This is a subject which is usually slurred over; therefore it is well to look it steadily in the face. First, from the least unpopular side, the injustice to the children. I do not hesitate to say that every fifth or sixth child is a deeply injured being. Indeed in most instances the case might be put more strongly. We are so accustomed to a low standard of physical and mental power, that few of us recognise the mischief, unless the child has fits or rickets, and then there is a lurking consolatory suspicion that he has them by the grace of God. Nobody counts the miseries caused by a low vitality, by an untoward start on the race of life, by a lack of that intelligent care which the most devoted mother in the world cannot give, if she has half-a-dozen other claimants to give it to, and no time or strength or heart to acquire the knowledge that must precede it. When shall we shake off the old notion, that maternal love makes up for the lack of common sense?

Now, from the unpopular standpoint, to face the question, the mother's sufferings. . . . It is a hideous ideal that we have set up for our women, and the world is wretched and diseased, because they have followed it too faithfully. An interval now of furious licence, if it must be, on the way to freedom, would be a kinder potion for this sick world than another century of "womanly" duty and virtue, as these have been provided hitherto. Happily there is no necessity to pass through such a terrible ordeal, socially or politically. The Anglo-Saxon race is not naturally addicted to "ideas," but it prefers them, if the worst comes to the worst, to revolutionary changes. A new order of life and thought first creeps in, and then floods all the heavens as the sun rises in the morning.

We have now considered two of the essential attributes of marriage as it stands – the wife's dependence, economic and social, and the supposed duty to produce as many children as Fate may decide. Take away from it these two solid props, and what but a scraggy skeleton remains of this plump and prosperous institution, appearing, if anything, a trifle over-fed, with one eye on the flesh pots, the other (when anyone is looking) on the stars? It is not yet recognised that what makes the "holy estate" so firm and inflexible are its atrocious injustices – to use no harsher word – and that if one firmly uses the surgeon's knife to these he destroys nearly all that holds the thing together. Suppose an opponent to grant this for the sake of argument; would he leave standing the institution, clamped and grappled by these injustices, rather than sacrifice its essentials? or would he say, "If this be so it cannot be a fair and sacred edifice, not having power to stand without such things!"

❋ ❋ ❋ ❋

There is, perhaps, no more difficult relation in the world than that of husband and wife. Peace is not so very hard to achieve, nor an apparent smoothness which passes for harmony. The really rare thing is a unity which is not purchased at the expense of one or other of the partners. The old notion that the man ought to be the commander, because one must have a head in every commonwealth, is an amusingly crude solution of the difficulty, to say nothing of its calm and complete injustice. Between two nations, it is easy to keep peace by disabling one of the combatants. That sort of peace, however, is of a somewhat "cheap and nasty" order, and can scarcely be described as international harmony. Between husband and wife it is absolutely degrading, not only to the disabled, but to him who disables. It is the fatal sense of power and possession in marriage which ruins so many unions and acts as a sort of disenchantment to the romance of pre-marital days. Through it the woman loses half her attraction, and it is this loss of attraction, observed *apart from its cause*, which creates so much fear of the effects of greater marital freedom. Ardent upholders of the present status point out that men would leave their wives without hesitation if they could, a curious admission that most marriages hold together by law rather than by affection.

What could possibly be more fatal to the wife's continued influence over her husband than the fact that she is *his* absolutely and for ever; that her beauty, her talents, her devotion are in duty bound dedicated to him for the rest of her life? He marries expecting exorbitantly. If the wife does not give him all he expects, he is disappointed and angry; if she does give it – well, it is only her duty, and he ceases to value it. It becomes a matter of course, and the romance and interest die out. The same thing in a lesser degree happens to the wife. She, too, may make vast claims upon her husband, curtail his liberty of action and even of thought; she may drag him about with her, on the absurd assumption that it is not "united" in husbands and wives to have independent tastes and pursuits, as other people have; she may even ruin a great talent, and fritter away an otherwise useful life, through her exactions.

Often indeed the claims on both sides are willingly recognised, but that saves neither of the pair from the narrowing influences of such a walled-in existence. Marriages of this kind are making life, as a whole, breathless and lacking in vitality; social intercourse is checked, the flow of thought is retarded; and these unions also have the very evil effect of cutting off, in a great measure, both the husband and wife from intimate relations with others. The complaint among friends is universal: when a man or woman marries a great curtain seems to fall; as human beings they have both lost their position; they are more or less shut away in their little circle and all the rest of the world is emphatically outside. As society is made up, to a large extent, of married couples – all tending to this self-satisfied isolation amidst the dust of undisturbed prejudices – it suffers from a sort of mental coagulation, whose effects we are all feeling in a thousand unsuspected ways. Life is tied up into myriads of tight little knots, and the blood cannot flow through the body politic. Ordinary social intercourse does little or nothing to loosen this stricture. The marital relationship of claims and restraints is, perhaps, in its vaunted "success" more melancholy to witness than in its failure.

In a marriage true to the modern spirit, which has scarcely yet begun to breathe upon this institution, husband and wife regard one another as absolutely free beings; they no more think of demanding subordination on one side or the other than a couple of friends who had elected to live together would mutually demand it. That, after all, is the true test. In love there ought to be *at least* as much respect for individuality and freedom as in friendship. Love may add to this essential foundation what it pleases, but to attempt to raise further structures without this as a basis, is to build for oneself a "castle in Spain." It cannot last, and it does not deserve to last. The more intensely humanity begins to feel its unity, its coherence, the more deep must be the reverence for each individuality.

Stolid peace, but not living harmony, is possible without it. Under the present set of ideas, there is something terribly disappointing in marriage even to those who start with the highest hopes and resolutions. Human nature is too severely tried. It finds itself in possession of almost irresponsible power, its claims (by supposition just) are innumerable; there is scarcely a moment in the life of husband or wife which cannot be brought to judgment and criticised. How is it possible for two people to satisfy one another in every word and look and deed? How can one invariably fit every detail of conduct to the preconceptions of the other, affected as each must always be by moods, health, chance influences, and hereditary feelings? It is simply insane, as well as a piece of intolerable impertinence to expect it. We do not ask our friends to shape their conduct always according to our opinion; neither ought those who are married and (presumably) anxious to be mutually helpful to lay this terrible burden on one another. How often is the courtesy and respect which is instinctively given to a mere acquaintance withheld from the husband or the wife! Roughness, lack of refinement in thought and word, which often disfigure this relationship, have much to do with the passing away of the first love and enthusiasm, the first so-called illusion, which was no illusion but the beautiful flower of life's poetry, deliberately crushed under foot. . . .

It would be madness indeed to ignore the licentious tendencies of mankind, but can we acquit the present restrictive dual-morality system of its share in increasing those tendencies? Can we forget how much the allotted scapegoats of society have to endure in the interests of purity among the elect?

Is this licentious element in human nature to be a perpetual stumbling-block, causing life to crystallize into hard patterns, separating people into inexorable groups, each with its evils, sorrows, limitations, despairs? This is what happens in consequence of our precautions against disorder. Does licentiousness indicate a state of physical and mental health or of disease? If a state of disease, is it incurable? What serious attempt have we ever made (except through asceticism, which is worse than useless) to cope with this dangerous force? We destroy a thousand possible joys, crib, cabin, and confine the lives of harmless people, set apart a great body of women for a purpose which we account disgraceful – and strange to say we make them no apology for our conduct, we only heap insults upon them – but what do we do to conquer this tyrant who destroys so much happiness, usurps so large a proportion of energy, runs amuck through all society? Our one idea is restraint, punishment, strict laws, suspicious, petty, watchful social usages.

All this emphasizes the idea it pretends to repudiate, and creates lip-service, while it gives sheltered hiding-places to the enemy. The atmosphere is growing daily more unwholesome; the finger of "Propriety" is leaving everywhere its stain. More liberty would mean less licence. In this matter women will have much to say and to do. Education – in its widest sense – must grapple with the problem; the tendencies, pleasures, interests of mankind must be raised to a higher level; the curtain that hides from vast multitudes of average men and women the marvels of nature, the dramatic splendours of life, must be lifted, and the art of living made familiar to all.

But practically, what is to be done? How would a free system work? We must face the unpalatable fact that a cut-and-dried scheme which will now seem plausible is just as impossible as our present state of society would have appeared to the "practical man" of the Middle Ages. Social changes are too gradual and subtle for such draughtsman-like forecasts to be of any use or meaning. All that can be done, at any given time in the world's history, is to indicate the next direction of development, initiate or emphasize the tendency of human thought, sentiment and institutions, for some new conception. Far more stupendous changes come to pass in average human action than any one would dare to predict, and even now a great movement affecting in the profoundest manner human ideals and standards is taking place. It is futile to say that human nature is incapable of this or that, since human nature is precisely the author and creator of the new heavens and the new earths.

I have suggested that the licentious element in mankind may be reduced to more manageable proportions; and this is surely not an entirely vain hope, unless it is also vain to hope to bring men and women into better conditions of mind and body; unless it is vain to hope that thought and will count for something in human destiny. The conditions of life, sentiment, fashion, which induced our ancestors to get drunk every night have passed away, and human nature on the whole finds that, without any conscious effort or restraint, the impulse to excessive drinking is no longer so imperious, and it will probably become progressively less so. The freer, richer, healthier, more full of interest a life becomes, the less need will there be to drown misery or chase away dulness by merely sensual pleasures. And for this rich and full life men need the society and influence of women, and women that of men, without let or hindrance. On matters of sex too much stress is laid by our network of laws and restraints. The Puritan spirit is greatly to blame for this; it casts an ugly, self-conscious light upon all things wherein men and women are concerned, creating evil where none need be; it fosters a heated, unnatural atmosphere, and makes artificial sins which are the parents of a swarm of unnecessary sorrows. The new ideas of education – the training of the mind in accordance with its own natural impetus, the awakening of vivid interests, the bringing forth of latent talent, and the powers of acquirement and concentration – all this, after a few generations, must have a profound influence upon the leading impulses and motives of mankind. Then we must remember that licentiousness is – in general – the preying of one sex upon the other; women, respectable and outcast alike, are dependent on men for their bread and butter. They have no voice in determining the relations they will bear to them. They are supported on the one condition: subjection of body and of soul. Were this dependence no longer existing, is it conceivable that women would continue to allow themselves to be doomed to so ghastly a fate? There are no doubt many prostitutes who crave for the excitement that their life affords, but is not this largely because Respectability carefully provides that the reputable life shall be so deadly dull? It is surely undeniable that if women were as free as men to say "Yes," and "No," the condition of society as regards these matters would be entirely transformed. It would not necessarily change in a direction to please Mrs. Grundy; in fact it would probably cause a serious shock to her nervous system; but it is almost inconceivable that the most ghastly evils would not disappear, for these are of a kind that implies a victim and an oppressor.

Does not, in fact, licentiousness have for a condition the subjection of women?

If this be admitted, there is comparatively little left to admit. If the independence of women had the effect of destroying or greatly lessening prostitution and mercenary marriage, what object would there be in binding people together by adamantine chains and subjecting them to vexatious rules and restrictions? Neither man nor woman would then submit to it.

Once more I must repeat that to demand what would appear to be an *immediately* workable system of free marriage is as unreasonable as it would be to ask a cattle-lifting clan of the Middle Ages to turn over a new leaf and earn their living on the Stock Exchange. The motives that are all potent to the Stockbroker are non-existent for the Highlander. Both conceptions of existence are, however, possible and workable, and both are the outcome of that most plastic material – human nature.

It would indeed be easy enough to suggest general outlines of a social system in which marriage should be free, but its workability entirely depends upon whether humanity is going to educate itself in that direction, whether it will take less jealous and possessive views of sex-relationship, and whether the conception of true liberty will penetrate from public into domestic life, where at present it is practically unknown. Love now comes with a vast bundle of claims in her hand, and she even passes on these claims to mere kinship, which presses them with the persistency of a Shylock. Free marriage is not for those who understand freedom no better than this. All such ideas of restriction and interference, on any plea whatsoever, must be swept away. If we cannot grant or claim liberty in one relation of life, we are incapable of it in another. This is a great lesson that has yet to be learnt. In learning it humanity will be fitting itself for the next development. But there is no reason why those who *do* understand the idea should not carry it into practice wherever individual circumstances permit.

When freedom is no longer merely political and civic, when it becomes as the breath of our nostrils in the most intimate relations of life, our notions of morality must undergo a very serious modification. A glimpse of the end of the twentieth century might puzzle even those who are most prepared for change.

It is impossible to be "practical" on this subject, if we consider its entire scope, for we are dealing with social movements affecting the beliefs, feelings, the very temperament of the whole people; we are not dealing with mere outward adjustments of the machinery. Critics generally assume that a change of machinery is chiefly demanded, and if it can be shown that, at the present moment, this would result in disorder, the whole doctrine is supposed to be crushed. This is simply to misunderstand the doctrine. It implies a complete revolution in our present conceptions of sex and family relationship, and therefore it is evident that no new law suddenly launched upon a people still under the spell of the old ideas could have any triumphant effect. The fears entertained of the working of a freer law are, I believe, wildly exaggerated, but it is certain that legal relaxation can never take the place of moral evolution. Still the law must not lag too far behind the change of thought, and there seems no reason why it should not at once become more flexible to individual needs in the marriage relation. This could be done without relinquishing the supervision and restraint which is still thought necessary on the part of the State. Less rigid divorce laws, equal for the two sexes; the right of the mother to the control of her children; these are the next practical steps which civilization demands. As soon as the principle of equality between the sexes is sincerely accepted, there remains no valid reason against the immediate adoption of contract-marriage under certain limitations. The idea of equality would at once sweep away the one-sided divorce laws, enabling man and woman to obtain divorce on the same grounds. Contract-marriage would permit them to agree upon these grounds, subject to certain restrictions which would guard against the selection of absurd or frivolous reasons.

A couple would draw up their agreement, or depute the task to their friends, as is now generally done as regards marriage-settlements. They agree to live together on such and such terms, making certain stipulations within the limits of the code. The breaking of any of these promises may or may not constitute a plea for separation or divorce – again according to agreement. The husband might bestow on the wife a certain sum as her exclusive property, this being her reward for her share in sustaining the household, and as the security for her independence. In case of the union proving unsuitable, a certain time shall be specified which shall elapse before application is made for divorce or separation, and the State would then demand a minimum interval between the notice and the divorce itself, if still desired after that interval is over.

---

78. Annie Matherson
A Song for Women

WITHIN a dreary narrow room
    That looks upon a noisome street,
    Half fainting with the stifling heat
A starving girl works out her doom.
        Yet not the less in God's sweet air
        The little birds sing free of care,
        And hawthorns blossom everywhere.

Swift ceaseless toil scarce wins her bread:
    From early dawn till twilight falls,
    Shut in by four dull ugly walls,
The hours crawl round with murderous tread.
        And all the while, in some still place,
        Where intertwining boughs embrace,
        The blackbirds build, time flies apace.

With envy of the folk who die,
    Who may at last their leisure take,
    Whose longed-for sleep none roughly wake,
Tired hands the restless needle ply.

But far and wide in meadows green
The golden buttercups are seen,
And reddening sorrel nods between.

Too pure and proud to soil her soul,
    Or stoop to basely gotten gain,
    By days of changeless want and pain
The seamstress earns a prisoner's dole.
        While in the peaceful fields the sheep
        Feed, quiet; and through heaven's blue deep
        The silent cloud-wings stainless sweep.

And if she be alive or dead
    That weary woman scarcely knows,
    But back and forth her needle goes
In tune with throbbing heart and head.
        Lo, where the leaning alders part,
        White-bosomed swallows, blithe of heart,
        Above still waters skim and dart.

O God in heaven! shall I, who share
    That dying woman's womanhood,
    Taste all the summer's bounteous good
Unburdened by her weight of care?
        The white moon-daisies star the grass,
        The lengthening shadows o'er them pass:
        The meadow pool is smooth as glass.

1891

79. Michael Field
from *Journal*

The moment we reach our hotel we are persuaded to scurry to the station
and catch a train that will bring us to Dresden by 11 in the morning. . . . O
weak, to be caught by such a bait! We have no evening meal – a bottle of
Nierstein and six "petits pains" are tumbled into our basket. At the station
we ourselves are deposited in a 1st class ladies' carriage by a compassionate

guard, who overlooks our 2nd class tickets. But the guard is too compassionate, and soon a 3rd class passenger enjoys his pity, and enters with
bundles, short hair, pallor and a cough. We think she has had the "grippe."

Darkness falls . . .

One is blown awake – the door opens to a lanthorn and a German face –
tickets are torn off. There is a bang and then the sleepy whirr goes on
under one. How far away are the horizons of that noiseless substance of
merely varying gloom that a few hours ago was the inhabited earth!

There are steady lights outside – there is a sound of illegitimate business,
against the laws of darkness, then moving lights and again the great dream
journey and its functional movement.

Across exhaustion shoots the pang of famine. We have no bread –
Nierstein is not a fortifying juice.

I watch the painful appearance of things visible – the world looks
common and very black – poor little patch as it is! One is hungry – one
feels that one's eyes are purple and swollen, as if one had fought with an
adversary. Suddenly there is sweetness in the world – the Sun himself
introduces isolated objects, and it is day. Then shame comes and one
hastens to the sponge, the comb, the mirror. One begins the comedy of
toilet in the space of a square yard – one re-seats oneself, curiously reconciled to the view and one's fellow-passengers.

But famine cries piteously in the currents of goodly morning air . . . and
we have no bread.

The train draws up at a lank station. We rush – I in hat, as befits one
who dislikes the ill-opinion of men – Sim in a "cloud" and the roughness
of her hair. Cups of coffee are seized, no bread can be bespoken on account
of the crowd, no bread is near at hand to be seized. Sim vanishes from my
side; I watch her rush down the room to a table appropriated by little
German soldiers – she breaks in between two of them with cries through
her teeth of "Brot, Brot!" The little German soldiers wonder naturally of
what kind this new Orlando comes, who darts on their feast and insists
ragingly that necessity must be served. As she bears off their rolls – "I
almost die for food, let me have it" – Teutonic amaze slackens into a disci-
plined smile and a few moments after develops into a titter. But the new
Orlando, the despiser of smooth civility, brings the food like a doe to its
fawn, unconscious of the regiment's laughter, or of the appearance made
by unfastened hair, excited eyes, and the bread, borne along in triumph.

❋ ❋ ❋ ❋

I lie on my bed, I gargle with eau-de-Cologne that increases the atrocious
pain in my throat. We have an early tea and start for *Tannhaüser*. . . . I sit

before Sim in a comfortable box – choking, suffering, full of gladness and divine unease . . . we reach the flat [*sic*]. A mustard plaster or the Doctor? . . . The Doctor comes. Herr Faust – a great, broad-cheeked Teuton who lisps English. *It is not diphtheria.* I instantly acknowledge the relief I have in the denial. I must go to bed and remain in bed. I have a bare, calm feeling as I go to our room . . . I have a fearful night.

I feel almost the patient agony of dying while we wait hour after hour for the Doctor. At last he comes and thinks I am going to have some infectious ailment. We ask what he means, "Oh, we call so many things infectious now," he replies evasively. Sim sits down and writes home I have a slight attack of pneumonia.

[*Next day.*] Again a long waiting for the Doctor – I lie almost voiceless. At last he comes, looks at my feet, and says that I have got scarlet fever, and I feel that a sentence is gathering against me. I know what it is. "You must go to the Hospital." Dismay scatters our fortitude. Sim goes out to speak to Fräulein. Doctor Faust implores me to influence her to go to the Hospital, he waits to hear me repeat his lesson. In weakness and impotence, I hesitate and am judged by the sturdy medico as if by a judgement-angel; a blast of condemnation reaches me, though he says not a word, and stalks out of the room with Sim. All is settled. I get up as if I were dressing for a great event – with the exaltation of a bride – I am dressing for the last time – but not as maiden, as mortal. . . . No one comes near us, not to the door. There is the silence, the sense of flight to far corners, that one feels in a house before a coffin is brought out . . . and yet our belongings and my yellow gown and my Love are so familiar in the midst of these tyrannous, appalling circumstances. . . .

Then a tiny room, a tiny bed on which I am stretched. We make the nurse understand we must have a larger room. . . . I dose my eyes in the hot joy of repose . . . my next remembrance is of a strong arm round me and white flaps above me – difficult, slow marching . . . a vast room with six beds, facing each other in couples, a few children's beds. . . . A very reasonable glance round to escape draughts and I choose a bed at the far end of the room . . . my Love is distracted and as Nurse told us afterwards, "said many things." Officialism has fed the sick at 12.30 – so it is impossible for me to have anything till 6.0 – even tea and coffee can only be ordered for the next day. Nurse brings a china spoon of wine and gives a draught to each. It is jacinth-brown, sweet, powerful, warm. . . .

In early morning light I open my eyes. Where am I? In a cabin! . . . I become aware that I am in hospital. . . . I feel a hunger that is a dreadful impotence . . . the nurse at last appears with a tray, I am raised to the coveted food and immediately, as if I were Tantalus himself, fail to eat a morsel

and drop back in a fainting condition. My Love resolves I shall have nourishment in the night – she will fight with all the weapons of her determination and of her German for the grace. I am revived by Greek wine and
Sister washes my face as one would wash coarse earthenware. . . .

My Love opens the striped blinds that I may watch the August full moon,
making a poetic daylight throughout the sky, defining with stern blackness
the roof of the near station and touching the green of the embowered
plane-trees till they are magical as an enchantress' robe in colour. I feel the
outside beauty has an ominous calm about it. I am fervidly hot; the white
beams lie on my brain and provoke it – they enter it clear, quiet, precise,
they make it vague, distracted, visionary. They evoke their contraries. I
create phantasies that come so fast that they form an element round me in
which I sink, sink – then float along under them and then sink again. . . .
My Love finding how it is with me lies on her bed and in a grave, low voice
recalls the lovely things we enjoyed in Italy. . . . As she speaks her words
turn into fair, hurrying visions. The moonlight through the blind becomes
more powerful – delirium is glorious, like being inspired continuously . . .
forms of art and poetry swim round and into me. Every moment is plastic.

❋ ❋ ❋ ❋

Pussie wakes from its "bye" and rings for Schwester, who comes straight
to grasp and kiss. She is like one who has been in a desert, who finds an
oasis and simply throws himself down and drinks. The kisses are almost
too rapid to have an aim. Suddenly she raises herself and says, in answer
to the forgotten ring of the bell, "Ein Wunsch?"

I go into the garden and watch the fish, leaving P. with Schwester, who
encloses her with passionate embrace and plunges down on her cheeks
with kisses, "Ich bin so hungrig," she says in a stifled sob that came out in
a smile of anxious love. P. kissed her cheeks, then, giving a little slap to the
round, honest cheek, kissed her lips. "Danke, danke," she said and it was
her heart that spoke. . . .

[*Edith writes:*] My experiences with Nurse are painful – she is under
the possession of terrible fleshly love, [which] she does not conceive [of]
as such, and as such I will not receive it.

Schwester, while my Love is in the garden, embraces me bodily and
from the outer precincts of language I catch the sound, "Eine mächtige
Liebe." She makes me shiver, but I play with her passion like a child and
she is utterly deceived in it herself – I am her child she has washed and
dressed with her piteous clinging hands; and her honest, stern eyes,
altered to a mother-hen's, belie the welling-up of all her frustrate nature at
the touch of first love for any mortal. . . . I must fight Nurse's unreason-

ableness. She comes while I am resting, throws herself about me and kisses me with the persistence of madness: I manage to make her understand she grieves and fatigues me – instantly with repentance she retires to the arm-chair and I pretend deep sleep with anxious ears. She strives with herself and scarcely ever breaks out after – but the strain makes me dull by the time my Love returns . . . [*Michael adds*] with fearful passion she threw P.'s hospital shirt away, saying, "Sie wollen das nicht mehr brauchen – fort!" ["Shirt, thou art no more needed – be off"! *Edith continues:*] This night Sister kissed me almost as we kiss the dying – gently, hopelessly, with dread – realising we shall never see a living face again greet us from their pillow.

---

80. Jane, Lady Wilde
from *George Eliot*

GEORGE ELIOT was decidedly the most popular of all the female novelists of recent times; and is still adored, as without rival or equal, by a vast world of fanatical worshippers. Her reputation was world-wide; and she exacted homage from all the leading men of the day, more, however, by her con-versation, which was singularly profound and interesting, than even by her works. She achieved also an unexampled financial success. No other woman, perhaps, of her generation realised forty thousand pounds by writing. And she deserved it, for she strove earnestly to perfect her work, though often in the effort to seem wise she attained only to being dull. Yet 'Romola' is a great book to add to literature; sufficient to ensure lasting fame to the author, even had she written nothing else; but in 'Daniel Deronda' and several of her later works she enforces her views with rather too much wearisome prolixity and assertive dogmatism. She is determined on teaching, and will interrupt a love-scene with a disquisition on the return of the Jews or the appearance of infusoria under the microscope.

She also abounds in commonplaces, delivered in language of oracular obscurity, as if they were deep truths brought to the surface for the first time, and given to us covered with the hard grit of primitive formations.

'Middlemarch' especially exhausts our patience by page after page of pretentious commonplace; and probably no amount of bribery would induce anyone to read it through a second time.

❋ ❋ ❋ ❋

George Eliot has a keen insight into ordinary human life and commonplace natures; some humour – a strong trenchant way of describing what lies on a certain low social level, and a sharp, rough power of sarcasm. These are her gifts as a writer, and not without fitness has she assumed a man's name, for she has more of the masculine nature, strong, hard, keen, and somewhat coarse, than of the passionate, glowing, sympathetic woman's intellect. . . .

Altogether, 'Middlemarch' is a dull book, without any development of that mystic working of a gifted woman's mind foreshadowed in the preface. Occasionally there are glimpses of that insight into life for which the author has been celebrated, as in the expression of truths like this: 'There is a wonderful frank charm in the intimacy between a man and a woman where there is no passion to hide or to confess.' But these passages of simple truth, expressed in clear, lucid language, are few and far between. George Eliot's style in general has the fatal affectation of being learned. There is an illustration, *à propos* of match-making, taken from vortices, hairlets, waterdrops, and infusoria, which has too much of a polytechnic flavour; also, her comparison of the mind of a woman to 'an irregular solid.' Women are very pretty story-tellers, but they are only good writers through sympathy and love. They should know the range of their limited mental powers, and keep within it if they wish to interest. An affectation of learning spoils them, because it is never more than an affectation; no woman is really learned; perhaps she would be very disagreeable if she were so. A logical dogmatic female is detestable. The great charm of the sex is in that light superficiality, which gives sympathy so readily; believes everything through love, and seeks no grounds for belief beyond faith in the one beloved. Our legions of female novelists – and they submerge the land – ought to know that their peculiar mission is to reveal and analyse the working of the heart; in this they may succeed better than men, but they can never expect to vie in power, knowledge of life, in the eloquence that comes by culture, or the wit that comes by nature, with the more richly endowed and more highly educated sex. Men are perpetually adding names to literature that will last for all time – women never. Amongst the male novelists of the day, this age crowns two at least with immortality – Bulwer and Disraeli – but not one woman, though they write by thousands. Not even George Eliot herself, called by the London critics the greatest female writer of the world, can hope to live beyond the passing moment. The fragrance distilled from the glowing feelings, crushed lives, and perhaps broken hearts of literary women may refresh a few idle hours of man's more earnest life. It is enough – the world asks no more from them than to amuse or soften through sympathy the powerful ruling race for whom woman was created only to be the helpmeet; but no one can be expected to care much or long for vanished fragrance, a crushed flower, a faded life, or the wrecks of broken hearts, from which most female writers draw their experiences, unless, indeed, the love tales were embalmed in such prose and verse as men only can write, and which women have never equalled. . . .

George Eliot has much of this fatal tendency to the insufferably prosy. She is always sermonising in an instructive, parochial way, and giving us her own views, in place of allowing her characters to reveal them by swift, dramatic touches. Nearly all the second volume, for instance, is entirely destitute of incident or scenic effect. . . .

All the characters talk with a ponderous verbosity in sentences of at least twenty lines long, and of the most involved construction, as if, like those of a legal document, they were to be paid for according to their obscurity and length.

✤ ✤ ✤ ✤

So the second volume ends, leaving a grand opening for a psychological study of human hearts, and a tragic involvement of human lives to be worked out in the concluding part of the work. George Eliot has a deep and penetrating insight into life. And so we leave the three principal actors in the drama to their fate in her powerful hands. Will she save or slay? Probably the latter, for such tragic involvements seldom end happily. Will the husband, from being only stern, become cruel? Will the lover – brilliant, reckless, loving, daring, passionate, and utterly unscrupulous – exert his fatal influence to the utmost? – and the woman, with all her noble resolves, her sacred, saintly sense of wedded vows, her devotion to the good, the beautiful, and the true – her lofty ideal of life – will she suffer herself to be led to the edge of the precipice whose depth is infinite, while all the time she fancies that her soul is springing forward on a path of light to loftier regions and a diviner life? The flame has been kindled, the spell has been woven, and the magnetic circle is closing around these three related lives; but we leave the reader to study the concluding volume, that will give an answer as to the final result.

81. Ménie Muriel Dowie
from *A Girl in the Karpathians*

Between eleven and twelve at night the train trailed into the station, slowly and dead-weary of the long level journey. Something had gone wrong with the carriage I was in: they had examined it in the afternoon during a leisurely pause we made, and had decided that it could hold out. Nevertheless, it came limping rather painfully in the rear, whining from time to time over its hurt, and holding up one paw, so to speak. Perhaps that made us so late. I stepped out into the dark of the platform, where a crowd of Jews and peasants jostled and shoved one another and yelled in common. I was oppressed by a strong smell of sheep and garlic, and was sensible of being in a crowd of extremely dirty persons; but with my valise in one hand, the green hunting sack and leather bag in the other, and some indefinite being in the rear carrying my saddle in its case, I threaded my way to the outer yard, and threw the things into a little two-horse fly, one of a waiting row. Though it was dark, the noisy but not particularly busy crowd had sighted or got wind of me, and several eager and disinterested members hung round to await developments.

Unaware whether the driver understood German, I intimated that my destination was "the best hotel," and listened while my audience wrangled as to which establishment deserved this title. It was just then that an impression was received by me which only deepened as my acquaintance with the people improved: they stood closer together, and made hotter, denser groups than any other people I had ever seen, and this was accounted for by their ravenous curiosity. Not one could bear the idea that any other should see or hear more of what was going forward than himself, so they leaned over one another's shoulders, and peered under one another's arms in an inconceivable fashion, until I dispersed them with a little homely German. Using a lofty and contemptuous tone constructed on the spur of the moment, I said, "Thut mir den Gefallen und gehet nur weiter?" and getting into the carriage bade the man go on.

He lashed his whip, there was a splash of tuneless music from the bells the two little horses had on their collars, I clutched my belongings and clung to the vehicle, and we dashed down the rutty road into the blue night. Behind me there was the aimless quarrelling of the crowd, in front a transparent indigo of utter vagueness lit only by some little stars.

The flatness of the surrounding landscape, more felt than seen, and the evenness of that same blue was broken only where a poplar traced itself darker than its background. Of mountains there was nothing to see, of town or hotel just as little. I had time for a long quiet laugh, and a sensation so delicious yet indescribable as no other experience has been able to produce.

But I was very hungry. Where was the hotel, and the town too? Would any one be awake when I arrived? Should I, in point of fact, ever arrive at all? Yes, it seemed so. The road became a street, lamps started up at long intervals, houses gleamed out on each side, but all with shut eyes and sleeping faces. It was so late. A rough macadam rattled under the horses' feet, and we flashed, quite suddenly, into what seemed a wide square. No fear that the town was abed! Why, the whole place echoed with noise, and when the carriage stopped before a door from which light and laughter streamed together, I knew that I had come to the hotel. Several servants ran out at the clang of the big bell my driver pulled, and I addressed myself with immense dignity to one of them in German, which the rest only partially understood – dignity, coolness, and a somewhat off-hand-not-to-be-trifled-with manner would, I fancied, meet the case.

Yes, I could have a room, "a magnificent guest chamber," said the head-waiter, only masking his curiosity till a more convenient moment; and after some further parley I was shown upstairs. The magnificent guest-chamber was on the first floor, and looked into the square. It had eight chairs and one sofa in white covers grouped round an oval table, and two white draped beds pushed into corners. Until the man lit the lamp I had the feeling that a spectre supper party had been surprised and had dispersed at our coming; but the lamp-light and the whole-souled stare of the head-waiter superseded this imaginative flight.

"The young lady belongs, no doubt, to the German Comedy Company?" he said, of course in German. Giving him to understand that I belonged exclusively to myself, I assumed the hauteur which used to be the property of people in novels, and which is, I hope, very foreign to my real nature, and ordered tea.

A little white pot with Polish tea, pale but potent, harmonised with the appointments of the room; and having observed the man fill with cold water an enormous blue glass hand-basin, I told him he might go, locked the doors, and opened the windows on to the balcony. Kolomyja is not early, and good, and quiet, as becomes a small white town; on the contrary, it is quite suggestively hilarious, and the square does not tuck itself in till after one.

I put my watch and money under the massive white pillow, with its strip of rich lace insertion to show the Turkey-red, laid my revolver and the matches on a chair, and spent an hour with the tea and my cigarettes, thinking amusedly over the situation and what it promised. That is the beauty of doing something which neither duty, necessity, nor pleasure distinctly demands: there is a margin of possibility with which no calculations or conjectures can fittingly deal. You are so out of your usual rut that legions of nameless adventures crowd indefinitely upon the immediate horizon. It does not matter if none of them ever come off. After all, adventure is not everything; there is incident, and the next half-hour must always bring that with it.

I went to bed smiling in anticipation of I knew not what – just what chanced to happen, since I had no builded schemes, would be sure to please me, I thought. Kolomyja tired of laughing and of howling; below my windows waverous footsteps and unsteady voices fell a prey to distance. A Polish bed, though resembling the shop-made raised pie on which the cover is laid so that you can lift it right off and put what you please inside, is not uncomfortable. The little red blanket, with a snowy sheet buttoned round it, and nothing tucking in anywhere, delighted me by its cleanness. It had been a long day, and I was soon asleep.

My regret is that I may not write of my unbroken repose. I should like to. In point of fact, I had not been sleeping two hours when I was rudely awakened – by fleas. Of course, everybody except me knew that was coming. I lit the lamp, and would have exchanged the revolver gladly for a tin of "Keating."

The Kolomyja flea deserves a paragraph: it is a speciality. Large and well-built, of a finer growth altogether than its western brother, it betrays little of his athleticism and baffling agility; it moves heavily and deliberately about its work with a due sense of what may be expected of it, and a fine consciousness of what a healthy flea can do, given time, opportunity, and the faculty of organisation. One of them discovered a piece of waste land, so to speak, upon my person, and laid me out in plots and spots, and sort of landscape-gardened me with exceptional taste and a far-sighted recognition of such advantages as the site offered.

Well, detail is superfluous. Only another thing that irritates me almost as much as a flea-bite is the way people complain of them who never suffer any inconvenience at all, – people who are tickled for five minutes, and can show a tiny red mark the size of a pin-prick, which they straightway forget. Others, again, ache for three weeks steadily: I am of these. This would not be referred to so particularly were it not for a circumstance that will be detailed later: only twice did Death come up and look very close at me during that summer, and he was nearest when he approached by this very avenue.

✿ ✿ ✿ ✿

The head-waiter nearly wept when I announced my intention of departing, and ordered horses and a man to take me further on my way. I could not share his depression, and when lunch, in the shape of two small ducks, fried whole in batter; the insidious boiled potato, against which seemingly the cuisine of no country is proof, and a dish of plums, conserved in vinegar by way of a vegetable, were sent up, I ordered a bottle of Hungarian wine in a reckless spirit, and prepared to take my farewell of civilised cookery.

Next, an adieu was bidden to the trappings of an average woman, and I indued myself with the tweed suit, skirt, coat, and knickerbockers in which I had decided to face every climatic possibility for two months.

With the heat, what it was, and what it was like to be, perhaps I had better say that for me no summer day in sun or shade was ever yet too warm, and many have been by far too cold.

Of my three shirts, one was silk, the other two pink flannel; the rest of me cased carefully in woollen. I have never envied a man his appearance, only the superior convenience of his clothing. In assuming a coat such as his, it is his pockets that I want. When I put on a shirt, I do it for its comfort, and with knickerbockers I only seek to equalise our chances of escape in case of tumbles.

This is not original that I know of. Most likely, other women who imitate in some sort their brothers would say as much, and sigh, at the same time, for the masculine vanity which fathers other views.

But discussion of this would be endless, even if the head-waiter had not just come in to say my carriage and a couple of good horses were at the door. Believe, at any rate, this much, that his vestural advantages and not his "points" are what I grudge a man sole possession of; if a woman's clothing offered any conveniences superior to their own, we should find men of sense desirous of imitating women. . . . At the lower door there awaited me the little conveyance, with half a haystack roped on behind, a driver who was said to know some German, and a curious and eager populace. The young man from the drapery establishment across the square, noting my tweeds, and having the usual rooted traditions about our countrywomen, murmured "Eine Engländerin," palpably for my benefit. I took a cigarette from my case and lit it, by this simple action dispelling for ever the notion that I hailed from certain respectable Islands. The case slipped from my hand as I was putting it in my pocket; in picking it up, the head-waiter noticed a coronet which happens to be engraved upon it, and at once received the impression that he had entertained a Russian Princess unawares.

But feeling that it was not fair to interrupt the market any longer, and cause, indeed, a stagnation of the town's whole business, I got in beside my hunting-sack, saddle and saddle-bag, and told the man to go on, remarking roomily "To the mountains!"

* * * *

EXPERIENCES of the mild and quiet nature that always occur to persons who go in search of adventure these unknightly days, heaped themselves upon me. Amongst them is a hygienic experience of which I am really proud. It relates to the way I preserved my skin. There blew almost always a searching wind, which burned and browned better than the fiercest sun and many patent ovens. I soon saw that to wash myself with the absurd frequency that I and other people do at home would be ridiculous. I found the way to encourage the skin to bear up against the weather is not to wash it. Let the skin alone – it knows how to keep itself clean, and how to stay on one's features, if it only gets the chance. The single daily bath in the river was quite sufficient; and before it was warm enough to bathe, I had a grand cold splash with my big blue glass basin, and the hard water from the well. There should be a word about these wells. They are square, built round with rough hewn logs; an immense crane, made of a pine-tree and very nicely adjusted, dumps the wooden jugs under the water, holding them firmly by one ear – much like the bathing women of my youth; it also lifts them up and swings them deftly to the edge.

But with the warmer weather my blue basin fell into disuse, and in the early morning, or about eleven, or previous to coffee at four, or in the evening, or the night, or indeed any time, I went straying over the ragged river-bed barefoot to the weir. The approach to the river on my side was flat; on the further, the hills rose. The sheer bank that overlooked the stream was sweet with wild strawberries, and I would swim across in a slanting line, buffeted by the current, and risking the queer whirlpools, to climb up with immense difficulty and eat all that were ripe.

Fine white river-sand, easily superseding every other material, was delicious to wash with, and left arms like satin that would not have shamed a nymph. Only the cows looked on, and sometimes the little peasant herds gathered to watch me swimming. I had never bathed just in this way before, and at first prowling in among the trout-fry and tadpoles was nervous work; but I found it most inspiring, often spending two hours in and out of the water; even the day I slipped on the bank when about to dress, falling upon a sunken pine-root which cut my side and bruised me badly, and that other day, when, having chosen a new spot, I was swept away by a current fiercer than I had known, and banged pretty severely upon some rocks – even upon these and minor accidental occasions I preferred my wild rivers to any seas that come and go upon wide beaches.

❈ ❈ ❈ ❈

Upon the principle – which I have heard voiced by certain reformers – that what is right for a man must be equally right for a woman, the Ruthenians would appear to be in advance of us; but perhaps the reformers carry their principle further, and decide that drunkenness is equally wrong and degrading for both.

"What do the men think when they see the young women drunk?" I asked, as I watched one of the prettiest girls reeling down the road about four o'clock in the afternoon, and suffered strange qualms of wrong-headed Western disgust. "Do they mind?"

"How should they mind?" was the answer. "Are they not drunk too?"

Well, yes; they certainly were. And I began to wonder why we express so much more horror at the sight of an intoxicated woman than an intoxicated man. Is it because we have been taught, with an amusing lack of reason, that a woman's standards ought to be higher, and that we have a right to expect a greater purity, a finer decency, in her than in him? I am afraid it is. And when I looked into it, it seemed to me that if the one sight shock us more, it should only be because it is so much less frequent; for surely what we want is not that a woman should be better than a man, but only that a man should be as good as a woman?

I'm only asking. Of course, I know what I want; but really I am not quite clear as to the general desideratum. The Ruthenian who gets drunk at least has the grace to permit a like indulgence to his wife and daughters – which is justice, at any rate; but then they all go down the hill together.

❀ ❀ ❀ ❀

Once in a way, it is as well to renounce the purely objective life of every day in favour of this other one. Ordinarily, you are scarcely on speaking terms with your real self; you catch hurried glimpses of it, darting before you, out of reach of touch and realisation, in the groves and alleys of commonplace concerns, among the brush and underwood of crowding "things to do," and you are barely acquaintances. But live alone for awhile, with no special pressing occupation, and how different it is. You have time to think over things that puzzled you, time to look into the conclusions you have had to jump at, leisure to unravel all the tangles that have pained you, opportunity to disinter the reason of your feelings for this and that. It is very good for man or woman to live alone, calmly and quietly, for a period, of whiles; to let their restlessness, their dissatisfaction, and their cares drop from them, "like the needles shaken from out the gusty pine." . . .

It is better to imitate Nebuchadnezzar – if you must imitate any one, and some people certainly must – and go out to grass for six weeks at least by yourself. Give your whims a loose rein, follow the promptings of that queer live soul in you which always retains its affinity to simpleness and green-growing things, and be prepared to be thought very odd when you come back.

You will have acquired a calm smile, an ability to suffer fools gladly, which will stand you in good stead. For, though with slight comment, loneliness is permitted to a man, it seems the opportunity for immense chaff to a woman. A public resents fiercely the conclusion that a woman, a fairly light-hearted young woman more especially, is happy alone and from choice. A preference of Nature to human nature, of green trees to people, and of her own reflections to their witless comments, is an oddity, a whimsical eccentricity which may be smiled upon, but which requires solid demonstration and justification before it be accepted and believed in.

"Well, but *why* did you go alone?" people will say, having heard all my high-falutin arguments; and they say it with an air of "Come now, you'll tell me, I know!" And I gaze at their indulgent, smiling eyes, and their self-satisfied faces, and I dare not tell them that I do it from sheer bald preference. I couldn't have the heart to wound and shock them so, and I say, what is perhaps also true, that I am driven to it, for nobody cares to come to the places I care to go to.

1893

82. Anne Thackeray Ritchie
from *Reminiscences of Julia Margaret Cameron*

Mrs Cameron's power was a peculiar one; many people can feel beauty and record it; she had an intuition, not only for appreciating, but for creating, with the materials at hand, something which was her own, and which she gave to us. She had a directness and originality which was all her own, which she applied to other things than chemicals; she made every day in the week a Saint's day, every commonplace event into something special, just as she transformed a village maiden into a Madonna, or a country bumpkin into a Paladin. English people as a rule, with all their appreciation and romantic aspirations, certainly do not possess this gift of daily life; they do not know how to mould surrounding circumstances to it, they have too much originality and too little. Enough to destroy the old traditions, not enough to withstand the meretricious drift of popular taste and fashion. At a time when a young lady's wildest aspirations did not reach beyond crinolines and frisettes, Mrs Cameron and other members of her family (of whom many used to come to the Island) realised for themselves the artistic fitness of things, the natural affinity between use and beauty, and being a very beautiful and interesting family of sisters, they were able to live out their own theories and to illustrate them. . . . To see one of this sisterhood float into a room with sweeping robes and falling folds, was almost an event in itself, and not to be forgotten. They did not in the least trouble themselves about public opinion (their own family was large enough to contain all the elements of interest and criticism). They had unconventional rules for life, which excellently suited themselves, and which also interested and stimulated other people. They were unconscious artists, divining beauty and living with it. It was this charming gift, this courage of good taste in Mrs Cameron, that gave her so much success in photography.

Something of what William Morris has done for the homes of intelligent people; what the aesthetic school ought to have done (only it took too long a step towards the sublime), these ladies were the first to suggest; and what some of her sisters did for everyday life, Mrs Cameron devised for the world of beautiful shadows which she loved so dearly.

This lady, as I have said, followed up her art with extraordinary trouble and devotion, and also expected much from her sitters. Sitting to her was a serious affair, and not to be lightly entered upon. We came at her summons, we trembled (or we should have trembled had we dared to do so) when the round black eye of the camera was turned upon us, we felt what consequences, what disastrous waste of time and money and effort, might ensue from any passing quiver of emotion. As I write, a respectable matron beside me exclaims at the remembrance of that solemn ordeal in the glass house, and the prick of the angel's wings fastened upon her bare shoulders in infant days. What was it to her in those times whether or not an exquisite little picture of cherubim or seraphim was given to the world, a picture which is now a delight and possession to her descendants in turn.

❊ ❊ ❊ ❊

It is delightful still to remember the photographer's delight in her work. She would come from the dark room holding the dripping glass before her, and calling us all to sympathise; husband, children, friends within the gate, maids from their work, the ox and ass were each summoned in turn. In one of her letters to her niece, Mrs Leslie Stephen, she says touchingly: 'While the spirit is within me, I must praise those I love'. And in the same way she seemed to live, and have her being, in the love and appreciation of those she cared for, without any great regard for persons. She was like Abou ben Adhem, who loved his fellow men. She could appreciate greatness, and she could appreciate smallness too. It was impossible for her to send anyone empty away who came to her, nor to leave any willingly out of the feast of life; and so the hungry guests crowded round about her path. Not unfrequently those kind hosts at Farringford must have suffered from our multiplications and untimely accompaniments. We used to go up with Mrs Cameron to Farringford in the dark after dinner, carrying lanterns along the lane, gathering as we went along, like the Pied Piper's followers. We were all anxious to accompany her, so the procession used to lengthen and multiply.

> Grave old plodders, gay young friskers,
> Father, mothers, uncles, cousins.

* * * *

Her vitality and keen interest in the common affairs of life seemed to be catching; she could get people to do things for her as nobody ever did before. She had a lawn laid out on one occasion in a single night as a surprise for her husband. I have seen a whole room full of people of different ages and standings, all helping to carry out her plans, and feeling a responsibility and unfeigned interest in their success, which their own affairs (perhaps more really important) entirely failed to create. I still remember a procession of young men, carrying foot-pans full of photographs by moonlight across the garden, when for some reason these photographs had to be moved. They were strange young men from Oxford and elsewhere, who had only called by chance, and for the first time; they are now grave and reverend signors, making speeches in Parliament, directing fleets, armies, and elections; also never were pans of photographs more carefully carried by moonlight. Indeed we all seemed to be performing parts in some fanciful pageant, making believe, and yet thoroughly in earnest as children at their play, and most entirely enjoying our holiday.

83. Eliza Lynn Linton
from *Our Past and Future*

At the present time [woman] is the absolute potentate of society; and the gravest of all the questions afloat is – Whether she shall or shall not become identical in power with man, and utterly removed from his protection and control?

There are many causes for the agitation of this question at this moment in England, but the main cause is the superabundance of women coincident with their want of independent means. There are not husbands for all, and fathers of the middle class as a rule make no provision for their daughters, but trust to the chances of their marrying, or else leave them as a legacy to their sons; there are no nunneries into which the unmarried can be drafted, or so few that they are not worth counting; life is so much more costly and luxurious than it was, and men in consequence so much more disinclined to marry on small incomes, that marriage, when even possible, is less frequent than at any other time in the history of the nation; all of which circumstances working together, leave a large mass of women doomed to celibacy and without the means of self-support. Hence the agitation for extended rights and independence as a logical sequence of their present condition, which is one neither of protection nor of independence, neither of dowered ease nor of possible earnings.

Again, there never was a time when women were so useless in their own homes, so idle, so unthrifty, so unwilling to perform their natural domestic duties; therefore, as they must do something, so mad in the pursuit of pleasure, or so frantic for abnormal work, as their tendencies chance to lie. This house idleness of theirs is due partly to the cheapness of labour and the consequent multiplication of domestic servants. If servants were more difficult to procure, and if wages were higher, ladies would be forced in self-defence to attend to their household duties more closely than they do now, and would be driven to do some amount of practical work. They would find too that practical work is not necessarily mindless work; and that to keep a house well takes more intellect and more knowledge than the foolish occupations to which they give themselves up now, under the name of work.

The old landmarks by which the reflected honour of woman was once determined, have been swept away. The days when the mother of many sons was blessed above the mother of but few, have gone; so have those when old maidenism was a scorn, and childlessness a curse. At least in England. We feel now that a large family is by no means the personal or national blessing it used to be; and that in this over-populated time of ours, those women are the greatest benefactresses who give fewest citizens to the clogged and loaded state. . . .

The great future before woman is undoubtedly a larger area of work – an increased power of self-support – and equality, not likeness, with man. Here lies the heart of the mistakes made by sundry of the aspiring and noble-minded sort, as by some of the foolish and unwomanly. Equality is what every large-hearted and large-minded man would wish to find in woman – but not likeness. Likeness indeed is impossible, and the assumption of it is therefore as ugly as it is silly. Two classes of women have to be got rid of before the truer sort can worthily flourish – the fine lady and the masculine women. The mere pretty puppet, with her head in her dress and her heart nowhere, silly, vain, idle, inconsequent, and hopelessly ignorant, unable to learn anything and unable to do anything useful, and putting her salvation in her eyes, her waist, and her toilette, is the worst enemy to her own sex that can be found. She it is who gives men the right to deride the whole world of women, to refuse them respect or honour as one refuses jewels and gold to a child. What can such small simpletons do with respect and honour? says the scornful man; would it not be casting pearls before swine to bestow on them power or influence? – giving infants priceless diamonds for playthings? Coarse and unlovely as is the masculine woman, she is at least a power, and one can easily imagine circumstances in which she would be useful, and able to be turned to good account. But the doll woman is hopeless from the beginning; of no value whatever, save as a toy to play with, and a pretty thing to look at.

As for the masculine woman who tries to make herself the bad copy of a man, who thinks delicacy folly, tenderness weakness, and womanly submission rank cowardice, she too fashions weapons for the enemy to use against herself and all her class; she repels and perhaps alarms men quite as much as the doll woman causes contempt. If that is to be the result of woman's rights, they say, we had better continue their wrongs; for assuredly these dreadful females who are neither men nor women – these awful creatures who cannot nurse a baby nor yet command an army – these halfway monsters, sphinxes, chimeras, Medusas, what not, are far less desirable in any sense than the silliest little doll, or the most lackadaisical fine lady we can find; both of whom at least would be good for petting if not for leading. Men are wrong there, so some of us think; but ninety-nine out of a hundred hold this opinion, and as an opinion it has to be respected and to have its own due weight.

✳ ✳ ✳ ✳

There is another question that must be touched on, – woman's political rights. Right or wrong, wise or foolish, I think all who can read present history will agree with me in saying that these will have to be conceded. No question of this kind was ever set afoot and striven for that was not ultimately successful. It all depends on the amount of fervour with which women seek political recognition, and the degree of central force existing in the demand – which is a very different thing from applied force. It may be put down for the present – set aside, postponed; but it will come up again year after year, till, perhaps bit by bit, perhaps in a sudden rush like our latest Reform Bill, the concession will be made, and the practical working of the principle tried. It is an instinctive utterance, and we shall have to reduce it to its proper level by giving it room for action. At present it is a superstition, a fetish that is to change the whole order of society: practicality alone will place it in the rank of an historic truth and a scientific experiment. A vast amount of rubbish is talked now about the handsome men getting all the votes, and wives voting blue while the husbands vote yellow, and so on; with the domestic quarrels that would ensue on such a splitting of votes. All these arguments are without weight, because they can be applied to other conditions, and their folly proved. A Turk would say the same thing if it was proposed that his Fatimas and Zuleikas should choose their own priest, or see and be seen by the doctor; but we do not find that European homes are made wretched, or that husbands are set at naught, because our women may choose their own religion, their own priest, and have unchecked intercourse with the family physician.

Is it impossible to imagine a woman sweet and yet strong, high-minded and yet modest, tender if self-reliant, womanly if well-educated? – would a fine political conscience necessarily deaden or depress the domestic one? Surely not! A fine political conscience would be only so much added – it would take nothing away. If women thought worthily about politics, as about smuggling and other things of the same class, they would be all the grander in every relation, because having so much clearer perception of baseness, and so much higher standard of nobleness.

At all events, the phase of woman's rights has to be worked through to its ultimate. If found impracticable, delusive, subversive, in the working, it will have to be put down again. It is all a question of power, both in the getting and the using. If women are really in earnest about it they will carry the day, because no power can withstand a compact organization or the moral pressure of a large class movement. If they are not in earnest, or rather while they are not in earnest, the boon will be either disdainfully conceded, even by its antagonists, under the conviction that it will prove useless, or that it will be misused, and so a case made out for withdrawal; or it will be withheld altogether. But the seed has been sown, and in time the prison flagstone will be lifted up. Meanwhile, all the best friends of women have but one duty to fulfil towards them; which is, to raise the standard of excellence among them, and to make them see for themselves that they can permanently gain their rights solely by means of the voluntary respect of men, and that respect is given only to those who deserve it.

Women are dissatisfied with things as they are, and with cause; but the remedy lies in their own hands, and is not to be looked for as a boon granted from the outside. When they will to be noble, free, respected and powerful, they can be all these; but they must will – not only wish; they must work towards the higher goal in earnestness of purpose and faithful self-devotion. They must remember that God helps those who help themselves, and that the secret of all success is in endeavour. And above all, they must leave off clinging to their faults as to so many special graces, and thinking themselves most lovely when they are most useless, and interesting in exact proportion to their weakness and their vanity.

---

84. Michael Field
from *Journal*

[*After the performance.*] It seems more natural to be dead than alive. We wake to the surprise of finding every morning paper against us.

Little Fleming falls before the crisis – he is too small a soul – but my Love is strong, pours him out his tea, cracks jokes with him, and is able to convey our gratitude for this Gray's Inn refuge. I am in helpless pain like a dumb animal at first. *The Times* and *Telegraph* are worthy of respect in their blame; they have some good words for us and our actors, the rest howl!

. . . there are caves in my brain, through which cruel tides swing and rave – my stomach feels as it does when anyone you love is dead; my throat is dry and quakes from time to time. I rise up from lunch and walk to the British Museum – the grim Egyptian Deities and the Branchidae Priests support me more than the Elgin Marbles – I long to lie in one of those sarcophagi, covered with hieroglyphics, and to know that the weight of ages would hold the lid down. I find, in the Metopes and Frieze of the Parthenon, a want of contagious life among the figures . . . gradually the stoniness of the sculpture strikes me with intolerable anguish, and I walk home for the first time to cry a few moments. My Love comforts me with tea, with a strong face and with tenderness. . . . Then my Love quails, she who has been so strong. The evening papers are worse than the morning. They are like a lot of unchained tigers We are hated, as Shelley was hated, by our countrymen, blindly, ravenously.

. . . We mark with a hall-mark, the people who have courage to stand by us. . . . Not a soul has been near us – our rooms are full of the sound of a winter-wind, on our desk are the Daily Journals . . . but though everything is against us, we are strong, thank Heaven and our race.

Act III was received silently, tensely . . . the curtain after all was too long in dropping, then applause boomed and the whole house gabbled. But no one came. At last old Miss Scott swelled over one of our front chairs, and she gave us compliments, and talked about her new house, and must have made the effect of a Turkey-hen from the theatre. . . . I felt suddenly as if I stood in a clearing where there was no humanity – where I was a mortal alone.

Act IV was lost from the beginning. The people resented Mrs. Creswick's old-fashioned method, and her costume (which we had never seen) was enough to kill any scene in which she took part. . . .

The applause must have been good, for the actors seemed warm. I cannot say I heard it, and not once did I catch the word "author," . . . a dampness quenched me within – I knew the play had failed with the critics. And little Fleming was a cold compress to any elation. With scarcely a word I bore his remarks, and went to bed as one does after a funeral. I woke feeling incomplete – I had lost my hope – any anticipation, and there was no triumph in its place.

---

85. Jane, Lady Wilde
from *Genius and Marriage*

But the artist . . . should beware of bondage to the emotions. He should stand apart from all human ties in order that he may more calmly analyse the workings of passion. His mission is to reveal the hidden mysteries of the soul, and, for the furtherance of philosophical analysis, he may even break a heart, but should never allow his own to be weakened by combat with inferior natures. . . .

For true spiritual natures pine in bondage. All routine of law and conventionalism is hateful and revolting to them. Their lives have no fixed orbit. They alternate in phases of ecstasy and agony, in storms and whirlwinds, or the gloom of a midnight despair; and for these beings of nerves and caprices a special type of women should be created; but the world seldom affords an example of such a type.

The daughters of men who wed with the sons of the gods, should have courage to face the lightnings and the thunders, if they dare to stand on the mountain height with an immortal husband. For such a man, and to insure his happiness, a woman should be ready to give her life with sublime self-immolation. At once an angel and a victim, sensitive to every chord of his nature, yet with a smile forever on the lip, no matter what anxieties may corrode the heart.

Genius is an exotic that requires to be nursed in sunshine, but the ordinary, common-place wife too often chills and blights the divine spirit through her shallow egotism, forever exacting, never giving; estimating work only, . . . by its money value; therefore she teases her husband to make busts of mediocrities, because they generally pay well, and to paint the faded, affected women of society, because it may bring him into fashion. And she insists on his going out with her, as she likes to be noticed as the wife of a celebrity. To all this the husband generally consents in a meek, submissive way; for, except in moments of passionate inspiration when the god descends on him, the artist is the weakest creature under heaven, so easily led and duped by a woman tyrant.

But some day he violently breaks the bonds, and a scene, a fracas, a separation is the result. . . .

The world says of the husband, 'How wicked of him to leave his wife, such an excellent woman, so active in her house, everything so orderly, and she never left him for a moment.'

Exactly, there was the horror of it. She never left him. He pined for solitude in those precious moments of intellectual excitement, when thought is organised to form only in divine stillness; but he never could attain it. She was there, always there, arranging and settling, methodical and punctual and orderly, abounding in all those virtues that kill great thoughts; incapable of sympathy, and entirely failing to comprehend the needs and peculiarities of the sensitive temperament of genius. So he fled. His life was wrecked, but his soul was liberated, and he was content. Solitude and liberty are for artists and gods.

Ill-assorted marriages torture the gifted in many other ways. The musician finds that his wife has no ear for music, and she always begins to chat with her friends, or declaim loudly to her refractory servants, when his soul is going forth into the infinite, and his hand 'loosens the notes in a golden shower.'

The poet's wife generally hates poetry, calls it 'stuff,' and laments that her husband cannot write, like other people, paragraphs and acrostics or prize parodies that bring in such quantities of money.

Even love marriages have no sure foundation in the intellectual temperament. To see, love and wed in a moment is ecstatic; but to live and not love for the whole after-term of human existence is a fearful reality, too often experienced, in all its dull depression, when unrelated souls are bound together by the irrefragable marriage chain.

A young writer of promise and rising fame sees a pretty shop-girl, a jeweller's daughter, and is fascinated at once. She was so gentle and insinuating, so charming, with her little curled head and her little white hands, daintily fingering the glittering trinkets, and her placid smile that always beamed a welcome. He fancies that under her rule the disorder of his bachelor home will be changed to a paradise of comfort, and they are married. But the sunshine came not; only a grey, watery atmosphere of fog seemed to envelop his life. When his clever friends came as usual, and thought flashed as at a Platonic symposium, the wife sat by and smiled her placid smile, and uttered the small platitudes of mediocre natures, the set colloquial phrases of commerce, with the most exasperating unconsciousness that she was a bore and wearisome to them all. On the contrary, she fancied she was quite an addition to the circle, so nice, ladylike and well bred.

Then the horror of a dreadful truth fell upon the husband's heart. He became conscious that he would have to sit opposite to this woman and look at her vapid smile, and listen to her flimsy talk, for, perhaps, half a century. There was no help for him. No release. Sometimes the tumult of his feelings raged in open war, and then she wept and lamented that she had not married one or other of the young shopmen who were dying about her, and were now so well off.

But after a time matters grew worse. She began to assume airs as the wife of an author, to give her opinion, and interrupt the conversation with her affected gush of praise. The husband could see the suppressed laughter on the lips of the Platonists, and their contempt for the little fool he had made his wife. This finished his agony. He gave up his friends. He gave up writing, fell into a state of morbid melancholy, and finally died, leaving all his precious manuscripts confused and incomplete. The widow crammed them all into the fire, smiled as before, and eventually married one, or, perhaps, both of the admiring shopmen. And she still utters her little platitudes of commerce, and refers, as to a martyrdom, to her first marriage with that poor scribbler who never could earn enough by anything he wrote to keep her in proper style.

But if the small common-place mind is exasperating, perhaps the untamed freedom of the half savage, the fearless passions of a daughter of the people, would suit the requirements of the exceptional soul of genius.

So thought a young French artist as he looked on the massive figure, the heavy coils of black hair, the grand limbs of a superb Tranteverine, as she stood in the mud of the shallows fishing for eels. How splendid she was in the flashing sunlight, with her great eyes, her scarlet bodice, her white chemisette tucked up high over the great sculptural arms, and then her mad, merry laughter that stirred the air like a rush of the breeze through the pine woods. He made a picture of her at once, which excited immense admiration at the Exposition. A glorious study of sky and air, and the full rich life of youth, in a flush of colour and a glow of light.

At last he had found an ideal to take into his life. He hated the false affected woman of society, but here was a beautiful savage, a child of the sun and the storms and the flowers; she would give his artist life eternal youth – so he married her. She had no possession save a big red cat, and he carried her and the cat to Paris.

But when she put on the Paris dress like other people, what a mournful transformation of the daughter of the sun. A great splendid animal in a little Paris bonnet, always tilting to one side over the heavy masses of hair was a failure, and the great Roman feet, made for splashing in the reeds and the rushes, limped sadly in the little Paris boots, and the effect of a Paris mantle on the great broad shoulders was altogether deplorable. Even her beauty seemed to have disappeared with the loss of her native picturesque surroundings. Then her coarse language, her large gestures, her bad French, all these things agonised him at every moment. A savage veneered is an artistic mistake.

He saw it all and sighed, and withdrew from the world where he could never bring a wife who talked as loud in society as if she were hailing a boat across the Tiber, and whose laugh shook the room like an earthquake.

However, they have got over ten years of married life. The heavy chin, the broad shoulders, the vulgar mouth, have become accentuated; still the eyes are splendid, and the artist-husband has learned to endure a good deal. She is so good-hearted and kind though when she claps him on the back, and presses him to eat some dish which she has spent all the morning preparing, he shudders, and a silent aspiration rises to his lips that he had left her on her own soil amid the reeds and the rushes, with her cat and the eels and the fishermen of the Tiber.

Other experiences in married life have proved equally uncongenial to the strange, sensitive, artistic nature. A young dramatist, with eyes of fire and soul of flame, fancies he will find his ideal in the first love of a pure young heart – a simple, docile girl, that he can mould as he chooses by his strong will, and breathe, as it were, a divine spirit into the clay.

'Yes,' he said to his friend, 'I liked her clear innocent eyes, her calm expression that no passions had ever disturbed; even her little provincial accent and ways I liked, for they suggested the pure innocence of the country life.

'And now to say that I hate her accent; I hate her ways; I hate this torpid soul that no effort of mine can wake to life or sensibility. I read my poem to her – my great, noble poem "How pretty," she said, and yawned.

'I could have killed her. But I was calm, and explained to her that poetry was the highest expression of the divine, and that she ought to strive to comprehend its depth and meaning. She smiled as if I were an idiot, and said she liked common sense, but what I read seemed all nonsense. Common sense, the instinct of common brains and cold hearts.

'She cared nothing for music, nor for art, nor even for dress, only for good solid household work, and economies above all. When our clever circle discussed art and literature with their usual fervent vehemence, she sat silent, stuck up in a corner at her eternal needlework, and looked on with such a contemptuous sneer that my friends began to hate the sight of her, and gave up their visits. Then she brought in her own set. Oh, heavens! The bathos of these mediocre souls, the torture of listening to the shallow talk of commonplace women. Can you wonder that I left her? The influence of a nature like hers on a man's intellect is like a slow poison. And why should I allow my soul to be slowly murdered by a woman, merely because she is called my wife? No, I tried honestly to lift her to my level, but she would not be lifted.

'So the horrible dream is over, and I am free. These obstinate, self-opinionated women, without sympathy or the power to appreciate, are a dull leaden weight on life; besides, she was not happy with me, and we are better parted.'

It is quite true that the temperament and ways of literary men are often very irritating to a woman, their disorder and recklessness, their utter want of a law of life, sometimes sitting up all night, or lying in bed all day or for days together, to finish an essay or a drama undisturbed, the atmosphere of cigars they live in, the fever and the fret, the sleeplessness and the stimulants, and their intense, ingrained, though unconscious selfishness, these things none but a woman nobly resolved to be a victim can endure. Yet the temperament only is to blame, the man never means to be unkind, or to make his wife walk on ploughshares. The artisan can work at all times with perfect freedom, but genius can only work in moments, in fits and spasms, when the idea must be caught flying, or it will come no more, and in these tempestuous moments of cerebral excitation the path must be left free for the rush of the chariot wheels, and all the home life must be hushed into a fearful silence lest the inspiration should be disturbed before the word of power has been uttered.

Then there are days of weird, wordless gloom, when a large parcel lies on the table, 'Declined with thanks,' and the wife knows it is there, like the corpse of a murdered innocent, but cares not to allude to it, only its presence is felt by the sombre silence that pervades the house, and the fitful temper at the dinner-table of the husband.

To some women the reflected glory of being the wife of a celebrity compensates for the actual discomfort, but unless a woman can accept immolation cheerfully, she becomes miserable herself, and a hindrance in place of a helpmeet to her husband. There is also the constant difficulty of getting money when there is no regular income, and one has to live on capital evolved from the brain in some happy fit of working power. And when money comes in, how recklessly it is spent! What ceaseless subscriptions for statues, tombs and memorials to the deceased brotherhood of genius. And what endless efforts to found a new 'literary review' which is to take the world by storm, always the craze of a young band of writers, though generally ending in failure, bitterness and bankruptcy.

Naturally, and by instinct, a woman has a strong tendency to look on a man of genius as a god, and to offer him worship as well as love; but in the fatal intimacy of daily life illusions soon vanish, and she finds that, except in moments of inspiration, her divinity is even weaker than an ordinary mortal, less able to guide or strengthen others; so she resents the knowledge that her idol is only made of clay, and her feelings alternate between contempt and dislike, especially if she is of a passionate, impulsive temperament.

An excellent man, an horticulturist, the head of a nursery garden, had a wife of this description – handsome, ardent, and about ten years his junior. Amidst her beautiful flowers in the silent garden she dreamed of the Paris world of splendour and celebrities, where even she also might reign as a queen, and be admired and flattered, were she only seen and known. Then the dream would vanish, and she saw only the bowed down back of her respectable husband over his flowers, and heard only the snipping of the hedges and the eternal drip of the watering-pot; and she wearied sadly over the gravel walks, the mathematical beds, the geometrical exercise, and the life regulated by the barometer.

So the years passed till she reached the *trente ans* – the fatal age when passion becomes reckless in the despair of vanishing youth.

Just then a poet arrives in the little provincial town, and is provincially lionised. A true poet of the *salons*, with cavernous eyes, floating hair, and a pale, sombre, fatal face. He is always perfectly dressed. No lyric disorder apparent, save in the somewhat careless tie of his cravat.

Everyone invited him; he always came late, between ten and midnight, and it was an impressive thing to see him as he leaned upon the mantelpiece, tossed back his long hair, and spoke, as if in a melancholy dream, of the soul of the poet tortured by passion and despair. But the excitement was at its height when he declaimed his celebrated poem, 'The Creed of Love,' beginning with the stupendous line, –

'I believe in Love as I believe in God.'

And all the pretty women in their full evening dress gathered round, and gazed at him with earnest, humid eyes.

Of course, the wife of the respectable horticulturist was vanquished at once. What woman of unfulfilled aspirations, whose husband only snipped and planted and watered, could resist the magic influence of this Orphic revelation?

After a few interviews she flung herself at the poet's feet, and declared that life was no longer endurable with 'this man' (on these occasions the husband is always 'this man,' even though he is a scientific gardener).

The poet was rather embarrassed by the gift of her devotion, but he could not refuse, so they departed together for Paris.

Now, she thought, the reign of intellectual splendour will begin; but how different was the reality. A mean apartment, a moody, irritable companion; no brilliant world waiting to receive her with homage and admiration. On the contrary, society treated her with the most supercilious impertinence, and she was left to an ignoble solitude, while the poet, faultlessly dressed, went out every evening and declaimed 'The Creed of Love' to other women, the elegant and fashionable women of society, who disdained to notice her existence. But even this might have been borne could she still have worshipped; but she found her idol querulous and fretful, hypochondriacal and abominably selfish. He was always imagining he was ill, and the table was covered with vials and powders, and the room kept at stove heat. What a change after her garden and the flowers and the pure air!

After a month or so of broken illusions, life became insupportable to her. She was stifled in the atmosphere of the close room, wearied with his temper, and she began to hate 'The Creed of Love.' How to escape was now her only thought. At length she wrote to her husband, told him all, entreated him to come for her. She had outlived her dreams, and would now be a good wife to him henceforth and for ever.

He was a philosopher; he forgave, and he came. One evening, while the poet was declaiming 'The Creed of Love' at an assembly of worshipping women, she left the house, found her excellent husband waiting with a carriage at the end of the street, and the midnight train whirled her back to peace, order, her beautiful gardens, and a happy, rational life. For, after all, a rational husband is the best companion for the life-long marriage state. The poet lover, with his moods and caprices, was only endurable when a glamour of glory covered him like a silver veil; and the veil, we know, is thrown on merely for society, and is never worn in the dull routine of common every-day life.

But it must be confessed that women have often many and grievous faults in married life, very irritating to a literary husband and a man of genius. . . .

Their chief fault is a childish jealousy of a man's life work, manifested in overt acts of ill-temper, and other modes of annoyance. This is the common failing of common minds. A woman has torn the canvas from the easel where her husband was at work in a fit of jealous rage. Another, with grim determination, always chose the time when the author sat down to write to practise her scales or pound at some terrible sonata. And one (though such cruel malignity is scarcely credible) has been even known to hum a tune in the very room where her poet husband was striving to finish a beautiful and elaborate sonnet. And all this out of spite and jealousy for some fancied neglect.

The best chance, perhaps, of domestic felicity is when all the family are Bohemians, and all clever, and all enjoy thoroughly the erratic, impulsive, reckless life of work and glory, indifferent to everything save the intense moments of popular applause.

Such a family may be met in the art circles of Paris. The mother had been a model and a beauty, and still posed as Hebe when she handed a cup of tea to a visitor. The daughters, handsome, brilliant and clever, as the children of artists always are, sing, act, recite, dance, dress better than anyone else. Everything looks picturesque on them. Fashionable ladies vainly desire the pattern of that flowing train, that lifted robe, that classic sleeve; but no pattern is to be had. All was arranged by the aid of a few pins in the caprice of the moment as the handsome girls chatted and laughed before the mirror in their little room. Youth, beauty, and artistic taste can work wonders with the most chaotic materials.

People asked how they managed to pay for everything; but they never paid. That was their magic secret.

Bills, of course, were endless; but when some particularly severe creditor appeared, one of the splendid daughters pleaded with such a bewitching smile that he would 'call next Monday' (it was the family formula), that he retired humbled and abashed from the glorious presence, as if his claim had been an impertinence.

There was no regular dinner hour. A kind of gipsy camp was held behind the screen, and nourishment was taken with lawless haste during the transition intervals of the drama of life.

When a good sum came in for a picture by the father, they spent it right royally; not, indeed, paying the School Board or the water rate, or the consolidated house taxes – such things depress genius – but in some splendid outlay of extravagant revelry, which kept them in high spirits for a week after, and they worked all the better for it.

The State, surely, ought to consider the importance of preserving genius from low cares; and Parliament might pass a bill to exempt the race of the gifted from taxation. For these brilliant beings are necessary to the world; they supply the life, the phosphorus, the divine fire, the grace, beauty, and charm of existence, and the nation in return should relieve them from all the mean burdens of prosaic and parochial claims.

The true joy of the artist is in work; and when every member of the family has a special gift, which is repaid by the world's praise, then everyone is happy. There is no idleness, no *ennui*. No one throws the burden of his life on another, no one needs a victim; all work and all triumph, and learn to live and reign alone. Even when youth has passed, artistic instincts still give grace and joy to life, and the world still continues its homage to the abdicated royalties of genius.

The more independent of each other each member of the household is, the greater the chance of happiness. If every wife had a definite employment, she would be less given to those little jealousies and watchings and pryings that fill up the time of vacant minds. . . .

The life-work should be the first; and the life-work need not hinder the beautiful ministrations of love, but it will make a woman stronger and nobler, more ready to pardon and help in moments of trial.

Unhappily, it is seldom that two equal and eternally related souls meet in the marriage state; but this age has given an example of at least one such divine marriage, when the great poet wedded the great poetess of England in bonds of mutual love and honour. No jealousy was possible, for each stood on the supreme height of fame, and no cares or troubles marred the flow of genius in a married life, made radiant by fortune, luxury, art, culture, travel, high social position, and the world's applause. Death made the memory of this union sad and sacred, but the love remained to the last; and the poet's genius gave it life and light. The most beautiful verses in Mr Browning's latest volume are consecrated to a thought of her who shared the glory of his life, and to an aspiration for their reunion.

Mrs Carlyle failed to reach happiness because she had ambition without fame, and intellect without a career, and was too self-conscious and proud to be content with a subordinate part in life. She ought to have considered that her existence was really of no importance to the universe; but, her husband's words and works had power to send the world on its path of progress with mighty tangential force, and to drive a current of new life into the heart of the century. He was necessary to humanity; but she was only necessary to smooth the path his soul travelled. In this line of duty lay the beautiful mission of a loving wife, and in this she ought to have found happiness; but she only thought of the small annoyances that lay in her own path, and pronounced herself 'miserable' – though holding the proud position of wife to the greatest man of the age! Yet she loved him as well as her nature would permit; but egotism can never nobly worship nor see the glory through the mist, and all the trials that made her 'miserable' resulted more from faults in her own disposition than from her husband's temper.

Had she married the village schoolmaster she might have been happier. A keen, clever, homely Scotchwoman, with her sharp tongue and her broad Scotch accent, she would have ruled the parish admirably. And this should have been her destiny; but Carlyle raised her to eminence as his wife, gave her station and dignity in the great capital of the world; and in return she darkened his fame, gave his name to the scoffers, and chilled the enthusiasm that would have raised memorials to his honour.

From the woman that stands beside the man of genius in life much is demanded. She is the angel of his destiny, and accountable to the world for the treasure committed to her care – the peace and serenity of his soul. Some men work, and the world crowns them – they have their recompense; others work and die in their youth, and the world weeps for them; but some work and suffer, and the world neither crowns nor weeps. For them, at least, let a woman live, or, if need be, let a woman die. The one supreme grace for the wife of a man of genius is the grace of immolation and self-sacrifice.

A woman is so easily replaced in the vast working world of life, but a great man's throne is vacant for evermore. Yet it must be remembered that under no circumstances can genius be made happy. The artist nature burns with an infinite desire for the infinite that nothing earthly can satisfy. Happiness is for the commonplace only – for the mechanical workers to whom success means wages, not glory. A victim upon whom can be laid all the burden of existence is needed by the high priest of genius, and a wife may not have the sacrificial vocation. Hence the sum of all experience is apparently rather against marriage for the race of the gifted; but the question still remains undecided. No new arguments have been adduced, and nothing stronger has been said on the subject by any modern writer than what Milton uttered two hundred years ago, when he wrote his celebrated treatise to prove that the loneliest life was better than an unsuited marriage, when two persons without any spiritual affinity were bound together in irrevocable bondage by the words of a ritual, 'to their unspeakable weariness and despair,' and life became to them, in Milton's expressive words, 'a drooping and disconsolate household captivity, without refuge or redemption.'

1895

86. Ouida
from *The New Woman*

IT can scarcely be disputed, I think, that in the English language there are conspicuous at the present moment two words which designate two unmitigated bores: The Workingman and the Woman. The Workingman and the Woman, the New Woman, be it remembered, meet us at every page of literature written in the English tongue; and each is convinced that on its own special W hangs the future of the world. Both he and she want to have their values artificially raised and rated, and a status given to them by favour in lieu of desert. In an age in which persistent clamour is generally crowned by success they have both obtained considerable attention; is it offensive to say much more of it than either deserves?

❋ ❋ ❋ ❋

The whole kernel of the question lies in this. The supporters of the New Woman declare that she will not surrender her present privileges, i.e., though she may usurp his professorial seat, and seize his salary, she will still expect the man to stand that she may sit; the man to get wet through that she may use his umbrella. Yet surely if she retain these privileges she can only do so by an appeal to his chivalry, i.e., by a confession that she is weaker than he. But she does not want to do this; she wants to get the comforts and concessions due to feebleness, at the same time as she demands the lion's share of power due to superior force alone. It is this overweening and unreasonable grasping at both positions which will end in making her odious to man and in her being probably kicked back roughly by him into the seclusion of a harem.

The New Woman declares that man cannot do without woman. It is a doubtful postulate. In the finest intellectual and artistic era of the world women were not necessary to either the pleasures or passions of men. It is possible that if women make themselves as unlovely and offensive as they appear likely to become, the preferences of the Platonic Age may become acknowledged and dominant, and women may be relegated entirely to the lowest plane as a mere drudge and child-bearer.

Before me at the moment lies an engraving from an illustrated journal of a woman's meeting; whereat a woman is demanding, in the name of her sovereign sex, the right to vote at political elections. The speaker is middle-aged and plain of feature; she wears an inverted plate on her head, tied on with strings under her double-chin; she has balloon-sleeves, a bodice tight to bursting, a waist of ludicrous dimensions in proportion to her portly person; her whole attire is elaborately constructed so as to conceal any physical graces which she might possess; she is gesticulating with one hand, of which all the fingers are stuck out in ungraceful defiance of all artistic laws of gesture. Now, why cannot this orator learn to gesticulate properly and learn to dress gracefully, instead of clamouring for a franchise? She violates in her own person every law, alike of common-sense and artistic fitness, and yet comes forward as a fit and proper person to make laws for others. She is an exact representative of her sex as it exists at the dawn of the twentieth century.

There have been few periods in which woman's attire has been so ugly, so disfiguring and so preposterous as it is in this year of grace (1894) at a period when, in newspaper and pamphlet, on platform and in dining-room, and in the various clubs she has consecrated to herself, woman is clamouring for her recognition as a being superior to man. She cannot clothe herself with common sense or common grace, she cannot resist the dictates of tailors and the example of princesses; she cannot resist the squaw-like preference for animals' skins, and slaughtered birds, and tufts torn out of the living and bleeding creature; she cannot show to any advantage the natural lines of her form, but disguises them as grotesquely as mantua-makers bid her to do. She cannot go into the country without making herself a caricature of man, in coat and waistcoat and gaiters; she apes all his absurdities, she emulates all his cruelties and follies; she wears his ugly pot hats, his silly, stiff collars; she copies his inane club-life and then tells us that this parody, incapable of initiative, bare of taste and destitute of common sense, is worthy to be enthroned as the supreme teacher of the world!

Woman, whether new or old, leaves immense fields of culture untilled, immense areas of influence wholly neglected. She does almost nothing with the resources she possesses, because her whole energy is concentrated on desiring and demanding those she had not. She can write and print anything she chooses; and she scarcely ever takes the pains to acquire correct grammar or elegance of style before wasting ink and paper. She can paint and model any subjects she chooses, but she imprisons herself in men's *atéliers* to endeavour to steal their technique and their methods, and thus loses any originality she might possess in art. Her influence on children might be so great that through them she would practically rule the future of the world; but she delegates her influence to the vile school boards if she be poor, and if she be rich to governesses and tutors; nor does she in ninety-nine cases out of a hundred ever attempt to educate or control herself into fitness for the personal exercise of such influence. Her precept and example in the treatment of the animal creation might be of infinite use in mitigating the hideous tyranny of humanity over them, but she does little or nothing to this effect; she wears dead birds and the skins of dead creatures; she hunts the hare and shoots the pheasant, she drives and rides with more brutal recklessness than men; she watches with delight the struggles of the dying salmon, of the gralloched deer; she keeps her horses standing in snow and fog for hours, with the muscles of their heads and necks tied up in the torture of the bearing rein; when asked to do anything for a stray dog, a lame horse, a poor man's donkey, she is very sorry, but she has so many claims on her already; she never attempts by orders to her household, to her *fournisseurs*, to her dependents, to obtain some degree of mercy in the treatment of sentient creatures and in the methods of their slaughter, and she continues to trim her court gowns with the aigrettes of ospreys.

The immense area for good influence which lies open to her in private life is almost entirely uncultivated, yet she wants to be admitted into public life. Public life is already overcrowded, verbose, incompetent, fussy and foolish enough without the addition of her in her sealskin coat with the dead humming bird on her hat. Women in public life would exaggerate the failings of men, and would not have even their few excellencies. Their legislation would be, as that of men is too often, the offspring of panic or prejudice; and women would not put on the drag of common-sense as men frequently do in public assemblies. There would be little to hope from their humanity, nothing from their liberality; for when they are frightened they are more ferocious than men, and, when they gain power, more merciless.

'Men,' says one of the New Women, 'deprived us of all proper education and then jeered at us because we had no knowledge.' How far is this based on facts? . . . In all eras and all climes a woman of great genius or of great beauty has done very much what she chose; and if the majority of women have led obscure lives, so have the majority of men. The chief part of humanity is insignificant whether it be male or female. In most people there is very little character indeed, and as little mind. Those who have much of either never fail to make their mark, be they of which sex they may.

The unfortunate idea that there is no good education without a college curriculum is as injurious as it is erroneous. The college education may have excellencies for men in its friction, its preparation for the world, its rough destruction of personal conceit; but for women it can only be hardening and deforming. If study be delightful to a woman, she will find her way to it as the hart to water brooks. The author of *Aurora Leigh* was not only always at home, but she was also for many years a confirmed invalid; yet she became a fine classic, and found her path to fame. A college curriculum would have done nothing to improve her rich and beautiful mind; it might have done much to debase it.

❀ ❀ ❀ ❀

Modesty is no doubt a thing of education or prejudice, a conventionality artificially stimulated; but it is an exquisite grace, and womanhood without it loses its most subtle charm. Nothing tends so to destroy modesty as the publicity and promiscuity of schools, of hotels, of railway trains and sea voyages. True modesty shrinks from the curious gaze of other women as from the coarser gaze of man. When a girl has a common bedchamber and a common bathroom with other girls, she loses the delicate bloom of her modesty. Exposure to a crowd of women is just as nasty as exposure to a crowd of men.

Men, moreover, are in all, except the very lowest classes, more careful of their talk before young girls than women are, or at least were so until the young women of fashion insisted on their discarding such scruples. It is very rarely that a man does not respect real innocence; but women frequently do not. The jest, the allusion, the story which sullies her mind and awakes her inquisitiveness, will much oftener be spoken by women than men. It is not from her brothers, nor her brother's friends, but from her female companions that she will understand what the grosser laugh of those around her suggests. The biological and pathological curricula complete the loveless disflowering of her maiden soul.

Everything which tends to obliterate the contrast of the sexes, like the mixture of boys and girls in American common schools, tends also to destroy the charm of intercourse, the savour and sweetness of life. Seclusion lends an infinite seduction to the girl, whilst the rude and bustling publicity of modern life robs woman of her grace. Packed liked herrings in a railway carriage, sleeping in odious vicinity to strangers on a shelf, going days and nights without a bath, exchanging decency and privacy for publicity and observation, the women who travel, save those rich enough to still purchase seclusion, are forced to cast aside all refinement and delicacy.

It is said that travel enlarges the mind. There are many minds which can no more be enlarged, by any means whatever, than a nut or a stone. What have their journeys round the world and their incessant gyrations done for the innumerable princes of Europe? The fool remains a fool, though you carry him or her about over the whole surface of the globe, and it is certain that the promiscuous contact and incessant publicity of travel, which may not hurt the man, do injure the woman. . . .

But every word, whether written or spoken, which urges the woman to antagonism against the man, every word which is written or spoken to try and make of her a hybrid, self-contained opponent of men, makes a rift in the lute to which the world looks for its sweetest music.

The New Woman reminds me of an agriculturist who, discarding a fine farm of his own, and leaving it to nettles, stones, thistles and wire-worms, should spend his whole time in demanding neighbouring fields which are not his. The New Woman will not even look at the extent of ground indisputably her own, which she leaves unweeded and untilled.

Not to speak of the entire guidance of childhood, which is certainly already chiefly in the hands of woman (and of which her use does not do her much honour), so long as she goes to see one of her own sex dancing in a lion's den, the lions being meanwhile terrorised by a male brute; so long as she wears dead birds as millinery and dead seals as coats, so long as she goes to races, steeplechases, coursing and pigeon matches; so long as she 'walks with the guns'; so long as she goes to see an American lashing horses to death in idiotic contest with velocipedes, so long as she curtsies before princes and emperors who reward the winners of distance-rides; so long as she receives physiologists in her drawing-rooms, and trusts to them in her maladies; so long as she invades literature without culture, and art without talent; so long as she orders her court-dress in a hurry, regardless of the strain thus placed on the poor seamstresses; so long as she makes no attempt to interest herself in her servants, in her animals, in the poor slaves of her tradespeople; so long as she shows herself, as she does at present, without scruple at every brutal and debasing spectacle which is considered fashionable; so long as she understands nothing of the beauty of meditation, of solitude, of Nature; so long as she is utterly incapable of keeping her sons out of the shambles of modern sport, and lifting her daughters above the pestilent miasma of modern society; so long as she is what she is in the worlds subject to her, she has no possible title or capacity to demand the place or the privilege of man, for she shows herself incapable of turning to profit her own place and her own privilege.

---

87. Louisa Sarah Bevington
Who Made The Cake?

"In the sweat of your brows," the rich man said, "ye who are useful shall eat your bread. In the sweat of your brows, too – don't mistake – we pastors and masters will live on cake." Year in, year out, the sweating was done; they toiled in the factory, toiled in the sun; for the master still left them a daily crust, and the pastor still preached that the text was just. Year in, year out, grew the pile of laws; this point grew weightier, clause by clause, "To him that holdeth shall more be given; from him that yieldeth take all but – heaven."

The Lord said, "Sweat of the brow brings bread." It was something shrewder the landlord said: – "Out of their sweat-won bread we'll draw cake for ourselves, and our rights by law." The parson in preaching quite left that out; the people were foolish and dull, no doubt; but landlords' hirelings have such an air when they mount in the pulpit or groan in prayer. They have lived on the fat of the land, you see, by letting the will of the landlord be, and by urging the winners of daily bread to bow to God's will in all they said.

Well, a new day dawned, and the people awoke, and found it was only old Mammon who spoke; they examined the swindle that held them fast, and got to the back of the trick at last. The sweat of the patient, toil-worn brow, buys more than the vouched-for bread by now. Surely, O world, there's a sad mistake, for where are the people who made the cake? How are they cared for, how are they fed? Care-worn and bound with their crust of bread; while the folk whom they feed make a law, you see, to keep themselves leisurely, merry, and free.

Men of the factory! men of the field! you who have won all this plentiful yield, cry to the world for your children's sake –

"Those who have made it shall taste of the cake!"

———

1896

88. Margaret Oliphant
from *The Anti-Marriage League*

This inclination towards the treatment of subjects hitherto considered immoral or contrary to good manners, in the widest sense of the words – and the disposition to place what is called the Sex-question above all others as the theme of fiction – has gradually acquired the importance of a *parti pris*. It may be said that this question has always been the leading subject of romance; but this never in the sense of the words as now used. Love has been the subject of romance, and all the obstacles that have always come in its way, and the devotion and faithfulness of Lovers, the chosen Two, the perennial hero and heroine in whom the simpler ideals of life have been concentrated. What is now freely discussed as the physical part of the question, and treated as the most important, has hitherto been banished from the lips of decent people, and as much as possible from their thoughts; but is now freely given forth as the favourite subject for the chatter of girls, who no doubt in a great number of cases know nothing about what they are talking of, and therefore are more or less to be pardoned for following a hideous fashion which has the never-exhausted charm of shocking and startling everybody around. Indeed one of the things most conspicuous in this new method is the curious development of shameless Innocence, more dangerous than folly, more appalling almost than vice, because one does not know at any moment into what miserable quagmire its bold and ignorant feet may stumble.

This is what the Young Person, the thought of whom put a bridle on the jaws of Mr Hardy and Mr Grant Allen for a certain period of their career, has come to, under their enlightening labours. For a long time it was She who was supposed to be spared by the painful subjection under which these accomplished writers declared themselves to be held for so many years in bondage. Now that they are emancipated She is emancipated too, and the great spectacle they have succeeded in setting before us is not even in the first place, what we may suppose them to have desired, the triumphs of their own genius – but the singular captive whom they have carried with them out of the battle, the most prized and precious of prisoners, the King's daughter, in whose safety the welfare of the race is concerned more than perhaps in that of any other hostage possible. At least this is what the alarmed spectator, always so timid and apt to fear the worst, is tempted to believe. I have the perfect conviction that it is not the Princess at all who is in their hands, but a false Duessa, always ready in all ages to trick herself in the garments of her mistress, and in reality only one Ignorance, a gipsy wench ever ready for mischief, who has bewildered the intelligence of all ages, and brought up a certain consistent breath of ill-fame from the very beginnings of the race, upon the Princess herself. The Red Cross Knight, it may be remembered, was himself taken in and woefully bewildered by this sham personage; but we have little doubt that Mr Hardy, and Mr Grant Allen, and Miss Ménie Muriel Dowie, and the other members of the band, believe that they have got the true.

I do not know, however, for what audience Mr Hardy intends his last work, which has been introduced, as he tells us, for the last twelve months, into a number of decent houses in England and America, with the most shameful portions suppressed. How they could be suppressed in a book whose tendency throughout is so shameful I do not understand; but it is to be hoped that the conductors and readers of 'Harper's Magazine' were so protected by ignorance as not to understand what the writer meant then – though he now states it with a plainness beyond mistake. I hesitate to confess that until the publication of Mr Hardy's last book, 'Tess,' I was one of those who had not been convinced of the extent of his power, or of the amount of real genius he possessed. The difference between that book and the former books from his hand was, it appeared to me, very great. It marked the moment of his supposed emancipation from prejudices of modesty which had previously held him (more or less, and sometimes rather less than more) from full enunciation of what was in him. And certainly the result of the *débordement* was very remarkable. To demonstrate that a woman, twice fallen from the woman's code of honour and purity, was by that fact proved to be specially and aggressively pure, was a task for a Hercules, and Mr Hardy has no more succeeded in doing this than others have done before him; but the rustic landscape, the balmy breathing of the cows, looming out of the haze in the mystery of the dawn – the rapture of the morning in the silent fields, the large figures of the men and women shaping out of the mist and dews – were things to call forth the enthusiasm of admiration with which indeed they were received. But I suppose Mr Hardy, like so many people, deceived by a simplicity which clings to genius, even when most self-conscious, was not aware what it was which procured him this fame, and ingenuously believed it to be the worser part, the doctrine he preached, and the very hideous circumstances of guilt, unjustified even by passion, of his theme, and not these better things – which thus uplifted him suddenly to the skies.

This perhaps explains, or partially explains, the tremendous downfall of the present book, which, by following 'Tess', accentuates its own grossness, indecency, and horror. Nothing, I think, but a theory could explain the wonderful want of perception which induces a man full of perceptions to make a mistake so fundamental; but it is done – and thus unconsciously affords us the strangest illustration of what Art can come to when given over to the exposition of the unclean. The present writer does not pretend to a knowledge of the works of Zola, which perhaps she ought to have before presuming to say that nothing so coarsely indecent as the whole history of Jude in his relations with his wife Arabella has ever been put in English print – that is to say, from the hands of a Master. There may be books more disgusting, more impious as regards human nature, more foul in detail, in those dark corners where the amateurs of filth find garbage to their taste; but not, we repeat, from any Master's hand. It is vain to tell us that there are scenes in Shakespeare himself which, if they were picked out for special attention, would be offensive to modesty. There is no need for picking out in the work now referred to. Its faults do not lie in mere suggestion, or any *double entendre*, though these are bad enough. In the history of Jude, the half-educated and by no means uninteresting hero in whose early self-training there is much that is admirable – Mr Hardy has given us a chapter in what used to be called the conflict between vice and virtue. The young man, vaguely aspiring after education, learning, and a position among the scholars and students of the land, with a piteous ignorance of the difficulties before him, yet that conviction of being able to triumph over them, which, as we know, has often in real life succeeded in doing so – is really an attractive figure at his outset. He is virtuous by temperament, meaning no evil; bent upon doing more than well, and elevating himself to the level which appears to him the highest in life. But he falls into the hands of a woman so completely animal that it is at once too little and too much to call her vicious. She is a human pig, like the beast whom in a horrible scene she and her husband kill, quite without shame or consciousness of any occasion for shame, yet not even carried away by her senses or any overpowering impulse for their gratification, so much worse than the sow, that it is entirely on a calculation of profit that she puts forth her revolting spell. After the man has been subjugated, a process through which the reader is required to follow him closely (and Jude's own views on this subject are remarkable), he is made for the rest of his life into a puppet flung about between them by two women – the fleshly animal Arabella and the fantastic Susan, the one ready to gratify him in whatever circumstances they may meet, the other holding him on the tiptoe of expectation, with a pretended reserve which is almost more indecent still. In this curious dilemma, the unfortunate Jude, who is always the puppet, always acted upon by the others, never altogether loses our esteem. He is a very poor creature, but he would have liked much better to do well if they would have let him, and dies a virtuous victim of the eternal feminine, scarcely ever blamable, though always bearing both the misery and the shame.

We can with difficulty guess what is Mr Hardy's motive in portraying such a struggle. It can scarcely be said to be one of those attacks upon the institution of Marriage, which is the undisguised inspiration of some of the other books before us. It is marriage indeed which in the beginning works Jude's woe; and it is by marriage, or rather the marrying of himself and others, that his end is brought about. We rather think the author's object must be, having glorified women by the creation of Tess, to show after all what destructive and ruinous creatures they are, in general circumstances and in every development, whether brutal or refined. Arabella, the first – the pig-dealer's daughter, whose native qualities have been ripened by the experiences of a barmaid – is the Flesh, unmitigated by any touch of human feeling except that of merciless calculation as to what will be profitable for herself. She is the native product of the fields, the rustic woman, exuberant and overflowing with health, vanity, and appetite. The colloquy between her and her fellows in their disgusting work, after her first almost equally disgusting interview with Jude, is one of the most unutterable foulness – a shame to the language in which it is recorded and suggested; and the picture altogether of the country lasses at their out-door work is more brutal in depravity than anything which the darkest slums could bring forth, as are the scenes in which their good advice is carried out. Is it possible that there are readers in England to whom this infamy can be palatable, and who, either in inadvertence or in wantonness, can *make it pay?* Mr Hardy informs us he has taken elaborate precautions to secure the double profit of the serial writer, by subduing his colours and diminishing his effects, in the presence of the less corrupt, so as to keep the perfection of filthiness for those who love it. It would be curious to compare in this unsavoury traffic how much of the sickening essence of his story Mr Hardy has thought his first public could stomach, and how many edifying details he has put in for the enlightenment of those who have no squeamish scruples to get over. The transaction is insulting to the public, with whom he trades the viler wares under another name, with all the sup-pressed passages restored, as old-book dealers say in their catalogues, recommending their ancient scandal to the amateurs of the unclean. It is not the first time Mr Hardy has adopted this expedient. If the English public supports him in it, it will be to the shame of every individual who thus confesses himself to like and accept what the author himself acknow-ledges to be unfit for the eyes – not of girls and young persons only, but of the ordinary reader, – the men and women who read the Magazines, the public whom we address in these pages. That the prophets should prophesy falsely is not the most important fact in national degradation: it is only when the people love to have it so that the climax is attained.

The other woman – who makes virtue vicious by keeping the physical facts of one relationship in life in constant prominence by denying, as Arabella does by satisfying them, and even more skilfully and insistently than Arabella – the fantastic *raisonneuse*, Susan, completes the circle of the unclean. She marries to save herself from trouble; then quits her hus-band, to live a life of perpetual temptation and resistance with her lover; then marries, or professes to marry him, when her husband amiably divorces her without the reason he supposes himself to have; and then, when a selfish conscience is tardily awakened, returns to the husband, and ends in ostentatious acceptance of the conditions of matrimony at the moment when the unfortunate Jude, who has also been recaptured by the widowed Arabella, dies of his cruel misery. This woman we are required to accept as the type of high-toned purity. It is the women who are the active agents in all this unsavoury imbroglio: the story is carried on, and life is represented as carried on, entirely by their means. The men are passive, suffering, rather good than otherwise, victims of these and of fate. Not only do they never dominate, but they are quite incapable of holding their own against these remorseless ministers of destiny, these determined operators, managing all the machinery of life so as to secure their own way. This is one of the most curious developments of recent fiction. It is perhaps natural that it should be more or less the case in books written by women, to whom the mere facility of representing their own sex acts as a primary reason for giving them the chief place in the scene. But it has now still more markedly, though much less naturally, become the method with men, in the hands of many of whom women have returned to the *rôle* of the temptress given to them by the old monkish sufferers of ancient times, who fled to the desert, like Anthony, to get free of them, but even there barely escaped with their lives from the seductions of the sirens, who were so audacious as to follow them to the very scene of the macerations and miseries into which the unhappy men plunged to escape from their toils. In the books of the younger men, it is now the woman who seduces – it is no longer the man.

This, however, is a consideration by the way. I have said that it is not clear what Mr Hardy's motive is in the history of Jude: but, on reconsideration, it becomes more clear that it is intended as an assault on the stronghold of marriage, which is now beleaguered on every side. The motto is, "The letter killeth"; and I presume this must refer to the fact of Jude's early and unwilling union to Arabella, and that the lesson the novelist would have us learn is, that if marriage were not exacted, and people were free to form connections as the spirit moves them, none of these complications would have occurred, and all would have been well. "There seemed to him, vaguely and dimly, something wrong in a social ritual which made necessary the cancelling of well-formed schemes involving years of thought and labour, of foregoing a man's one opportunity of showing himself superior to the lower animals, and of contributing his units of work to the general progress of his generation, because of a momentary surprise by a new and transitory instinct which had nothing in it of the nature of vice, and could be only at the most called weakness." This is the hero's own view of the circumstances which, in obedience to the code of honour prevalent in the country-side, compelled his marriage. Suppose, however, that instead of upsetting the whole framework of society, Jude had shown himself superior to the lower animals by not yielding to that new and transitory influence, the same result could have been easily attained: and he might then have met and married Susan and lived happy ever after, without demanding a total overthrow of all existing laws and customs to prevent him from being unhappy. Had it been made possible for him to have visited Arabella as long as the new and transitory influence lasted, and then to have lived with Susan as long as she pleased to permit him to do so, which was the best that could happen were marriage abolished, how would that have altered the circumstances? When Susan changed her mind would he have been less unhappy? when Arabella claimed him again would he have been less weak?

Mr Hardy's solution of the great insoluble question of what is to be the fate of children in such circumstances brings this nauseous tragedy suddenly and at a stroke into the regions of pure farce – which is a surprise of the first quality, only too grotesque to be amusing. There are children, as a matter of course: a weird little imp, the son of Arabella, and two babies of Susan's. What is the point of the allegory which Mr Hardy intends us to read in the absurd little gnome, nicknamed Old Father Time, who is the offspring of the buxom country lass, is a secondary subject upon which we have no light: but it is by the means of this strange creature that the difficulty is settled. In a moment of dreadful poverty and depression, Susan informs her step-son, whom she loves and is very kind to, of the severe straits in which she is. The child – he is now fourteen – asks whether himself and the others are not a great burden upon the parents who are already so poor; and she consents that life would be easier without them. The result is that when she comes in after a short absence she can find no trace of the children, until she perceives what seems to be, at first, suits of their clothes hanging against the wall, but discovers to be the children themselves, all hanged, and swinging from the clothes-pegs: the elder boy having first hanged them and then himself to relieve the parent's hands. Does Mr Hardy think this is really a good way of disposing of the unfortunate progeny of such connections? does he recommend it for general adoption? It is at least a clean and decisive cut of the knot, leaving no ragged ends; but then there is no natural provision in families of such a wise small child to get its progenitors out of trouble. . . . Mr Hardy knows, no doubt as everybody does, that the children are a most serious part of the question of the abolition of marriage. Is this the way in which he considers it would be resolved best?

89. Mary E. Coleridge
Gone

ABOUT the little chambers of my heart
Friends have been coming – going – many a year.
    The doors stand open there.
Some, lightly stepping, enter; some depart.

Freely they come and freely go, at will.
The walls give back their laughter; all day long
    They fill the house with song.
One door alone is shut, one chamber still.

⎯⎯

90. Mary E. Coleridge
To Memory

STRANGE Power, I know not what thou art,
Murderer or mistress of my heart.
I know I'd rather meet the blow
Of my most unrelenting foe
Than live – as now I live – to be
Slain twenty times a day by thee.

Yet, when I would command thee hence,
Thou mockest at the vain pretence,
Murmuring in mine ear a song
Once loved, alas! forgotten long;
And on my brow I feel a kiss
That I would rather die than miss.

⎯⎯

1898

91. Sarah Grand
from *The Modern Man And Maid*

THOSE who look upon the modern girl as in some sort the result of their
own efforts for the emancipation of her sex watch her progress with very

mixed feelings. In so far as she is an improvement on the girls of other days, it is a joy to contemplate her; but in view of her failings there is cause for disheartenment. We must remember, however, that she is so much stronger, so much more pronounced in every way than her colourless predecessor, that what would have passed for an amiable trait in a girl of the last generation stands out as a fine quality in the girl of today; while, on the other hand, those little weaknesses which provoked the mild recurrent ridicule of our ancestors threaten now to develop into faults or failings with which society will have to reckon.

Strength is one of the coming characteristics of the modern English girl. It is as if nature were fitting her to be the mother of men who will keep us in our proud place as the dominant race. She begins already to show herself superior to the girls of other nations in her courage, and the fineness of her physique, in the soundness of her judgment, in her knowledge of life, and in her capacity for dealing with the problems which beset her.

There was a picture, some little time ago, in illustration of an article by Mrs. Lynn Linton, in one of the weekly papers, which showed very happily the difference between the two girls. The picture was divided into two sections. In the one an old-fashioned girl, very gentle, sweet, and helpless in appearance, stood beside her mother, by whom she was being sheltered from contact with the outside world. She knew nothing, she was fearful of everything, her intelligence was undeveloped, her character unformed – and in that state she was expected to remain up till the time of her marriage, when she was required to blossom forth of a sudden into a fully formed woman, and take upon herself successfully the difficult and complicated duties of mistress of a household and mother of children, as if the necessary knowledge came by instinct. Such was the reason and logic of her day. No wonder that in the result she became a subject for ridicule to those who had not heart enough to perceive that she was a subject for sorrow. In the other section of the picture a girl comes riding down the road alone on her bicycle, a slight strong figure, alive, alert, her superabundant vitality, her joy in life and action visible in her whole pose. One knew that she would steer her way through life, as she was steering her way through the traffic of the crowded street, with grace and skill, and arrive at last at her destination, her place of rest, the brighter and the better for all that she had encountered and accomplished and survived.

Which is the better part? The elderly woman of a passive generation, who is out of sympathy with the active service of this and who sees only the dangers which undoubtedly surround our advance, holds up the ideal of the sheltered girl. She would have girls to continue delicate, supersensitive – leave them with every nerve exposed to suffer the jars and shocks of a world they cannot avoid, a world which was arranged to make them suffer rather than for their benefit. Happily it is for the girl herself to choose which she would be: the gentle namby-pamby, of little consequence, never at ease, incapable of independent action, unfitted for liberty, a dependent and a parasite from the cradle to the grave, or that nobler girl who is not the less tender because she is self-reliant, nor the less womanly because she has the power to resent insult and imposition. A woman cannot be developed into a man; therefore, when a woman is strengthened she is strengthened in womanliness, which surely is a desirable consummation. But just as there were fine characters developed by the old inadequate system of education, so may there be much that is regrettable brought out as a result of the new and better method. What should be guarded against is letting go: let nothing go that is good.

A truism of culture insists that it is good to be gracious, gentle, loving, kind, and true; these are qualities of noble womanhood which should be jealously guarded by women. One of the great difficulties of education is that the same training results in quite opposite effects on different characters. What produces the happiest results on one temperament may be disastrous to another; ideas which make one girl a capable gentlewoman will make another a vulgar hoyden; and there is no help for it in the system. The same, broadly speaking, must be applied to all. There may be modifications to suit special cases, but the modifications must be managed by individuals at their own discretion. The different effects are probably due to personal equation, natural bent, something in the blood; but they are also due to the girl's own ideal of life, and to the influence of associates who are either helping her instructors or are at war with them. It is a thankless task to find fault with others; but with ourselves or our work, when we find fault, the tonic property of the discipline helps us to bear it. Still it goes against the grain to have to admit that our countrywomen are inferior in anything to the women of other nations; but it is well to be watchful, especially at the present period of their progress, lest they become so. So far they have not deteriorated, and there is good hope that they will not deteriorate, but, on the contrary, advance in spite of the dangers that beset them. At the present time, however, they seem to have entered upon what threatens to be an ugly phase.

On the finer characteristics of the modern girl there is no need to dilate; she has won for herself an assured position, and now commands respect where it was supposed she could only provoke ridicule. None of the terrible things foretold of her, if she went her way, have come to pass. Indeed, one has to flip through the back numbers of our national humour to fully realize the fearful havoc prophesied to fall upon public morality should a girl bestride a bicycle. The comic press, and that part of the press not ostensibly comic, still attack her at times after the manner of the last generation, and with the same old jibes; but they are powerless to raise a laugh at her expense; the cap does not fit, and these efforts of an antiquated humour to disport itself recoil upon the humorist, exposing him in his turn to ridicule as being behind the times. But the modern girl has her failings, else she would not be human. I believe, however, that there is nothing ingrained in even the worst of her kind, and certainly she might easily escape, if she would, from the ugly phase to which I have already alluded.

On returning to England after a prolonged absence, one is painfully struck by the fact that there is an attribute in which the modern English girl, with all her advantages, tends to be deficient: and that is charm of manner. The boy remains much the same, but the girl has lost a good deal of the natural dainty diffidence of youth; she thinks too much of herself, too little of other people; and that this should be the case is anything but a credit to her. In return for all that society concedes to her to-day in the way of education, physical training, and independence, she should at least show a desire to please. She has a great objection to disagreeable people, yet she takes no trouble to make herself agreeable. When she is out of temper she does not conceal the fact. In her home life she is apt to be selfish, and in society she is only genial when it suits herself. She walks with a stride, she elbows people about in a crowd, she asserts herself on all occasions, and there is a conceited "I'm as good as you are" sort of air about her, a want of becoming deference to people older than herself, which is peculiarly unlovely, not to say offensive, and proclaims her at once underbred and ungenerous – ungenerous in that she accepts every privilege bestowed upon her but offers nothing in return, cultivates none of the gentle dignity, the grace, with which women can add so much to the beauty of life. In this world, if we would be happy, we must give as well as take; but, for the moment, the policy of the modern girl seems to be to take all that she can get, and give nothing.

❀ ❀ ❀ ❀

THE education of young people in the matter of their social relations – their duties as members of the community – when it is not altogether neglected, is usually quite superficial. Marriage, for which they ought to be prepared as they are for confirmation, is not even mentioned to them. All their knowledge of the subject they obtain haphazard, and often from the most undesirable sources. This is especially the case with girls. Hitherto, in England, such information as a girl has been able to obtain on the subject of marriage has for the most part been admirably calculated to mislead her. Her only outlook upon life has been through the novels of the day, which as a rule give but a poor, fragmentary, and altogether primitive view of it. Of men she has no knowledge at all. She is left to choose a husband as she might choose a parrot, for his power to please, his talk and his plumage, so to speak. Her feelings are her only guide; and having no idea of the way in which they may mislead her, she confides in them utterly, and only too often to her own destruction. When a lover presents himself, she does not see the man, or only sees him through a haze of illusions. It is her natural instinct to believe in him, to consider him a superior being, to look up to him. In her misguided ignorance she is not only liable to take him at his own valuation, which will be high in proportion to his worthlessness, but to invest him with all the attributes of all her favourite heroes of romance. Many a charming girl and rich throws herself away on a glib scamp, who, as he protests, marries her for the pleasure of possessing her (there being no other way), but casts her aside without compunction when the pleasure palls and the money is spent. We know what sort of women such girls become: wrecks ruined and deserted, or wreckers preying on society. It is generally said of one of these wretched wives that she has nobody to blame but herself: she chose him, she would have him, she would not be advised. Naturally not. Because she did not even know enough to enable her to realize how very much more there was to know. Even if she were an intelligent girl, she could exercise no discretion in the matter, because, having nothing but the most superficial acquaintance with men, either practically or theoretically, she was quite unable to compare one man with another, and judge of their respective merits. In fact, she had less power to choose a husband than she had to choose a horse, for with regard to the horse external appearance is some guide. Fortunately, now-a-days, parents and guardians get their proper amount of blame and discredit for their neglect of duty in such cases. The children themselves rise up and call them anything but blessed. For a girl has a right to demand of those in authority over her the knowledge requisite to enable her to choose a husband properly when the time comes. Marriage is not at present a perfect institution, and it is an injustice to let a girl believe that it is. She should know what it means exactly – know its advantages and drawbacks; know enough not to be victimised. It is no use warning a girl after she has fallen in love with the wrong man. The knowledge must come first to prevent her falling in love with him; she should have her principles ready for the occasion. And even then she should know better than to rely altogether upon herself, because it is impossible to make her understand beforehand what the force of her own feelings will be, and how much her decision will be influenced by her inclinations.

In the choice of a husband one of the golden rules for a young and inexperienced girl is to be advised.

But she should be careful as to whom she consults. She should beware of the advice of any one whose interest it is to persuade her to marry – to "get her off," to use the vulgar trade expression of certain mothers. She should consult some quite disinterested persons – the more the better – and take the advice of the majority. "In the multitude of counsellors there is safety." The general opinion of a man is pretty certain to be the right one. To this rule, however, there are exceptions – as, for instance, in the case of the good-fellow sort of man, and nobody's-enemy-but-his-own. These men have one recommendation usually which covers all defects in the estimation of their casual acquaintances – they are amusing. The community is always kindly disposed towards its entertainers. But men who are brilliant abroad are often deadly dull bores at home, even when they are no worse. It is there that their nerves recover from the strain they put upon them in society; and their wives get the benefit of the reaction. They live for themselves, alone. All they care about is to shine, to win applause, and when their wives are their only audience they do not trouble themselves to please unless there is something special to be gained. The jolly-good-fellow in society has seldom anything in him that makes for pleasure in permanent companionship.

It is dangerous for a girl to allow herself to be influenced by anything a man's particular friends may say about him if it does not agree with the general opinion; any one of them may be consulting his interests rather than hers, and this is particularly likely when the friend is also a man. Girls must remember that men hang together. It is their habit to sacrifice women for their own or each other's benefit. . . . Happily a change for the better is taking place slowly in this respect. Girls are being taught that they have a right to know all about the men who propose to marry them; moreover, that it is their duty to know. If anything important concerning a man is either misrepresented to a girl or concealed from her, she is the victim of a fraud which robs her of the power to decide whether the man is a suitable person to marry.

It is easy enough to prove to a girl that men in the abstract are apt to be mercenary. She sees that the rich girls of her acquaintance, even when they are unattractive, are courted and wed, while the poor ones, however charming, are pretty generally neglected and left. There is nothing that a girl despises more than a mercenary man, and yet somehow, when a lover presents himself, if he please her, she is very ready to acquit him of mean motives. A generous girl will take it for granted that he is an exception, and a vain one will be prepared to believe that it is herself alone that he is after.

When a girl has money, it should invariably be settled on herself and her children. This is an infallible test of a man's disinterestedness. The man who is worth anything would prefer to have it so settled, while the mercenary man will betray his cupidity when the question is raised. . . . Moral qualities make the man. A woman should be very careful when one of these gentry from the sewers of society presents himself as a lover. He is pretty sure to be a plausible person; but his habit is to protest too much, and by that he may be known; and also by the habit of the friendly narrow-heads, who "give him away" unwittingly and with enthusiasm, calling him "a bit of a dog, don't you know," averring that "he has lived his life," "been about a bit," "knows a thing or two," and so on. There is a long list of such euphemisms, which, being interpreted, mean that the man is horribly stale, his finer feelings are blunted, there is no human experience that can come to him afresh. The girl who is just beginning to live her life will be woefully disappointed in any lover of whom it can be said that he has "been a bit of a dog"; and she will find herself with but a very second-hand sort of husband if she takes all that is left of a man who has been the sport of other women's caprices. He will plead to be reformed, perhaps; but we know what that means. Once a dog, always a dog. No better epithet was ever chosen to describe a characteristic.

It is a source of weakness in women that they so often abase themselves before the undeserving. They will give themselves to men who have nothing adequate in the way of merit to offer them in return, who are not on the same plane with them, who are much lower morally, if not intellectually, in the scale of development. I would say to every girl: Do not be too easily pleased in a man; be fastidious, have a high ideal. That a man is agreeable is not reason enough for accepting him; he must have some higher recommendation. His power to make himself agreeable may be a mere trick, which he could not keep up in domestic life for want of the qualities of head and heart, such as truthfulness, unselfishness, refinement, sympathy, and affection, which go to make good manners genuine. It is easy to make sure of a man in this respect. If he talks about old people contemptuously, and pays them no kindly attention, and if he is not consistently polite to everybody, have nothing to do with him. His manners are a poor veneer which will not stand the slightest friction. Notice, too, if a man adores you for nothing but your beauty, and speaks of other women as if physical charm were all he cared for, and beware of him. That kind of man is a mere animal, who will disgust you in a month, and tire of you in a year – if you can stand him so long.

Men may be delightful at balls and parties, charming and indispensable

317

on all occasions of pleasure; but when it comes to business with them, why, be advised by them, and remember that business is business. It is startling, perhaps, to see marriage ranked as a business; but in one of its aspects it certainly is a business – the great business of life and everything depends upon how it is conducted. I am not using the word "business" in the sordid sense; there is a business of preparation for the most sacred occasions. The business of preparation for a happy marriage is to make sure of the character of the man you are marrying. Of all the tests to which ladies put their lovers long ago, the time-test seems to me to have been the most satisfactory; and for that the modern girl is happily situated. Now that marriage is no longer the only career open to her, she can take time to make her choice, and time to be sure of herself as well. She should never marry a man because she has a passion for him; she should wait until she is sure that she can love him. Passion and love are not the same thing. Passion is a transient state of feeling, a mere physical condition, which usually precedes but does not necessarily resolve itself into love. It is a form of intoxication which includes all the evils of other forms of intoxication – the loss of self-control, of the power to think, of dignity, of self-respect. Love is the higher state, the spiritual, which ennobles the one that loves.

. . . Unfortunately, there are only certain broad lines on which it is possible to indicate to girls in the abstract the sort of men they should accept or reject. The best adviser a girl can have is the person who inspires her with a sense of her own responsibility, and teaches her to be self-reliant; who says to her: You are here to enjoy life, and to help others to enjoy it; you have duties public as well as private, responsibilities, and rights. It is impossible to have nobody to please but yourself, and nobody to injure; every move you make [a]ffects other people. When you marry, you take the most serious step in life. Not only your own happiness, but the happiness of countless generations depends upon your discretion in the matter. Therefore study the subject, and do not allow yourself to be persuaded to marry until you know exactly what you are doing. And remember that marriage is not a four weeks' honeymoon – but a lifetime's comradeship, or a lifetime's antagonism.

1899

92. Margaret Oliphant
from *Autobiography*

With that year began a new life, one of which I cannot speak much. That was the burden and heat of the day: my anxieties were sometimes almost more than I could bear. I had gone through many trials, as I thought, and God knows many of them had been hard enough, but then I knew to the depths of my heart what the yoke was and how heavy. Many times I have woke in the morning feeling in myself that image of Shelley's "Prometheus," which in my youth I had vexed my husband by not appreciating, except in what seemed to me the picture rather than the poem, the man chained to the rock, with the vultures swooping down upon him. Their cruel beaks I seemed to feel in my heart the moment I awoke. Ah me, alas! pain ever, for ever, God alone knows what was the anguish of these years. And yet now I think of *ces beaux jours quand j'étais si malheureuse*, the moments of relief were so great and so sweet that they seemed compensation for the pain, – I remembered no more the anguish. Lately in my many sad musings it has been brought very clearly before my mind how often all the horrible tension, the dread, the anxiety which there are no words strong enough to describe, – which devoured me, but which I had to conceal often behind a smiling face, – would yield in a moment, in the twinkling of an eye, at the sound of a voice, at the first look, into an ineffable ease and the over-whelming happiness of relief from pain, which is, I think, our highest human sensation, higher and more exquisite than any positive enjoyment in this world. It used to sweep over me like a wave, sometimes when I opened a door, sometimes in a letter, – in all simple ways. I cannot explain, but if this should ever come to the eye of any woman in the passion and agony of motherhood, she will more or less understand. I was thinking lately, or rather, as sometimes happens, there was suddenly presented to my mind, like a suggestion from some one else, the recollection of these ineffable happinesses, and it seemed to me that it meant that which would be when one pushed through that last door and was met – oh, by what, by whom? – by instant relief. The wave of sudden ease and warmth and peace and joy. I felt, to tell the truth, that it was one of them who brought that to my mind, and I said to myself, "I will not want any explanation, I will not ask any question, – the first touch, the first look, will be enough, as of old, yet better than of old."

I do injustice to those whom I love above all things by speaking thus, and yet what can I say? My dearest, bright, delightful boy missed somehow his footing, how can I tell how? I often think that I had to do with it, as well as what people call inherited tendencies, and, alas! the perversity of youth, which he never outgrew. He had done everything too easily in the beginning of his boyish career, by natural impulse and that kind of genius which is so often deceptive in youth, and when he came to that stage in which hard work was necessary against the competition of the hard working, he could not believe how much more effort was necessary. Notwithstanding all distractions he took a second-class at Oxford, – a great disappointment, yet not disgraceful after all. And I will not say that, except at the first keen moment of pain, I was in any way bitterly disappointed. *Tout peut se réparer.* I always felt so to the end, and perhaps he thought I took it lightly, and that it did not so much matter. Then it was one of my foolish ways to take my own work very lightly, and not to let them know how hard pressed I was sometimes, so that he never, I am sure, was convinced how serious it was in that way, and certainly never was convinced that he could not, when the moment came, right himself and recover lost way. But only the moment, God bless him! did not come till God took it in His own hands. Another theory I have thought of with many tears lately. I had another foolish way of laughing at the superior people, the people who took themselves too seriously, – the boys of pretension, and all the strong intellectualisms. This gave him, perhaps, or helped him to form, a prejudice against the good and reading men, who have so many affectations, poor boys, and led him towards those so often inferior, all inferior to himself, who had the naturalness along with the folly of youth. Why should I try to explain? He went out of the world, leaving a love-song or two behind him and the little volume of "De Musset," of which much was so well done, and yet some so badly done, and nothing more to show for his life. And I to watch it all going on day by day and year by year!

My Cecco took the first steps in the same way; but, thanks be to God, righted himself and overcame – not in time enough to save his career at Oxford, but so as to be all that I had hoped, – always my very own, my dearest companion, choosing me before all others. What a companion he was, everybody who knew us knows: full of knowledge, full of humour – a most accomplished man, though to me always a boy. He did not make friends easily, and he had few; but those whom he had were very fond of him, and all our immediate surroundings looked up to him with an affectionate admiration which I cannot describe. "I don't know, but I will ask Cecco," was what we all said. He had not much more than emerged from the desert of temptation and trial, bringing balm and healing to me, when he fell ill. When his illness first was declared, it seemed to me that

my misery was more than I could bear. I remember that we all went to the
Holy Communion together the Sunday before we left for Pau, and that as
I went up to kneel at the altar I was so nearly overcome, that Cyril put his
hand on my arm and gripped it almost roughly to recall me to myself. And
then the whole world seemed to come back again into the sun after a time;
he got so much better, and the warm summer of the Queen's Jubilee year
seemed to complete what Pau had begun. And he passed his examination
for the British Museum, coming out first, and his life seemed now to be
ordered in a safe place – in the work he loved. Alas! Then Sir Andrew
Clark would not pass him, but other doctors gave the best of hopes. And
he did a great deal of good work, and finally went to the Royal Library
here; and we had many blinks of happiness, both in the winter on the
Riviera and at home. I cannot tell what he was to me – consulting me
about everything, desiring to have me with him, to walk with me and talk
to me, only put out of humour when I was drawn away or occupied by
other things. When he was absent he wrote to me every day. I never went
out but he was there to give me his arm. I seem to feel it now – the dear,
thin, but firm arm. In the last four years after Cyril was taken from us, we
were nearer and nearer. I can hear myself saying "Cecco and I." It was the
constant phrase. But all through he was getting weaker; and I knew it, and
tried not to know.

And now here I am all alone.

I cannot write any more.

1900

93. Sarah Grand
from *The Human Quest*

All through the ages human beings have made extraordinary efforts to be
miserable. They know themselves to be gregarious animals who are bound
to pass their lives in a community; they know that to a great extent their
happiness must depend upon each other; and yet by far the commonest
attitude of one human being to another is offensive. The art of happiness
is in its infancy, but everybody knows how to be disagreeable.

Take a very ordinary household in which there are father and mother, sons
and daughters, and servants. The happiness of that household obviously

depends upon the way in which those people conduct themselves, upon their attitudes towards each other; and also, of course, upon the way they do such duties as fall to their share. If there is a good tone in the house, if the master and mistress, the young people and the servants are all well-disciplined, and courtesy is the general attitude of one towards the other, if all are attempting to live up to some respectable ideal of life, that house-hold must go smoothly.

But, unfortunately, one of the rarest things in human intercourse is the desire to please – I mean the disinterested desire to please. Plenty of people do their best to be pleasant when it suits themselves, and fail, because the power to please comes of practice only. The power to please is the outcome of many qualities of head and heart which cannot be assumed. Charm of manner cannot be put on and taken off, like a garment, at will; it can only be the result of an habitual attitude. The woman in society, who cold-shoulders this person, will not be perfectly agreeable to that one, in spite of all her efforts, because the desire to please in her case is not ingrained in the character, it is not a radical grace, but a trumpery assumption. Were it radical, all would be benefited by it.

Beware of people who play the agreeable from self-interested motives only, for sooner or later they will play you false. 'One of the most abhorred things in nature', says Lavater, 'is the face that smiles abroad, and flashes fury when it returns to the lap of a tender, hapless family'. And, in quite another vein, a victim has defined 'Mock Turtle' as calling a husband *My Dear* in public and *You Brute* in private.

We find in the commonplaces of humorists the key to the major miseries of life. An astounding amount of misery may be concealed in a standing joke. The things in life that are oftenest jested about are our misery-making propensities; the sources of poverty, crime, and disease. The stock-in-trade of a comic paper, principle and interest, consists for the most part in three subjects only: upon these three subjects, the changes are rung with wearisome iteration.

There is, first of all, the mother-in-law. A great lawyer, being asked in court what was the ordinary punishment for bigamy, smartly answered: 'Two mothers-in-law'.

But how tired one is of that mother-in-law! What a happy release it would be if the law decreed that all the chestnuts on the subject should be burnt! She has been kept too long a jest, that mother-in-law, and has become an offence.

So also have the married people who practice more or less contemptible deceptions upon each other – particularly the husband who stays out late at night, amusing himself in a disreputable manner, and excuses himself to his wife on the plea that he had been detained by business. This man is a hardy perennial, I don't know why, for he is a dull fellow. But the sense of humour seems to suffer eclipse in the offices of the comic papers, it is worked to death, perhaps.

Then, thirdly, there is the ever-recurrent attempt to make merriment out of drunkenness. . . In a casual search for jests by way of illustration of this point, I could scarcely find any which were not drawn from the lowest stratum of society, which I take to be a hopeful sign that this unseemly subject for mirth has sunk so low in the world that we may shortly expect it to die out altogether.

Jests at the expense of marriage are many and significant. People, as a rule, marry in the hope of happiness. Marriage is the most perfect state, and were the conduct of it right, happiness must ensue. Yet a voice comes from the Colonies crying: 'Send us wives!' and a thousand Benedicks reply: 'Take ours!'

Then, on the other hand, 'I cannot live without him', the despairing wife exclaims: 'I cannot live without him – I haven't a penny!'

It is the economic position in marriage from which the wife is credited with suffering most; her own pennilessness and her husband's meannesses are the commonest subjects of jest; while the husband, honest man, is supposed to be most oppressed by a check upon his favourite vices.

❋ ❋ ❋ ❋

Happiness has many enemies bent upon its destruction; and idleness is one of them. Idleness is at the bottom of the gluttony, the sensuality, the drunkenness, and the base intrigue, which are compassing the destruction of a certain section of society today.

Those who would be happy will find it essentially necessary to cultivate regular habits of work and regular habits of play. Lives that are perfectly balanced throb between exertion and repose, between work and play. The mistake that people often make when they do work is that they do not play enough. We require pleasure as much for our mental health and strength as we require salt for our food. . . .

We hear little of the curse of labour nowadays, because we are inclined to call things by their right names, and labour was never a curse. The curse was in the conditions under which labour was done, the curse which human beings at their vilest impose upon each other when they treat the workers with less consideration than we treat our beasts of burden.

When the labourers were herded together indecently like cattle, in insanitary hovels on the rich man's estate; when the master goaded the mechanic to madness with the threat that meant starvation; when the conditions imposed even on little children were so cruel that we recoil now from the very description of them – the conditions that wrung from Elizabeth Barrett Browning that *Cry of the Children* which resounded throughout the whole civilised world; when those who worked were called contemptuously 'the common people' by those who ground them down and lived in luxury on their toil and saw them suffer and were not ashamed.

Idleness is at the bottom of that form of heart-ache which is peculiarly the lot of women; the heart-ache which comes of an empty, purposeless existence. I don't think any part of the misery that need not be is more acute than that which comes from the want of a settled purpose in life. When men have no regular occupation – nothing to do that they must do – if they do not make work for themselves they generally deteriorate.

Women who suffer from want of steady purpose in life, sometimes look forward to marriage in the hope that it will cure them; but when they marry they generally find, when the novelty of the change of position has worn off, that the old malady recurs. They still want something – they don't know what. In our own day we have seen them running hither and thither in search of this elusive something. Some of them think that if they had the suffrage *that* would cure them. Some of them look to cigarettes. These are the women who have not formed the habit of living for others, and rounding their day with many duties. They are not necessarily the idle and frivolous, but rather the untrained and undisciplined – those who try to skip the details of life in an attempt to arrive prematurely at the great events. They have no proper sense of proportion. A sense of proportion is what they should cultivate in order that their lives may be properly balanced.

❈ ❈ ❈ ❈

There are those who question our right to be happy. Whatever religion we may profess, I take it that we all acknowledge that there is good and evil, right and wrong. Those who question our right to be happy might satisfy their doubts with the certainty that the highest form of happiness is the noblest. If we analyse happiness, if we pick it to pieces, we shall find that it has been composed for us of various experiences: that it comes from a mixture of sensations and sentiments, every one of which is elevated, is of the kind which the best men and women in all ages have agreed to respect and admire. Fidelity in friendship; love in marriage; the bond of affection between parents and children; moral courage; courteous sympathy in social intercourse; devotion to duty; and absolute sincerity in every relation in life: these are the ingredients of which a happy life is made.

The sensations which make for happiness are all the sensations which, in their perfect form, make for the well-being of body and soul . . . I maintain that we do not make ourselves happy, but that we might and ought; that there is an art and duty of happiness which we should be practising from the cradle to the grave.

---

94. Ouida
from *The Ugliness of Modern Life*

Amongst even the most cultured classes few have really any sensibility to beauty. Not one in a thousand pauses in the hurried excitements of social life to note beauty in nature; to art there is accorded a passing attention because it is considered *chic* to do so; but all true sense of art must be lacking in a generation whose women wear the spoils of tropical birds, slain for them, on their heads and skirts, and whose men find their principal joy for nearly half the year in the slaughter of tame creatures, and bespatter with blood the white hellebore of their winter woods.

Beauty is daily more and more withdrawn from the general life of the people. Fidgety and repressive bye-laws tend to suppress that element of the picturesque which popular life by its liberties, and by its open-air pastimes and peddlings, created for itself. The police are everywhere, and street-life is joyless and colourless. Even within doors, in the houses of poor people, the things of daily usage have lost their old-world charm; the ugly sewing-machine has replaced the spinning-wheel, the cooking-range the spacious open hearth, the veneered machine-made furniture the solid home-made oaken chests and presses, a halfpenny newspaper the old family Bible; whilst out of doors the lads and lasses must not sing or dance, the dog must not play or bark, the chair must not stand out on the pavement, the bells must not ring their chimes, only the cyclist, or the automobilist, lord of all, may tear along and leave broken limbs and bruised flesh of others behind him at his pleasure.

If all feeling for grace and beauty were not extinguished in the mass of mankind at the actual moment, such a method of locomotion as cycling could never have found acceptance; no man or woman with the slightest æsthetic sense could assume the ludicrous position necessary for it. Nor would the auto-car with its stench of petroleum be tolerated for an instant in lanes and roads. Nor could modern dress be endured for a day were there any true sense of fitness, of harmony, and of colour extant in modern times. Even the great Catholic pageants are spoiled in their grouping and splendour by the dull crowds of ill-dressed, dingily clad townsfolk which drown their effect like a vast tide of muddy water rising over a garden of flowers. . . .

A gorgeous spectacle of the streets now, whether it be popular, military, or religious, is swamped in the mass of dull-coloured hues, and grotesquely ugly head-gear, common to the whole population of a city. Its effect may struggle as it will: it sinks under the preponderating mass as a butterfly will be beaten down under a dirty, drenching, city rain. . . .

Follow the architectural history of any city, and you find it during the last half-century the sorrowful record of a pitiful destruction. The great gardens are always the first thing sacrificed. They are swept away, and their places covered by brick and mortar with an incredible indifference. Fine houses, even when of recent construction, like the Pompeiian house of Prince Napoleon in Paris, are pulled down out of a mere speculative mania to build something else, or to cut a long, straight street as uninteresting and as unsuggestive as the boxwood protractor which lies on a surveyor's desk.

The greatest crime, or one of the greatest crimes (for there are others black as night), of which the nineteenth century has been guilty has been the driving of the people out of long familiar homes in the name and under the pretext of hygiene, but in fact for the enrichment of contractors, town councillors, and speculators of every kind. It began with Haussmann; it has continued in Paris, and everywhere else, with delirious haste ever since his time, as a burglar may drag a greybeard to his death. The modern ædiles with their court of ravenous parasites cannot understand, would not deign even to consider, the sorrow of a humble citizen driven out of a familiar little home with nooks and corners filled with memories and a roof-tree dear to generations. Go into an old street of any old city you will, and you will almost certainly find a delight for the eye in archway and ogive, in lintel and casement, in winding stair and leaning eave; in the wallflowers rooted in the steps, in the capsicum which has seeded itself between the stones, in the swallows' nests under the gargoyle, in the pots of basil and mignonette on the window-sills. But the modern street with its dreary monotony, its long and high blank spaces, its even surfaces where not a seed can cling or a bird can build, what will it say to your eyes or your heart? You will see its dull, pretentious uniformity repeated on either side of you down a mile-long vista, and you will curse it.

It is natural that the people shut up in these structures crave for drink, for nameless vices, for the brothel, the opium den, the cheap eating-house and gaming booth; anything, anywhere, to escape from the monotony which surrounds them and which leaves them no more charm in life than if they were rabbits shut up in a physiologist's experimenting cage, and fed on gin-soaked grains. No one in whom the æsthetic sense was really awakened could dwell in a manufacturing city, or indeed in any modern town. The 'flat,' whether in a 'first-class mansion,' or in a 'block' for the working man, would be more intolerable than a desert island to anyone with a sense of the true charm of life, or, one may add, any sensitiveness to the meaning of the word 'home'; that word which is to be found in every language, though the English people do not think so, and which is one of the sweetest and most eloquent in all tongues. The Americans attach extreme pride to the fact that their 'sky-scrapers' are so advanced that your horses and carriage can be carried up on a lift to the highest storey, and the nags, if it do not make them dizzy, can survey the city in a bird's-eye view. But even this supreme achievement of architects and engineers cannot lend to the cube, shared with a score of others, the charm, the idiosyncrasy, the meaning, the soul, which exhale from the smallest cottage where those who love dwell all alone, through whose lattices a candle shines as a star to the returning wanderer, and on whose lowly roof memory lies like a benediction.

According to the statistics of modern cities the mass of middle-class and labouring-class people change their lodgings or tenements every two or three years; three years is even an unusually long time of residence. What can a people who flit like this, continually, know of the real meaning of a home?

The same restlessness and dissatisfaction which make these classes change their residence so frequently, make the wealthier classes flit in another way, from continent to continent, from capital to capital, from one pleasure-place to another, from one house-party to another, from the yacht to the *rouge-et-noir* tables, from the bath to the coverside, from the homewoods to the antipodes, in an endless gyration which yields but little pleasure, but which they deem as necessary as cayenne pepper with their hot soup.

I believe that this monotony and lack of interest in the towns which they inhabit fatally affect the minds of those whose lot it is to go to and from the streets in continual toil, and produce in them fatigue, heaviness and gloom; what the scholar and the poet suffer from articulately and con- sciously, the people in general suffer from inarticulately and unconsciously. The gaiety of nations dies down as the beauty around them pales and passes. They know not what it is that affects them, but they are affected by it none the less, as a young child is hurt by the darkness, though it knows not what dark or light means.

Admit that the poorer people were ill-lodged in the Middle Ages, that the houses were ill-lit, undrained, with the gutter water splashing the thresh- old, and the eaves of the opposite houses so near that the sun could not penetrate into the street. All this may have been so, but around two-thirds of the town were gardens and fields, the neighbouring streets were full of painted shrines, metal lamps, gargoyles, pinnacles, balconies of hand-forged iron or hand-carved stone, solid doors, bronzed gates, richly-coloured frescoes; and the eyes and the hearts of the dwellers in them had where-withal to feed on with pleasure, not to speak of the constant stream of many-coloured costume and of varied pageant or procession which was for ever passing through them. Then in the niches there were figures; at the corners there were shrines; on the rivers there were beautiful carved bridges, of which examples are still left to our day in the Rialto and the Vecchio. There were barges with picture-illumined sails, and pleasure-galleys gay to the sights, and everywhere there were towers and spires, and crenulated walls, and the sculptured fronts of houses and churches and monasteries, and close at hand was the greenness of wood and meadow, the freshness of the unsullied country. Think only what that meant; no miles on miles of dreary suburban waste to travel; no pert aggressive modern villas to make day hateful; no underground railway stations and subways; no hissing steam, no grinding and shrieking cable trams; no hell of factory smoke and jerry-builders' lath and plaster; no glaring geometrical flower beds; but the natural country running, like a happy child laden with posies, right up to the walls of the town.

The cobbler or craftsman, who sat and worked in his doorway, and saw the whole vari-coloured life of a mediæval city pass by him, was a very different being to the modern mechanic, a cypher amongst hundreds, shut in a factory room, amongst the deafening noise of cogwheel and pistons. Even from a practical view of his position, his guilds were a very much finer organisation than modern trades-unions, and did far more for him in his body and his mind. In the exercise of his labour he could then be individual and original, he is now but one-thousandth part of an inch in a single tooth of a huge revolving cogwheel. The mediæval house might be in itself nothing more than a cover from bad weather, but all about it there was infinite variety; all life in the street or alley was richly coloured, even the gutter brawls were medleys of shining steel, and broken plumes, and many-coloured coats, and broidered badges, a whirl of bright hues, which sent a painter in joy to his palette.

Indoors there were the spinning-wheel, the copper vessels, the walnut presses, the settle by the wide warm hearth, the shrine upon the stairs which the women made fresh with flowers. The river was gay with blazoned hulls and painted sails; over its bridges the processions of church or guild passed like embroidered ribbons slowly unrolling; the workman had a busy life, and often a perilous life, but one still blent with leisure; and the mariners' tales of wondrous lands unknown lent to life that witchery of the remote and unattainable, that delightful thrill of mystery and awe, which to the omniscient and cynical modern soul seem childishness too trivial for words.

❋ ❋ ❋ ❋

There can be, I think, no hope that this loss of beauty will not be greater and greater with every year. The tendency, continually increasing in the modern character, is to regard beauty and nature with cynical indifference, stirred, when stirred at all, into active insolence; such insolence as was expressed in the joke of the Chicago citizen who called the plank-walks of his city 'the reafforesting of our town.' It is a temper not merely brutal, but with a leer in it which is more offensive than its brutality.

The great beauty which animal and bird life lends to the earth is doomed to lessen and disappear. The automatic vehicle will render the horse useless; and he will be considered too costly, and too slow, to be kept even as a gambling toy. The dog will have no place in a world which has no gratitude for such simple sincerity and faithful friendliness as he offers. When wool, and horn, and leather, and meat foods have been replaced by chemical inventions, cattle and sheep will have no more tolerance than the wild buffalo has had in the United States. What are now classed as big game will be exterminated in Asia and Africa, and already in Europe we are told that the pleasure it affords to people to kill them is the sole reason why stags, foxes, and gamebirds are allowed to exist and multiply under artificial protection. All the charm which the races of 'fur and feather' lend to the earth will be lost for ever; for a type destroyed can never be recalled.

Every invention of what is called science takes the human race farther and farther from nature, nearer and nearer to an artificial, unnatural and dependent state. One seems to hear the laugh of Goethe's Mephistopheles behind the hiss of steam; and in the tinkle of the electric bell there lurks the chuckle of glee with which the Tempter sees the human fools take as a boon and a triumph the fatal gifts he has given.

What shall it profit a man if he gain the whole world and lose his own soul? What shall it profit the world to put a girdle about its loins in forty minutes when it shall have become a desert of stone, a wilderness of streets, a treeless waste, a songless city, where man shall have destroyed all life except his own, and can hear no echo of his heart's pulsation save in the throb of an iron piston.

The engine tearing through the disembowelled mountain, the iron and steel houses towering against a polluted sky, the huge cylinders generating electricity and gas, the network of wires cutting across the poisoned air, the overgrown cities spreading like scurvy, devouring every green thing like locusts; haste instead of leisure, Neurasthenia instead of health, mania instead of sanity, egotism and terror instead of courage and generosity, these are the gifts which the modern mind creates for the world. It can chemically imitate every kind of food and drink, it can artificially produce every form of disease and suffering, it can carry death in a needle and annihilation in an odour, it can cross an ocean in five days, it can imprison the human voice in a box, it can make a dead man speak from a paper cylinder, it can transmit thoughts over hundreds of miles of wire, it can turn a handle and discharge scores of death-dealing tubes at one moment as easily as a child can play a tune on a barrel organ, it can pack death and horror up in a small tin case which has served for sardines or potted herrings, and leave it on a window-sill, and cause by it towers to fall, and palaces to crumble, and flames to upleap to heaven, and living men to change to calcined corpses; all this it can do, and much more. But it cannot give back to the earth, or to the soul, 'the sweet wild freshness of morning.' And when all is said of its great inventions and their marvels and mysteries, are they more marvellous or more mysterious than the changes of chrysalis and caterpillar and butterfly, or the rise of the giant oak from the tiny acorn, or the flight of swallow and nightingale over ocean and continent?

1901

95. Michael Field
from *Journal*

Our beloved Queen is dying. . . . Our Beloved, our Sovereign Lady. God knows I would die now, this moment, if so she might be spared in full brain power and strength of soul till she could pray that good prayer – "Lord, now lettest Thou Thy servant depart in peace." How pathetic that our people, as soon as they knew their Queen was seriously ill, took to singing everywhere the National Anthem.

How moving too that she is said to have asked Princess Beatrice if her people still loved her . . . that last doubt of the aged and dying if they are still loveable. Loveable! The young are loveable because the spring is still with them; the old are loveable because God in His Beauty is still with them.

For us the rest of our lives can be but sequels – the big volume is closed.

Le Matin says, "The end approaches. Europe waits. The world is about to breathe again." Yes, the world of small vermin; all lice and scorpions, all things of creeping filth and slime. Oh, that England may learn hatred! Hatred and fierceness and pitilessness – that we may all learn God-like hardship and simplicity and sternness with our children. At present they are taught to make money – not serve either their country or their God.

Our Great Queen is dead. I – I have no tears. She sweeps away with her into the locked land, my life, my youth, my breathing. I have no allegiance to any other. I love her. She is as simply my Queen, as God is my God. . . .

The great illusion of the Victorian age is the illusion of progress. Because at the beginning of her reign our streets were paved with cobbles – therefore . . .

Growth of suburbs, growth of education among the poor, an unmitigated evil – extension of franchise and growth of free trade, unmitigated disasters – the growth of Trades Unions, the damnation of the future.

The growth of sentimentality towards crime; and of science-craft (the priest-craft of the Victorian age), insidious, berotting influences.

The synthesis of the reign – Imperialism.

The great virtue to be cultivated – "hardiness" and the love of beauty. . . .

It is a pity the Queen is not consigned to her grave to-day. There is something impious in delaying burial. It is like painting age, it is a horrible reversal of dueness. The Gods infect the land – disgust at the unlawful pause breeds farce.

NOTES

1. Text: *The Girlhood of Queen Victoria: A Selection from Her Majesty's Diaries between the Years 1832 and 1840*, ed. Viscount Esher (2 vols, Murray, London, 1912), vol. i pp. 195–6
   Archbishop of Canterbury] William Howley (1766–1848)
   Lord Conyngham] Francis C, Second Marquis Conyngham (1797–1876)
2. Text: *Phantasmion* (W. Pickering, London, 1837) p. 68
3, 4. Text: *Ethel Churchill; or, The Two Brides* (2 vols, Colburn, London, 1837), vol. ii pp. 117, 157
5. Text: *Winter Studies and Summer Rambles in Canada* (3 vols, Saunders & Otley, London, 1838), vol. i pp. 82–7, 112–18, vol. ii pp. 267–70; vol. iii pp. 197–200, 298–312
   Context: AJ had travelled to Canada for an attempted (but abortive) reconciliation with her husband
   I am translated . . . ass's head] alludes to the scene in *A Midsummer Night's Dream* (III. i. 108–12) in which Bottom is given an ass's head by Puck
   Lethe] the river of forgetfulness (Gr myth)
   Fanny Butler] Frances Anne Kemble, AJ's friend, who had visited the Falls in 1833 (see(63))
6. Text: *Retrospect of Western Travel* (3 vols, Saunders & Otley, London, 1838), vol. i pp. 228–33, vol. ii pp. 52–55
   a story against slavery] 'Demerara', in HM's *Illustrations of Political Economy* vol. ii (1834)
7. Text: *Caroline Clive: From the Diary and Family Papers of Mrs Archer Clive (1801–1873)*, ed Mary Clive (Bodley Head, London, 1949), pp. 70–1
   Context: CC had been visiting France, and had embarked from St Malo for Jersey
   Garçon . . . bassin] Boy, another basin
   'ce que vous appelez'] what you call
8. Text: as (1), vol. ii pp. 268–9
   'das Leben . . . zubringen'] 'to spend my life with you'
9. Text: *The Poetical Works of Percy Bysshe Shelley* (2nd edn, Moxon, London, 1840) pp. vii–x, 301–2, 328
   Obstacles] PBS's father, Sir Timothy S, had made it a condition of the allowance that he paid for MS's son, Percy Florence (b. 1819) that MS should not publish an edition of PBS's poems.

331

errors of action] presumably the elopement of PBS with MS, which was followed not long after by the suicide of his wife Harriet

$τὸ \ldots καλὸν$] the good and the beautiful

ameliorations . . . country] the Reform Bill of 1832 extended the franchise to all propertied adult males

Arno] river flowing through central Italy

Maremma] marshy region near the sea

'Ma va per la vita!'] 'But go for life!'

'I love . . . billows'] PBS, *Julian and Maddolo* (1818) 11.14–19

He spent . . .] the last part of MS's account is reprinted from her edition of Shelley's *Posthumous Poems* (1824)

Williams] Edward W, drowned with Shelley

10. text: as (1) vol. ii pp. 818–21

    Lord Melbourne] William Lamb, Viscount Melbourne (1779–1848), the Prime Minister

11. Text: *Woman and her Master* (Colburn, London, 1840) pp. 8–18

    femme sole . . . couverte] single woman . . . married woman

12. Text: *The Women of England, their Social Duties and Domestic Habits* (2nd edn, Fisher, London, 1842) pp. 53, 145–6, 166–8, 344–7

13. Text: as (7) pp. 147–9

    Archer] CC's husband

14. Text: as (7) p. 167

15. Text: *Poems* (2 vols, Moxon, London, 1844) vol. ii, pp. 219–222

    Context: See Biographical Note on Letitia Landon (and see 41)

16. Text: *Quarterly Review* lxxvi, No cli, pp. 98–103, 136–7

    our own] like many women journalists of the period writing anonymously, ER adopts a male persona

    ladies . . . themselves] an ironic reference to the usual disclaimer that the work was published at the urging of friends or family

17. Text: as (7) p. 223

    Mr Lockhart] John Gibson Lockhart (1794–1854), best known for his biography of Walter Scott (1838)

    Mr Kinglake . . . *Eothen*] Alexander William Kinglake (1809–91), military historian; his *Eothen* (1844) describes an Eastern tour

    Lady Duff Gordon] Lady Lucie Duff-Gordon (1821–69), author and translator. She and her husband kept open house for literary celebrities in London

    guipure] lace

    Mrs Norton] for Caroline N, see (28) and Biographical Note

18, 19. Text: *Poems by Currer, Ellis, and Acton Bell* (Aylott & Jones, London, 1846) pp. 107–110, 31–2

20. Text: *Quarterly Review* vol. lxxxii, no. clxiv (Dec 1847–Mar 1848) pp. 432–4, 435–7

    Coleridge] Samuel Taylor C (1772–1834), SC's father

    Southey] Robert S (1774–1843), SC's uncle

21. Text: *Quarterly Review* vol. lxxxiv, no. clxvii (Dec 1848–Mar 1849) pp. 162–3, 166–7, 172–7

little Becky] heroine of W. M. Thackeray's *Vanity Fair* (1847)

the authorship] CB published the novel under the pseudonym Currer Bell

métier] job, business (i.e. cookery)

beau idéal] perfect excellence

22.   Text: *Sartain's Union Magazine* v (July 1849); reprinted in *Cranford*, World's Classics (Oxford University Press, Oxford, 1971) pp. 161–8

The town . . . resided] EG was brought up in Knutsford, Cheshire

ci-devant] former

Mrs Grundy] archetypal narrow-minded person

Lilliputian] tiny (from Swift's *Gulliver's Travels*, in which the land of Lilliput has minute inhabitants) (see also below)

calash and pattens] hooped hood and clogs

Preference] card game

comme il faut] proper

haute volée] high rank

Betty or Molly] generic names of housemaids

post-chaise] coach for transporting mail and passengers

Adam . . . weather-glass] form of barometer with two figures, one of which comes out to forecast rain and the other to forecast sun

dram-shop] public house

brobdignagian] huge (from Brobdignag, land visited by Gulliver, where the inhabitants were enormous)

23.   Text: *Westminister Review* 52 (October 1849–January 1850) pp. 380–3, 396–7, 406–7

a movement] the so-called 'Oxford Movement', a revival of Anglo-Catholicism centred in Oxford in the 1830s and 40s

'obstinate questionings'] Wordsworth, 'Ode: Intimations of Immortality' (1807) 1.142

Micah] Old Testament prophet

Carlyle . . . *Resartus*] Thomas C (1795–1881); *Sartor Resartus* (1833–4) is a semi-autobiographical account of a spiritual crisis

'dies irae'] 'day of wrath'

'Lux . . . ei'] 'they will be lit with perpetual light'

24.   Text: *Eliza Cook's Journal*, vol. i no. 12 (July 21, 1849) pp. 177–9

25.   Text: 'Editor's Preface', Emily Brontë, *Wuthering Heights* (Smith, Elder, 1850) pp. xvii–xxiv

Ellis Bell] pseudonym of Emily Brontë

'a horror . . . darkness'] *Genesis* 15:12

Lascar] East Indian Sailor

Afreet] powerful evil demon (Arab myth)

'to harrow . . . furrow'] *Job* 39:10

'laughs . . . driver'] *Job* 39:7

Pluto . . . Jove] ruler of the underworld and king of the gods (Greek and Roman myth)

Tisiphone . . . Psyche] one of the Furies and goddess of the soul (Greek myth)

26.   Text: *Poems* (2 vols, Chapman & Hall, London, 1850) vol. ii p. 451

27. Text: *A Brief Summary in Plain Language of the most important Laws Concerning Women* (Chapman, London, 1854) pp. 13–15, 17–18

28. Text: *English Laws for Women in the Nineteenth Century* (printed for private circulation, London, 1854) pp. 1–3, 24–7, 31–7, 41–3, 49–53
     my grandfather] Richard Brinsley Sheridan (1751–1816), playwright and, from 1780, Whig politician
     my first poem] *The Sorrows of Rosalie* (1829)
     Miss Vaughan] Norton's mistress
     the trial] Norton had unsuccessfully brought an action for adultery against CN's friend Lord Melbourne

29. Text: *Leader* vol. vi (13 October 1855) pp. 988–9
     Context: This essay appeared as a review of *Woman in the Nineteenth Century* (1855) by the American feminist Margaret Fuller (1810–50). Mary Wollstonecraft (1759–97), British feminist writer, published her *Vindication of the Rights of Woman* in 1792.

30. Text: *Blackwood's* 77 (May 1855) pp. 554–5, 557–9, 568
     Place aux dames!] Make way for the women!
     Jacob . . . Rachel] *Genesis* 29–35
     Hogarth men] as depicted in the works of the painter and engraver William Hogarth (1697–1764) who specialised in depicting the seamier side of life
     'Rights of Woman'] Mary Wollstonecraft, *Vindication of the Rights of Woman* (1792)
     Sebastopol] port on the Black Sea, besieged for eleven months (1854–5) during the Crimean War before being captured and destroyed by British, French and Turkish forces

31. Text: Mrs A. Ireland, *Life of Jane Welsh Carlyle* (Chatto and Windus, London, 1891) pp. 235–242
     Context: The troubled marriage of the Carlyles had worsened owing to TC's (apparently non-sexual) involvement with Lady Harriet Ashburton, and JWC was unwell and unhappy. Her 'Budget' was handed to TC on 12 February 1855 and, according to her biographer: 'Carlyle received it with roars of laughter and promptly complied with the modest demands made on him. "Excellent", he says, "my dear, clever Goody; thriftiest, wittiest and cleverest of women". He did not feel the hidden bitterness of the whole thing' (p. 235)
     Femme Incomprise] a woman misunderstood, not appreciated

32. Text: *Westminster Review*, lxvi (October 1856) pp. 442–61
     mauvais moments] bad moments
     Belgravia] fashionable area of London
     très vrai] very true
     Laura Gay] anonymous novel (1856)
     noumenon] intuited essence
     'Moi . . . flute'] 'I play the flute too'

33. Text: *The Life of Charlotte Brontë* (2 vols, Smith, Elder, London, 1857) vol. i pp. 51–2, 99–100, 308–11, 330–3; vol. ii pp. 36–7, 83–4
     Shirley] eponymous heroine of CB's novel (1849)
     Tabby] servant to the Brontës

the woman . . . intrigued] Lydia Robinson. EG was forced to revise this passage out of the second edition

34.   Text: *Athenaeum* No. 1635, 26 February 1859, p. 284

'To see . . . see us'] Robert Burns, 'To a Louse'

Sancho Panza] loyal servant to Don Quixote in Cervantes' novel (1605, 1616)

35.   Text: *Suggestions for Thought to the Searchers after Truth among the Artizans of England* (3 vols, Eyre and Spottiswood, London, 1860), vol. ii, 'Cassandra', Section IV

36.   Text: *Beeton's Book of Household Management*, (Beeton, London, 1861) pp. 1, 1001–5, 1092

37.   Text: *Legends and Lyrics* (2nd series, Bell and Daldy, London, 1861) pp. 119–20

38.   Text: *More Leaves from the Journal of a Life in the Highlands* (4th edn, Smith, Elder, London, 1884) pp. 1–2

Context: Albert had died on 14 December 1861

Bertie] the Prince of Wales, later Edward VII (1841–1910)

39.   Text: *Goblin Market and Other Poems* (Macmillan, London, 1862) pp. 110–11

40.   Text: *The Diaries of Hannah Cullwick, Victorian Maidservant*, ed. Liz Stanley, Virago, London, 1984, pp. 124–6, 138–9

Massa] Arthur Munby (see Biographical Note on HC)

chains and padlocks] see Biographical Note on HC

41.   Text: *Victoria Magazine* I (1863) pp. 40–1

Context: See Biographical Note on Letitia Landon and cf (15) from which CR misquotes 1.39 as her epitaph)

scathe] injury

42.   Text: *English Women of Letters* (2 vols, Hurst & Blackett, London, 1863) vol. ii pp. 188–93, 232–6

Aphra Behn] playwright, poet, novelist (1640–1689). Her *Oroonoko; or the Royal Slave* (1688) referred to below is often regarded as the first anti-slavery fiction

Uncle Tom's Cabin] anti-slavery novel (1852) by Harriet Beecher Stowe

Mademoiselle de Scudéry] Madeleine de Scudéry (1607–91), author of fashionable and influential French romances

43.   Text: *Journal of a Residence on a Georgian Plantation* (Longman, Green, Longman, Roberts & Green, London, 1863) pp. 31–8, 121–131, 289–93

Context: In 1838 FAK, with her two young daughters, accompanied her husband on a visit to his plantation in Georgia. Her pro-abolitionist views were greatly intensified by what she found there, and this journal, addressed to her friend Elizabeth Dwight Sedgwick, was the result. In deference to her husband's family it remained in manuscript until 1863 when FAK, by now divorced, decided to publish it in support of the movement for emancipation during the American Civil War

Oh God . . . them!] echoes the words of Jesus on the cross (*Matthew* 27.45, *Mark* 15.34), themselves an echo of *Psalms* 22.1

Mr –] Pierce Butler, FAK's husband

M–] Margery O'Brien, FAK's nursemaid

vain appeals] Butler had forbidden FAK to plead on behalf of the slaves

my past profession] before her marriage FAK had been a hugely successful actress

immondezzio] rubbish

femme couverte] legal term for a married woman

44.   Text: *Cornhill Magazine*, vol. viii (December 1863) pp. 733–7

Mrs Siddons] FAK's aunt Sarah Siddons (1755–1831), the most celebrated actress of her day

Garrick] David Garrick (1717–1779), celebrated actor and producer

garble . . . the masterpieces] like many eighteenth-century producers, Garrick rewrote Shakespeare's plays to suit the supposed taste of the times

Kean] Edmund Kean (1787–1833) celebrated actor

Mdlle Rachel] Élisa Félix R (1820–58), famous French tragedienne

Pasta] Guidotta P (1798–1865), leading Italian opera singer

'*Vous avez . . . senti*'] 'You have made a great study of antiquity' 'I have felt it greatly'

The younger . . . combine] unidentified

45.   Text: *The Autobiography and Letters of Mrs M. O. Oliphant*, ed. Mrs Harry Coghill (Blackwood, Edinburgh, 1899) pp. 92–4

Context: MO's beloved only daughter Maggie, aged nine, died of scarlet fever on a family holiday in Rome

The Principal] John Tulloch (1823–86)

'In Memoriam'] *In Memoriam AHH* (begun in 1833, published 1850), Tennyson's elegy on his friend Arthur Hallam, who died at the age of 22. The poem deals with questions of faith and doubt in the face of the death of a loved one

46.   Text: *Autobiography, Poems and Songs* (William Love, Glasgow, 1867) pp. 4–15

'Dainty Davie'] EJ's dog

the suffering . . . tormentor] presumably sexual abuse by her stepfather, the 'mystery of my life' referred to several times in the account

When . . . to die] Oliver Goldsmith, *The Vicar of Wakefield* (1764) p. 29

47.   Text: as (46) pp. 44–5

Context: see (46) and Biographical Note on EJ

48.   Text: 'La Femme Passée', *Saturday Review* 26.663 (11 July 1868) pp. 49–50

raison d'être] reason for living

beauté du diable] devilish beauty

la femme passée] the woman who is 'past it'

et ridicule] and ridiculous

quid pro quo] something given in compensation

49.   Text: *The Education and Employment of Women* (Brackell, Liverpool, 1868) pp. 3–9, 17–18, 22–4, 25–6

Bethlehem Hospital] mental asylum in London (popularly known as Bedlam)

'A wall . . . there'] unidentified

'**tripos'ed**'] having passed the honours degree examination at Cambridge University

50.   **I am . . . serveth**'] *Luke* 22: 27

Text: Josephine Butler: *An Appeal to the People of England, on the Recognition and Superintendence of Prostitution by Governments. By an English Mother* (Banks, Nottingham, n.d., [1869]), pp. 4–5, 14–15

Context: The Contagious Diseases Acts of 1866 and 1869 proposed to deal with the problem of venereal disease by enforcing prostitutes to submit to physical examinations, seen by JB as equivalent to rape

51.   Text: *Edinburgh Review* cclxvi (October 1869) pp. 572–4, 582–9, 595–9

52.   Text: as (40) pp. 152–3

Massa] see note to (40)

such a little boy] i.e. not a strong man for heavy work

Adam Bede] novel (1859) by George Eliot

53.   Text: *The Life of Frances Power Cobbe. By Herself* (2 vols, Bentley, London, 1894), vol. ii, pp. 105–6

Context: Addressed to Elizabeth Garrett Anderson (1836–1913), the pioneering woman physician, on the occasion of her marriage to J. G. S. Anderson, the poem wittily parodies the earlier 'Excelsior' by Henry Wadsworth Longfellow. As FPC remarks, EGA 'occupied a particularly prominent place in our eyes, succeeding as she did in obtaining her medical degree in Paris, and afterwards a seat on the London School Board, which last was quite a new kind of elevation for women' (p. 105). FPC's fears that marriage would put an end to her career proved unfounded.

54.   Text: *Medical Women: Two Essays* (Oliphant, Edinburgh; Hamilton Adams, London, 1872) pp. 7–11, 34–40, 49a–50, 68–70

David's words] see *Psalms* 35:22

'**To the pure . . . pure**'] *Titus* 1.15

'***Honi . . . pense***'] 'evil be to him who evil thinks'

my own experience as a medical student] SJB had studied medicine in Edinburgh, 1869–72 (see Biographical Note)

but two women] Elizabeth Garrett Anderson (see (53)) and Elizabeth Blackwell (1821–1910), who qualified as a doctor in New York City but returned to her native England in 1869 and co-founded the London School of Medicine for Women with SJB in 1874

55.   Text: *Poems by the Author of John Halifax, Gentleman* (Samson and Low, Marston, Low & Searle, London, 1872) pp. 180–3

Tantalus-cup] King Tantalus was punished by perpetual close proximity to water which receded as he tried to drink it (Greek myth)

Galvanic] produced by electric shock

56.   Text: *Memoir and Letters of Sara Coleridge*, ed. E. Coleridge (2 vols, Henry King, London, 1873) vol. i, pp. 17–21, 24–6

Allan Bank] home of William Wordsworth and his family between 1808 and 1811

Dorothy] known as Dora (1804–47)

domesticated . . . Wordsworths] Coleridge had separated from SC's mother in 1807

John] Wordsworth's elder son (1803–75)

Mr De Quincey] Thomas De Quincey, essayist (1785–1859)

my uncle Southey] Robert Southey (1774–1843) poet, married to SC's aunt

Sarah Hutchinson] Coleridge had fallen in love with SH in 1799

Edith] Edith Southey (b.1804), SC's first cousin

57. Text: as (40) pp. 271–3

Context: HC and Munby were now married (see Biographical Note on HC)

Massa] See note to (40)

whose face . . . fire] HC believed she had had a vision of Munby several years before their first meeting

58. Text: *Gerard's Monument and Other Poems* (Trübner, London, 1873) p. 181

59. Text: *Fraser's Magazine*, December 1874, pp. 763–766

cornets] military musicians

the Dundreary pattern] resembling Lord Dundreary, a foolish aristocrat in T. Taylor's comedy *Our American Cousin* (1858)

primogeniture] law whereby property passed to the eldest son

60. Text: *The Hawaiian Archipelago: Six Months among the Palm Groves, Coral Reefs and Volcanoes of the Sandwich Islands* (John Murray, London, 1875) pp. 138–43, 162–74

Context: IB (wearing a Hawaiian riding costume with divided skirt and riding astride on a Mexican saddle) was travelling through the mountains of Hawaii accompanied by a male guide, Kaluna, and a native female companion, Deborah

a-a] jagged impassable rock

pali] precipice

kalo] arum esculentum

poi] national Hawaiian dish, a fermented pasted made from *kalo* root;

ti] tree of genus *cordyline terminalis*

the Moriston] river feeding Niagara Falls

61. Text: *Autobiography* (2 vols, Smith, Elder, London, 1877), vol. i, pp. 18–20, 62–5, 117–20, 131–3, 400–2, vol. ii, pp. 433–5

62. Text: *Why Women Desire the Franchise* (National Society for Women's Suffrage, London, 1877) pp. 1–4

the last Reform Bill] the Reform Act of 1867 extended the franchise to all male householders satisfying a one-year residential qualification

Miss Somerville] Mary Somerville (1780–1872), scientific writer

Lady Coutts] Angela Burdett-Coutts (1814–1906), philanthropist, used her large inheritance to found a shelter for fallen women and build model homes. She was created Baroness in 1871

Belgravian] inhabitant of Belgravia, a fashionable district of London

63. Text: *Record of a Girlhood* (3 vols, Bentley, London, 1878) vol. iii pp. 309–312

Context: FAK visited Niagara on her American tour of 1833, but this account remained unpublished until her 1878 momoirs

Mr Trelawney] FAK and her father had been joined on their travels by

Edward Trelawney (1792–1881), author and friend of the Shelleys, whom they had met in New York

perfect love . . . fear] I *John* 4.18

64. Text: *Contemporary Review*, vol. xxxii (April, 1878), pp. 55–87

Context: FPC's article appeals for assault to be made a ground for legal separation

'trop . . . service'] 'only too happy to be of service'

imbroglio] confusion

au désespoir] deeply sorry (literally 'in despair')

père de famille] father of a family

ultima ratio] final appeal

Afreet] powerful evil demon (Arab myth)

'puddlers'] iron-foundry workers

65. Text: *A Lady's Life in the Rocky Mountains* (Murray, London, 1879) pp. 250–7, 259–61, 266–7, 272–8

Context: In November, after three months in the Colorado Rockies, IB found herself in severe financial straits: the banks in Denver had suspended payment and she was owed $100 by an acquaintance. With only 26 cents to her name, she returned to a cabin inhabited by two young men in the remote valley of Estes Park, 'where I can live without ready money', to sit out the increasingly severe weather and await some financial improvement.

Edwards] owner of the cabin

Birdie] IB's trusty and much-loved horse

write to you] IB's book is in the form of letters to her sister

'Jim's' mood] IB had befriended the notorious Mountain Man 'Mountain Jim' Nugent, attractive, well-born and cultivated but given to black moods related to alcoholism

the former one] IB had been shocked and fascinated by some of Nugent's revelations about his past

unchinked] made from uncut logs, leaving gaps for the wind and snow to come in

articular] needle-shaped

the spectre of the Brocken] atmospheric phenomenon in which the observer's shadow appears huge against the clouds

'Ring'] Nugent's dog

Doré] Gustave Doré (1832–83), French artist celebrated for his grotesque illustrations

66. Text: *Poems and Music* (Kegan Paul, London, 1880) p. 27

67. Text: *A Pageant and Other Poems* (Macmillan, London, 1881) p. 45

68. Text: *The Nineteenth Century*, vol. ix no. li (May 1881) pp. 782–6

Context: Written a few months after GE's death (December 1880). For ES's feelings for GE, see Biographical Note on ES

Mr Lewes] George Henry Lewes (1817–78), GE's common-law husband

Middlemarch] novel by GE (1871–2)

Life of Goethe] published 1855

esse is *percipi*] existence is as it is perceived

par-dessus le marché] above the crowd

deus ex machina] a god introduced into a play by mechanical means to resolve the plot

Meliorist] one who hopes for human betterment

69. Text: *Songs and Sonnets of Springtime* (Kegan Paul, London, 1881) pp. 81–4

70. Text: *Poems* (Satchell, London, 1881) pp. 49–54

71. Text: *Lays and Legends* (Longmans, Green, London, 1886) pp. 82–3

72. Text: *The World and its Gods* (Freethought Publishing, London, 1886) pp. 3–4, 13–19, 24

73. Text: *Dreams to Sell* (Longmans, Green, London, 1887) pp. 38–9

    plaque] small plaster cast made as a hobby

    Newton . . . Spenser] Isaac Newton (1643–1727), philosopher and scientist; Edmund Spenser (?1552–99), poet

74. *Songs, Ballads, and a Garden Play* (Fisher Unwin, London, 1888) p. 36

75. Text: *The Nineteenth Century* v.25 (May 1889) pp. 667–71

    Bryant and May] match-factory where the female workers, organised by Annie Besant, went on strike for fair wages in 1888

76. Text: *Long Ago* (Bell, London, 1889) pp. 95–6

77. Text: *The Fortnightly Review*, vol. xlvii n.s. (March 1890) pp. 311–15, 319–25

    Mrs Grundy] archetypal narrow-minded person

    Shylock] grasping money-lender in Shakespeare's *Merchant of Venice*

78. Text: *The Religion of Humanity* (Percival, London, 1890) pp. 7–8

79. Text: *Work and Days: From the Journal of Michael Field*, ed. T and D. C. Sturge Moore (Murray, London, 1933) pp. 44–7, 49–54, 62–4

    Nierstein . . . 'petits pains'] German white wine and small bread rolls

    'grippe'] form of influenza

    Sim] Katherine (see Biographical Note)

    '*Brot, Brot!*'] 'bread, bread'

    new Orlando] see *As You Like It* II. vii. 88ff

    Tannhäuser] opera by Wagner

    Pussie] Edith (see Biographical Note)

    Schwester] the nurse

    '*Ein Wunsch?*'] a desire?

    '*Ich bin so hungrig*'] 'I am so hungry'

    '*Danke . . .*'] thank you

    '*Eine mächtige Liebe*'] 'a powerful love'

80. Text: *Notes on Men, Women and Books* (Ward & Downey, London, 1891) pp. 171–7, 179

    Romola . . . Daniel Deronda . . . Middlemarch] novels by GE, 1863, 1876, 1871

    Bulwer and Disraeli] Edward Bulwer-Lytton (1803–73), novelist and statesman; Benjamin Disraeli (1804–1881) novelist and later Prime Minister

    we leave the reader . . .] given JW's admitted boredom with the novel, there seems a strong possibility that she had not read beyond the second volume (of three)

81.　Text: *A Girl in the Karpathians* (2nd edn, Philip, London, 1891) pp. 5–11, 16–19, 52–4, 101–3, 107–10

Context: the Carpathian mountains, in Central Europe, form a semi-circle through Czechoslovakia, Poland (where MMD began her journey), the USSR and Romania

'*Thut mir den Gefallen und gehut nur weiter?*'] 'Will you do me a favour and just walk on?'

'Keating'] patent flea powder

'*Eine Engländerin*'] an Englishwoman

Nebuchadnezzar] king of Babylon, 605–562 BC

82.　Text: *Alfred Lord Tennyson and his Friends*, ed. H. H. Hay Cameron (Fisher & Unwin, London, 1893) pp. 12–14

Context: Julia Margaret Cameron (1815–79), celebrated photographer and friend of Tennyson and his circle. Her niece Julia Duckworth (the mother of Virginia Woolf) was the second wife of Leslie Stephen, whose first wife 'Minny' (d. 1875) was ATR's sister

Paladin] knightly champion

frisettes] artificial curly fringes worn on the forehead

the Island] the Isle of Wight, where JMC had a house

William Morris] (1834–96), poet, painter, craftsman and designer

Abou ben Adhem] eponymous hero of a poem by Leigh Hunt

the Pied Piper] in the poem (1842) by Browning, based on a German legend, the piper lures away the children of Hamelin after the mayor refuses to honour his promise of payment. ATR quotes 11.114–15 below.

83.　Text: *Ourselves: Essays on Women*, 2nd edn (Chatto and Windus, London, 1893) pp. 247–51, 254–7

chimeras, Medusas] fabulous mythical beasts

our latest Reform Bill] The Reform Act of 1884 in which suffrage was extended to all male members of households of voting age

84.　Text: as (79)

Context: Written after the opening night of MF's play *A Question of Memory*

85.　Text: *Social Studies* (Ward and Downey, London, 1893) pp. 30–52

Platonic symposium] intense philosophical discussion between Plato and his followers

Tranteverine] Italian peasant woman

'Declined with thanks'] stock phrase of rejection of a literary manuscript

trente ans] thirty years

salons] fashionable gatherings of literary people

Orphic] enchanting, melodious (from Orpheus, legendary poet and lyre-player [Greek myth])

Hebe] goddess of youth and Spring (Greek myth)

ennui] boredom

great poet . . . poetess] Robert and Elizabeth Barrett Browning, whose elopement and marriage had already become a romantic legend

Mrs Carlyle] see (31) and Biographical Note on JWC

celebrated treatise] Milton, *The Doctrine and Discipline of Divorce* (1643)

86. Text: *Views and Opinions* (Methuen, London, 1895) pp. 205, 208–13, 219–22

mantua-makers] dressmakers

ateliers] artists' studios

gralloched] disembowelled

fournisseurs] tradesmen

the author of *Aurora Leigh*] Elizabeth Barrett Browning

87. Text: *Chiefly a Dialogue Concerning Some Difficulties of a Dunce* (Freedom Office, London, 1895) p. 15

'To him . . . heaven'] paraphrases *Matthew* 25:29

'Sweat . . . bread'] cf *Genesis* 3:19

Mammon] false god of riches and greed (*New Testament*)

88. Text: *Blackwood's*, January 1896, pp. 136–142

parti pris] set prejudice

Mr Hardy and Mr Grant Allen] Thomas Hardy's *Jude the Obscure* and Grant Allen's *The Woman Who Did* (both 1895) portray 'advanced' New Women

Duessa . . . The Red Cross Knight] characters in Edmund Spenser, *The Faerie Queen*, Book One (1590)

Miss Ménie Muriel Dowie] see (81) and Biographical Note on MMD

the most shameful portions] Hardy was forced to censure *Jude the Obscure* for magazine publication the America

Tess] *Tess of the D'Urbervilles: A Pure Woman* (1891)

débordement] bursting forth

Zola] Émile Zola (1840–1902), French novelist whose works graphically depict human vices and misery

raisonneuse] logician

89, 90. Text: *Fancy's Following* (Daniel, Oxford, 1896) pp. 1, 4

91. Text: *The Modern Man and Maid* (Marshall, London, 1898) pp. 11–24, 75–96

rise up . . . blessed] cf. *Proverbs* 31.28

92. Text: as (45) pp. 146–50

With that year . . . much] In 1875 MO's elder son Cyril (b. 1856) had begun the alcoholism which destroyed his promising academic career

ces beaux . . . malheureuse] 'those beautiful days when I was so unhappy' (adapted from a poem by Claude de Rulhière (1735–91))

Tout . . . réparer] Everything can be remedied

God . . . own hands] Cyril died in November 1890

volume of 'De Musset'] presumably a translation of the poems of Alfred De Musset (1810–57) which remained unpublished

My Cecco] nickname of MO's second surviving son Francis (b. 1859)

Pau] mountain town in South-West France where MO had taken Cecco in search of health

Sir Andrew Clark] (1826–93), celebrated physician

And now... any more] MO ended her autobiography with this passage, written shortly after Cecco's death in October 1894

93. Text: *The Human Quest: Being Some Thoughts in Contribution to the Subject of the Art of Happiness* (Heinemann, London, 1900) pp. 10–13, 25–8, 38–9

Lavater] J. K. Lavater (1741–1801), Swiss theologian and author. SG quotes his *Aphorisms on Man*

Benedicks] in *Much Ado About Nothing*, Benedick declares against marriage

Cry of the Children] EBB's poem (1843) against child labour

94. Text: *Critical Studies* (Unwin, London, 1900) pp. 215–23, 235–7

Haussmann] George, Baron H. (1809–91), town planner responsible for improving Paris

ædiles] municipal architects

ogive] diagonal rib of a vault

capsicum] plant bearing the sweet pepper

rouge-et-noir] roulette

crenulated] notched or battlemented

Goethe's Mephistopheles] the devil in *Faust* (1808, 1832) by J. W. von Goethe

What shall . . . soul?] *Mark* 8.36

girdle . . . forty minutes] *Midsummer Night's Dream* II. i. 174–5

Neurasthenia] neurosis

'the sweet . . . morning'] unidentified

95. Text: as (79)

BIOGRAPHICAL NOTES

Items marked with an asterisk can be found in this anthology

Beeton, Isabella Mary, née Mayson (1836–1865)
Educated in London and later in Heidelberg, she was the eldest of a family of four sisters, four step-siblings and thirteen half-siblings. After her marriage in 1856 to Samuel Orchart Beeton, publisher, she began contributing articles to various of the periodicals which he owned. These included the *Englishwoman's Domestic Magazine*, for which she became first the fashion correspondent and later the editor, the *Young Englishwoman*, and the *Queen*. Her *Book of Household Management*, aimed at middle-class Victorian housewives and covering not only recipes but also medical matters and servants' duties, was published in monthly parts in 1859 and in volume form in 1861. The book became a huge success, with over 60,000 copies sold in the first year. She later published *The Englishwoman's Cooking-Book* (1862) and *A Dictionary of Every-day Cookery* (1865). Her first two children died before the age of three; a third was born in 1863; and IB died of puerperal fever, aged twenty-eight, following the birth of her fourth.
    See: Spain (1948); Hyde (1951); Freeman (1977)

Besant, Annie, née Wood (1847–1933)
Born in London of Irish parentage, she was educated by the evangelist Ellen Marryat. In 1867, she married Frank Besant, schoolmaster and later clergyman, by whom she had two children. The marriage was unhappy, owing largely to her growing religious scepticism, and the couple separated in 1873 following her publication of a pamphlet entitled *The Deity of Jesus of Nazareth by the Wife of a Benificed Clergyman*. She lost the custody of both her children shortly afterwards when she formed a relationship with a leading atheist, Charles Bradlaugh, and joined the National Secular Society. She published *The Gospel of Atheism* in 1877, and together with Bradlaugh edited the *National Reformer* until 1885, when she separated from Bradlaugh and joined the Fabian Society. A celebrated public speaker, she organised the successful Bryant and May match-girls' strike in 1888 and worked on behalf of homeless girls in London. She then became a theosophist, and was elected President of the Theosophical Society in 1907. She visited India in 1893 and subsequently considered it as her home, founding schools, setting up journals, and forming a Home Rule for India League in 1916. She died in India, a few weeks away from her eighty-sixth birthday.

Despite having published over a hundred pamphlets and books, she is best remembered as a social reformer, orator and propagandist.

See: Nethercot (1961) and (1963); Dinnage (1986); Wessinger (1988); Taylor (1992)

Bevington, Louisa Sarah, later Guggenberger (1845-1895)

Born in London, the eldest of a family of eight, she began publishing poetry in the Quaker journal *Friends Monthly Examiner*. Her first book of poems, published under the pseudonym 'Arbor Leigh', appeared in 1876, followed by *Key-Notes* (1879) and *Poems, Lyrics and Sonnets* (1882). Called by an admiring contemporary 'the poetess of evolutionary science', she published several articles questioning established Christianity. Her marriage to the Munch artist Ignatz Guggenberger in 1893 was short-lived. In the last years of her life she became involved with London-based anarchist groups and contributed to *Liberty*, the journal of 'Anarchist Communism'. Her final book was a collection of poems, *Liberty Lyrics*, published in the year of her death, 1895.

See: Blain et al. (1990); Armstrong et al. (1996)

Bird, Isabella, later Bishop (1831-1904)

The most intrepid of the numerous lady travellers of the period, she was a clergyman's daughter and lived in Yorkshire, Cheshire, Birmingham and Huntingdonshire at various times in her childhood. Travel was recommended as a help to her long-standing spinal complaint, and she spent seven months in America in 1854, producing her first travel book, *The Englishwoman in America* (1856) as a result. Her health was always precarious in England but improved overseas, and she spent the rest of her life taking numerous journeys to such out of the way places as Australia, New Zealand, the Sandwich Islands and the Rocky Mountains, publishing accounts of her travels on her return (**The Hawaiian Archipelago* [1875] and **A Lady's Life in the Rocky Mountains* [1879]). She married her sister's medical advisor, Dr John Bishop, in 1881: she was forty-nine and he was ten years younger. After her marriage she visited Japan, Malaya and Egypt (more publications) and, after his death in 1886, went to Tibet (*Among the Tibetans* [1894]), India, Persia, Kurdistan, Korea and China (*The Yangtzee Valley and Beyond* [1899]). Her last major expedition was made at the age of sixty-nine, when she travelled to Morocco, mostly on horseback, although illness prevented her from completing another book on the subject. She died at seventy-three, not having achieved her ambition of revisiting China.

See: Stoddart (1906), Middleton (1965), Barr (1970), Foster (1990)

Black, Clementina (1855-1923)

Born in Brighton, she was the eldest of eight children, one of whom was the translator Constance Garnett. After her mother's death she lived mainly in London, where she studied in the British Museum and moved in socialist and Fabian circles. She was a tireless social reformer on behalf of women and worked for two years as Secretary of the Women's Provident and Protective League before leaving in 1888 to form the Women's Trade Union Association. She published seven novels and a collection of stories between 1877 and 1911, but her best known works are her publications on behalf of women's suffrage.

See: Glage (1981); Blain et al. (1990)

Bodichon, Barbara, née Leigh Smith (1827-1891)
Born in Sussex, she was the eldest of the five illegitimate children of the Unitarian and Radical MP Benjamin Leigh Smith and his common-law wife Annie Longden, who died when BB was seven. Initially educated at home by a tutor, she was later enrolled in the Ladies' College in Bedford Square, London, where she studied painting and drawing, skills which she practised successfully throughout her life. Her father settled £300 on her when she came of age, and gave her the deeds of the Westminster Infant School, which led to her foundation of the Portman Hall non-denominational, co-educational school. A tireless campaigner on feminist issues, her first publication was *A Brief Summary in Plain Language of the Most Important Laws Concerning Women* (1854), followed by *Women and Work* (1857). The same year she married a French Algerian, Dr Eugene Bodichon (their honeymoon in America provided material for her *American Diary, 1857-8*) and thereafter spent part of every year in Algeria. With her friend Bessie Rayner Parkes she founded, in 1858, the *English Woman's Journal*. Her interest in women's education led to her establishment, with her friend Emily Davies, of Girton College, Cambridge, to which she left a large sum of money realised from the sale of her paintings.

See: Burton (1949); Hertein (1985); Blain et al. (1990); Shattock (1993)

Brontë, Charlotte, later Nicholls (1816-1855), and Emily Jane (1818-1848)
Born in Yorkshire, they were the third and fourth of six children of the Revd Patrick Brontë. Their mother died in 1821, and the children were brought up by an aunt, and educated at home apart from a brief period for the four eldest at Cowan Bridge clergy school. The two elder sisters died of consumption the following year, and CB and EB were removed and taught at home by their father. Solitary and imaginative, the sisters, together with their brother Branwell, created imaginary kingdoms about which they wrote at length. CB worked for a time as a governess, and then, planning to start their own school, she and EB went to Brussels in 1842 to improve their language skills. CB fell in love with the principal of the school, Constantin Heger, and stayed on in Brussels for two years until poor relations with Mme Heger forced her to leave. The school failed to materialise, and Branwell, dismissed from a tutor's post for a liason with his employer's wife, sank increasingly into alcohol and drug addiction, from which he was to die in 1848. In 1846, together with their youngest sister Anne, they published a volume of *Poems* by 'Currer, Ellis and Acton Bell', which went almost unnoticed. The following year AB's novel *Agnes Grey*, EB's *Wuthering Heights* and CB's *Jane Eyre* (the only one to meet real critical acclaim) were published. EB died of consumption in December 1848, aged thirty, and AB, whose second novel, *The Tenant of Wildfell Hall* appeared in 1848, died of the same disease in May 1849 aged twenty-nine. CB published two further novels, *Shirley* (1849) and *Villette* (1853). In June 1854 she married her father's curate, Arthur Bell Nicholls, but died in March

of the following year from pregnancy complications. Her friend Elizabeth Gaskell's *Life of Charlotte Brontë* (1857) was written at the request of her father.

> See: (among many others) Chitham (1991); W. Gerin (1967, 1971); Nestor (1985, 1987); Gordon (1994); Davies (1988); Pykett (1989); Tayler (1990); Alexander and Sellars (1995); Bristow (1995); Blain et al. (1990); Shattock (1993); Leighton and Reynolds (1995); Armstrong et al. (1996).

Browning, Elizabeth Barrett, née Moulton-Barrett (1806–1861)

Descended from slave-owning families on both sides, she was born in County Durham, the oldest of a family of eleven children. Precociously intelligent, she was educated at home and, allowed to share her brother's classics tutor, she became proficient in Latin and Greek. A serious illness in her teens left her more or less bedridden for many years. In the early 1830s her father suffered financial reversals, and after several unsatisfactory moves, the whole family settled in Wimpole Street, London in 1835. EBB had been publishing poetry with increasing success since 1820, when her epic *The Battle of Marathon* was privately printed. Her fame was established with her *Poems* of 1844, which led the poet Robert Browning to write to her. Their secret courtship, elopement and marriage in 1846 have become legendary. The couple, who had one son in 1849, settled in Florence, where EBB's most admired work was produced, including *Poems* and *Sonnets from the Portuguese* (both 1850), *Casa Guidi Windows* (1851), *Aurora Leigh* (1856) and the posthumous *Last Poems* (1861).

> See: Kenyon (1897); Karlin (1987); Taplin (1957); Leighton (1986); David (1987); Cooper (1988); Mermin (1989); Bristow (1995); Blain et al. (1990); Shattock (1993); Leighton and Reynolds (1995); Armstrong et al. (1996).

Butler, Josephine, née Grey (1828–1906)

Daughter of John Grey, a radical agricultural reformer and Whig agent, she was born in Northumberland and educated mainly at home. Her husband, George Butler, whom she married in 1852, was an educator and a clergyman. Her interest in helping destitute women and prostitutes began in 1866 after a move to Liverpool. She argued that lack of employment and education for women frequently led to prostitution, which denied women's rights and kept them enslaved to male lust. She worked in support of higher education for women, but she is best known for her campaign for the abolition of the Contagious Diseases Acts, and wrote numerous pamphlets to that end. After the repeal of the Acts, she established and edited two periodicals, *The Dawn* (1888–96) and *The Storm Bell* (1898–1900), with the view of ensuring that the Acts would not be re-introduced. She wrote several biographies, and her autobiography, *Personal Reminiscences of a Great Crusade* (1896).

> See: Johnson (1909); Petrie (1976); Blain et al. (1990)

Caird, Mona, née Alison (1858–1932)

Born on the Isle of Wight, she lived in Australia for part of her childhood, and wrote about the experience in her first novel, *Lady Hetty* (1875), published when she was seventeen. Two years later she married Alexander Henryson-Caird, by whom she had one son. She wrote eight further novels, many of which argue against marriage and women's victimization by men: the most successful was *The Daughters of Danaeus* (1894). Her anti-marriage essays, collected as *The Morality of Marriage* (1897), caused a heated controversy. She also wrote against vivisection in three books (1895, 1897 and 1903), and published a travel book, *Romantic Cities of Provence*, in 1906. *The Great Wave*, her last novel, in which her latent mysticism comes to the fore, was published the year before her death.

See: Gullette (1989); Blain et al. (1990); Shattock (1993)

Carlyle, Jane, née Welsh (1801–1866)

Born in East Lothian, Scotland, she was the only child of a doctor. Precociously intelligent, she attended Haddington School from the age of four, and insisted on learning Latin. She was devastated by her father's death, from typhus, in 1819. In 1821 she met the essayist and historian Thomas Carlyle and they married four years later, despite her mother's opposition and the fact that their relationship was already a stormy one. They lived in Scotland for the next eight years, JC's health and spirits being increasingly undermined by a combination of financial problems and Carlyle's irritability. In 1834 they moved to London where their house became a centre for the literary intelligensia of the day. One of her closest friends was *Geraldine Jewsbury, to whom, among others, she confided the anguish she suffered owing to Carlyle's attachment, in the 1850s, to Lady Harriet Baring, Lady Ashburton. She died suddenly in 1866 after rescuing a dog from an oncoming carriage. The tensions in the Carlyles' marriage were revealed in various memoirs and editions by the historian J. A. Froude (1881, 1883, 1903), who caused a furore by suggesting that the unsatisfactoriness of the marriage may have been the result of Carlyle's impotence.

See: Hanson (1952); Collis (1971); Hardwick (1974); Clarke (1990); Blain et al. (1990); Shattock (1993)

Clive, Caroline, née Meysey-Wigley (1801–1873)

Born into a wealthy landowning family in Worcestershire, she contracted polio at the age of three which left her permanently lame. Reputedly an unattractive, lonely and melancholy child, she became determinedly independent, taking up riding and travelling abroad alone despite her disability. Given to passionate friendships in her early years, including one for the novelist Catherine Gore, she married at the relatively late age of thirty-nine the handsome rector of Solihull, Archer Clive, with whom she had previously, and unconventionally, toured Europe. The marriage, which produced two children, appears to have been a very happy one, as her *Diary* shows. In 1840 she published her first book, *IX Poems by V*, which was well received and led to several subsequent volumes under the same pseudonym. Her best-known work, however, is *Paul Ferroll* (1855), now regarded as the first 'sensation' novel. Three further novels in the same vein followed before CC was partly paralysed by a stroke at the age of sixty-four. She died eight years later as a result of a fire at her home.

See: Partridge (1932; 1970); Blain et al. (1990); Shattock (1993); Leighton and Reynolds (1995); Armstrong et al. (1996).

Cobbe, Frances Power (1822–1904)
Born in Dublin, into an Evangelical landowning family, she was educated at home apart from a brief period at an expensive but ineffectual English boarding school. She developed religious doubts in her early twenties, ceased church-going, and set out her position in *An Essay on Intuitive Morals* (1855), which alienated her from her father. After his death two years later she began what would become a lifetime's interest in travel to Europe and the Middle East. She settled in Bristol, where she became involved with various philanthropic causes on behalf of sick and unemployed women. By the early 1860s she had become a vociferous writer on women's issues: some of the pamphlets and essays she published, such as 'What Shall We Do with our Old Maids' (1862), 'Criminals, Idiots, Women and Minors' (1868) and *'Wife Torture in England' (1878) were highly influential. She also wrote in favour of university education for women, campaigned against vivisection, and was active in the Suffrage League. She supported herself by her journalism until a legacy in 1884 enabled her to retire to Wales with Mary Lloyd, her companion of over twenty years. Her *autobiography appeared in 1894.
See: Manton (1976); Caine (1992); Blain et al. (1990); Shattock (1993)

Coleridge, Mary (1861–1907)
Born in London, she was the great-niece of *Sara Coleridge and the great-great niece of Samuel Taylor Coleridge. Educated at home by a tutor, the poet William J. Cory, she began writing poems and stories at an early age. She lived at home all her life, and taught from 1895 at the Working Women's College. She published at least five novels, of which the first was *The Seven Sleepers of Ephesus* (1893) and the last the admired *Lady on the Drawing-Room Floor* (1906). She began publishing poetry under a pseudonym: her first collection, *Fancy's Following* (1896), was moderately successful, and a selection, with seven new poems, appeared the following year as *Fancy's Guerdon*. She wrote for several magazines and periodicals, published a collection of prose sketches in 1900, and had just finished a *Life of Holman Hunt* (1908) before her sudden death, from appendicitis, at the age of forty-five. Her *Poems, Old and New* was published posthumously in 1907, and a posthumous collection of prose writings as *Gathered Leaves* in 1910. Her poetry has been much admired in the twentieth century, and her *Collected Poems*, ed. T. Whistler, appeared in 1954.
See: Bridges (1931); Gilbert and Gubar (1979); Blain et al. (1990); Shattock (1993); Leighton and Reynolds (1995); Armstrong et al. (1996)

Coleridge, Sara (1802–1852)
The daughter of Samuel Taylor Coleridge, she was born in Keswick, Cumberland, and educated at home, partly by means of her uncle Robert Southey's library. Formidably intelligent, she became fluent in several languages, including Latin and French, and her first publications were translations from those languages in 1821 and 1825. In 1829 she married her cousin Henry Nelson Coleridge, a barrister, by whom she had two children. In 1834 she published a book of educational poetry for children, but her best-known original work is *Phantasmion* (1837), a fairy tale with lyrics. She edited her father's works after his death, bringing out several important editions of his

writings both published and unpublished. She also wrote reviews for the *Quarterly*. Her *Memoirs and Letters*, edited by her daughter Edith, show her interest in a wide range of issues from theology to politics.

See: Griggs (1940); Mudge (1989); Lefebure (1986); Blain et al. (1990); Shattock (1993); Leighton and Reynolds (1995); Armstrong et al. (1996)

Cook, Eliza (1818–1889)

Born in London, she was the youngest of eleven children of a brazier and tinman who retired when she was nine, moving his family to a farm in Sussex. Intelligent and gifted, she was encouraged by her mother, and published her first volume of poetry, *Lays of a Wild Harp* (1835) at the age of seventeen. Numerous poems, signed only by her initials, appeared in various newspapers and journals where they were much admired and compared to the work of Robert Burns. A second collection, *Melaia and Other Poems*, appeared in 1838. In 1849 she founded and edited *Eliza Cook's Journal*, a weekly publication most of which was written by herself and which voiced a moderate support for women's rights. Despite its high circulation, said to have exceeded Dickens' *Household Words*, the journal folded in 1854 owing to EC's ill health. Extracts were republished later as *Jottings from my Journal* (1860) and *Diamond Dust* (1865). She never married, but is reputed to have had a 'romantic friendship' with the American actress Charlotte Cushman. She wrote little in later life, and was awarded a civil-list pension of £100 a year in 1864.

See: Mitchell (1981); Blain et al. (1990); Shattock (1993); Leighton and Reynolds (1995); Armstrong et al. (1996)

Craik, Dinah, née Mulock (1826–1887)

Born in Staffordshire, she was the daughter of an Irish non-conformist minister whose mental instability led first to the loss of his chapel and later to his committal as a pauper lunatic. By the age of thirteen, DC was teaching Latin to the pupils at her mother's school. In 1845 she assumed responsibility for her two younger brothers, whom she undertook to support by writing. She moved the family to London and worked as a journalist, and in 1849 published the first of over twenty novels, *The Ogilvies*. In 1865 she married George Lillie Craik, eleven years her junior, and the couple adopted a daughter four years later. Her most successful novel was the best-selling *John Halifax, Gentleman* (1858), but many of her other novels are more overtly feminist: *Agatha's Husband* (1853) and *Christian's Mistake* (1865), for example, portray disastrous marriages, while *A Brave Lady* (1870) supports the Married Women's Property Act. Her pamphlet *A Woman's Thoughts about Women* (1858) pleads for better opportunities for women's education and employment. Although best remembered for her novels, she also published several successful volumes of poetry.

See: Parr (1897); Mitchell (1983); Showalter (1975); Blain et al. (1990); Shattock (1993); Armstrong et al. (1996)

Cullwick, Hannah, later Munby (1833–1909)

Born in Shropshire, the daughter of a housemaid and a saddler, she went into domestic service at the age of eight and remained a lower servant for most of her life, working variously as pot-girl, maid-of-all-work, cook, housemaid, and housekeeper. In 1854 she met the upper-class barrister and poet Arthur Munby, whose lifetime obsession with working-class women led him to form a relationship with her (during part of which she wore chains and padlocks as a sign of her willing servitude to him) which lasted until her death in 1909. After eighteen years of secret courtship, during which he encouraged her to write a series of *diaries detailing her daily life of work and drudgery, they married. However the relationship still remained secret, with HC appearing to be Munby's servant and living in the basement kitchen of his chambers. After four years the couple separated and HC moved to Shropshire, eventually retiring to a cottage rented for her by Munby. He visited her there frequently, especially towards the end of their lives. After his death in 1910, the relationship came to light by means of his will, and caused a furore. The Munby collection, in Trinity College Cambridge, contains thousands of pages of her diaries and numerous letters.

See: Stanley (1984); Hudson (1972); Davidoff (1979); Blain et al. (1990)

Dowie, Ménie Muriel, later Norman, later Fitzgerald (1866–1945)

A novelist, short-story writer, and travel writer, she was born in Liverpool, and educated in Germany and France. Her popular *A Girl in the Karpathians (1891) is based on a journey she made alone at the age of twenty, and depicts a young woman travelling alone, dressing like a man, smoking and drinking. Her novels and stories demonstrate an interest in women's rights: they include Gallia (1895), which argues for the separation of love and motherhood; The Crook of the Bough (1898); and Love and His Masks (1901). Her first marriage ended in divorce, and she lived for several years in India after her second marriage. She became a successful cattle breeder after her return to England towards the end of her life.

See: Blain et al. (1990); Mix (1960); Sutherland (1988)

Eastlake, Elizabeth, Lady, née Rigby (1809–1893)

One of twelve children of a Norwich doctor, she began reviewing in 1836 and became a regular reviewer of English and European literature for the Quarterly Review, for which she continued writing until the 1880s. She travelled to Russia in 1838 and based her First Residence on the Shore of the Baltic (1841) and her two works of fiction (The Jewess (1843) and Livonian Tales (1846)) on her experiences there. In 1849 she married Sir Charles Eastlake, a painter, who became the Keeper of the National Gallery. She translated and edited several works on painting, including two by her husband (1870 and 1874) after his death in 1869. A series of essays was republished as Five Great Painters in 1883, as a result of her shocked response to Rossetti's exhibition of that year. Her nephew Charles Eastlake Smith brought out an edition of her Journals and Correspondence in 1895, two years after her death.

See: Lochhead (1961); Shattock (1993)

'Eliot, George' (Mary Anne Evans), later Cross (1819–1880)

Born and brought up in rural Warwickshire, where her father was a land-agent, she was educated at various boarding-schools. Her mother died in 1836, and she returned home to look after her father, at the same time educating herself by means of a formidable reading list including English and German literature, theology and philosophy. Having become strongly Evangelical at the age of fifteeen, she lost her faith in the early 1840s. In 1844 she undertook a translation of D.F. Strauss's controversial *Das Leben Jesus*, published in 1846. Following her father's death in 1849 she moved to London and began writing for the *Westminster Review*, of which she became the unofficial editor in 1851 and for which she wrote a number of important review articles. In 1854, having had a series of unsatisfactory relationships, she entered a happy and stable common-law marriage with the writer George Henry Lewes (who was unable to obtain a divorce since he had condoned his wife's adultery), which lasted until his death in 1878. Her first fiction, published under her pseudonym, was *Scenes of Clerical Life* (1858). A series of hugely successful novels followed, including *Adam Bede* (1859), *The Mill on the Floss* (1860), *Silas Marner* (1861), *Middlemarch* (1871–2), and *Daniel Deronda* (1876). Lewes's death in 1878 devastated her. Two years later she married John Walter Cross, twenty years her junior, but died suddenly of a kidney infection after only seven months.

See: (among many others) Haight (1954–79 and 1968); Pinney (1963); Beer (1986); David (1987); Blain et al. (1990); Shattock (1993); Leighton and Reynolds (1995); Armstrong et al. (1996)

Ellis, Sarah, née Stickney (1812–1872)

Born in Yorkshire, she rejected her Quaker upbringing and joined the Congregationalist church. Her husband William Ellis, whom she married in 1837, was a missionary and had worked in the South Seas and in Madagascar. Her earliest publications were moral tales, collected as *Pictures of Private Life* (1833–7), and three volumes of poetry, *The Sons of the Soil* (1840), *The Island Queen* (1846), and *Janet: One of Many* (1862). She is best remembered for her numerous, highly conservative, conduct books aimed at middle-class women, which advocate submission to the husband and a life devoted to domesticity and parenthood. **The Women of England, their Social Duties and Domestic Habits* (1839) was followed by *The Daughters of England* (1842), *The Mothers of England* and *The Wives of England* (both 1843). Many of her over 30 books are 'improving' works. She was also concerned with, among other things, working-class women's education, and temperance.

See: Ellis (1893); Blain et al (1990); Shattock (1993); Armstrong et al. (1996)

Evans, Anne (1820–1870)

The daughter of linguist, musician, professor of classics and later headmaster Dr Arthur E, she was educated at home. After her father's death in 1855 she moved to London with her mother and some of her five siblings. She became a companion to the daughters of the novelist William Makepeace Thackeray (one of whom was the writer Anne Thackeray, later Ritchie), and travelled abroad with them. At this time she wrote a short story, 'The Rose and the Ring', which she showed to Thackeray in manuscript. Her story never appeared in print, but Thackeray later published a work of the same name. She suffered from long periods of ill health, and died in London aged fifty. Her only published work was *Poems and Music*, which appeared posthumously in 1880 with a preface by Anne Thackeray Ritchie.

See: Blain et al. (1990), Armstrong et al. (1996)

'Field, Michael' (Katherine Harris Bradley [1846–1914] and Edith Emma Cooper [1862–1913])

An aunt and niece, they lived together and collaborated on their large output of poetry and drama under the joint name of Michael Field. KB was born in Birmingham, but moved into her elder sister's house in Warwickshire just before EC's birth, and passed on her own impressive learning to her niece. She published her first book of poems, *The New Minnesinger* (1875) under the pseudonym Arran Leigh. The two women attended classes at University College, Bristol, in 1878, and apparently became lovers at about this time. Their first collaborative work as Michael Field was a play, *Callirrhoe* (1884), highly acclaimed and the first of their twenty-seven poetic dramas. A few years later they published *Long Ago* (1889), a volume of poems which rewrite the legend of Sappho following Henry Wharton's edition of 1885 which restored the female pronoun to the addressee of the Greek poetess. Eight more joint poetic volumes followed, including *Sight and Song* (1892) and *Underneath the Bough* (1893). Living quietly together in Surrey, they also travelled widely and had a wide cricle of literary friends including the Brownings and Oscar Wilde. They supported the suffrage movement and the anti-vivisection league, and converted to Roman Catholicism in 1907, after which their work became less sensual and more pious. They died within months of each other, both from cancer. Selections from their manuscript *journal, which is in the British Library, were published in 1933 as *Work and Days*, ed. T. and D. C Sturge Moore.

See: Sturgeon (1922); Faderman (1981); Leighton (1992); Blain et al. (1990); Shattock (1993); Leighton and Reynolds (1995); Armstrong et al. (1996)

Gaskell, Elizabeth Cleghorn née Stevenson (1810–65)

Born in London, she was brought up by an aunt in Knutsford, Cheshire (which she later fictionalised in *Cranford* (1855)), following her mother's death when she was a year old. She was happily married to William Gaskell, a Unitarian minister, and had four daughters and a son. She started writing her first novel, *Mary Barton* (1848), following the death of her son from scarlet fever. Much of her fiction (notably the industrial novels *Mary Barton* and *North and South* (1855)) is set in Manchester, where she lived. Her other novels include the controversial *Ruth* (1853), the story of an unmarried mother; *Sylvia's Lovers* (1863); and *Cousin Phyllis* (1864). Her numerous short stories frequently deal with unorthodox subjects: *Lizzie Leigh* (1850) tackles prostitution, for example. She befriended Charlotte Brontë in 1850, and published her much-admired *Life of Charlotte Brontë* in 1857. She died suddenly, aged fifty-five, leaving her final novel, *Wives and Daughters* (1865) incomplete.

See: Blain et al. (1990); Chapple and Pollard (1966); Easson (1979); Nestor (1985); Shattock (1993); Spencer (1993); Stoneman (1987); Sutherland (1988); Uglow (1993)

'Grand, Sarah' (Frances Elizabeth McFall, née Clarke) (1854–1943)

Born in Northern Ireland to English parents, she moved to Yorkshire after the death of her father, a naval officer, when she was seven. Badly and unhappily educated at two boarding schools, she married at sixteen an army surgeon twenty-three years her senior, Lieutenant Colonel David McFall, who was a widower with two children. The marriage, which produced one son, was unhappy. Her first novel, *Ideala*, published anonymously, appeared in 1888, and the profits enabled her to leave her husband and move to London with her son. Her most celebrated works are two feminist novels, published under her carefully chosen pseudonym, *The Heavenly Twins* (1893), which caused a scandal for its treatment of venereal disease and women's rights, and which sold 20,000 copies in its first year, and *The Beth Book* (1897), a thinly disguised autobiography. She became an active campaigner on behalf of women's suffrage and lectured tirelessly in England and overseas for twenty years. Her last years were spent in Bath, where she was elected mayoress six times.

See: Cunningham (1978); Huddleston (1979); Kersley (1983); Blain et al. (1990); Shattock (1993)

Jameson, Anna Brownell, née Murphy (1794–1860)

Born in Dublin, she published a fictionalised version of her journal, describing travels through France and Italy as a governess, as *A Lady's Diary* (1826). She married Robert Jameson, a barrister, in 1825, but separated after four years. She wrote prolifically, producing *Loves of the Poets* (1829), *Memoirs of Celebrated Female Sovereigns* (1831); *Characteristics of Women* (1832), *Visits and Sketches at Home and Abroad* (1834), and **Winter Sketches and Summer Rambles in Canada* (1838). In 1842 she published the first of her six books on art, of which the most celebrated is the four-part *Sacred and Legendary Art* (1848–64), the last part being completed after her death by her friend **Elizabeth Eastlake. Increasingly involved with the 1850s women's movement, she published articles on women's rights as well as two important lectures, *Sisters of Charity* (1855) and *The Communion of Labour: Social Employment of Women* (1856).

See: Erskine (1915); Thomas (1967); Blain et al. (1990); Shattock (1993)

Jewsbury, Geraldine Endsor (1812–1880)

Born in Derbyshire, she moved with her family to Manchester in 1818. After her mother's death the following year, she and her four brothers were brought up by their oldest sister, the poet and prose writer Maria Jane Jewsbury. Educated at boarding-school and 'finished' in London, she was intended for a governess but took over running her father's household in 1832 following her sister's marriage and departure for India (where she was to die after only six months). After her father's death in 1840, GJ ran her brother Frank's household in Manchester, which became a lively intellectual and social centre, until his marriage in 1854. She then moved to Chelsea, in London, to be near to her close friend **Jane Carlyle. Her first novel, *Zoe* (1845) was considered shocking in its questioning of religious orthodoxy, and her second, *The Half-Sisters* (1848) explored the options open to women in society. *Marion Withers*

(1851) is an industrial novel which draws on her experience of Manchester life. She wrote three more novels and two childrens' books, but perhaps her most important work, though least known to her contemporaries, was her journalism (including over 1,600 reviews for *The Athenaeum*) and her influential position as reader for the publisher Bentley's from 1858 until her death.

See: Ireland (1892); Woolf (1932); Howe (1935); Fryckstedt (1986); Clarke (1990); Blain et al. (1990); Shattock (1993)

Jex Blake, Sophia (1840-1912)
Born in Sussex, she attended Queen's College in London and stayed on to become a tutor in mathematics. In 1865 she travelled to New York City to study medicine under the English-born Elizabeth Blackwell. In 1869, she and five other women were allowed to matriculate at Edinburgh University, where she continued her medical studies until 1873 when the university authorities reversed their decision. She then campaigned for medical education for women, and opened the London School of Medicine for Women in 1874. In 1876 her campaign succeeded when the law was changed to allow medical examiners to examine women students. In 1886 she founded a medical school in Edinburgh.

See: Todd (1918)

Johnston, Ellen ('The Factory Girl') (1835-1873)
Born in Scotland, she was the only child of a stonemason who emigrated to America when she was seven months old, leaving her with her mother who had decided at the last minute not to go. Some years later, after supporting herself and EJ by dressmaking, her mother heard reports of her husband's death and married a man who appears to have physically and probably sexually abused her daughter, forcing the child to take up factory work at the age of eight. Her father later proved not to have died, and committed suicide on hearing that his wife had remarried. In 1852, at the age of seventeen, EJ gave birth to an illegitimate daughter and then turned her attention to earning money by means of her poetry. She published a number of poems in newspapers and magazines, although she was later forced to return to factory work. In 1867 she brought out a collection by subscription under the title *Autobiography, Poems and Songs*. She removed the revelations of her unmarried motherhood from the second edition two years later. She died in a Glasgow poorhouse in 1873, at the age of thirty-eight.

See: Vicinus (1974); Swindells (1985); Boos (1995); Leighton and Reynolds (1995); Armstrong et al. (1996)

Kavanagh, Julia (1824-1877)
Born in Ireland, she was brought up in England and later in Paris. JK began a literary career in London in the 1840s after she and her mother, who was an invalid, separated from her father. Her childrens' book, *The Three Paths*, appeared in 1848 and in the same year she published her first novel, *Madeleine*. At least six more novels followed, several of which had French settings: one in particular, *Nathalie* (1850), was admired

by Charlotte Brontë, who first met JK in 1850. Her non-fictional works undertake to restore women to their rightful place in historical writing and to celebrate their achievements. They include *Woman in France during the Eighteenth Century* (1850), *French Women of Letters* (1862) and **English Women of Letters* (1863). At the end of her life she moved back to France, and died in Nice.

See: Sergeant (1897); Blain et al. (1990); Shattock (1993)

Kemble, Frances Anne ('Fanny'), later Butler (1809–1893)
Born in London, she was the daughter of the actor-manager Charles Kemble and his Viennese actress wife Marie Thérèse Kemble, and the niece of the famous actress Sarah Siddons. Brought up and educated by an aunt in France, she wrote a verse melodrama, *Francis I*, at the age of eighteen. Two years later she began a highly successful theatrical career (which saved her father's company from bankruptcy) with her Covent Garden debut as Juliet. On a successful American tour in the early 1830s she met Pierce Butler, a wealthy Southern plantation-owner, whom she married in 1834. Her *Journal of a Residence in America* (1835) criticises American institutions, and the sequel, **Journal of a Residence in a Georgian Plantation, 1838–9* was suppressed until 1863 owing to its outspoken anti-slavery views. The marriage was not a success and in 1845 the couple separated. After her divorce in 1848 Butler kept custody of her two daughters. For many years she divided her time between England and America, at times denied access to her children, with whom she was, however, reunited when they attained majority. For twenty years she undertook a series of successful readings from Shakespeare in both England and America, and also published three volumes of *Poems* (1844, 1865, 1883), and three more of reminiscences (1878, 1882, 1890). Her first novel, *Far Away and Long Ago* (1889) appeared in her eightieth year.

See: Marshall (1977); Furnass (1982); Blain et al. (1990); Shattock (1993); Leighton and Reynolds (1995); Armstrong et al. (1996)

Kendall, 'May' (Emma Goldworth) (1861–1943)
The daughter of a Wesleyan minister, she was born in Bridlington, Yorkshire, and lived in York for most of her life. Her first publication was *That Very Mab* (1885), a volume of poems and satirical essays written in collaboration with Andrew Lang. In 1887 **Dreams to Sell*, her first volume of poems, some reprinted from *Punch* and *Longmans*, appeared. Her first novel, *From a Garret*, a 'New Woman' fiction, was published the same year. Two more novels, also concerned with women's issues, were published in 1889 and 1893. The following year she published a second collection of poems, *Songs from Dreamland*. A collection of her short stories, *Turkish Bonds* (1898) supports the cause of the Armenians. She became increasingly involved with philanthopy in later life, and collaborated with B.S. Rowntree on two surveys, *How the Labourer Lives* (1913) and *The Human Needs of Labour* (1819). She apparently died in poverty, and is buried in an unmarked grave in York cemetery.

See: Briggs (1961); Green (1946); Blain et al. (1990); Leighton and Reynolds (1995); Armstrong et al. (1996)

Landon, Letitia Elizabeth ('L. E. L.'), later Maclean (1802–38)
Born and educated in London, she began publishing in the *Literary Gazette* in 1820, and her first volume, *The Fate of Adelaide*, appeared the following year. She was a prolific writer, going on to publish six more volumes of poetry as well as numerous poems in various annuals. She also wrote a number of novels, including the historical *Ethel Churchill* (1837), edited and contributed to *Fisher's Drawing Room Scrapbook* (1832–9), *Heath's Book of Beauty* (1833) and the *New Juvenile Keepsake* (1838). Her earnings at the peak of her career were estimated at over £2500, enough to support her mother and brother in separate households and to buy her brother a clerical living. Her personal life was surrounded by gossip and scandal, and a rumoured affair put an end to her engagement to Dickens's future biographer John Foster. Shortly afterwards she married George Maclean, Governor of Cape Coast Castle (now Ghana). She travelled to Africa after her marriage in July 1838, and in October of the same year was found dead in her room, a bottle of prussic acid in her hand. Accidental death, suicide and murder have all been put forward as possible causes. Her popularity remained high throughout the nineteenth century, with many collections of her work appearing posthumously.
See: Blanchard (1841); Ashton (1936); Blain et al. (1990); Leighton (1992); Shattock (1993); Ashfield (1995); Leighton and Reynolds (1995); Armstrong et al. (1996); Stephenson (1996)

Linton, Eliza Lynn, née Lynn (1822–1898)
Born in Cumberland, she was the twelfth child of a vicar. Her mother died when she was still an infant, and she educated herself, gaining an impressive command of several European languages as well as some Greek and Latin. In 1845 she moved to London where she began a career as a journalist, and published her first novel, *Azeth the Egyptian*, in 1846. Her next two novels (1848 and 1850) were criticised for radical feminist views. She married the engraver and writer William Linton in 1858, but parted from him amicably in 1864. Her later fiction also confronts women's issues, but she became increasingly conservative in later life and is best remembered today for her article 'The Girl of the Period', first published in the *Saturday Review* in March 1868, the first of a series in which she attacked the 'New Woman' for aggressiveness and hysteria. Her last novels (1894 and 1895) continued the attack. Her autobiography, *My Literary Life* (1899), was published posthumously.
See: Layard (1901); van Thal (1979); Anderson (1987); Blain et al. (1990); Shattock (1993)

Martineau, Harriet (1802–76)
Born in Norwich, into a leading Unitarian family, she suffered from chronic ill-health and deafness for most of her life. Her first publications were essays in the *Monthly Repository*. These were followed by a collection of moral tales, *Illustrations of Political Economy* (1832–4). Her *Society in America* (1837) and **A Retrospect of Western Travel* (1838) criticised American society, which she had experienced during a tour a few years earlier. She began writing fiction with *Deerbrook* (1839), and subsequently published *The Hour and the Man* (1841), *The Playfellow* (1841) and *Forest*

and Game-Law Tales (1845–6). She settled in Ambleside, where she became a friend of Wordsworth's, in 1844. She published the radical *History of England 1816–1846* in 1848–50 and, having lost her religious faith, the anti-theological *Laws of Man's Nature* in 1851. She was a prolific writer for periodicals, and some of her articles were published as *Biographical Sketches* in 1867. Thinking she was dying she wrote her **Autobiography* in 1855, but lived another twenty-one years: the work was published posthumously in 1877.

See: Sanders (1986 and 1990); Webb (1960); Pichanick (1980); David (1987); Blain et al. (1990); Shattock (1993)

Matheson, Annie (1853–1924)
Born in London, she was brought up in Shropshire where her father was a Congregationalist minister. Her first book of poems, mainly on religious issues, appeared in 1890 as **The Religion of Humanity*. *Love's Music* followed in 1894, and *Love Triumphant* in 1898. Her selected poems, *Roses, Loaves, and Old Rhymes*, came out in 1899. She also published numerous essays on social issues to various journals and periodicals, later collected in book form and published as *Leaves of Prose* (1912). She wrote biographies of Florence Nightingale (1913) and Elizabeth Fry (1920), edited some of George Eliot's works, and published books for children.

See Blain et al. (1990), Armstrong et al. (1996)

Morgan, Sydney, Lady, née Owenson (1776–1859)
The daughter of an Irish actor, she was born and educated in Dublin. Her first publication was *Poems* (1801), followed by *Twelve Original Hibernian Melodies* (1805). She also wrote fiction, and her third novel, *The Wild Irish Girl* (1806) brought her considerable success. She continued to write on Irish themes, publishing *The Lay of an Irish Harp* (1807), and several Irish novels, all of which were attacked by Tory reviewers for their strong Irish nationalist views. She published several travel books on France, Italy and Belgium, and two collections of articles, essays and sketches (1827, 1829) An important late work arguing for the equality (or superiority) of women was **Woman and her Master* (1840). *Geraldine Jewsbury helped her to complete *Passages from my Autobiography* in 1859. She married Sir Charles Morgan in 1812, and died in London at the age of seventy-six. Her *Memoirs*, ed. H. Dixon, appeared in 1862.

See: Fitzpatrick (1860); Stevenson (1936); Campbell (1988); Newcomer (1990); Moskal in Feldman and Kelley (1995); Sha in Feldman and Kelley (1995); Blain et al. (1990); Shattock (1993)

Naden, Constance (1858–1889)
An only child, she was born at Edgbaston, Birmingham, and brought up by her mother's parents. She was educated at a Unitarian day school, and later studied botany at the Birmingham and Midland Institute and modern languages at Mason College. A large inheritance from her grandmother in 1887 enabled her to travel widely in Europe and Asia, and later to buy a house in Grosvenor Square, London,

where she became involved in women's causes. A friend of the doctor and suffrage campaigner Elizabeth Garrett Anderson, she helped to establish the New Hospital for Women in Marylebone, London. She published two volumes of poetry, *Songs and Sonnets of Springtime* (1881) and *A Modern Apostle* (1887), after which she gave up poetry in favour of campaigning, although her complete poems were republished in 1894. She also published *What is Religion? A Vindication of Free Thought* (1883) and a book of essays, *Induction and Deduction* (1890)

See: Armstrong et al. (1996); Blain et al. (1990), Hughes (1890)

Nesbit, E[dith], later Bland, later Tucker (1858–1924)

Born in London, she was educated in convents, mainly abroad, after her father's death when she was three. Her family later settled in Kent, where she was to live for most of her life. In 1876 she published her first story, in the *Sunday Magazine*, but she really began writing professionally in the mid-1880s, following her marriage in 1880 to the socialist Hubert Bland who proved unable to support their growing family. The couple were active in the forming of the Fabian Society in 1884. In the 1890s her childrens' fiction, especially her two trilogies, *The Treasure Seekers*, *The Wouldbegoods*, and *The New Treasure Seekers* (1899, 1901, 1904) and *Five Children and It, The Phoenix and the Carpet*, and *The Story of the Amulet* (1902, 1904 and 1907) became extremely successful, and has remained popular ever since. She published several volumes of poetry, including *Lays and Legends* (1886) and *Ballads and Lyrics of Socialism* (1908). Her home life was unsettled: she had to cope with Bland's sometimes violent temper, and brought up two of his illegitimate children in addition to her own four. After his death she married the marine engineer Thomas Tucker.

See: Armstrong et al. (1996); Blain et al. (1990); Briggs (1989); Moore (1933); Nesbit (1987); Shattock (1993)

Nightingale, Florence (1820–1910)

Born in the city after which she was named, she was brought up in her family's two country houses in Derbyshire and Hampshire, where she received an unusually wide education. Her frustration with the idleness of upper-class female life is expressed in *Cassandra*, part of a larger religious and philosophical work, *Suggestions for Thought to Searchers after Truth among the Artizans of England*. Her nursing career began (following much parental opposition) in Germany in 1851, and in 1853 she became Superintendent of the Hospital for Gentlewomen in London. In 1854 she was invited to undertake the overall supervision of nursing in the Crimean war. She was nationally acclaimed for her achievements in the Crimea, and popularly celebrated as 'The Lady with the Lamp'. Following her return to England in 1856 she worked tirelessly to improve nursing conditions at home and abroad for the remainder of her life, founding the Nightingale School of Nursing in 1860 and publishing several works on the subject, including *Notes on Nursing* (1860).

See: Cook (1913), Woodham-Smith (1950), Vicinus and Nergaard (1990), Blain et al. (1990), Shattock (1993)

Norton, Caroline, née Sheridan, later Stirling-Maxwell (1808–1877)
One of three sisters celebrated for their extraordinary beauty, she was the grand-daughter of the playwright and politician Richard Brinsley Sheridan. She was married at the age of nineteen to the Honourable George Norton, a barrister, whom she hardly knew, and had three children in 1829, 1831 and 1833. The marriage was unhappy from the start, owing to Norton's violent temper and his inability to support her and her children. For several years she supported him through her writing, publishing numerous stories and poems in various annuals as well as several volumes of poetry. The marriage finally broke down in the mid-1830s, but Norton forced her to return home by refusing to allow her to see her children, of whom the law gave him custody. He then accused her of adultery with the Prime Minister Lord Melbourne, and although he lost his case against Melbourne for £10,000 'compensation', CN's reputation never fully recovered. Several of her novels dramatise unhappy marriages, and her later poetry deals increasingly with social issues. She also wrote several pamphlets in support of the Divorce Bill and the Married Women's Property Act. Her husband died in 1875, and she married an old friend, Sir William Stirling-Maxwell, in 1877, but died only four months later.
    See: Perkins (1909); Acland (1948); Hoge and Olney (1974); Hoge and Marcus (1978); Chedzoy (1992); Blain et al. (1990); Shattock (1993); Leighton and Reynolds (1995); Armstrong et al. (1996)

Oliphant, Margaret née Wilson (1828–97)
Born in Scotland, she published her first novel, the successful *Margaret Maitland* (1849), at the age of twenty one. She moved to London after her marriage to her cousin Francis Wilson Oliphant, a stained-glass engraver, in 1852, and produced a number of novels, the income from which helped to support not only her husband and children but also her alcoholic brother. Widowed in her early thirties, and left virtually penniless, she supported her children (and, later, her widowed brother's children) by writing, becoming one of the most prolific and skilful of Victorian writers and Queen Victoria's favourite novelist. Of her almost 100 novels, the series known as the 'Chronicles of Carlingford' is the best known, and includes *The Rector and The Doctor's Family* and *Salem Chapel* (both 1863), *The Perpetual Curate* (1864), *Miss Marjoribanks* (1866) and *Phoebe Junior* (1876). She also published several volumes of short stories (her ghost stories, collected as *Stories of the Seen and Unseen* (1885), are considered among her best), literary histories, art criticism, several biographies, travel works and two *autobiographies (1868 and 1899). She also wrote over 200 articles for *Blackwood's*, and edited their Foreign Classics Series. Her history of Blackwood's, *Annals of a Publishing House* (1897), is much admired. Her *Autobiography* was edited by her nieces after her death.
    See: Blain et al. (1990); Colby (1966); Haythornthwaite (1990); Homans (1986); Jay (1995); Shattock (1993); Showalter (1978; 1982); Sutherland (1976, 1988); Trela (1994); Williams (1986)

'Ouida' (Marie Louise de la Ramée) (1839–1908)
She was born in Suffolk to a Guernsey-born father, who was a teacher, and an English

mother. She was a precocious child and her father was largely responsible for her education, encouraging her interest in French fiction, politics and history. Her first story, 'Dashwood's Drag', serialised in *Bentley's Miscellany* in 1859, led to a highly successful career as a novelist and short-story writer. Most of her forty-seven novels have conventional plots involving aristocratic heroes, love intrigues, suspense and melodrama: the most successful, *Under Two Flags* (1867) sold over two million copies. From the 1860s she spent increasing amounts of time in Italy, settling permanently near Florence, in considerable style and surrounded by numerous dogs, in 1874. Her popularity declined with the replacement, in the 1890s, of the three-volume novel by the one-volume format, and she turned increasingly to writing for various reviews and journals. Her essays, on subjects such as anti-vivisection, women's suffrage (to which she was opposed) and South African politics, were collected as *Views and Opinions* (1895) and *Critical Studies* (1900). The extreme extravagence of her lifestyle eventually led to her spending the last years of her life in poverty, although she was awarded a civil-list pension (which pride almost caused her to refuse) in 1906.

See: Lee (1914); ffrench (1938); Bigland (1950); Stirling (1957); Sutherland (1988); Blain et al. (1990); Shattock (1993)

Pfeiffer, Emily, née Davis (1827–1890)

Born in London, she was the daughter of a wealthy landowner who was plunged into poverty following the failure of his father-in-law's bank, which prevented her from having any formal education. In 1843 she produced a volume of her own writing, *The Holly Branch: An Annual for 1843*, after which she published nothing for fourteen years. She married Jurgen Pfeiffer, a German banker resident in London, in 1853. Two works, *Valisneria*, a fantasy, and *Margaret; or the Motherless*, a narrative poem, appeared in 1857 and 1861, but it was another twelve years before she published again. From 1873 onwards she produced a number of volumes of poetry, including *Gerard's Monument* (1873), *Poems* (1876), *Sonnets and Songs* (1880), and *Under the Aspens* (1882). Her strong feminist sympathies are apparent in many of her poems and also in her essays, reprinted as *Women and Work* (1887). She published a travel book based on a journey round the world, *Flying Leaves from East and West* (1885), and her final collection of poems, *Flowers of the Night*, in 1889. She was devastated by her husband's death the same year, and died herself the year after, leaving a large sum of money to support education for women.

See: Robertson (1883); Hickok (1984); Blain et al. (1960); Shattock (1993); Leighton and Reynolds (1995); Armstrong et al. (1996)

Probyn, May (dates unknown)

Born and brought up at Weybridge in Surrey, she published three volumes of poetry: *Who Killed Cock Robin* (1880), *A Ballad of the Road* (1883), and *Pansies* (1895).

See: Leighton and Reynolds (1995)

Procter, Adelaide (1825–1864)

Born in London, she was the eldest child of the solicitor Bryan W. Procter, who published poetry as Barry Cornwall. Her parents' home was the centre of a lively literary circle which included Dickens and Thackeray. She began writing poetry early, and published her first poems in *Heath's Book of Beauty* in 1843, when she was eighteen. In 1853 she sent some poems to Dickens under the pseudonym Mary Berwick: he was impressed, published them and subsequent others in *Household Words*, and did not learn her identity for eighteen months. In 1858 her two volume collection *Legends and Lyrics* appeared, and rapidly became extremely popular, going through at least twelve editions. She also contributed to the *English Woman's Journal*, and campaigned actively for women's rights as Secretary of the Society for Promoting the Employment of Women and by editing a volume of prose and verse, *Victoria Regia* in 1861, produced by the women of Emily Faithfull's Victoria Press. The proceeds of her last volume, *A Chaplet of Verses* (1862), went to a Catholic night shelter for women. One of the most popular poets of the mid-century, and still being anthologised in the 1920s, she died at home after many years suffering from tuberculosis.

See: Hickok (1984); Blain et al. (1990); Shattock (1993); Leighton and Reynolds (1995); Armstrong et al. (1996)

Ritchie, Anne, Lady, née Thackeray (1837-1919)

Born in London, she was the daughter of the novelist William Makepeace Thackeray. Her mother's mental illness meant that she lived with her grandparents in Paris until the age of ten, when she returned to London to live with her father, acting as his secretary and amanuensis from 1851 until he died in 1863. Her earliest publications were essays in the *Cornhill* magazine, edited initially by her father and later by her brother-in-law Leslie Stephen. She wrote five novels between 1863 and 1885, of which the most successful were *The Village on the Cliff* (1867) and *Old Kensington* (1873). In 1875 her sister died and ATR spent two years looking after her children before marrying, in 1877, at the age of forty, her cousin Richmond Ritchie, a civil servant seventeen years her junior. After her marriage, which was happy and successful, she turned increasingly to writing memoirs and biographies, including *A Book of Sybils* (on English women writers) in 1881, *Records of Tennyson, Ruskin, and Robert and Elizabeth Browning* (1892) and *Lord Tennyson and his Friends* (1893). She wrote biographical and critical introductions to her father's works (1894–5) and published two collections of essays (1908 and 1913).

See: Ritchie (1924); Gerin (1981); Blain et al. (1990); Shattock (1993)

Robinson, A. Mary F., later Darmester, later Duclaux (1857-1944)

Born in Warwickshire into a cultured family (her parents' friends included the Brownings and Oscar Wilde) she was later educated in Belgium and Italy before spending seven years studying classical literature at University College London. Her first husband, James Darmester, was a Professor of Persian in Paris, where AMFR ran a literary salon for the six years before his death in 1895. Remaining in France, she remarried in 1901 and moved to the Cantal region. She published poetry in both English and French. Among her many publications are several collections of poetry including *A Handful of Honeysuckle* (1878), *The New Arcadia* (1884), *An Italian Garden* (1886) and *Collected Poems* (1902). She also published a novel, *Arden* and a biography of Emily Brontë (both 1883).

See: Blain et al. (1990), Armstrong et al. (1996), Robertson (1883)

Rossetti, Christina (1830–1894)
Born in London, her father Gabriele R was an Italian political refugee and poet who became professor of Italian at King's College London. Her brothers were Dante Gabriel R, poet and painter, and William Michael R, critic and editor, who largely supported the family following their father's severe ill-health in the 1840s and 50s. She began publishing her poems privately at the age of sixteen, and contributed poems under the pseudonym Ellen Alleyne to her brother DGR's journal *The Germ* in 1850. Critical acclaim came with the publication of *Goblin Market and Other Poems* (1862), followed by *The Prince's Progress* (1866), *Sing-Song* (poems for children) (1872), and *A Pageant* (1881). She also published a number of prose works (1870, 1874, 1879). She never married: an engagement to the painter James Collinson foundered in 1850 owing to her staunch commitment to Anglicanism and his Roman Catholicism. A later relationship with the agnostic translator and scholar C. B. Cayley also failed owing to her refusal to marry anyone who did not share her religious beliefs, although they remained close friends until his death in 1883. She died of cancer in 1894.
    See: Crump (1979–90); Harrison (1988); Kent (1989); Jones (1992); Leighton (1992); Bristow (1995); Blain et al. (1990); Shattock (1993); Leighton and Reynolds (1995); Armstrong et al. (1996)

Shelley, Mary, née Godwin (1797–1851)
Daughter of the writer and philosopher William Godwin and of the feminist writer Mary Wollstonecraft, who died ten days after her birth. She eloped to the continent with the poet Shelley in 1814, accompanied by her step-sister Claire Clairmont, and published an account of their journey as *History of a Six Weeks Tour* in 1817. She married Shelley after his first wife committed suicide in 1816. They had four children, only one of whom, Percy, survived. Her most famous work is *Frankenstein; or The Modern Prometheus*, begun when she was eighteen and published in 1818. After Shelley's death in 1822 she largely supported herself and her son, managing to send him to Harrow and Cambridge, by writing. She wrote several other novels, including *Valperga* (1823), *The Last Man* (1826), *Lodore* (1835) and *Falkner* (1837), published a number of stories in various annuals and periodicals, and contributed to Lardner's *Cabinet Cyclopedia*. Her important editions of Shelley's *Poetical Works* (1839) and of his *Essays, Letters from Abroad, Translations and Fragments* (1840) remain standard today. Her last major work was *Rambles in Germany and Italy* (1844). She never remarried, and died in London at the age of fifty-three.
    See: Bennett (1980–8); Feldman and Scott Kilvert (1987); Crook (1995–); Mellor (1988); Stephen Behrendt in Feldman and Kelley (1995); Blain et al. (1990); Shattock (1993)

Simcox, Edith (1844–1901)
Extremely well-educated and knowledgeable, she taught herself Latin, Greek, Italian and Flemish in addition to the French and German she learned at school, and was well versed in political and social matters as well as issues relating to literature and the arts. She became a journalist on *The Academy*, for which she wrote for over quarter of a century. With her friend Mary Hamilton she started a shirt-manufacturing

co-operative in London in 1875, offering decent conditions of employment to women who would otherwise have worked in sweat-shops. Her interest in trades unionism led to her attending numerous congresses both at home and abroad, on which she wrote reports for the *Manchester Guardian*. A meeting with George Eliot precipitated her into a passionate devotion to the novelist, which she recorded in the unpublished 'Autobiography of a Shirt Maker'. After Eliot's death she fictionalised her intense feelings in *Episodes in the Lives of Men, Women and Lovers* (1882).

See: Blain et at. (1990), McKenzie (1961)

Thomas, Bertha (1845–1918)

Born into a wealthy clerical family (her grandfather was Archbishop of Canterbury, two uncles were bishops and her father Canon of Canterbury from 1862) she wrote for enjoyment rather than financial need. She contributed to several magazines including *Fraser's*, *Cornhill* and the *National Review*. Her twelve novels include *Proud Maizie* (1876), *The Violin-Player* (1880) and *Son of the House* (1900). She also published a study of George Sand for the Eminent Women Series in 1883. Her final work, *Picture Tales from the Welsh Hills*, came out in 1912.

See: Blain et al. (1990)

Victoria, Queen (1819–1901)

Granddaughter of George III, she succeeded to the British throne in 1837 at the age of eighteen. Three years later she married Prince Albert of Saxe-Coburg-Gotha: the marriage was a happy one, and she was devastated by his death in 1861. A prolific letter-writer, she also kept a *journal from her childhood to the end of her life. Selections were published, with the editorial assistance of Arthur Helps, in 1868 as *Leaves from a Journal of our Life in the Highlands 1848–1861*, which became an instant bestseller, as did the following volume, *More Leaves* (1883). Selections from her journals and correspondence appeared in 1907, edited by A. C. Benson and R. B. B. Esher

See: Sitwell (1936); Cooper (1961); Strachey (1921); Longford (1964); Woodham-Smith (1972); Thompson (1990); Blain et al. (1990); Shattock (1993)

Wilde, Jane Francesca, Lady, née Elgee (1826–1896)

Born into a conventional Anglo-Irish family (both her grandfathers were clergymen) she was converted to nationalism as a young woman and contributed inflammatory poems and articles to the journal *The Nation* in the 1840s under the pseudonym Speranza. The journal was suppressed and its editor arrested following the publication of her 1848 essay 'Jacta Alea Est' ('The Die is Cast'), which urged the Irish to take up arms. In 1851 she married the eminent surgeon William Robert Wills Wilde, and had three children, one of whom was the poet and dramatist Oscar Wilde (1854–1900). Strikingly tall, eccentric in her appearance and known for her wit, she espoused feminist causes and held literary salons in Dublin and later in London, where she moved after her husband's death in 1879. She published two volumes of poems (1864 and 1867), and two of Irish folklore (1887 and 1890). Her essays were collected as *Men, Women and Books* (1891) and *Social Studies* (1893). Her finances decreased considerably towards the end of her life and although in receipt of a Royal Literary Fund grant in 1888 and a civil-list pension from 1890, she died in poverty during her son's imprisonment.

See: Wyndham (1951); Ellmann (1987); Blain et al. (1990); Shattock (1993); Leighton and Reynolds (1995); Armstrong et al. (1996)

BIBLIOGRAPHY

References

Acland, Alice (1948), *Caroline Norton*, London: Constable.

Alexander, Christine, and Jane Sellars (1995), *The Art of the Brontës*, Cambridge: Cambridge University Press.

Anderson, N. F. (1987), *Woman against Women in Victorian England: A Life of Eliza Lynn Linton*, Bloomington: University of Indiana Press.

Armstrong, Isobel (1993), *Victorian Poetry: Poetry, Poetics and Politics*, London: Routledge.

Armstrong, Isobel and Joseph Bristow, with Cath Sharrock, (eds) (1996), *Nineteenth-Century Women Poets: An Oxford Anthology*, Oxford: Clarendon Press.

Ashfield, Anthony, (ed.) (1995), *Romantic Women Poets 1770–1838: An Anthology*, Manchester and New York: Manchester University Press.

Ashton, H.(1936), *Letty Landon*, London: Collins.

Barr, Pat (1970), *A Curious Life for a Lady: The Story of Isabella Bird*, London: Macmillan: Murray.

Beer, Gillian (1986), *George Eliot*, Brighton: Harvester Press.

Bennett, Betty T., (ed.) (1980–8) *Letters of Mary Wollstonecraft Shelley*, 3 vols, Baltimore: Johns Hopkins University Press.

Bigland, E. (1950), *Ouida: The Passionate Victorian*, London & New York: Jarrolds.

Blain, Virginia, Patricia Clements and Isobel Grundy, (eds) (1990), *The Feminist Companion to Literature in English: Women Writers from the Middle Ages to the Present*, London: Batsford.

Blanchard, S. L. (1841), *Life and Literary Remains of L. E. L.*, 2 vols, London: Colburn.

Boos, Florence (1995), 'Cauld Engle-Cheek: Working-Class Women Poets in Victorian Scotland', *Victorian Poetry 33*.

Bridges, Robert (1931), *Collected Essays*, vol 6, London: Oxford University Press.

Briggs, Asa (1961), *Social Thought and Social Action: A Study of the Work of B. Seebohm Rowntree*, London: Longmans.

Briggs, Julia (1989), *A Woman of Passion: The Life of E. Nesbit 1858–1924*, Harmondsworth: Penguin.

Bristow, Joseph, (ed.) (1995), *Victorian Women Poets: Emily Brontë, Elizabeth Barrett Browning, Christina Rossetti*, New Casebooks, Basingstoke: Macmillan.

Burton, Hester (1949), *Barbara Bodichon 1827–91*, London: Murray.

Caine, Barbara (1992), *Victorian Feminists*, Oxford: Oxford University Press.

Campbell, M. (1988), *Lady Morgan*, London: Pandora.

Chapple, J. V. and A. Pollard, (eds) (1966), *The Letters of Elizabeth Gaskell*, Manchester: Manchester University Press.

Chedzoy, Alan (1992), *A Scandalous Woman: the Story of Caroline Norton*, London: Allison & Busby.

Chitham, E. (1987), *A Life of Emily Brontë*, Oxford: Blackwell.

Clarke, Norma (1990), *Ambitious Heights: Writing, Friendship, Love: The Jewsbury Sisters, Felicia Hemans and Jane Welsh Caryle*, London & New York: Routledge.

Colby, V. and R. A. Colby (1966), *The Equivocal Virtue: Mrs Oliphant and the Victorian Literary Market-Place*, Hamden, CT: Archon Books.

Collis, J. S. (1971), *The Carlyles*, London: Sidgwick & Jackson.

Cook, E. T. (1913), *The Life of Florence Nightingale*, London: Macmillan.

Cooper, Helen (1988), *Elizabeth Barrett Browning, Woman and Artist*, Chapel Hill & London: University of North Carolina Press.

Cooper, L. (1962), *The Young Victoria*, London: Parrish.

Crook, Nora, (ed.) (1995–), *Works of Mary Wollstonecraft Shelley*, London: Pickering & Chatto.

Cross, Nigel (1985), *The Common Writer; Life in Nineteenth-Century Grub Street*, Cambridge: Cambridge University Press.

Crump, Rebecca W., (ed.) (1979–90) *Complete Poems of Christina Rossetti*, 3 vols, Baton Rouge: University of Louisiana Press.

Cunningham, Gail (1978), *The New Woman and the Victorian Novel*, London: Macmillan.

David, Deirdre (1987), *Intellectual Women and Victorian Patriarchy: Harriet Martineau, Elizabeth Barrett Browning, George Eliot*, London: Macmillan.

Davidoff, Leonore (1979), 'Class and Gender in Victorian England: The Diaries of Arthur J. Munby and Hannah Cullwick', *Feminist Studies* 5, p. 105.

Davies, Stevie (1988), *Emily Brontë*, Hemel Hempstead: Harvester Wheatsheaf.

Dinnage, Rosemary (1986), *Annie Besant*, Harmondsworth: Penguin.

Easson, Angus (1979), *Elizabeth Gaskell*, London: Routledge and Kegan Paul.

Ellis, Sarah (1893), *The Life and Letters of Mrs Ellis*, compiled by her nieces, London: Nisbet.

Ellmann, Richard (1987), *Oscar Wilde*, London: Hamilton.

Erskine, Mrs S. (1915), *Anna Jameson: Letters and Friendships 1812–60*, London: Unwin.

Faderman, Lilian (1981), *Surpassing the Love of Men: Romantic Friendship and Love between Women from the Renaissance to the Present*, New York: Morrow.

Feldman, P. R. and D. Scott Kilvert, (eds) (1987), *Journals of Mary Wollstonecraft Shelley*, 2 vols, Oxford: Clarendon Press.

Feldman, Paula R. and Theresa M. Kelley, (eds) (1995), *Romantic Women Writers: Voices and Countervoices*, Hanover, NH: University Press of New England.

ffrench, Y. (1938), *Ouida: A Study in Ostentation*, London: Corben Sanderson.

Fitzpatrick, W. J. (1860), *Lady Morgan*, London: Skeet.

Foster, Shirley (1990), *Across New Worlds: Nineteenth-Century Women Travellers and their Writings*, Hemel Hempstead: Harvester Wheatsheaf.

Freeman, S. (1977), *Isabella and Sam: The Story of Mrs Beeton*, London: Gollancz.

Fryckstedt, Monica (1986), *Geraldine Jewsbury's Athenæum Reviews: A Mirror of Mid-Victorian Attitudes to Fiction*, Stockholm: Almquist & Wiksell.

Furnass, J. C. (1982), *Fanny Kemble: Leading Lady of the Nineteenth Century Stage*, New York: Dial Press.

Gerin, W. (1967), *Charlotte Brontë: The Evolution of Genius*, Oxford: Oxford University Press.

Gerin, W. (1972), *Emily Brontë: A Biography*, Oxford: Oxford University Press.

Gerin, W. (1981), *Anne Thackeray Ritchie: A Biography*, Oxford: Oxford University Press.

Gilbert, Sandra M. and Susan Gubar (1979), *The Madwoman in the Attic*, New Haven: Yale University Press.

Glage, Liselotte (1981), *Clementina Black*, Heidleberg: C. Winter.

Gordon, Lyndall (1994), *Charlotte Brontë: A Passionate Life*, London: Chatto and Windus.

Green, Roger Lancelyn (1946), *Andrew Lang*, E. Ward, Leicester.

Griggs, E. L. (1940), *Coleridge Fille: A Biography of Sara Coleridge*, London: Oxford University Press.

Gullette, M. M., (ed.) (1989), Mona Caird, *The Daughters of Danæus*, New York: Feminist Press at City University of New York.

Haight, G. S. (1954–79), *Letters of George Eliot*, 9 vols, London: Oxford University Press.

Haight, G. S. (1968), *George Eliot: A Biography*, Oxford: Clarendon Press.

Hanson, L. and E. (1952), *Life of Jane Welsh Carlyle*, London: Constable.

Hardwick, E. (1974), *Seduction and Betrayal*, London: Weidenfeld & Nicolson.

Harrison, A. H. (1988), *Christina Rossetti in Context*, Brighton: Harvester Press.

Haythornethwaite, J. (1990), 'Friendly Encounters: A Study of the Relationship between the House of Blackwood and Margaret Oliphant in her Role as Literary Critic', *Publishing History* vol.28, pp. 79–88.

Hertein, Sheila R. (1985), *A Mid-Victorian Feminist: Barbara Leigh Smith Bodichon*, New Haven, CT: Yale University Press.

Hickok, Kathleen (1984), *Representations of Women: Nineteenth-Century British Women's Poetry*, Westport, CT: Greenwood Press.

Hoge, J. O. and C. Olney, (eds) (1974), *Letters of Caroline Norton to Lord Melbourne*, Columbus, OH: Ohio University Press.

Hoge, J. O. and J. Marcus, (eds) (1978), *Selected Writings of Caroline Norton*, Columbus, OH: Ohio University Press.

Homans, Margaret (1986), *Bearing the Word: Language and Female Experience in Nineteenth-Century Women's Writing*, Chicago: University of Chicago Press.

Houghton, Walter (1979), *Wellesley Index to Victorian Periodicals*, 4 vols, vol. ii, Toronto: University of Toronto Press; London: Routledge.

Howe, Susanna (1935), *Geraldine Jewsbury: Her Life and Errors*, London: Allen & Unwin.

Huddleston, Joan (1979), *Sarah Grand 1854–1943: A Bibliography*, Victorian Fiction Research Guides No. 1, St Lucia, Australia: University of Queensland Press.

Hudson, Derek (1972), *Munby: Man of Two Worlds*, London: Murray.

Hughes, W. R. (1890), *Constance Naden: A Memoir*, London: Dickers & Son.

Hyde, H. M. (1951), *Mr and Mrs Beeton*, London: Harrap.

Ireland, Mrs A., (ed.) (1892), *Selections from the Letters of Geraldine Endsor Jewsbury and Jane Welsh Carlyle*, London and New York: Longmans Green.

Johnson, G. W. & L. A., (eds) (1909), *Josephine Elizabeth Butler: An Autobiographical Memoir*, Bristol: Arrowsmith.

Jones, K. (1992), *Learning not to be First: The Life of Christina Rossetti*: Gloucestershire: Windrush Press.

Karlin, D. (1987), *Robert Browning and Elizabeth Barrett: The Courtship Correspondence*, Oxford: Clarendon Press.

Kelley, Philip and Scott Lewis, (eds) (1992), *The Brownings' Correspondence*, vol. 10, Winfield, Kan: Wedgestone Press.

Kent, D. A., (ed.) (1989) *The Achievement of Christina Rossetti*, Ithaca, NY: Cornell University Press.

Kenyon, F. G. (1897), *Letters of Elizabeth Barrett Browning*, 2 vols, London: Murray.

Kersley, Gillian (1983), *Darling Madame: Sarah Grand and Devoted Friend*, London: Virago.

Layard, G. S. (1901), *Mrs Lynn Linton: Her Life, Letters and Opinions*, London: Methuen.

Lee, F. (1914), *Ouida: A Memoir*, London: Fisher Unwin.

Lefebure, Molly (1986), *The Bondage of Love: A Life of Mrs Samuel Taylor Coleridge*, London: Gollancz.

Leighton, Angela (1986), *Elizabeth Barrett Browning*, Brighton: Harvester Press.

Leighton, Angela (1992), *Victorian Women Poets: Writing Against the Heart*, Hemel Hempstead: Harvester Wheatsheaf.

Leighton, Angela, and Margaret Reynolds, (eds) (1995), *Victorian Women Poets: An Anthology*, Oxford and Cambridge, MA: Blackwell.

Lewes, George Henry (1847), 'The Condition of Authors in England, Germany and France', *Frasers's* vol. xxxv, pp. 285–95.

Lewes, George Henry (1850), 'A Gentle Hint to Writing Women', *Leader* I, pp. 929–30.

Lochhead, M. (1961), *Elizabeth Rigby, Lady Eastlake*, London: Murray.

Longford, Elizabeth (1964), *Victoria R.*, London: Weidenfeld & Nicolson.

Manton, Jo (1976), *Mary Carpenter*, London: Heinemann Educational.

Marshall, Dorothy (1977), *Fanny Kemble*, London: Weidenfeld and Nicholson.

McKenzie, K. A. (1961), *Edith Simcox and George Eliot*, London: Oxford University Press.

Mellor, A. K. (1988); *Mary Shelley: Her Life, Her Fiction and her Monsters*, London: Methuen.

Mermin, Dorothy (1989), *Elizabeth Barrett Browning: The Origins of a New Poetry*, Chicago & London: University of Chicago.

Mermin, Dorothy (1993), *Godiva's Ride: Women of Letters in England, 1830–1880*, Bloomington and Indianapolis: Indiana University Press.

Middleton, Dorothy (1965), *Lady Travellers*, London: Routledge and Kegan Paul.

Mitchell, Sally (1981), *The Fallen Angel: Chastity, Class and Women's Reading 1835–1880*, Bowling Green, Ohio: Bowling Green University Popular Press.

Mitchell, Sally (1983), *Dinah Mulock Craik*, Boston: Twayne.

Mix, Katherine (1960), *A Study in Yellow: The Yellow Book and its Contributors*,

Lawrence, KS: University of Kansas Press.

Moore, Doris Langley (1933; rev. 1964), *E. Nesbit: A Biography*, London: Benn.

Mudge, B. K. (1989), *Sara Coleridge: A Victorian Daughter: Her Life and Essays*, New Haven, CT & London: Yale University Press.

Nesbit, E. (1987), *Long Ago when I was Young*, London: Beehive.

Nestor, Pauline (1987), *Charlotte Brontë*, Basingstoke: Macmillan Educational.

Nestor, Pauline (1985), *Female Friendships and Communities: Charlotte Brontë, George Eliot, Elizabeth Gaskell*, Oxford: Clarendon Press.

Nethercot, A. H. (1961), *The First Five Lives of Annie Besant*, London: Hart Davis.

Nethercot, A. H. (1963), *The Last Four Lives of Annie Besant*, London: Hart Davis.

Newcomer, J. (1990), *Lady Morgan the Novelist*, London: Associated University Presses.

Parr, Louisa (1898), 'The Author of *John Halifax, Gentleman*' in A. Sergeant, (ed.) *Women Novelists of Queen Victoria's Reign*, London: Hurst and Blackett.

Partridge, Eric (1932; 1970), 'Mrs Archer Clive', *Literary Sessions*, London: Scholartis Press.

Perkins, Jane Gray (1909), *Caroline Norton*, London: Murray.

Petrie, G. (1976), *A Singular Iniquity: The Campaigns of Josephine Butler*, London: Macmillan.

Pichanick, V. K. (1980), *Harriet Martineau: The Woman and her Work*, Ann Arbor, Mich.: University of Michigan Press/London: Heinemann.

Pinney, T, (ed.) (1963), *Essays of George Eliot*, London: Routledge & Kegan Paul.

Pykett, Lyn (1989), *Emily Brontë*, Basingstoke: Macmillan.

Pykett, Lyn (ed.) (1996), *Reading Fin-de-Siècle Fictions*, London: Longmans.

Ritchie, Anne Thackeray (1924), *Letters*, London: Murray.

Robertson, E. S. (1883), *British Poetesses*, London: Cassell.

Sanders, Valerie (1986), *Reason over Passion: Harriet Martineau and the Victorian Novel* , Brighton: Harvester Press.

Sanders, Valerie (1989), *The Private Lives of Victorian Women: Autobiography in Nineteenth-Century England*, Hemel Hempstead: Harvester Wheatsheaf.

Sanders, Valerie, (ed.) (1990), *Selected Letters of Harriet Martineau*, Oxford: Clarendon Press.

Sergeant, A., (ed.) (1897), *Women Novelists of Queen Victoria's Reign*, London: Hurst and Blackett.

Shattock, Joanne, (ed.) (1993), *The Oxford Guide to British Women Writers*, Oxford and New York: Oxford University Press.

Showalter, Elaine (1975), 'Diana Mulock Craik', *Feminist Studies 2*.

Showalter, Elaine (1978), *A Literature of their Own*, London: Virago.

Sitwell, Edith (1936), *Victoria of England*, London: Faber & Faber.

Spain, Nancy (1948), *Mrs Beeton and her Husband*, London: Collins.

Spencer, Jane (1993), *Elizabeth Gaskell*, Basingstoke: Macmillan.

Stanley, Liz, (ed.) (1984), *The Diaries of Hannah Cullwick, Victorian Maidservant*, London: Virago.

Stephenson, Glenys (1996), *Letaitia Landon: The Woman behind L. E. L.*, Manchester: Manchester University Press.

Stevenson, L. (1936), *The Wild Irish Girl*, London: Chapman & Hall.

Stirling, M. (1957), *The Fine and the Wicked: The Life and Times of Ouida*, London: Gollancz.

Stoddart, Anna (1906), *The Life of Isabella Bird (Mrs Bishop)*, London: Murray.

Stoneman, Patsy (1987), *Elizabeth Gaskell*, Brighton: Harvester Press.

Strachey, Lytton (1921), *Queen Victoria*, London: Chatto & Windus.

Sturgeon , M. (1922), *Michael Field*, London: Harrap.

Sutherland, John (1976), *Victorian Novelists and Publishers*, London: Athlone Press.

Sutherland, John (1988), *The Longman Companion to Victorian Fiction*, Harlow: Longman.

Swindells, Julia (1985), *Victorian Writing and Working Women: The Other Side of Silence*, Cambridge: Polity Press.

Taplin, Gardner B.(1957), *Life of Elizabeth Barrett Browning*, London: John Murray.

Tayler, Irene (1990), *Holy Ghosts: The Male Muses of Emily and Charlotte Brontë*, New York: Columbia University Press.

Taylor, Anne (1992), *Annie Besant: A Biography*, Oxford: Oxford University Press.

Thomas, Clara (1967), *Love and Work Enough: The Life of Anna Jameson*, London: Macdonald.

Thompson, Dorothy (1990), *Queen Victoria: Gender and Power*, London: Virago.

Todd, Margaret G. (1918), *The Life of Sophia Jex Blake*, London: Macmillan.

Trela, D., (1994), *Margaret Oliphant: Critical Essays on a Gentle Subversive*, Selinsgrove, PA: Susquehanna University Press.

Uglow, Jennifer (1993), *Elizabeth Gaskell: A Habit of Stories*, London: Faber and Faber.

van Thal, H. (1979), *Eliza Lynn Linton: The Girl of the Period*, London: Allen & Unwin.

Vicinus, Martha and Nergaard, B, (eds) (1990), *Ever Yours, Florence Nightingale: Selected Letters*, London: Virago.

Vicinus, Martha (1974), *The Industrial Muse: A Study of Nineteenth-Century British Working-Class Literature*, London: Croom Helm.

Webb, R. K.(1960), *Harriet Martineau: A Radical Victorian*, London: Heinemann.

Wessinger, Catherine L. (1988), *Annie Besant*, Lewiston, NY: E. Mellen Press.

Williams, Merryn (1986), *Margaret Oliphant: A Critical Biography*, Basingstoke: Macmillan.

Wyndham, H. (1951), *Speranza: A Biography of Lady Wilde*, London: Boardman.

Woodham-Smith, Cecil (1950), *Florence Nightingale*, London: Constable.

Woodham-Smith, Cecil (1972), *Queen Victoria: Her Life and Times*, 2 vols, London: Hamilton.

Woolf, Virginia (1932), 'Geraldine and Jane', *The Common Reader: Second Series*, London: Hogarth Press.

Further Reading

Benstock, Shari, (ed.) (1988), *The Private Self: Theory and Practice in Women's Autobiographical Writings*, Chapel Hill: University of North Carolina Press.

Cline, Cheryl (1989), *Women's Diaries, Journals and Letters: An Annotated Bibliography*, New York: Garland.

Flint, Kate (1993), *The Woman Reader, 1837–1914*, Oxford: Clarendon Press.

Gilmour, Robin (1993), *The Victorian Period: The Intellectual and Cultural Context of English Literature, 1830–1890*, London: Longman.

Helsinger, E. K. et al. (1983), *The Woman Question: Society and Literature in Britain and America, 1837–1883*, 3 vols, Manchester, Manchester University Press.

Hollis, Patricia, (ed.) (1979), *Women in Public, 1850–1900: Documents of the Victorian Women's Movement*, London: Allen & Unwin.

Hughes, Linda K, (ed.) (1995), *Victorian Poetry* (special issue on women poets), 33.

Levine, Philippa (1987), *Victorian Feminism, 1850–1900*, London: Hutchinson.

Mitchell, Sally (1988), *Victorian Britain: An Encyclopedia*, New York & London: Garland.

Mitchie, Elsie B. (1993), *Outside the Pale: Cultural Exclusion, Gender Difference, and the Victorian Woman Writer*, Ithaca, NY: Cornell University Press.

Poovey, Mary (1988), *Uneven Developments: The Ideological Work of Gender in Mid-Victorian England*, Chicago: University of Chicago Press.

Rendell, Jane (1985), *The Origins of Modern Feminism: Women in Britain, France and the United States, 1780–1860*, Basingstoke and London: Macmillan.

Rendell, Jane, (ed.) (1987), *Equal or Different? Women's Politics 1800–1914*, Oxford: Blackwell.

Strachey, Ray (1928), *The Cause: A Short History of the Women's Movement in Great Britain*, London: Bell.

Vicinus, Martha, (ed.) (1972), *Suffer and Be Still: Women in the Victorian Age*, Bloomington: University of Indiana Press.

Vicinus, Martha (1980), *A Widening Sphere: Changing Roles of Victorian Women*, London: Methuen.

INDEX OF AUTHORS

Numbers refer to individual items, not pages

INDEX OF THEMES

Numbers refer to individual items, not pages

abuse, physical and sexual 28, 46, 64
autobiography 9, 18, 28, 44, 46, 56, 61, 63, 92
biography, memoirs 9, 25, 33, 68, 82
death 19, 38, 45, 92, 95
diaries, journals 1, 7, 8, 10, 13, 14, 17, 38, 40, 45, 52, 57, 79, 84, 95
education, teachers, governesses 18, 21, 49, 54, 61
love, sexuality 2, 19, 26, 37, 39, 67, 76, 79
male poets 9, 20, 56
marriage 3, 8, 10, 12, 28, 31, 38, 53, 64, 71, 77, 85, 88, 91
motherhood 13, 14, 45, 47, 92
position of women 7, 11, 12, 24, 27, 28, 35, 37, 46, 48, 49, 50, 51, 53, 54, 55, 58,
    59, 62, 64, 66, 69, 71, 73, 75, 77, 78, 83, 86, 88, 91, 93
religion 23, 61, 72
servants 24, 36, 40, 52, 57
slavery 6, 43
social comment, social class 22, 24, 27, 36, 46, 50, 64, 87, 94
travel writing 5, 6, 7, 16, 60, 63, 65, 81
women, law and the franchise 27, 28, 50, 59, 62, 64, 75, 77
women and medicine 53, 54, 69
women writers and women as writers 4, 15, 21, 25, 29, 30, 32, 34, 41, 42, 61, 68,
    80 (*see especially*: Jane Austen 42; Charlotte Brontë (*as subject*) 21, 30, 33;
    Emily Brontë (*as subject*) 25; George Eliot (*as subject*) 34, 68, 80; Letitia Landon
    (*as subject*) 15, 41; Mary Wollstonecraft 29, 30